ICSA
STUDY TEXT

Foundation Paper 3

Introduction to English and EU Law

New in this September 1999 edition

- Recent statute and case law

- Notes on the Woolf reforms

- Thorough and reliable updating of material

FOR 2000 EXAMS

BPP Publishing
September 1999

First edition 1993
Fifth edition September 1999

ISBN 0 7517 5017 4 (previous edition 0 7517 5100 6)

British Library Cataloguing-in-Publication Data
A catalogue record for this book
is available from the British Library

Published by

BPP Publishing Limited
Aldine House, Aldine Place
London W12 8AW

http://www.bpp.co.uk

Printed in England by
THE BOOK FACTORY
35/37 Queensland Road
London N7 7AH
(0171) 700 1000

We are grateful to the Institute of Chartered Secretaries and Administrators for permission to reproduce past examination questions. The suggested solutions have been prepared by BPP Publishing Limited.

We are also grateful to the Institute of Chartered Secretaries and Administrators for permission to reproduce past examination questions. The suggested solutions have been prepared by BPP Publishing Limited.

HOW TO USE THIS STUDY TEXT

Aims of this Study Text

To provide you with the knowledge and understanding, skills and application techniques that you need if you are to be successful in your exams

This Study Text has been written around the **Introduction to English and EU Law** syllabus (reproduced on page (ix), and cross-referenced to where in the text each topic is covered).

- It is **comprehensive**. We do not omit sections of the syllabus as the examiner is liable to examine any angle of any part of the syllabus - and you do not want to be left high and dry.

- It keeps you **up-to-date** in developments in English and EU law and the way in which the examiner is examining the subject, together with relevant legislation.

- And it is **on-target**. We do not include any material which is not examinable. You can therefore rely on the BPP Study Text as the stand-alone source of all your information for the exam, without worrying that any of the material is irrelevant.

To allow you to study in the way that best suits your learning style and the time you have available, by following your personal Study Plan (see page (viii))

You may be studying at home on your own until the date of the exam, or you may be attending a full-time course. You may like to (and have time to) read every word, or you may prefer to (or only have time to) skim-read and devote the remainder of your time to question practice. Wherever you fall in the spectrum, you will find the BPP Study Text meets your needs in designing and following your personal Study Plan.

To tie in with the rest of the BPP Effective Study Package to ensure you have the best possible chance of passing the exam

Recommended period of use	Elements of the BPP Effective Study Package
3-12 months before exam	**Study Text** Use the Study Text to acquire knowledge, understanding, skills and the ability to use application techniques.
1-3 months before exam	**Practice & Revision Kit** Attempt the tutorial questions and read the helpful checklists which are provided for each topic area in the Kit. Then try the numerous examination questions, for which there are realistic suggested answers. 2000 examinees will find the 2000 edition of the Kit invaluable for bringing them up-to-date.

Settling down to study

By this stage in your career you are probably very experienced at learning and taking exams. But have you ever thought about *how* you learn? Let's have a quick look at the key elements required for effective learning. You can then identify your learning style and go on to design your own approach to how you are going to study with this text - your personal Study Plan.

Key element of learning	Using the BPP Study Text
Motivation	You can rely on the comprehensiveness and technical quality of BPP material. You've chosen the right Study Text - so you're in pole position to pass your exam!
Clear objectives and standards	Do you want to be a prizewinner or simply achieve a moderate pass? Decide.
Feedback	Work through the examples in this text and do the Exercises and Test your knowledge quizzes. Evaluate your efforts critically - how are you doing?
Study Plan	You need to be honest with yourself about your progress - don't be over-confident, but don't be negative either. Make your Study Plan (see below) and try to stick to it. Focus on the short-term objectives - completing two chapters a night, say - but beware of losing sight of your study objectives.
Practice	Use the Test your knowledge quizzes and Chapter roundups to refresh your memory after you have completed your initial study of each chapter.

These introductory pages let you see exactly what you are up against. But however you study, you should:

- **read through the syllabus [and syllabus commentary]** - these will help you to identify areas you have already covered, perhaps at a lower level of detail, and areas that are totally new to you;

- **study the examination paper section**, where we show you the format of the exam (how many and what kind of questions) and analyse the recent papers **including the one set in June 1999**.

Key study steps

The following steps are, in our experience, the ideal approach to studying for professional exams but you can of course adapt it for your particular learning style (see page (viii)). Tackle the chapters in the order you find them in the Study Text. Taking into account your individual learning style, follow these key study steps for each chapter.

Key study steps	Activity
Step 1 *Chapter topic list*	Study the list. Each numbered topic is a numbered section in the chapter.
Step 2 *Introduction*	Read through it. It is designed to show you *why* the topics in the chapter need to be studied - how they lead on from previous topics, and how they lead into subsequent ones.
Step 3 *Knowledge brought forward boxes*	In these we highlight information and techniques that it is assumed you have 'brought forward' with you from your earlier studies. If there are topics which have changed recently due to legislation for example, these topics are explained in full. Do not panic if you do not feel instantly comfortable with the content of the box - it should come back to you as we develop the subject for this paper. If you are really unsure, we advise you to go back to your previous notes.
Step 4 *Explanations*	Proceed methodically through the chapter, reading each section thoroughly and making sure you understand. Where a topic has been examined, we state the month and year of examination against the appropriate heading. You should pay particular attention to these topics.
Step 5 *Note taking*	Take brief notes if you wish, avoiding the temptation to copy out too much.
Step 6 *Examples*	Follow each through to its solution very carefully.
Step 7 *Case examples*	Study each one, and try to add flesh to them from your own experience - they are designed to show how the topics you are studying come alive (and often come unstuck) in the real world.
Step 8 *Exercises*	Make a very good attempt at each one in the chapter. These are designed to put your knowledge into practice.
Step 9 *Solutions*	Check yours against ours, and make sure you understand the reasons why they may differ.
Step 10 *Chapter roundup*	Work through it very carefully, to make sure you have grasped the major points it is highlighting.
Step 11 *Test your knowledge quiz*	When you are happy that you have covered the chapter, use the Test your knowledge quiz to check how much you have remembered of the topics covered. The answers are in the paragraphs in the chapter that we refer you to.
Step 12 *Illustrative questions*	Either at this point, or later when you are thinking about revising, make a full attempt at the question(s) suggested at the very end of the chapter. You can find these at the end of the Study Text, along with the answers so you can see how you did.

Developing your personal Study Plan

Preparing a Study Plan (and sticking closely to it) is one of the key elements in learning success. First you need to be aware of your style of learning. There are four typical learning styles. Consider yourself in the light of the following descriptions and work out which you fit most closely. You can then plan to follow the key study steps in the sequence suggested.

Learning styles	Characteristics	Sequence of key study steps in the BPP Study Text
Theorist	Seeks to understand principles before applying them in practice	1, 2, 3, 4, 6, 7, 8, 9, 10, 11, 12 (5 continuous)
Reflector	Seeks to observe phenomena, thinks about them and then chooses to act	
Activist	Prefers to deal with practical, active problems; does not have much patience with theory	1, 2, 8/9 (read through), 6, 7, 10, 3, 4, 8/9 (full attempt), 11, 12 (5 continuous)
Pragmatist	Prefers to study only if a direct link to practical problems can be seen; not interested in theory for its own sake	8/9 (read through), 2, 6, 7, 10, 1, 3, 4, 8/9 (full attempt), 11, 12 (5 continuous)

Next you should complete the following checklist.

Am I motivated? (a) ☐

Do I have an objective and a standard that I want to achieve? (b) ☐

Am I a theorist, a reflector, an activist or a pragmatist? (c) ☐

How much time do I have available per week, given: (d) ☐

- the standard I have set myself

- the time I need to set aside later for work on the Practice and Revision Kit

- the other exam(s) I am sitting, and (of course)

- practical matters such as work, travel, exercise, sleep and social life?

Now:

- take the time you have available per week for this Study Text (d), and multiply it by the number of weeks available to give (e). (e) ☐

- divide (e) by the number of chapters to give (f) (f) ☐

- set about studying each chapter in the time represented by (f), following the key study steps in the order suggested by your particular learning style.

This is your personal Study Plan.

Moving on...

However you study, when you are ready to embark on the practice and revision phase of the BPP Effective Study Package, you should still refer back to this Study Text, both as a source of reference (you should find the index particularly helpful for this) and as a refresher (the Chapter roundups and Test your knowledge quizzes help you here).

And remember to keep careful hold of this Study Text - you will find it invaluable in your work.

SYLLABUS

General guidance

Note that the following general stipulations are made in the ICSA's 1999/2000 syllabus booklet.

'All syllabi are based on English and EC derived law and practice, except where specifically stated.'

'Students are expected to keep abreast of changes in the law affecting the modules which they are studying. Generally, however, a detailed knowledge of new legislation will not be expected in examinations held within six months of the passing of the relevant Act. Syllabus changes will be notified to teaching establishments and will be published for the information of students in the Institute's journal *CS Student*.' You are also strongly advised to read the official journal of the Institute, *Chartered Secretary*.

Objective

To provide a broad understanding of the sources and administration of English Law and the impact of the European Community, in preparation for a more detailed and specialised study of law at later stages.

		Covered in Chapter
Nature and sources of law		
(i)	Development of common law and equity	1
(ii)	Legislation	3
(iii)	Interpretation of statutes	3
(iv)	Delegated legislation	3
(v)	EU Institutions, their roles and impact on UK law	4
(vi)	Case law	3
(vii)	Doctrine of precedent	3
(viii)	Hierarchy of the courts	2
(ix)	Tribunals and Arbitration	2
(x)	The judiciary and legal profession	2
(xi)	Criminal and civil liability	1
Introduction to property law		
(i)	Real and personal property	5
(ii)	Choses in possession and choses in action	5
(iii)	Freehold and leasehold estates	6
Trusts		
(i)	Kinds of trusts; creation; rights of beneficiaries; role and duties of trustees	7-9
Business associations		
(i)	The legal framework of companies, partnerships and business associations	10
Contract		
(i)	Introduction to the law of contract	11
(ii)	Offer and acceptance	12
(iii)	Intention to create legal relations	13
(iv)	Consideration	14
(v)	Capacity	15
(vi)	Formalities	16
(vii)	Privity	14

Torts

THE EXAMINATION PAPER

Paper format

The paper consists of ten questions, from which students must choose any six. All questions carry equal marks.

Analysis of past papers

The analysis below shows the topics which have been examined to date.

June 1999

1   *Business associations-* veil of incorporation
2   *Contract-* offer and invitation to treat; revocation of offer
3   *Nature and sources of law-* High Court
4   *Nature and sources of law-* EU law; European Court of Justice
5   *Tort-* defamation
6   *Trusts-* types of trust
7   *Contract-* sufficiency of consideration
8   *Property law-*estate and interest in land; freehold and leasehold
9   *Nature and sources of law-* English legal profession
10 *Tort-* negligence

December 1998

1   *Trusts-* trustees and their duties
2   *Business associations* – public and private companies; procedures and documentation
3   *Contract-* acceptance
4   *Tort* – duty of care
5   *Sources of English law* – the role of the judiciary
6   *Contract and tort-*excluding or restricting liability
7   *Property-* legal and equitable rights
8   *Contract and tort-* remoteness of damage
9   *Tort-* duty of care to visitors
10 *Sources of English law-* role of EC law

June 1998

1   *Nature and sources of law* - doctrine of precedent
2   *Nature and sources of law* - civil and criminal law
3   *Tort* - liability for employee's injuries
4   *Nature and sources of law* - EU law and institutions
5   *Tort* - liability for negligent advice
6   *Nature and sources of law* - Arbitration Act 1996
7   *Contract* - remedies for breach of contract
8   *Trusts* - apportionment and removal of trustees
9   *Contract* - void, voidable and unenforceable
10 *Business associations* - ultra vires and limited companies

December 1997

1   *Nature and sources of law* - equity and common law
2   *Tort* - negligence and vicarious liability
3   *Law of property* - principles of property law
4   *Contract* - consideration
5   *Nature and sources of law*- civil courts
6   *Business associations* - legal personality
7   *Contract* - frustration of contract
8   *Nature and sources of law* - EU law
9   *Tort* - defamation
10 *Trusts* - public and private trusts

June 1997

1   *Business associations* - creation of partnerships and companies
2   *Land* - types of estate
3   *Tort* - remoteness of damage
4   *Nature and sources of law* - industrial tribunal
5   *Nature and sources of law* - interpretation of statue
6   *Nature and sources of law* - supremacy of Community Law
7   *Contract* - privity
8   *Contract* - intention to create legal relations
9   *Tort* - duty of care
10 *Trusts* - breach of trust

December 1996

1   *Nature and sources of law* - case law and statute
2   *Contract* - exclusion clause
3   *Nature and sources of law* - EU law
4   *Tort* - duty of care to visitors
5   *Contract* - arbitration
6   *Tort* - standard of care
7   *Nature and sources of law* - delegated legislation
8   *Property law* - types of property and interests in land
9   *Trusts* - implied trusts
10 *Business associations* - partnership and limited company

June 1996

1   *Contract* - consideration
2   *Contract* - offer and invitation to treat; timing of acceptance
3   *Tort and contract* - contrasting rules on remoteness of damage
4   *Tort* - negligence; duty of care of one road user to another
5   *Nature and sources of law* - doctrine of precedent
6   *Trusts* - definition; classification; creation
7   *Property law* - types of property; ownership v possession
8   *Nature and sources of law* - primacy of Community law
9   *Business associations* - company v partnership
10 *Tort* - vicarious liability

Part A
Nature and sources of law

Chapter 1

THE ENGLISH LEGAL SYSTEM

This chapter covers the following topics.

1   Criminal and civil liability

2   Features of English law

3   The development of English law

4   The relationship between equity and the common law

Introduction

For most people outside the legal profession, the legal system is a mystery of archaic language and costumes. In fact, for the most part it consists of practical and down-to-earth sets of procedures and rules designed to provide resolutions to ordinary problems.

Publicity tends to focus on the higher courts, such as the Court of Appeal and the House of Lords. However the vast majority of cases are heard in the magistrates' courts or the county courts.

Many people, when they think of the law, have an image in their minds of judge and jury, or of 'cops and robbers'. These are manifestations of criminal law. Business conduct, on the other hand, is generally regulated by civil law.

The distinction between criminal and civil law is fundamental to the English legal system. In order to understand the court system therefore, it is necessary to understand the differences between criminal and civil cases. In this chapter, we explain the distinction and provide a brief review of the development of the English legal system. We will look at the present court system in detail in Chapter 2 and discuss the ways in which law is currently created in Chapters 3 and 4.

---

1   CRIMINAL AND CIVIL LIABILITY   *6/98*

1.1   The distinction between criminal and civil liability is central to the legal system and to the way in which the court system is structured. Civil and criminal law have different objectives.

Criminal law

1.2   *A crime is conduct prohibited by the law.* In a criminal case the State is usually the prosecutor because it is the community as a whole which suffers as a result of the law being broken. *Persons guilty of crime are punished by fines or imprisonment.*

1.3   Usually criminal proceedings are started by the *State*, although in rare cases they may be brought by a private person. The *police* or the *Director of Public Prosecutions* take the initial decision to prosecute, but this is then reviewed by the Crown Prosecution Service, which will subsequently conduct the case. Although most crimes have a victim - be it someone who has been mugged or a company which has been defrauded - the victim does not have a say in whether a prosecution is brought. In addition, the victim does not benefit from a conviction, since fines are payable to the State.

1.4   In a criminal trial, the burden of proof to convict the *accused* rests with the State (the *prosecution*), which must prove its case *beyond reasonable doubt*. A criminal case might be referred to as *R v Smith*. The prosecution is brought in the name of the Crown (R signifying *Regina*, the Queen).

Civil proceedings

1.5   *Civil law* exists to regulate disputes over the rights and obligations of persons dealing with each other. The State has no direct role in a dispute over, for instance, breach of contract. It is up to the persons involved to settle the matter in the courts if they so wish. The general purpose of such a course of action is to impose a settlement on matters, sometimes by financial compensation in the form of damages, sometimes by injunctions or other orders. There is no concept of punishment.

1.6   In civil proceedings, the case must be proven on the *balance of probability*. The party bearing the burden of proof is not required to produce absolute proof, nor prove the issue beyond reasonable doubt. He must convince the court that it is more probable than not that his assertions are true.

1.7   Terminology is different from that in criminal cases; the *plaintiff* sues the *defendant*, and the burden of proof may shift between the two. A civil case would therefore be referred to as, for example, *Smith v Megacorp plc*.

1.8   One of the most important areas of civil liability for business, and for professional staff in particular, is the law of *contract*. A second area, of which you should be aware, and which is also contained within the syllabus, is the law of *tort*. Both are forms of relationship between persons.

(a)   A *contract* is a relationship between two parties. It is a legally binding agreement, breach of which infringes one person's legal right given by the contract to have it performed.

(b)   A *tort* is a wrong committed by one person against another, infringing the general rights given to him by the law. There does not need to have been any pre-existing relationship between plaintiff and defendant before the tort was committed. The most significant tort in modern times is the tort of *negligence*.

Distinction between criminal and civil cases

1.9   It is important to bear in mind that it is not an act or event which creates the distinction, but the legal consequences of the act or event. A single event might give rise to criminal and civil proceedings.

1.10   For example, a broken leg caused to a pedestrian by a drunken driver is a single event which may give rise to a criminal case (prosecution by the State for the offence of driving with excess alcohol), and a civil case (the pedestrian sues for compensation for pain and suffering caused by the wrong).

1.11   The two sorts of proceedings are usually easily distinguished by the fact that the courts, the procedures and the terminology are different. As noted above, the burden of proof is different in each case, and the rules of evidence are also different. In criminal cases the rules of evidence are very strict; for example a confession will be carefully examined to see if any pressure was brought to bear upon the accused, but an admission in a civil case will not be subjected to such scrutiny.

2   FEATURES OF ENGLISH LAW

2.1   There are a number of important characteristics of English law, which, although individually not unique, together distinguish the English legal system from most other systems.

Continuity

2.2   England was last conquered in 1066. Since then there have not been any major changes imposed on the legal system, and so there is a progression in the development of the law over a long period. Principles of English law do not become inoperative through the lapse of time. Thus in *R v Casement 1916*, the Treason Act 1351 was consulted. This does not just apply to Acts of Parliament, but also to case law. The outcome of *Pinnel's case 1602* is still important today when examining the law of contract.

Judicial precedent

2.3   The doctrine of judicial precedent means that a judge is bound to apply decisions from earlier cases to the facts of the case before him, provided, among other conditions, that there is no material difference between the cases.

Common law and equity

2.4   The earliest element of the legal system to develop was the *common law*, a harsh system incorporating rigid rules applied by royal courts after the Norman conquest. Equity was developed, several hundred years later, as a system of law applied by the Chancellor where for some reason justice did not appear to be done under common law principles. The rules of *equity* were more flexible, based on the principles of equality and good conscience.

Codification

2.5   On occasion, the law in a particular area may be *codified*; the relevant rules as derived from existing legislation and from case law may be set out anew in a single codifying statute. *Case law* is law made in the courts. *Legislation*, or *statute*, is made by Parliament, the supreme law-making body in the United Kingdom. Codification should not be confused with consolidation, which is a process of bringing together statutory provisions (not case law) on a particular topic.

2.6   In some countries most of the law has been *codified*, or reduced to written codes which contain the whole of the law in a particular area. This is not generally the case in England. Examples of codification which has taken place are the Bills of Exchange Act 1882 and the Sale of Goods Act 1893 (the latter being subsequently *consolidated* into the Sale of Goods Act 1979). The resource required to codify key areas of the law is now thought to be too great to allow it; it is unlikely for example that the law of contract will be codified, although certain areas of criminal law may be addressed in the foreseeable future.

The courts

2.7   The *courts* have to be organised to accommodate the working of the legal system. There are four main functional aspects of the court system which underlie its structure.

     (a)   *Civil and criminal law* differ so much in substance and procedure that they are best administered in separate courts. However, there is no clear division into criminal courts and civil courts, although certain courts may have jurisdiction primarily in one area.

     (b)   *Local courts* allow the vast bulk of small legal proceedings to be decentralised. But important civil cases, in which large sums of money are at stake, begin in the High Court in London.

     (c)   Although the courts form a single system (as a result of the Judicature Acts 1873-1875), there is some *specialisation* both within the High Court (split into three divisions) and in other courts with separate functions.

(d) There is a system of *review by appeals* to higher courts. However, there is no clear division between courts of first instance and appeal courts; some courts function as both.

Exercise 1

While on a sales trip, one of your employees is involved in a car accident. The other vehicle involved is damaged and it is alleged that your employee is to blame. What legal proceedings may arise as a result of this incident?

Solution

Your employee may be guilty of a driving offence such as careless driving. The police, to whom the incident should be reported, will investigate, and if the facts indicate a driving offence, will prosecute him, probably in the local magistrates' court. The owner of the damaged vehicle (or his insurers) may sue the driver at fault in civil proceedings to recover damages. A claim would probably be brought in the county court.

---

3 THE DEVELOPMENT OF ENGLISH LAW

3.1 As noted earlier, English law has developed in an unbroken progression over a period of some 900 years. There are two *historical* sources of law, common law and equity. These comprise the procedures, rules and ways of thinking which have given rise to today's *legal* sources.

Common law

3.2 At the time of the Norman Conquest in 1066 there was no system of law common to the whole country. Rules of local custom were applied by local manorial courts. To improve the system, the King sent royal commissioners on tour (circuit) of different parts of the realm to deal with crimes and civil disputes.

3.3 These commissioners, who often heard their cases with the assistance of a local jury, at first applied the local customary law of the neighbourhood. On their return from circuit the commissioners sat in the royal courts at Westminster to try cases there.

3.4 In time the commissioners in their judicial capacity developed rules of law, selected from the differing local customs which they had encountered, as a common law *(ius commune)* which they applied uniformly in all trials (before the King's courts) throughout the kingdom.

Problems

3.5 (a) Common law was often *inflexible*. Before he could bring an action, a plaintiff had to obtain a *writ* (an order issued under the King's authority). Writs covered only a limited number of matters. If there was no appropriate writ form, an action could not be brought.

(b) Only a *limited remedy*, damages (compensation), was available. Common law could not stop a person doing something or compel him to do something.

(c) There was *too much emphasis on procedure*. A plaintiff might lose his case because of a minor technicality or wording. The system was open to bribery and corruption.

Equity

3.6 Citizens who could not obtain redress for grievances in the King's common law courts petitioned the King to obtain relief by direct royal intervention. These petitions came before the King in Council and by custom were referred to the principal civil minister - the Chancellor, who was usually a cleric.

3.7 In dealing with each petition his concern was to establish the truth of the matter and then to impose a just solution without undue regard for technicalities or procedural points.

3.8 Because the principles on which the Chancellor decided points were based on fair dealing between two individuals as equals, it became known as *equity*.

3.9 The system of equity, developed and administered by the Court of Chancery, was not a complete alternative to the common law. It was a method of adding to and improving on the common law.

This interaction of equity and common law produced three major changes.

New rights

3.10 Equity recognised and protected rights for which the common law gave no safeguards. If, for example, Sam transferred property to the legal ownership of Tom to pay the income of the property to Ben (in modern law Tom is a trustee for Ben) the common law simply recognised that Tom was the owner of the property at common law and gave no recognition to Tom's obligations to Ben. Equity recognised that Tom was the owner of the property at common law but insisted, as a matter of justice and good conscience, that Tom must comply with the terms of the trust imposed by Sam (the settlor) and pay the income to Ben (the beneficiary).

Better procedure

3.11 As explained above, equity could be more effective than common law in bringing a disputed matter to a decision.

Better remedies

3.12 The standard common law remedy for the successful plaintiff was the award of monetary compensation, damages, for his loss. The Chancellor developed remedies not available in other courts. Equity was able to order the defendant:

(a) to do what he has agreed to do (*specific performance*);
(b) to abstain from wrongdoing (*injunction*);
(c) to alter a document so that it reflected the parties' true intentions (*rectification*); or
(d) to restore the pre-contract status quo (*rescission*).

3.13 The development of equity was based on a number of 'equitable maxims', or principles. These are still applied today if an equitable remedy is sought. The following are examples.

(a) *He who comes to equity must come with clean hands.* To be fairly treated, the plaintiff must have acted fairly himself.

(b) *Equality is equity.* The law attempts to play fair and redress the balance; hence what is available to one person must be available to another. As an example, this principle can be observed in relation to contracts of minors. Equity does not allow the remedy of specific performance to be granted against a minor, and so it does not allow a minor to benefit from the remedy either.

(c) *He who seeks equity must do equity.* Similar to (a) above, this means that a person wanting equitable relief must be prepared to act fairly in future himself. For example, a mortgagor wishing to redeem his security under the principle of 'equity of redemption' must give reasonable notice of this to the mortgagee.

(d) *Equity looks at the intent, not the form.* However a person may try to pretend that he is doing something in the correct form, equity will look at what he is actually trying to achieve. For example, if an agreed damages clause in a contract is not a genuine pre-estimate of likely loss, equity will treat the clause as a penalty clause.

4 THE RELATIONSHIP BETWEEN EQUITY AND THE COMMON LAW 12/97

4.1 Equity and common law often *conflicted*. The rivalry between Chancery and common law courts was resolved in 1615 by a decision of the King (in the *Earl of Oxford's* case) that *where common law and equity conflict, equity must prevail*. This is still the rule today.

4.2 Equity was not in its origins a consistent code of law: it was simply disconnected intervention in legal disputes. Each Chancellor (and the Chancery judges acting under his authority) applied a personal and sometimes arbitrary standard of what he considered fair. However, under common law influence, equity become a consistent body of doctrine and at least as technical as the common law.

4.3 Thus the common law, administered in royal courts, was supplemented and sometimes overruled by principles of equity administered in the Court of Chancery. A plaintiff who began proceedings in one set of courts might after years of expensive litigation find that for some technical reason, he could not obtain the desired result but must abandon his case and begin again in the other courts.

4.4 This dual court system was ended by the Judicature Acts 1873 - 1875 which amalgamated the English courts. It is now possible to rely on any principle of common law or equity in any court of law in which the principle is relevant.

4.5 Although the courts have been amalgamated, common law and equity remain distinct. Where *common law* applies it tends to be *automatic* in its effect. *Equity* recognises the common law, as it always did; it sometimes offers an alternative solution but the court has *discretion* as to whether or not it will grant an equitable remedy in lieu of a common law one.

4.6 If, for example, breach of contract is proved, the plaintiff will at least get common law damages as compensation for his loss automatically; in certain circumstances the court may, at its discretion, provide an alternative remedy of equity. It may, for instance, order the defendant to perform the contract rather than allow him to 'buy his way out' of his contractual obligations by paying damages. The discretionary nature of equitable remedies means that a person who wins an action will not necessarily get the remedy he wants.

> *Miller v Jackson 1977*
> The Court of Appeal held that a village cricket club had committed both negligence and nuisance by allowing cricket balls to be struck out of the ground into the plaintiff's adjoining premises. However, the court refused to grant the injunction that the plaintiff had sought. They awarded damages of £400 instead on the grounds that the interest of the public in being able to play and watch cricket on a ground where it had been played for over 70 years should prevail over the hardship of a few individual householders who had only recently purchased their homes.

Exercise 2

What was the effect of the decision in the *Earl of Oxford's* case?

Solution

In the case of a conflict between common law and equity, equity must prevail.

Chapter roundup

- The distinction between criminal and civil liability is central to the English legal system.

- Crime is conduct prohibited by law. The State is the prosecutor, the perpetrator is punished and fines are payable to the State. There is an accused and a prosecution, and the case must be proved beyond reasonable doubt. The courts must be used to settle the matter.

- Civil law regulates disputes over the rights and obligations of persons dealing with each other. The State has no role, there is no concept of punishment and compensation is owed to the wronged person. There is a plaintiff and a defendant, and the case must be proved on the balance of probabilities. The parties are free to settle the dispute outside the court system.

- English law has developed over many centuries. Common law and equity, before 1875, were administered by two separate court systems. Since their amalgamation it has been possible to rely on a legal or an equitable principle in any court, though in the case of conflict *equity* (fairness) *prevails*.

- *Common law* (legal rights) is applied automatically and comprises a complete system of law. Rights are enforceable against anyone and everyone, regardless of their knowledge that the rights exist; rights must be exercised within a 3, 6 or 12 year limitation period. Remedies, for example damages, are given against property.

- *Equity* (equitable rights) is applied at the court's discretion and does not comprise a complete system of law. Rights are enforceable only against those persons who know or ought to know of their existence and must be exercised without undue delay. Remedies, for example an injunction, are given against the person.

Test your knowledge

1   Who conducts a criminal prosecution? (see para 1.3)

2   What is the standard of proof in civil proceedings? (1.6)

3   What is meant by codification? (2.6)

4   What are the two historical sources of law? (3.1)

5   Give three examples of equitable remedies (3.12)

6   Give three examples of equitable maxims (3.13)

7   What important principle was established by the *Earl of Oxford's* case? (4.1)

Now try illustrative question 1 at the end of the Study Text

Chapter 2

THE SYSTEM OF COURTS

This chapter covers the following topics

1   The structure of the courts

2   Magistrates' courts

3   The County Court

4   The Crown Court

5   The High Court

6   The Court of Appeal

7   The House of Lords

8   The Woolf reforms

9   Other courts and tribunals

10   Arbitration

11   The legal profession

Introduction

In the first chapter of this part of the syllabus, we examined the difference between civil and criminal proceedings. We saw how criminal actions are brought by the State, and how, in the event of a successful prosecution, the accused person is liable to punishment. Some crimes, for example murder, have a victim, while others, for example speeding, can be committed without causing loss to any particular person.

Civil law, as we have also seen, regulates disputes over the rights and obligations of persons dealing with each other. The State has no direct role and it is up to the persons involved to settle the matter in the courts if they so wish. Nearly all important court cases are reported by a system of law reports, described later on. Only a very few civil cases are reported in the general press or on television. You may remember, for example, the High Court case involving French champagne growers and a small vineyard in South-East England which wished to call one of its products 'Elderflower champagne'.

The publicity afforded to court cases, nearly all of which are open to reporters and the public, and the fact that even cases of local interest may be reported in the regional press - precisely in the area where a company operates - means that many companies prefer not to become involved in court proceedings. There are other options open to them, sometimes described collectively as *alternative dispute resolution*.

In this chapter, we start by describing the court system. We have included both criminal and civil courts, as some courts fulfil both roles, but it is more important that you understand the role of the civil courts, particularly the county court and the High Court which are of greatest practical relevance.

In the second part of the chapter we look at the two key alternatives to the court system: arbitration and tribunals. Arbitration gives greater privacy and often allows the parties to resolve a dispute on their own terms; tribunals are a kind of specialised court offering a procedure which may be quick, cheap and informal by comparison with the normal court system. You may, for example have heard of industrial tribunals or rent tribunals.

1   THE STRUCTURE OF THE COURTS   *12/95*

1.1   The English court system is quite complex. It has four basic levels.

(a)   The House of Lords.
(b)   The Court of Appeal.
(c)   The High Court (including the Crown Court).
(d)   The inferior courts (including county courts and magistrates' courts).

1.2   Within this structure there is neither a clear division into criminal courts and civil courts, nor a division into courts of first instance and appeal courts. The Queen's Bench Division of the High Court provides an example of this. It hears civil cases *and* criminal cases, and in its civil jurisdiction it operates as a court of first instance *and* as a court hearing appeals from the county courts. However, the vast majority of cases are heard in the magistrates' courts or the county courts.

1.3   A *court of first instance* is the court where the case is originally heard in full. The *appeal court* is the court to which an appeal is made against the ruling or the sentence.

1.4   If the appeal court finds in favour of the party making the appeal (the appellant), the original decision is *reversed*. This is different from *overruling* which, as we shall see, happens when a higher court finds a lower court's precedent to be wrong. Although the precedent is overruled and hence not followed again, the overruling has no effect on the actual outcome of the original case.

The civil courts   *12/97*

1.5   The following diagram sets out the English civil court structure.

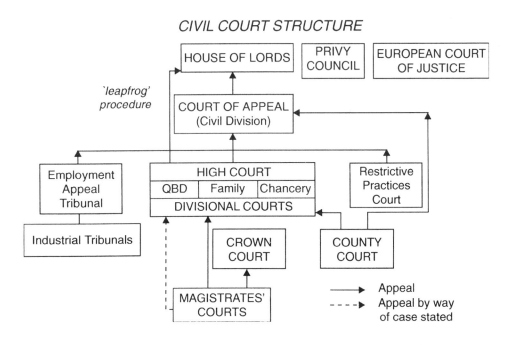

CIVIL COURT STRUCTURE

The criminal court structure   *6/98*

1.6   The following diagram sets out the English criminal court structure.

CRIMINAL COURT STRUCTURE

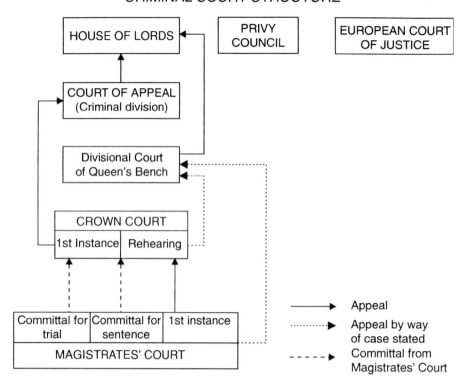

2   MAGISTRATES' COURTS

2.1   Magistrates' courts are the inferior criminal courts. In addition they exercise certain family law, administrative law and minor civil functions.

Criminal jurisdiction

2.2   Magistrates courts deal with criminal cases as follows.

(a)   They try summarily (without a jury) all minor offences.

(b)   They conduct *committal proceedings*, which are preliminary investigations of the prosecution case, when the offence is triable only on *indictment* (by a Crown Court). Committal proceedings are due to be replaced by a 'transfer for trial' procedure when the relevant provisions of the Criminal Justice and Public Order Act 1994 come into effect.

(c)   Certain offences are '*triable either way*'. This means that they are triable summarily or on indictment with a jury. If the accused consents and the magistrates' court considers that the case is suitable for trial in that court, then they may try such a case summarily. If the magistrates are satisfied that such a case should not be tried summarily, or if the accused insists on his right to trial by jury, they commit the defendant for trial in a Crown Court. (Again, this procedure will be replaced by a 'transfer for trial'.)

Proceedings concerning juveniles

2.3   Criminal proceedings cannot be instituted against children under ten years of age: it is presumed that they cannot be guilty of any offence. Children between 10 and 14 may be prosecuted if it can be shown that they were of 'mischievous discretion', and 'young persons' over 14 are regarded as fully responsible for their acts.

Penalties

2.4   The maximum penalties which *magistrates* may impose on a defendant convicted summarily of a criminal offence are *six months' imprisonment* or a *fine of up to £5,000*. The magistrate also has discretion to order the defendant to compensate his victim, up to

£5,000. If in a summary trial the magistrates consider that their sentencing powers are inadequate they may convict and commit the defendant to a Crown Court for sentence.

Civil jurisdiction

2.5 Magistrates' civil jurisdiction includes family proceedings, various types of licensing and enforcement of local authority charges and rates.

Family proceedings

2.6 Magistrates have an extensive jurisdiction in family law matters. Their powers include powers to make orders for financial provision for, or protection of, parties to a marriage and children of a family for the custody or supervision of children and for guardianship orders and adoption orders.

Appeals

Criminal cases

2.7 A defendant convicted on a criminal charge has a general right to a rehearing by a Crown Court. Either the defendant or the prosecution may appeal on a point of law only by way of 'case stated' to a divisional court of the Queen's Bench Division.

2.8 A 'case stated' appeal is based on the idea that magistrates or the Crown Court have wrongly interpreted the law. The magistrate produces written reasons for the way in which he decided the case. These, together with the facts, are considered by the Divisional Court to ensure that the law was correctly applied. If not, then the case may be sent back to the lower court with instructions as to how it should be decided.

Civil cases

2.9 On family matters, appeals are to a divisional court of the Family Division of the High Court.

Staffing

2.10 *Lay magistrates* (the majority) are not legally qualified and sit part-time. They are appointed by the Lord Chancellor on the advice of local advisory committees and are assisted by a salaried, legally qualified *clerk*, who must be a solicitor or barrister of at least five years' standing. *Stipendiary magistrates* sit in large towns and are salaried. They must be solicitors or barristers of at least seven years' standing. Lay magistrates sit two or three to a court, stipendiary magistrates sit alone.

3 THE COUNTY COURT

Jurisdiction

3.1 *County courts* have *civil jurisdiction only* but deal with almost every kind of civil case arising within the local areas for which the courts are established. In some matters the jurisdiction is exclusive, in others it is exercised concurrently with the High Court. In the latter event, there are criteria laid down to determine which court hears a case.

3.2 The practical importance of the county courts is that they deal with *the majority of the country's civil litigation.* Over one and a half million actions are commenced each year (about one million are for debt), although only about 5% result in trials since most actions are discontinued or settled out of court before the trial stage is reached.

3.3   The county court is involved in:

(a)   *Contract and tort* claims (see below).

(b)   *Equitable matters* concerning trusts, mortgages and partnership dissolution up to £30,000, unless the parties waive the limit.

(c)   Disputes concerning *land* where the capital value of the land is less than £30,000, although there is unlimited jurisdiction where the Rent Acts are concerned, or where the parties agree.

(d)   *Undefended matrimonial* cases.

(e)   *Probate matters* (disputes concerning the grant of authority to personal representatives etc) where the estate of the deceased is estimated to be less than £30,000.

(f)   *Miscellaneous matters* conferred by various statutes, for example the Consumer Credit Act 1974 (no limit on jurisdiction).

(g)   Some *bankruptcy*, company winding-up and admiralty cases.

(h)   '*Small claims*' of up to £5,000 (revised from £3,000 since 26th April 1999).

Contract and tort

3.4   Actions in contract and tort worth *less than £25,000* must normally be tried in a *county court* and those worth *£50,000 or more* must normally be tried in the *High Court*, with those in between going either way, subject to:

(a)   the 'financial substance' of the action;
(b)   whether questions of public interest are raised;
(c)   the complexity of the facts, the legal issues, procedures or remedies involved; and
(d)   whether transfer is likely to result in a more speedy trial.

3.5   These criteria may also be used to transfer an action worth less than £25,000 to the High Court or an action worth over £50,000 to the county court.

The county court and the High Court

3.6   Allocation of cases between the High Court and the county court is made on the basis of the principles laid down in the High Court and Country Court Jurisdiction Order 1991. For example, actions in respect of personal injuries are to be commenced in a county court unless the claim is worth £50,000 or more.

The Small Claims Court

3.7   To assist litigants who decide to conduct their case in person the county court registrar may, if the amount involved *does not exceed £5,000* or if the parties agree, refer a case to an arbitrator to hear and decide informally in a Small Claims Court.

(a)   The arbitrator is usually the district judge himself but may be another person chosen by the parties. The arbitrator's award is recorded as a county court judgement.

(b)   This is a cheaper and quicker way of settling small claims in an informal atmosphere.

(c)   Personal injury claims, claims for possession of land, housing disrepair claims and harrassment claims may be dealt with by the small claims procedure only if they fall below £1,000. Any such claim between £1,000 and £15,000 is likely to be dealt with under the 'fast track' procedure introduced by the Woolf reforms (see section 8).

Appeals

3.8 From the county court there is a right of appeal direct to the Civil Division of the Court of Appeal. In bankruptcy cases an appeal goes to the Chancery Division of the High Court.

Staffing

3.9 A *circuit judge* presides, being a barrister of at least ten years' standing. A *recorder*, a part-time appointment in the Crown Court, is a solicitor or barrister of at least ten years' standing, and may be appointed as a circuit judge after three years' experience as a recorder. A *district judge* (previously known as a registrar), who must be a solicitor or barrister of at least seven years' standing, assists the circuit judge. The circuit judge normally sits alone, although in a limited number of civil cases (fraud, libel, slander) there may be a *jury* of eight persons. The district judge may hear small claims, or any other with the consent of the parties.

4   THE CROWN COURT

4.1 The Crown Court is theoretically a single court forming part of the *Supreme Court*, but in fact it comprises *local courts* in large towns and also the *Central Criminal Court* (the Old Bailey) in the City of London.

Criminal jurisdiction

4.2 It tries all indictable (serious criminal) offences with a jury and hears appeals and deals with committals for sentencing from magistrates' courts.

4.3 There are four classes of offence triable in the Crown Court.

(a) *Class 1 offences* are the *most serious offences* such as murder and treason. A High Court judge must preside.

(b) *Class 2 offences* include serious offences such as rape and manslaughter. Cases are usually presided over by a High Court judge.

(c) *Class 3 offences* are *less serious* offences which must be tried on indictment (not summarily). Examples are robbery and grievous bodily harm. A High Court judge, circuit judge or recorder may preside.

(d) *Class 4 offences* are those offences which may be tried on indictment or summarily (triable either way) such as burglary and reckless driving. Usually a circuit judge or recorder presides, though a High Court judge may do so.

Civil jurisdiction

4.4 The Crown Court deals with a few types of civil cases, being appeals from the magistrates' court on matters of affiliation, betting, gaming and licensing.

Appeals

4.5 From the Crown Court there is a right of appeal on criminal matters to the Criminal Division of the Court of Appeal. An appeal by way of 'case stated' on a point of law may also be made to a Divisional Court of the Queen's Bench Division.

Staffing

4.6 A High Court Judge, a circuit judge or a recorder may sit in the Crown Court, depending on the nature of the offence being tried. Sometimes lay magistrates also sit. All indictable offences will be heard by a judge with a *jury* of 12 persons.

5   THE HIGH COURT   *6/94, 6/99*

5.1   The *High Court* is organised into three divisions - Queen's Bench, Chancery and Family. Except where other special courts have exclusive jurisdiction, the High Court can deal with any civil matter.

Queen's Bench Division

Civil jurisdiction

5.2   The Queen's Bench Division (QBD) deals mainly with common law matters such as actions based on contract or tort. It also has a supervisory jurisdiction over all applications for judicial review, and a supervisory role over other courts. It is the largest of the three divisions, having 54 judges. The division also includes two separate courts.

5.3   It includes a separate *Admiralty Court* to deal with shipping matters such as charterparties, salvage and collisions at sea.

5.4   There is also within the Queen's Bench Division an important *Commercial Court* which specialises in commercial cases, for example insurance claims. The Commercial Court offers a rather simpler trial procedure to meet business needs. Judges of the Commercial Court may also sit as arbitrators.

Supervisory role

5.5   A Divisional Court of QBD has a supervisory role over other courts. It may issue a writ of *habeas corpus,* which is an order for the release of a person wrongfully detained, and also prerogative orders against inferior courts, tribunals and other bodies such as local authorities, insofar as they have a duty to exercise a discretion fairly. There are three types of *prerogative order.*

(a)   *Mandamus* requires the court or other body to carry out a public duty. For example, a tribunal may be ordered to hear an appeal which it has wrongly refused to do or a local authority may be ordered to produce its accounts for inspection by a ratepayer.

(b)   *Prohibition* prevents a court or tribunal from exceeding its jurisdiction (before it has done so).

(c)   *Certiorari* orders a court or tribunal which has taken action to submit the record of its proceedings to the High Court for review. The High Court may then quash the decision but cannot substitute its own decision (as it can under ordinary appeal procedure). The exact scope of this power of review is not clearly defined. It is exercised when an inferior court has acted illegally, exceeded its jurisdiction or reached its decision contrary to the principles of natural justice - without giving the person concerned the right to know of and reply to the case against him. Essentially, it is a review of what has been done after it has been done.

Criminal (appellate) jurisdiction

5.6   The division hears appeals by way of case stated from the magistrates' courts and the Crown Courts.

Chancery division

5.7   This division deals with traditional equity matters.

(a)   Trusts and mortgages.
(b)   Revenue matters.
(c)   Bankruptcy (though outside London this is a county court subject).
(d)   Disputed wills and administration of estates of deceased persons.
(e)   Partnership and company matters.

5.8 There is a separate *Companies Court* within the division which deals with liquidations and other company proceedings, and a Patents Court established under the Patents Act 1977. This division also hears *appeals* from the county court on bankruptcy matters.

Family division

5.9 This division deals with matrimonial cases (though most undefended divorce cases are heard in the county court), family property cases, and proceedings relating to children (wardship, guardianship, adoption, legitimacy etc). It has long been suggested that the family division should be merged with the county court matrimonial jurisdiction to create a separate family court.

5.10 The division hears appeals from magistrates' courts and the county court on family matters.

Appeals

5.11 Appeals are made from the High Court as follows.

Civil cases

5.12 Appeals may be made to the *Court of Appeal (Civil Division)* or to the *House of Lords*, under what is known as the 'leapfrog' procedure. For the leapfrog procedure to be followed, all parties must give their consent to it, and the case must involve a point of law of general public importance. The House of Lords must also give their leave to this.

Criminal cases

5.13 Appeals are made direct to the House of Lords where the case has reached the High Court on appeal from a magistrates' court or from the Crown Court.

Staffing

5.14 The High Court is staffed by no more than 98 puisne (pronounced 'puny') judges, who must be barristers of at least ten years' standing. QBD has 54 judges and is presided over by the Lord Chief Justice. Chancery has 13 judges and is presided over (nominally) by the Lord Chancellor. Family Division has 16 judges and its President presides. At least two judges must sit in each divisional court, but a single judge may hear a case at first instance.

Exercise 1

What are the four areas of jurisdiction of the Queen's Bench Division?

Solution

(a) Original civil jurisdiction.
(b) Appellate civil jurisdiction.
(c) Appellate criminal jurisdiction.
(d) Supervisory jurisdiction.

---

6 THE COURT OF APPEAL

6.1 The Court of Appeal was divided into two divisions in 1966.

Civil Division

6.2   The Civil Division of the Court of Appeal can hear appeals from the High Court, county courts, and from certain other courts and special tribunals. It does not conduct a complete re-hearing but reviews the record of the evidence in the lower court and the legal arguments put before it. It may uphold or reverse the earlier decision or order a new trial. A majority decision is sufficient, and a judge who disagrees gives an express dissenting judgment.

Criminal Division

6.3   The Criminal Division of the Court of Appeal hears appeals from the Crown Court. It may also be invited to review a criminal case by the Home Secretary (as in *R v Maguire 1991*) or to consider a point of law at the request of the Attorney General. Its powers and procedures are very similar to those of the Civil Division.

Appeals

6.4   Appeals lie to the House of Lords, with the leave of the House of Lords or the Court of Appeal, on a point of law.

Staffing

6.5   There are 29 *Lord Justices of Appeal*, promoted from the High Court. Three judges normally sit together. In the Criminal Division, the *Lord Chief Justice* presides. In the Civil Division the *Master of the Rolls* presides. A majority decision is sufficient and dissenting judgments are expressed.

Exercise 2

Find out the names of the current Lord Chief Justice and the Master of the Rolls.

Solution

At the time of writing, the Lord Chief Justice is Sir Thomas Bingham and the Master of the Rolls is Lord Woolf.

---

7   THE HOUSE OF LORDS   *12/94*

7.1   The House of Lords has two separate roles, and it is important that these are not confused.

   (a)   It has a *legislative* role, as one of the two Houses of Parliament.

   (b)   It has a *judicial* role, as the highest appeal court of the English, Scottish and Northern Irish legal systems.

The judicial committee of the House of Lords

7.2   Apart from the limited jurisdiction of the European Court, the Judicial Committee of the House of Lords is the highest court of appeal. It hears appeals from both the civil and the criminal divisions of the Court of Appeal (and, under the leapfrog procedure, direct from the High Court, although this is rare).

Staffing

7.3   Judges are usually promoted from the Court of Appeal to be members of the House of Lords. They are known as *Lords of Appeal in Ordinary*, or *Law Lords*. Five judges normally sit together, though there may only be three. Majority decisions hold and dissenting judgments are made.

The judicial committee of the Privy Council

7.4 Some countries of the Commonwealth (about 25) still retain a right of appeal from their national court to the Queen's Privy Council. Canada and India abolished appeals in 1949 and Australia in 1986. The Judicial Committee (with a slightly different representative membership) is in effect the same body as the corresponding Committee of the House of Lords. It also deals with appeals from the English ecclesiastical courts.

Exercise 3

List the court (or courts) to which an appeal may be made from each of the following:

(a)   The county court.
(b)   The High Court (civil cases).

(Refer to the court structure diagram on page 11)

Solution

(a)   The Court of Appeal (Civil Division) or the High Court (Chancery - for bankruptcy cases).
(b)   The Court of Appeal (Civil Division) or the House of Lords.

---

8   THE WOOLF REFORMS

8.1 Major changes to the system of civil justice in England and Wales took effect from 26 April 1999, bringing in new *procedure rules* for the High Court and County Courts. The reform of civil justice was first proposed by Lord Woolf in his 1996 report *Access to Justice*

8.2 Under the reforms, the Court will have the power to control every aspect of the litigation process, shifting responsibility away from the litigants and their advisers. This will affect a wide range of commercial disputes.

8.3 The new procedures are designed to lead to *quicker and less confrontational* settlement of disputes at the beginning of a case, to encourage parties to consider *alternative methods* of dispute resolution, and to avoid the excessive expense of litigation, which Lord Bingham has called "a cancer eating at the heart of the administration of justice". A recent survey of 217 cases by a firm of solicitors acting for plaintiffs in personal injury cases found average costs to be £836, whilst damages recovered were on average only £694.

8.4 Examples of some of the changes are as follows.

   (i)   The court will allocate cases to new 'tracks' – the *small claims track*, the *fast track* or the *multi-track*.

   (ii)   The expanded small claims track will deal with claims of not more than £5,000.

   (iii)   The fast track limit will be £15,000. This will be a strictly limited procedure, designed to take cases to trial within a short but reasonable timescale. The hearing will be no more than one day and costs will be fixed.

   (iv)   Larger claims will be allocated to the multi-track. This will span both High Court and county court cases, and will cover most commercial claims. There will be an initial 'case management conference' to encourage parties to settle the dispute or to consider alternative dispute resolution (such as mediation or arbitration).

   (v)   The trial judge in a multi-track trial will set a budget and a final timetable for the trial.

8.5   The court's management of a case will be achieved by the setting up of *codes of practice* with which the parties must comply, and which will ensure effective exchange of information before the proceedings begin.

8.6   Litigants will have to be much better prepared before going to court. One consequence of this is that costs of litigation will be largely known in advance. For example, the court's permission will now be needed to call expert witnesses, and the court can compel the parties to use a single joint witness. The names of court documents and applications are to be changed to make them more user friendly.

8.7   There will be a new senior judge with overall responsibility for civil justice, to be known as the *Head of Civil Justice*. His appointment is designed to raise the status of civil justice, which has long been in the shadow of the criminal justice system.

8.8   The detail presented here on the Woolf reforms is mainly included for your background information, so that you are aware of the principles involved. You should note that the changes are mainly *procedural* (ie how cases are to be conducted). You will not need a detailed knowledge of the Woolf reforms to pass this exam but it will impress the examiner if you can refer to them (where relevant of course!) in an answer on the English legal system. The main point to remember is that the reforms hope to encourage *speedy dispute resolution* without recourse to the courts, by forcing litigants to be much *better prepared in advance* and to really think about what they are getting themselves into.

9   OTHER COURTS AND TRIBUNALS   6/97

9.1   There is a number of other courts and tribunals which feature prominently in the English legal system, either because they have a relatively important status (for example, the Employment Appeal Tribunal is of equal status with the High Court) or because they have a heavy caseload (Industrial Tribunals hear nearly 10,000 cases per annum).

Industrial tribunals

9.2   Industrial Tribunals were established by the Industrial Training Act 1964. They have a wide jurisdiction over most disputes between *employee and employer*. They are now called *employment tribunals*.

   (a)   Disputes about redundancy pay.
   (b)   Complaints of unfair dismissal.
   (c)   Questions as to terms of contracts of employment.
   (d)   Equal pay claims.
   (e)   Appeals against health and safety notices.
   (f)   Complaints about sex and race discrimination.
   (g)   Contractual claims (ie claims for wrongful dismissal) of up to £25,000.

9.3   There is a right of appeal to the *Employment Appeal Tribunal*.

9.4   Each tribunal is staffed by a legally qualified *chairman* and two other persons, one representing the employer and one representing the employee. Under the Trade Union Reform and Employment Rights Act 1993, the chairman can sit alone in certain types of case.

Employment Appeal Tribunal (EAT)

9.5   In spite of its name, this is a court of equal status with the High Court. It was established by the Employment Protection Act 1975. It hears appeals from industrial tribunals mainly on employment matters (claims for unfair dismissal, redundancy pay, sex discrimination etc).

9.6 A *High Court judge* and two *lay assessors* from a panel appointed on the Lord Chancellor's recommendation sit. From the EAT there is a right of appeal to the Court of Appeal.

Social security appeal tribunals

9.7 A variety of cash benefits are available under the Social Security Act 1975 (including unemployment benefit, invalidity and sickness benefit and retirement pensions) and the Social Security Act 1986 (including income support, family credit and housing benefit). Questions may arise in the administration of these benefits, claims being submitted to an *adjudication officer*.

9.8 The Social Security appeal tribunals hear appeals arising from the adjudication process. The tribunal consists of a chairman (usually a lawyer) and two members from panels representative of employers and of employees. Either party may appeal from the decision of the tribunal to the Social Security Commissioners. On a point of law there is a further right of appeal to the High Court.

Lands Tribunal

9.9 This tribunal deals with disputes over the value of property, for example for compulsory purchase. It is usually composed of three members, being experienced lawyers and qualified valuation experts.

The restrictive practices court

9.10 This is not part of the High Court but is co-ordinate in status with it; appeals from it go to the Court of Appeal. It investigates the merits (if any) of agreements registered under the Competition Act 1998. In these functions it is required to have regard to EC law.

9.11 Usually a *High Court judge* and two *lay assessors* from a panel appointed on the Lord Chancellor's recommendation sit.

Supervision

9.12 The working of the system of tribunals is supervised by a *Council on Tribunals*. In many instances, especially industrial tribunals, there is of course a statutory right to appeal from a tribunal to a higher court on points of law. The High Court may also make prerogative orders to prevent or remedy errors and injustices. At the appeal stage (but not usually in the proceedings before the lower tribunal) the applicant may be able to obtain legal aid which is the professional services of legal advisers and advocates provided at public expense.

Instituting proceedings

9.13 A person who wishes to bring a claim must present an 'originating application' to the appropriate regional office. The application must be in writing and must set out:

   (a) the name and address of the applicant;
   (b) the names and addresses of the person or persons against whom relief is sought;
   (c) the grounds on which relief is sought.

ACAS

9.14 ACAS (the *Advisory, Conciliation and Arbitration Service*) has a positive role to play in 'promoting the improvement of industrial relations'. As an independent body, it can be required under the Act to settle trade union recognition issues, by holding inquiries and publishing recommendations. It may also be involved in individual conciliation cases, prior to hearing by tribunal: it is frequently called in, for example, over unfair dismissal complaints.

9.15 ACAS may thus intervene with:

(a) *conciliation* (getting conflicting parties together);
(b) *arbitration* (assisting in the appointment of arbitrators); or
(c) *mediation* (offering middle ground for settlement).

9.16 Although recorded disputes have fallen to very low levels - giving the impression that conflict at work has largely disappeared - there is a still a high demand for ACAS's services on a personal level, in matters of unfair dismissal, equal pay and sex and race discrimination. In 1993, 47% of ACAS' completed *collective* conciliation cases related to pay and employment conditions disputes, 20% to redundancy and only 9% to union recognition. ACAS hit the headlines in 1994 with its successful intervention in the Railtrack dispute with rail union RMT.

10   ARBITRATION

10.1   It is common practice to include in commercial contracts a clause providing that any dispute is to be settled by arbitration under the relevant legislation. There is therefore a growing tendency for business people to settle disagreements using alternative methods of dispute resolution, in particular forms of *arbitration*.

10.2   Arbitration is settlement of a dispute by an independent person usually chosen by the parties themselves. A dispute may be referred to arbitration either by *agreement* out of court, or *compulsorily*. Arbitration is governed by the rules set out in the Arbitration Acts 1950 to 1996.

Voluntary agreements

10.3   The Arbitration Act 1996, which came into force in January 1997, aimed to introduce *greater speed and flexibility* into the arbitration process, in particular by conferring upon the parties the right to make their own agreement on virtually all aspects of the arbitration (section 1). It contains provisions for the appointment and removal of arbitrators, and the power to appoint experts (s 37), advisers and assessors. It turned the courts' role into a supervisory rather than an interventionist one. Under this Act, the parties may choose to dispense with formal hearings and strict rules of evidence and procedure (s 46).

10.4   Under the 1996 Act, an arbitration agreement is a separate agreement which can outlive the original contract that gave rise to the arbitration proceedings.

10.5   The main advantage of the arbitration procedure is *privacy*, since the public and the press have no right to attend a hearing before an arbitrator.

10.6   An arbitrator is usually an expert in the field of dispute. The parties may name their arbitrators or provide that some other person, say the President of the Law Society, shall appoint him. The High Court has power to appoint an arbitrator.

10.7   Unless otherwise agreed, a hearing before an arbitrator follows the same essential procedure as in a court of law. However, following the Arbitration Act 1996, the arbitrators and parties can settle on the form of the arbitration.

10.8   There may be an appeal to the High Court on a preliminary point of law only if both parties consent or if the High Court gives leave to appeal. There is a further restricted right of appeal from the High Court to the Court of Appeal. The right to appeal against an award made in arbitration is restricted. The 1996 Act provides for the immunity of the arbitrator, stating that he is not liable for anything that is done or not done while he is arbitrator, as long as he always acted in good faith.

Compulsory arbitration

10.9 In addition to voluntary arbitration as described above, compulsory arbitration may be enforced in the following circumstances.

(a) Certain statutes provide for arbitration on disputes arising out of the provision of the statute.

(b) The High Court may order that a case of a technical nature shall be tried (or investigated with report back to the court) by an Official Referee or other arbitrator.

(c) A county court may order that a small claim (not exceeding £5,000) shall be referred to arbitration, under the small claims court procedure.

Employment disputes

10.10 New measures to improve dispute resolution in employment matters came into force in August 1998 with the Employment Rights (Dispute Resolution) Act 1998. Under its provisions there will be encouragement of greater use of voluntary alternatives, and tribunal procedures have been revised. Cases may now be determined on the basis of written evidence, and ACAS has the power to provide an arbitration service for unfair dismissal, unlawful discrimination and redundancy entitlement.

10.11 Where a tribunal finds that an applicant was unfairly dismissed but that he did not use the employer's internal procedures for appealing, any compensatory award will be reduced. In addition, the Employment Appeal Tribunal can now hear appeals from tribunals in breach of contract (ie wrongful dismissal) cases.

Exercise 4

What are the relative advantages of court proceedings and arbitration?

Solution

The *court system* may be cheaper than arbitration, where the arbitrator's remuneration and all the venue costs must be met. More importantly the rights to appeal from a court decision are more entrenched, the judge's interlocutory powers are greater and a judge may grant interim relief or even make a summary judgement. A judge may be better qualified to assess evidence and apply rules of law. Although this would also be true of legally qualified arbitrators, an arbitrator who is not so qualified may decide a case on what he thinks to be a fair basis only. This may make the results of arbitration proceedings even less easy to predict than court proceedings.

Under *arbitration*, the parties to a contract may provide for disputes to be settled by *a third party* giving them greater control. This person is likely to be an expert in the issue in question, which may be invaluable in complex cases. Arbitration proceedings are usually *private affairs*, with none of the publicity which surrounds most court proceedings. This may be especially desirable when the dispute involves 'sensitive' material. An *arbitrator's decision* may, if the parties agree, be final, with no right of appeal. Venue and timing may be more flexible. There is more likelihood of a compromise, as proceedings are less adversarial in nature.

---

11   THE LEGAL PROFESSION   6/99

11.1 It is clearly not intended that everyone who studies the law for professional examinations should be an expert lawyer, able to deal with the most complex legal issues unaided. What is important is that you should be aware when legal problems arise and be able to judge when outside assistance is required. In these circumstances you should be better able to communicate with lawyers.

11.2   The legal profession is divided into two mutually exclusive groups - barristers and solicitors.

Solicitors

11.3   Solicitors are the general practitioners of the legal profession and provide many services to their clients which do not involve them in court proceedings. Generally solicitors may only appear as advocates for their clients before magistrates' and county courts, although some do have rights of higher audience and can appear in the High Court. In most other court proceedings the solicitor prepares the case and retains one or more counsel (barristers) to appear in court as advocates for his client. The individual conduct and collective affairs of solicitors are subject to regulation (partly on a statutory basis) by the Law Society. It is common for solicitors to practise as partners of a firm, but they may not carry on business through companies.

Barristers

11.4   Barristers are specialists in advocacy in court, but much of their working time is spent in chambers conducting conferences with their instructing solicitors and their clients on the affairs of the latter. There is also a great deal of paperwork, for example drafting legal documents and advisory 'opinions'. Barristers are consultants who usually (but not always) deal with lay clients only through solicitors. The Bar Council has approved proposals which allow direct access by certain professionals (for example accountants and engineers) to seek an opinion.

Exercise 5

It is not possible for anyone to be qualified as a solicitor and a barrister at the same time. What do you think might be the advantages and disadvantages of the present division of the legal profession into two branches?

Solution

The present system gives greater access to barristers than a 'fused' system would. Under fusion, leading barristers would probably join the larger firms of solicitors. The present system, by keeping advocacy in the hands of 'specialists' , also means that judges hear clear arguments in trials.

Those who argue in favour of fusion would point to duplication of effort, unnecessary division of responsibilities, and the higher cost of paying more than one expert.

Chapter roundup

- Four functional aspects of the court system underlie its structure. Civil and criminal law differ and are best administered separately. Local courts allow smaller civil proceedings and criminal cases to be decentralised. Specialisation is necessary, hence the split nature of the High Court. Higher courts represents a system of appeals.

- The civil court structure contains the following courts.

  o Magistrates' courts mostly deal with small domestic matters.

  o County courts hear claims in contract and tort, equitable matters, land and probate disputes among others.

  o The Crown Court hears appeals from magistrates' courts

  o The High Court is divided into three specialist divisions.

  o The Court of Appeal hears appeals from the County Court, the High Court, the Restrictive Practices Court, and from the Employment Appeal Tribunal.

  o The House of Lords hears appeals from the Court of Appeal and the High Court.

- The criminal court structure comprises the following.

  o Magistrates' courts hear summary offences and committal proceedings for indictable offences

  o The Crown Court tries serious criminal (indictable) offences and hears appeals from the magistrates' court.

  o The Divisional Court of QBD hears appeals by way of case stated from magistrates' courts and the Crown Court.

  o The Court of Appeal hears appeals from the Crown Court.

  o The House of Lords hears appeals from the Court of Appeal or a Divisional Court of QBD.

- The Woolf reforms have proposed changes to civil court procedure.

- The court system is not the only way to settle disputes, *Administrative tribunals*, such as social security appeal tribunals and industrial tribunals deal with the administration of Acts of Parliament and delegated legislation - that is, disputes between individuals and government agencies or between two individuals. *Arbitration* allows parties to bring their dispute before a non-legal independent expert so that he may decide the case, although an arbitrator's award may be enforced in the same manner as a High Court judgment.

Test your knowledge

1   What is meant by the inferior courts? (see para 1.1)

2   Sketch a diagram of the civil court structure (1.5)

3   What are the two categories of magistrate? (2.10)

4   What is the jurisdiction of the county court over actions in contract and tort? (3.4)

5   What is the Small Claims Court? (3.7)

6   What are the three divisions of the High Court? (5.1)

7   To what court may appeals be made from the High Court in civil cases? (5.12)

8   What kind of judge sits in the House of Lords? (7.3)

9   What are the 'tracks' introduced by the Woolf reforms? (8.4)

10 What is the EAT? (9.5)

Now try illustrative question 2 at the end of the Study Text

Chapter 3

SOURCES OF ENGLISH LAW

This chapter covers the following topics

1 Legislation

2 Delegated legislation

3 The interpretation of statutes

4 Rules of statutory interpretation

5 Presumptions of statutory interpretation

6 Other assistance in interpretation

7 Case law

8 The doctrine of binding precedent

9 The advantages and disadvantages of precedent

10 Custom

11 Subsidiary sources of law

Introduction

In Chapter 1, we traced the development of, and the relationship between, common law and equity. The law is not static but changes and develops, reflecting the values and institutions of each era. Until Parliament was reformed in the nineteenth century, the main purpose and effect of English was to define and safeguard rights of property and to uphold public order. Since that time there has been an increasing flow of new laws designed, for example, to deal with social problems and to develop the national economy. Many old laws have been repealed; for instance, a broken promise of marriage was formerly actionable by the jilted woman as a breach of contract, but this is no longer so.

There are four current (legal) sources of law. These are the means by which the law is currently brought into existence. The two most important sources of law today are case law and legislation. Custom is of little practical importance as a source of law, but is still classified as a current source. The impact of the EC, the fourth current source of law, is increasing. We examine the first three in this chapter and discuss EC law in Chapter 4.

Legislation is made by Parliament, the supreme law making body in the United Kingdom. There are two types of legislation, Parliamentary and delegated legislation. Delegated legislation comes into being when Parliament confers on persons or bodies, particularly Ministers of the Crown, powers to make regulations for specific purposes.

Case law is made in the courts. Although it can be argued that the function of judges is to apply the law and not to make it, there are inevitably disputes which come to be decided in areas where there is no existing statutory provision and no existing relevant case.

Subsidiary sources of law are not currently responsible for the direct creation of law. They are described briefly at the end of this chapter.

---

1 LEGISLATION   *6/95, 12/95, 12/96, 12/98*

1.1 Statute law is made by Parliament (or in exercise of law-making powers delegated by Parliament). Until the United Kingdom entered the European Community in 1973 the UK Parliament was completely *sovereign* - its law-making powers were unfettered. In that respect there was a marked contrast with the position in some other countries, such as the USA, where there is a written constitution and it is possible to challenge in the courts (as unconstitutional) legislation made by the statutory law-making body.

1.2   In recent years however, UK membership of the European Community has restricted the previously unfettered power of Parliament. There is an obligation, imposed by the Treaty of Rome, to bring UK law into line with the Treaty itself, and with directives. On certain subjects regulations, having the force of law in every member state, may be made under provisions of the Treaty of Rome.

Parliamentary sovereignty

1.3   Parliamentary sovereignty gives rise to a number of consequences. Parliament is able to make the law as it sees fit. It may repeal earlier statutes, overrule case law developed in the courts or make new law on subjects which have not been regulated by law before. Thus the War Damage Act 1965, removing rights to compensation from the Crown, reversed the decision of the House of Lords in *Burmah Oil v Lord Advocate 1965*.

1.4   No Parliament can legislate so as to prevent a future Parliament changing the law.

Vauxhall Estates v Liverpool Corporation 1932
If compensation for compulsory purchase were assessed under an Act of 1919 the plaintiffs would receive £2,370, whereas if it were assessed under an Act of 1925 they would only receive £1,133. The Act of 1919 provided that any Act inconsistent with it would have no effect.

Held: this provision in the 1919 act did not apply to subsequent Acts because Parliament cannot bind its successors. In addition the 1925 Act by implication repealed the 1919 Act so far as it was inconsistent with it. The plaintiffs therefore received £1,133.

1.5   The courts are bound to apply the relevant statute law however distasteful to them it may be. But the judges have to *interpret* statute law and they may find a meaning in a statutory rule which those Members of Parliament who promoted the statute did not intend.

1.6   The validity of an Act of Parliament cannot be questioned.

Cheney v Conn 1968
The plaintiff objected to his tax assessment under the Finance Act 1964 because some of the tax collected was used by the government to fund the manufacture of nuclear weapons. He alleged that this was contrary to the General Conventions Act 1957 and in conflict with international law.

Held: the 1964 Act gave clear authority to collect the taxes and prevailed over the 1957 Act. 'It is not for the court to say that a parliamentary enactment, the highest law in this country, is illegal.'

1.7   In practice, Parliament usually follows certain conventions which limit its freedom. It does not usually enact statutes which alter the law with retrospective effect or deprive citizens of their property without compensation.

1.8   In addition to making new law and altering existing law, Parliament may make the law clearer by passing a codifying statute (such as the Sale of Goods Act 1979) to put case law on a statutory basis, or a consolidating statute to incorporate an original statute and its successive amendments into a single statute (such as the Companies Act 1985).

Parliamentary procedure

1.9   A proposal for legislation is originally aired in public in a Government Green Paper. After comments are received a White Paper is produced, which sets out the intended aim of the legislation. It is then put forward in draft form as a Bill, and may be introduced into either the House of Commons or the House of Lords. When the Bill has passed through one House it must then go through the same stages in the other House.

1.10   In each House the successive stages of dealing with the Bill are as follows.

Stage 1   *First reading.* Publication and introduction into the agenda; no debate.

Stage 2   *Second reading.* Debate on the general merits of the Bill; no amendments at this stage.

Stage 3   *Committee stage.* The Bill is examined by a Standing Committee of about 20 members, representing the main parties and including some members at least who specialise in the relevant subject. The Bill is examined section by section and may be amended. If the Bill is very important all or part of the Committee Stage may be taken by the House as a whole sitting as a committee.

Stage 4   *Report stage.* The Bill as amended in committee is reported to the full House for approval. If the government has undertaken in committee to reconsider various points it often puts forward its final amendments at this stage.

Stage 5   *Third reading.* This is the final approval stage at which only verbal amendments may be made.

1.11   When it has passed through both Houses it is submitted for the *Royal Assent* which in practice is given on the Queen's behalf by a committee of the Lord Chancellor and two other peers. It then becomes an Act of Parliament (or statute) but it does not (unless the Act itself so provides) come into operation until a commencement date is notified by statutory instrument.

1.12   Statute law has the following advantages and disadvantages:

(a) *Advantages*

     (i)   The House of Commons is elected at intervals of not more than five years. Hence the law making process is theoretically responsive to public opinion.

     (ii)   Statute law can in theory deal with any problem.

     (iii)   Statures are carefully constructed codes of law.

     (iv)   A new problem in society or some unwelcome development in case law can be dealt with by passing an Act of Parliament.

(b) *Disadvantages*

     (i)   Statutes are bulky (about 70 public statutes are passed each year and the complete set of statutes runs to more than 40 volumes of several hundred pages each).

     (ii)   Parliament often lacks time to consider draft legislation in sufficient detail Statutes are sometimes found to be badly drafted, ambiguous or inconsistent.

     (iii)   A substantial statute can take up a lot of Parliamentary time. It is often not possible to enact amending legislation within the lifetime of one parliament. However, where there is political agreement on one matter a Bill may be enacted very quickly.

     (iv)   Statute law is a statement of general rules. Those who draft it cannot anticipate every individual case which may arise. The more detail introduced into statue law, the more rigid it becomes. There is then the burden of elaborating general propositions to fit individual cases.

1.13   Most Bills are *Public Bills* of general application, whether introduced by the government or by a private member. They are referred to as Government Bills or Private Members' Bills respectively. An example of a Private Members' Bill is the Abortion Act 1967, sponsored by David Steel MP. A *Private Bill* (*not* the same as a Private Members' Bill) has a restricted application: for example, a local authority may promote a Private Bill to give it special powers within its own area.

1.14   If the House of Commons and the House of Lords disagree over the same Bill, the House of Lords may delay its passing for a maximum of one year (only one month if it is a financial measure, such as the annual Finance Act). It may veto any bill which tries to extend the life of Parliament beyond five years, and it may veto any Private Bill.

Exercise 1

What are the five stages of dealing with a Bill in each of the Houses of Parliament?

Solution

First Reading
Second Reading
Committee Stage
Report Stage
Third Reading

---

2   DELEGATED LEGISLATION   *12/94, 12/96*

2.1   To save time in Parliament, Acts usually contain a section by which power is given to a minister, or public body such as a local authority, to make subordinate or delegated legislation for specified purposes only.

2.2   *Delegated legislation* therefore means rules of law, often of a detailed nature, made by subordinate bodies to whom the power to do so has been given by statute.

2.3   Delegated legislation appears in various forms.

(a)   Ministerial regulations are promulgated as *statutory instruments* (as are emergency powers of the Crown contained in *Orders in Council*).

(b)   *Local authorities* are given statutory powers to make *bye-laws*, which apply within a specific locality.

(c)   Parliament gives power to certain *professional bodies* to regulate their members' conduct. The Law Society has such powers, as has the Securities and Investments Board.

(d)   *Rules of Court* may be made by the judiciary to control court procedure, such as the Supreme Court rules made under the Supreme Court Act 1981.

Control over delegated legislation

2.4   Parliament does exercise some control over delegated legislation by restricting and defining the power to make rules and by keeping the making of new delegated legislation under review as follows.

(a)   Some statutory instruments do not take effect until approved by affirmative resolution of Parliament.

(b)   Most other statutory instruments must be laid before Parliament for 40 days before they take effect. During that period members may propose a negative resolution to veto a statutory instrument to which they object.

2.5   There are standing Scrutiny Committees of both Houses whose duty it is to examine statutory instruments with a view to raising objections if necessary, usually on the grounds that the instrument is obscure, expensive or retrospective.

2.6   As explained above, the power to make delegated legislation is defined by the Act which confers the power. A statutory instrument may be challenged in the courts on the grounds that it is *ultra vires* - ie, it exceeds the prescribed limits or has been made without due compliance with the correct procedure. If the objection is valid the court declares the statutory instrument to be void.

2.7   Both statutes and delegated legislation under it are expressed in general terms. It is not possible to provide in the Act for each eventuality of human endeavour which falls within its remit. It therefore often falls to judges to interpret Acts. The legal reasoning used to do this is covered later.

Advantages and disadvantages

2.8   Delegated legislation is unavoidable and has the following advantages.

(a)   Parliament does not have time to examine these matters of detail.

(b)   Much of the content of delegated legislation is technical and is better worked out in consultation with professional, commercial or industrial groups outside Parliament.

(c)   If new or altered regulations are required later, they can be issued without referring back to Parliament, and in much shorter time than is needed to pass an amending Act.

(d)   The system allows the law to be enacted quickly in an emergency.

2.9   The disadvantages of the system are as follows.

(a)   In practice it is not easy to exert effective *pressure* on ministers who are in theory responsible for the process of delegating law-making to civil servants in consultation with interested pressure groups. A minister could be challenged in Parliament if objectionable changes are made.

(b)   Because delegated legislation can be produced in large amounts, the *volume* of such law-making becomes unmanageable and it is impossible to keep up-to-date. Even lawyers have difficulty in keeping track of law-making by this means - or at best they discover what has been done when it is too late to express informed criticism and opposition.

(c)   The system is *unrepresentative* in that power is given to civil servants who are not democratically elected, and Parliament finds it difficult to scrutinise and control it effectively.

(d)   The different sorts of delegated legislation which may be produced by virtue of one statue can greatly *confuse* users.

3   THE INTERPRETATION OF STATUTES   6/97

3.1   Statutes, including delegated legislation, are expressed in general terms. For example, a Finance Act may impose a new tax on transactions described as a category; it does not expressly impose a tax of specified amount on the particular transaction of a particular person. If a dispute arises as to whether or how a statute applies to particular acts or events, the courts must interpret the statute, determine what it means and decide whether or not it applies to a given case.

3.2   In the interpretation of a statute the court has always been concerned with what the statute itself provides. Lord Reid said the following in *Black-Clawson International Ltd v Papierwerke Waldhof-Aschaffenburg AG 1975*.

> 'We often say that we are looking for the intention of Parliament, but that is not quite accurate. We are seeking the meaning of the words that Parliament used. We are seeking not what Parliament meant but the true meaning of what they said.'

3.3   However a landmark decision of the House of Lords in *Pepper v Hart 1992* ruled that *Hansard*, the official journal of UK Parliamentary debates, can be used to assist in interpreting legislation. Three criteria must be satisfied.

(a)   The legislation must be ambiguous or obscure

(b)   The material relied upon must consist of one or more statements by a minister or other promoter of the Bill

(c)   Statements relied upon must be clear.

It is not yet clear to what extent this practice will become adopted or to what extent it is actually necessary.

3.4   There are a number of situations which might lead to a need for statutory interpretation.

(a)   *Ambiguity* might be caused by an error in drafting whereby the words used are capable of two or more literal meanings.

(b)   *Uncertainty* may arise where the words of a statute are intended to apply to a range of factual situations and the courts must decide whether the case before them falls into any of these situations.

(c)   There may be *unforeseeable developments*, which the parliamentary draftsmen cannot be expected to address. Thus, although the Telegraph Act 1869 was passed before the invention of the telephone, it was held to confer certain powers concerning telephone usage on the Postmaster General: *Attorney-General v Edison Telephone Co 1880*.

(d)   The draftsmen may use a *broad term*. Thus, the word vehicle, usually accepted as covering cars, buses and motorcycles, may need to be considered in relation to the use of unicycles or skateboards.

3.5   There are a number of different sources of assistance for a judge in his task of statutory interpretation. These are, collectively, the principles of statutory interpretation, and consist of:

(a)   rules;
(b)   presumptions; and
(c)   other aids, which may be:
    (i)   intrinsic; or
    (ii)   extrinsic.

4   RULES OF STATUTORY INTERPRETATION

4.1   In interpreting the words of a statute the courts have developed a number of well-established general principles. These provide a framework for the solution of interpretative problems.

The literal rule

4.2   Words should be given their plain, ordinary or literal meaning. Normally a word should be construed in the same literal sense wherever it appears throughout the statute. The courts will use standard dictionaries to aid them in their interpretation. If the words used are clear the courts must apply them even if the result is absurd or if they do not like the statute. Thus if the meaning of a taxation statute is clear it must be adhered to even if it allows a loophole for fraud against the Inland Revenue: *Barnard v Gorman 1941*.

The golden rule

4.3   A statute should be construed to avoid a manifest absurdity or contradiction within itself.

> *Re Sigsworth 1935*
> There is a principle that, on grounds of public policy, a murderer cannot benefit under his victim's *will*. The golden rule was applied to prevent a murderer from inheriting on the *intestacy* of his victim although he was, as her son, her only heir on a literal interpretation of the Administration of Estates Act 1925.

The mischief rule

4.4   If the words used are ambiguous and the statute discloses, in its preamble, the purpose of the statute, the court will adopt the meaning which is likely to give effect to the purpose or reform which the statute is intended to achieve. This is to take account of the mischief or weakness which the statute is explicitly intended to remedy.

> *Gardiner v Sevenoaks RDC 1950*
> The purpose of an Act was to provide for the safe storage of inflammable cinematography film wherever it might be stored on 'premises'. A notice was served on the plaintiff who stored film in a cave, requiring him to comply with the safety rules. He argued that 'premises' did not include a cave and so the Act had no application to his case.
>
> *Held*: the purpose of the Act was to protect the safety of persons working in all places where film was stored. Insofar as film was stored in a cave, the word 'premises' included the cave.

4.5   The mischief rule is sometimes referred to as 'the rule in *Heydon's Case*' (1584) which provides that judges should consider three factors:

(a)   What the law was before the statute was passed;
(b)   What 'mischief' the statute was trying to remedy;
(c)   What remedy Parliament was trying to provide.

The statute should then be interpreted so as to solve the problem.

The contextual rule

4.6   A word should be construed in its context: it is permissible to look at the statute as a whole to discover the meaning of a word in it. The courts have been paying more attention to what Parliament intended in recent times. In 1988, for example, the Attorney-General issued a statement interpreting the word 'obtain' in the Company Securities ((Insider Dealing) Act 1985. This was in order that the courts should apply the law for the purpose for which it was enacted by Parliament. A more purposive approach is also being taken because so many international and EC regulations come to be interpreted by the courts.

> *Re Attorney-General's reference (No 1 of 1988) 1989*
> The accused had received unsolicited information from a merchant banker telling him of a forthcoming merger. He knew that this was price-sensitive information and instructed his broker to buy shares in one of the companies, later netting a profit of £3,000. The Act sets out the offence of 'knowingly obtaining' such information. His defence was that he had obtained it passively, not actively.
>
> *Held*: both the Court of Appeal and the House of Lords rejected this interpretation on the grounds that the effect of the legislation would be lessened if it was followed.

The *eiusdem generis* rule

4.7   Statutes often list a number of specific things and end the list with more general words. In that case the general words are to be limited in their meaning to other things of the same kind (Latin: *eiusdem generis*) as the specific items which precede them.

> *Evans v Cross 1938*
> E was charged with driving his car in such a way as to 'ignore a traffic sign'. He had undoubtedly crossed to the wrong side of a white line painted down the middle of the road. 'Traffic sign' was defined in the Act as 'all signals, warning signposts, direction posts, signs or other devices'. Unless, therefore, a white line was an 'other device', E had not ignored a 'traffic sign' and had not committed the offence charged.

Held: 'other device' must be limited in its meaning to a category of signs in the list which preceded it. Thus restricted it did not include a painted line which was quite different from that category.

Expressio unius est exclusio alterius

4.8   To express one thing is by implication to exclude anything else. For example, a statutory rule on 'sheep' does not include goats.

Noscitur a sociis

4.9   A word draws meaning from the other words around it. If a statute mentioned 'children's books, children's toys and clothes' it would be reasonable to assume that 'clothes' meant children's clothes.

In pari materia

4.10 If the statute forms part of a series which deals with similar subject matter, the court may look to the interpretation of previous statutes on the assumption that Parliament intended the same thing.

5   PRESUMPTIONS OF STATUTORY INTERPRETATION

5.1   Unless the statute contains express words to the contrary it is assumed that the following presumptions or 'canons' of statutory interpretation apply, each of which may be rebutted by contrary evidence.

5.2   *A statute does not alter the existing common law*. If a statute is capable of two interpretations, one involving alteration of the common law and the other one not, the latter interpretation is to be preferred.

5.3   *If a statute deprives a person of his property*, say by nationalisation, he is to be compensated for its value.

5.4   *A statute is not intended to deprive a person of his liberty*. If it does so, clear words must be used. This is relevant in legislation covering, for example, mental health and immigration.

5.5   *A statute does not have retrospective effect* to a date earlier than its becoming law. This means for example that a statute creating a new crime does not make unlawful an act carried out before the Act came into force. Conversely, if an Act were to abolish a crime by repealing an earlier statute, an offence committed before the repeal would remain an offence. Some legislation is made specifically retrospective in operation, for example the War Crimes Act 1991.

5.6   *A statute does not bind the Crown*. In certain areas, the Crown's potential liability is great and this is therefore an extremely important presumption. In those areas the Crown is expressly bound; relevant legislation includes, for example, the Occupiers' Liability Acts 1957 and 1984 and the Equal Pay Act 1970.

5.7   *A statute has effect only in the UK*; it does not have extraterritorial effect. However a statute does not run counter to international law and should be interpreted so as to give effect to international obligations.

5.8   *A statute cannot impose criminal liability* without proof of *mens rea* (guilty mind or intention). Many modern statutes rebut this presumption by imposing strict liability, say for dangerous driving under the Road Traffic Act.

5.9   *A statute does not repeal other statutes.*

5.10   Any point on which the statute leaves *a gap or omission is outside the scope of the statute.* In practice a statute usually deals expressly with all matters other than this one to remove any possible doubt.

6   OTHER ASSISTANCE IN INTERPRETATION

6.1   The Interpretation Act 1987 defines certain terms frequently found in legislation. These definitions are to be used in construing any Acts which contain these words or expressions. The Act also states that, unless a specific intention to the contrary exists, the use in a statute of masculine gender terminology also includes the feminine, and *vice versa.* Similarly, words in the singular include plurals, and *vice versa.*

6.2   *Intrinsic aids* to statutory interpretation consist of the following.

(a)   The *long title* of an Act, which may give guidance as to the Act's general objective.

(b)   The *preamble* of an Act often directs the judge as to its intentions and objects; private Acts must have a preamble, public ones recently have just contained long titles. But preambles may only be used to resolve an ambiguity - they may not be used when the enacted words are already clear: *Attorney-General v Ernest Augustus (Prince) of Hanover 1957.*

(c)   *Interpretation sections* to Acts - particularly long, complicated and wide-ranging Acts often contain self-explanations; for instance, s 207 of the Financial Services Act 1986 defines 'authorised persons' and 'recognised investment exchanges' for its purposes.

(d)   *Sidenotes* - statutes often have summary notes in the margin - these may be used to give a general interpretation of the clauses to which they are attached.

6.3   *Intrinsic* aids are those words contained in the Queen's Printer's copy of the statute. *Extrinsic aids* are those found elsewhere. Traditionally, the use of extrinsic aids has been very restricted. There are now signs that such restrictions are being relaxed, enabling judges to look at the background to an Act. Extrinsic aids include the following.

(a)   Reports of the Law Commission, royal commissions, the Law Reform Committee and other official committees: the *Black-Clawson* case.

(b)   *Hansard*, as described earlier. There are concerns that this could add significantly to the length and cost of legislation.

(c)   *Travaux préparatoires*, which are preparatory works leading to legislation. These can be used in the interpretation of international conventions only.

7   CASE LAW   *6/95, 12/96, 12/98*

7.1   It is generally accepted that consistency is an important feature of a good decision-making process. Similar cases should be treated in the same way. However, the passage of time, or changing circumstances, may cause a case to offer a solution which no longer appears just. One of the main functions of the higher courts is to give an authoritative decision on disputed questions of law.

7.2   A court's decision is expected to be *consistent* (or at least not unjustifiably inconsistent) *with previous decisions* and to provide an opinion which the parties, and others, can use to direct their future relationships. This is the basis of the system of *judicial precedent.*

7.3   Both common law and equity are the product of decisions in the courts. They are judge-made law but based on a principle of consistency. Once a matter of principle has been decided (by one of the higher courts) it becomes a precedent. In any later case to which that principle is relevant the same principle should (subject to certain exceptions) be applied. This doctrine of consistency, following precedent, is expressed in the maxim *stare decisis* - 'to stand by a decision'.

7.4   Judicial precedent is based on three elements.

(a)   There must be adequate and reliable *reports* of earlier decisions.

(b)   There must be *rules for extracting* from each earlier decision on a particular set of facts the *legal principle* to be applied in reaching a decision on a different set of facts.

(c)   Precedents must be classified into those which are *binding* and those which are merely *persuasive*.

Law reports

7.5   There are major series of law reports on general law published weekly and then bound as annual volumes. At a hearing in court, the barrister who cites a case as a precedent upon which he relies will read aloud from the reports the passage from the reported judgment.

7.6   Every case has a title, usually (in a civil case) in the form *Carlill v Carbolic Smoke Ball Co*. This denotes Carlill (plaintiff) versus Carbolic Smoke Ball Co (defendant). In the event of an appeal, the plaintiff's name is still shown first, whether he is the *appellant* or the respondent.

7.7   Some cases are cited (for technical reasons of procedure) by reference to the subject matter. Thus case names have included *Re Barrow Haematite Steel Co* (a company case), *Re Adams and Kensington Vestry* (a trust case) (*Re* means 'about') and in shipping cases the name of the ship, eg *The Wagon Mound*.

7.8   Some older cases may be referred to by a single name, for example *Pinnel's case*. In a full citation the title of the case is followed by abbreviated particulars of the volume of the law reports in which the case is reported, eg. *Best v Samuel Fox & Co Ltd (1952)* 2 All ER 394 (The report is at p 394 of Vol. 2 of the All England Reports for 1952).

7.9   The same case may be reported in more than one series of law reports and sometimes under different names.

7.10   As regards content a full law report includes the following.

(a)   The names of the parties
(b)   The court in which the case was decided
(c)   The judge or judges
(d)   The date of the hearing
(e)   A summary (*head note*) of the points of law established by the case
(f)   A list of the earlier cases cited as precedents at the hearing
(g)   The previous history of the litigation
(h)   The facts
(i)   The names of counsel and their arguments
(j)   The verbatim text of the judgment (or judgments if more than one)
(k)   The order of the court
(l)   Whether leave to appeal was granted
(m)   The solicitors
(n)   The reporting barrister

7.11   It is only decisions of the higher courts - the High Court, the Court of Appeal and the Judicial Committee of the House of Lords - which are included in the general law reports. Only the important cases (in the effect on the law) are included in the law reports (though certain libraries hold a copy of the judgments in unreported cases also).

7.12   Students are often perplexed as to how much they are expected to memorise of cases referred to in textbooks or teaching manuals. The important aspect of a leading case is what it was about: its essential facts and the point of law which it illustrates or establishes. It is always useful to preface the mention of a case (in a written answer) by citing the name of the case. But if you cannot remember the name you can say 'in a decided case...'.

Exercise 3

What do you think are the advantages of case law as a source of law?

Solution

The law is decided fairly and *predictably*, so that businessmen and individuals can regulate their conduct by reference to the law. The *risk* of mistakes in individual cases is reduced by the use of precedents. Case law can *adapt* to changing circumstances in society, since it arises directly out of the actions of society. Case law, having been developed in *practical* situations, is suitable for use in other practical situations.

---

8   THE DOCTRINE OF BINDING PRECEDENT   *6/94, 6/96, 6/98*

8.1   The doctrine of judicial precedent is based on the view that the function of a judge is to *decide* cases in accordance with existing rules. This is the basis for the doctrine of *stare decisis*.

8.2   The doctrine of judicial precedent is designed to provide *consistency* in the law. In order that this should be done in a coherent manner, four things must be considered when examining a precedent before it can be applied to a case.

(a)   It must be a *proposition of law*.

(b)   It must form part of the *ratio decidendi* of the case.

(c)   The *material facts* of each case must be the same.

(d)   The preceding court must have had a *superior (or in some cases, equal) status* to the later court, such that its decisions are binding on the later court.

Proposition of law

8.3   A decision must be based on a *proposition of law* before it can be considered as a precedent. It may not be a decision on a *question of fact*. The distinction is not straightforward. An issue is a finding of fact where it depends on the credibility of direct evidence or on deductions drawn from circumstantial evidence. For example, a judge may, from the direct facts of weather conditions and the length of skidmarks, infer that a driver has been negligent. This finding of fact is not binding and so a judge in a later case involving the same conditions and facts need not be bound by the earlier decision. It is the *ratio decidendi* which is binding.

Ratio decidendi

8.4   A judgement will start with a description of the facts of the case and probably a review of earlier precedents and possible alternative theories. The judge will then make statements of law applicable to the legal problems raised by the material facts. Provided these statements are the basis for the decision, they are known as the *ratio decidendi* of the case. The *ratio decidendi* (which literally means 'reason for deciding') is the vital element which binds future judges. A definition of the *ratio decidendi* (often shortened to *ratio*) widely recognised in English law is as follows.

> 'The *ratio decidendi* of a case is any rule of law expressly or impliedly treated by the judge as a necessary step in reaching his conclusion, having regard to the line of reasoning adopted by him, or a necessary part of his direction to the jury.'(Cross: *Precedent in English law*.)

8.5 Statements made by a judge are *ratio decidendi* or *obiter dicta*. There are two types of *obiter dicta*.

    (a) A judge's statements of legal principle might not form the basis of the decision. For example a dissenting (minority) judgment might be made by one judge when three or five judges are sitting together.

    (b) A judge's statements might not be based on the existing material facts but on hypothetical facts. In either case, the judge's statements are known as *obiter dicta* statements - something said 'by the way'. A later court may respect such statements, but it is not bound to follow them. They are only of persuasive authority.

> *Rondel v Worsley 1969*
> The House of Lords stated an opinion that a barrister might be held liable for negligence when not acting as an advocate, and that a solicitor might be immune from such an action when acting as an advocate. Since the case actually concerned the liability of a barrister when acting as an advocate these opinions were *obiter dicta*. The proposition was wider than necessary for the facts of the case.

8.6 It is not always easy to identify the ratio decidendi. The same judgment may appear to contain contradictory views of the law in different passages. In decisions of appeal courts, where there are three or even five separate judgments, the members of the court may reach the same conclusion but give different reasons. In such a case there may be two different *rationes*. Often, the *ratio* will be intermingled with *obiter* statements. To assist the process of legal reasoning, many judges indicate in their speeches which comments are *ratio* and which *obiter*.

Distinguishing the facts

8.7 Although there may arguably be a finite number of legal principles to consider when deciding a case, there are necessarily an infinite variety of facts which may be presented. Apart from identifying the *ratio decidendi* of an earlier case, it is also necessary to consider how far the facts of the previous and the latest case are similar. Facts are never identical. If the differences appear significant the court may 'distinguish' the earlier case on the facts and thereby avoid following it as a precedent.

Status of the court

8.8 Not every decision made in every court is binding as a judicial precedent. The court's status has a significant effect on whether its decisions are binding, persuasive or disregarded.

Magistrates' courts and county courts

8.9 The decisions of magistrates' courts and county courts are usually only reported in local newspapers. They do not constitute precedents binding on anyone. They do not even bind themselves, although it is of course expected that magistrates and county court judges will attempt to show consistency in reaching decisions.

8.10 Magistrates' courts and county courts are bound by decisions of the High Court, the Court of Appeal and the House of Lords.

Crown Court

8.11 The decisions of Crown Courts are reported more frequently, many criminal cases being reported nationally. Judges are often High Court judges and their pronouncements are more authoritative. However, Crown Court decisions are only of persuasive authority, as evidenced by a series of cases on marital rape in 1990 and 1991.

8.12   The Crown Court is bound by decisions of the High Court (QBD), the Court of Appeal and the House of Lords.

The High Court

8.13   A decision of a High Court judge sitting alone is binding on inferior courts, but not on other High Court judges. This may create conflict. For example in the 1970s, before the wearing of seat-belts became compulsory in the UK, a number of cases addressed the question of whether failure to wear a seat-belt in a car could amount to contributory negligence. Ultimately, the matter had to be settled by the Court of Appeal: *Froom v Butcher 1976*. If a decision is reached by two or more High Court judges sitting together as a divisional court, the decision is binding on any other divisional court and on a single High Court judge sitting alone.

8.14   A single High Court judge is therefore bound by the divisional court, the Court of Appeal and the House of Lords. A divisional court is itself bound by the House of Lords, the Court of Appeal and its own previous decisions.

The Court of Appeal

8.15   The Court of Appeal's decisions are binding on all English courts (except the House of Lords). In *Young v Bristol Aeroplane Co 1944* it was held that the civil division is usually bound by its own decision and by those of the House of Lords, except where:

(a)   two of its previous decisions are in conflict with each other (it must decide which to follow);

(b)   the previous decision conflicts with a subsequent House of Lords judgment; or

(c)   the previous decision was made *per incuriam*, through lack of care, for example failure to observe some relevant statute or precedent: *Young v Bristol Aeroplane Co 1944*.

It is bound to follow the House of Lords. In *Broome v Cassell Co Ltd 1971* a case before the Court of Appeal, Lord Denning, in considering *Rookes v Barnard 1964*, an earlier House of Lords case, said 'I think the difficulties presented by *Rookes v Barnard* are so great that the judges should direct the juries in accordance with the law as it was understood before *Rookes v Barnard*.' When the case in question reached the House of Lords, Lord Hailsham dismissed this, saying 'it is not open to the Court of Appeal to give gratuitous advice to judges of first instance to ignore decisions of the House of Lords in this way and, if it were open to the Court of Appeal to do so, it would be highly undesirable'.

The House of Lords

8.16   The Judicial Committee of the House of Lords stands at the apex of the judicial system. Its decisions are binding on all other English courts.

8.17   In *London Tramways v London County Council 1898*, (sometimes referred to as *London Street Tramways*), the House of Lords held that it was bound by its own previous decisions in the interests of finality and certainty in the law, although it was at the same time accepted that a decision could be questioned where it was made *per incuriam* or where it conflicted with another decision. This situation continued until 1966, when a Practice Statement on Judicial Precedent was issued. Lord Gardiner, then Lord Chancellor, made the statement as follows.

'Their Lordships regard the use of precedent as an indispensable foundation upon which to decide what is the law and its application to individual cases. It provides at least some degree of certainty upon which individuals can rely on the conduct of their affairs, as well as a basis for orderly development of legal rules.

Their Lordships nevertheless recognise that too rigid adherence to precedent may lead to injustice in a particular case and also unduly restrict the proper development of the law. They propose, therefore, to modify their present practice and, while treating former decisions of this House as normally binding, to depart from a previous decision when it appears right to do so.

In this connection they will bear in mind the danger of disturbing retrospectively the basis on which contracts, settlements of property and fiscal arrangements have been entered into and also the especial need for certainty as to the criminal law.

This announcement is not intended to affect the use of precedent elsewhere than in this House.'

8.18   It is therefore possible that the House could overrule its own earlier decision, but the power has in practice been invoked on average less than once a year. Examples are as follows.

(a)   In *Anderton v Ryan 1985,* a criminal case, the House of Lords misinterpreted the Criminal Attempts Act 1981 in holding that a defence of impossibility in the criminal law had survived the Act. The decision was criticised for ignoring the bulk of the relevant academic literature, the Law Commission report which preceded the Act and the plain words of the Act itself. In *R v Shivpuri 1987,* their Lordships acknowledged that, while there was no valid ground on which the later case could be distinguished, the earlier decision should be overruled.

(b)   In *Murphy v Brentwood District Council 1990,* the House of Lords overruled its earlier decision in *Anns v Merton London Borough 1977* on the common law liability of local authorities for the inspection of building foundations. In the earlier case it was held that the local authority had a common law duty of care to the owner and occupier of a building to ensure that the foundations complied with building regulations. In the later case, this decision was overruled on the basis that there had been no damage to property or injury to persons and that a purely economic loss did not create a liability for the local authority.

(c)   The decision in *Congreve v Inland Revenue Commissioners 1948* was overruled in *Vestey v Inland Revenue Commissioners (Nos 1 and 2) 1980* on the ground that the earlier decision had led to results which were 'arbitrary, potentially unjust and fundamentally unconstitutional'.

The European Court of Justice

8.19   Decisions of the European Court of Justice are binding on all English courts, including the House of Lords:

(a)   on the interpretation of Community treaties; and
(b)   on the validity and interpretation of secondary community legislation.

The European Court is not bound by its own decisions. It is described further in Chapter 4.

Persuasive precedents

8.20   Apart from binding precedents as described above, reported decisions of any court (even if lower in status) may be treated as *persuasive* precedents - they may be, but need not be followed in a later case. Reported decisions of the Judicial Committee of the Privy Council (which is technically a court of appeal from certain Commonwealth countries), of higher courts of Commonwealth countries which have a common law legal tradition and of courts of the United States of America may be cited as persuasive precedents. With persuasive precedents much depends on the personal reputation of the judge whose earlier decision is cited.

8.21   A court of higher status is not only free to disregard the decision of a court of lower status. It may also deprive it of authority and expressly overrule it. Remember that this does not reverse the previous decision; overruling a decision does not affect its outcome as regards the defendant and plaintiff in that earlier decision.

8.22 If, in a case before the House of Lords, there is a dispute about a point of European Community law it must be referred to the European Court for a ruling. English courts are also required to take account of principles laid down by the European Court in so far as these are relevant. The European court does not, however, create or follow precedents as such, and the provisions of EC directives should not be used to interpret UK legislation.

8.23 A case in the High Court may be taken on appeal to the Court of Appeal. If the latter reverses the former decision, that first decision cannot be a precedent, and the reversed decision becomes a precedent. However, if the original decision had been reached by following precedent, then reversing that decision overrules the precedent which formed the ratio. Overruling a precedent does not affect the parties in that original precedent's case, but the parties in the reversed decision are affected by the new decision.

Avoidance of a binding precedent

8.24 Even if a precedent appears to be binding, there are a number of grounds on which a court may decline to follow it:

(a) It may be able to *distinguish the facts* (see above).

(b) It may declare the *ratio decidendi* obscure, particularly when a Court of Appeal decision by three or five judges gives as many *rationes*.

(c) It may declare the previous decision made *per incuriam* - without taking account of some essential point of law, such as an important precedent.

(d) It may declare it to be in *conflict with a fundamental principle of law;* for example where a court has failed to apply the doctrine of privity of contract: *Beswick v Beswick 1968*.

(e) It may declare an earlier precedent to be *too wide* - for example, the duty of care to third parties, first propounded in *Donoghue v Stevenson 1932*, has since been considerably refined.

(f) The earlier decision may have been *subsequently overruled* by another court or by statute.

Exercise 4

Match each of the following definitions to the correct term.

(a) A court higher up in the hierarchy overturns the decision of a lower court on appeal in the same case.

(b) A principle laid down by a lower court is overturned by a higher court in a different, later case.

(c) A judge states that the material facts of the case before him are sufficiently different from those of an earlier case as to enable the application of a different rule of law.

(1) Distinguishing

(2) Overruling

(3) Reversing

Solution

(a) (3)
(b) (2)
(c) (1)

---

9   THE ADVANTAGES AND DISADVANTAGES OF PRECEDENT

9.1 Many of the strengths of judicial precedent as the cornerstone of English law also indicate some of its weaknesses.

Certainty

9.2 The whole point of following binding precedent is that the law is decided fairly and predictably. In theory therefore it should be possible to avoid litigation because the result is a foregone conclusion. The doctrine gives guidance to judges and reduces the risk of mistakes in individual cases. *However, judges may sometimes be forced to make illogical distinctions to avoid an unfair result*, which combined with the wealth of reported cases serves to complicate the law. Lord Diplock warned of the 'danger of so blinding the court with case law that it has difficulty in seeing the wood of legal principle for the trees of paraphrase': *Lambert v Lewis 1981.*

Clarity

9.3 Following only the reasoning in *ratio* statements should lead to statements of principle for general application. This is why the Court of Appeal must usually adhere to its own previous decisions and the House of Lords departs from its own previous decisions only infrequently. In practice, however, *the same judgment may be found to contain propositions which appear inconsistent with each other or with the precedent which the court purports to follow.*

Flexibility

9.4 The real strength of the system lies in its ability to change with changing circumstances in society since it arises directly out of the actions of society. The counter-argument is that the *doctrine limits judges' discretion* and they may be unable to avoid deciding in line with a precedent which produces an unfair result. Often this may only be resolved by passing a statute to correct the law's failings.

Detail

9.5 Precedent states how the law applies to facts, and it should be flexible enough to allow for details to be different, so that the law is all-encompassing. As has been noted above, however, judges often distinguish on facts to avoid a precedent. The wealth of detail is also a drawback in that it produces a *vast body of reports* which must be taken into account; again, statute can help by codifying rules developed in case law - this, for instance, was the source of the Sale of Goods Act 1979.

Practicality

9.6 Case law is based on the experience of actual cases brought before the courts, not on logic or theory. This is an advantage as against legislation, which is sometimes found wanting when tested. There is currently debate about the adequacies and possible need for revision of a number of statutes, for example the Consumer Credit Act 1974 and the Criminal Justice Act 1991.

9.7 The most famous (adverse) description of case law is that made by the eighteenth century philosopher and jurist Jeremy Bentham, when he called it 'dog's law'. Precedent follows the event, just as beating a dog follows the dog disobeying his master - before the dog transgressed, the offence did not exist.

Exercise 5

The English courts are looking to decisions of Commonwealth, Scottish and United States courts increasingly for guidance in cases which appear to 'break new ground' in England. What is the effect of the decisions of such courts on English law?

Solution

They are of persuasive authority.

---

10   CUSTOM

10.1   In early mediaeval times the courts created law by enforcing selected customs. Custom is now of little importance as a source of law, but it is still classified as a legal source of law. In disputes over claims to customary rights, such as to use the land of another or to remove things from it, the alleged custom may be established subject to certain conditions.

10.2   It must have existed since *time immemorial* (in theory since 1189 AD). It usually suffices to show that the custom has existed without interruption from as far back as records (if any) exist. The custom must have been enjoyed *openly as of right*. If it has only been enjoyed secretly, by force, or with permission of the landowner, it is not a custom which amounts to a right.

10.3   In determining what are the implied terms of a contract, the court may take account of local or trade customs which the parties intended should be part of their contract.

> *Hutton v Warren 1836*
> The parties were landlord and tenant of a farm. The landlord gave notice to the tenant to quit. Disputes arose as to the tenant's obligation to continue to cultivate the farm until the notice expired and as to his entitlement to allowances for work done and seed supplied.
>
> *Held*: these matters were to be resolved according to local custom which had been incorporated in the contract.

11   SUBSIDIARY SOURCES OF LAW

11.1   You should be aware of the existence of a further category of sources of law, not currently responsible for the direct creation of law. A number of *subsidiary sources* of law have had some influence on the law's development, and are still recognisable today.

Law Merchant

11.2   In mediaeval times, traders submitted their disputes to courts at main ports, fairs and markets which applied mercantile custom. The law of negotiable instruments was brought to England as a commercial practice recognised by bankers and traders in Northern Italy, Germany and elsewhere in late mediaeval times. The work of these courts was absorbed (with the Law Merchant) into common law in the seventeenth century. But a separate Court of Admiralty existed - to deal with shipping matters - down to modern times and still exists as a special court within the Queen's Bench Division of the High Court.

Roman law

11.3   Although it is the basis of most European systems of law, Roman law is of little importance as a source of English law. Its influence was mainly felt in the ecclesiastical courts and in the rules relating to the requirements of a valid will. A soldier's privileged will (a verbal will) is an example of a current law which has Roman origins.

Canon law

11.4   Like the courts of the Law Merchant, the ecclesiastical courts were independent of the common law courts. They mainly dealt with offences against morality, such as adultery and slander. They also had jurisdiction over the law of succession. They kept this jurisdiction until 1857 when the Divorce Court and the Probate Court were established. Their jurisdiction is now confined to church matters.

Chapter roundup

- One of the major legal sources of law is legislation. UK statute law may take the form of Acts of Parliament, or delegated legislation under the Acts, for example statutory instruments or bye-laws.

- Statutes are not always clear nor clearly relevant to the case in hand. There are certain well established principles of interpretation, such as the literal, golden, contextual, mischief and *eiusdem generis* rules. Judges interpret statute according to the 'canons of statutory interpretation'.

- To assist the judges in interpretation there are the Interpretation Act 1978 and interpretation sections, preambles and sidenotes in the Acts themselves.

- Decisions made in the courts are case law, which is judge-made law based on the underlying principle of consistency. Once a legal or equitable principle is decided by an appropriate court it is a judicial precedent.

- In order that judicial precedent provides consistency in the law, a precedent must be carefully examined before it can be applied to a particular case. It must be a proposition of law. The *ratio decidendi* must be identified. The material facts must be the same. The status of the court which set the precedent must be such as to bind the present court.

- *Ratio decidendi* are the reasons for the decision being made - they alone are binding. *Obiter dicta* are comments made by the deciding judge in passing and are persuasive only.

- It is important to be aware of which courts' decisions are binding on which other courts. The House of Lords binds itself (but may depart from its own decisions) and all lower courts. The Court of Appeal binds itself and all lower courts. A Divisional Court of the High Court (two or more judges) binds itself and all lower courts. The High Court (single judge) binds all lower courts. Crown Court decisions may be of persuasive authority. The county court and magistrates' courts do not make binding precedent.

- Even where a precedent appears to be binding rather than merely persuasive, the court may decline to follow it by distinguishing the facts, by declaring the *ratio* obscure, by declaring that it was made without taking account of some essential point of law, by declaring it in conflict with a fundamental principle of law, by declaring it too wide or because it has been overruled.

Test your knowledge

1   Give three consequences of Parliamentary Sovereignty (see paras 1.3-1.6)

2   What is a consolidating statute? (1.7)

3   What is the final step in the life of a Bill? (1.10)

4   Distinguish a Private Bill from a Private Members' Bill. (1.13)

5   Give two examples of delegated legislation. (2.3)

6   How is delegated legislation controlled? (2.4)

7   What is Hansard? (3.3)

8   List four rules of statutory interpretation. (4.2 - 4.10)

9   Give six presumptions of statutory interpretation. (5.2 - 5.10)

10   What is an intrinsic aid to statutory interpretation? (6.2)

11   What does *stare decisis* mean? (7.3)

12   If a court finds for the plaintiff, and the defendant appeals, what terms are used to describe these two parties in the appeal case? (7.6)

13   What is *ratio decidendi*? (8.4)

14   When is the Court of Appeal not bound by its own previous decisions? (8.15)

15   Is the House of Lords bound by its own previous decisions? (8.17)

Now try illustrative question 3 at the end of the Study Text

Chapter 4

EUROPEAN COMMUNITY LAW

This chapter covers the following topics.

1   The European Community

2   Community institutions

3   EC law

4   EC law in the UK

5   Interpretation of EC law

Introduction

In Chapter 3 we saw the legislative role of Parliament. In this chapter we examine how membership of the EC and of the EU has affected parliamentary sovereignty.

The European Community exists to promote free trade and competition, economic integration and the harmonisation of law. Political union is a possible long-term goal. It has 15 European states as members. The United Kingdom joined in 1973. The six original members were France, Germany (then West Germany), Italy and the 'Benelux' countries (Belgium, the Netherlands and Luxembourg). The UK, Eire and Denmark joined in 1973, Greece in 1981 and Spain and Portugal in 1986. Legislation was passed in 1994 to allow Norway, Austria, Finland and Sweden to join following national approval within each of those countries. Austria, Finland and Sweden duly joined on 1 January 1995, but Norway remains outside the EC following a negative vote in a referendum.

There are actually three communities, the European Community (formerly the European Economic Community), the European Coal and Steel Community and the European Atomic Energy Community, but for our purposes we can regard them all as one, which we shall refer to as the European Community (the EC).

The EC was set up by the Treaty of Rome, and this treaty is the legal foundation for the powers of EC institutions. The original treaty has been amended, most notably by the Treaty on European Union (the Maastricht treaty).

In accordance with the requirement that all member states (then numbering 12) ratify its terms, the Treaty on European Union came into force on 1 November 1993, after the last constitutional objections to ratification were eliminated in individual states. Since this date, the EC has not ceased to exist, but has been subsumed within the European Union. The term European Union should be used to refer to the whole European organisation consisting of the three original communities and the Maastricht areas of co-operation. The Maastricht areas of co-operation include such matters as politics, foreign affairs, defence and conventions.

---

1   THE EUROPEAN COMMUNITY

1.1   The EC generates much law, mainly on economic and social matters such as competition between businesses, working conditions and the free movement of people within the European Union. The legislative process is independent of national legislatures, such as the United Kingdom Parliament, although it is controlled by government ministers from the member states. EC law can be enforced through the national courts in the member states and through the European Court of Justice.

1.2   If EC law conflicts with national law, EC law takes priority. EC law should thus be seen as a separate system of law, independent of national systems and overriding them where necessary.

2 COMMUNITY INSTITUTIONS 6/95, 6/98

2.1 There are four main institutions established by the Treaties. Three are *political* institutions: the Commission, the Council of Ministers and the European Parliament. The fourth is the European Court of Justice.

The European Commission

2.2 The European Commission is the executive body of the Community. Its main activities are 'formulating proposals for new community policies, mediating between the Member States to secure the adoption of these proposals, co-ordinating national policies and overseeing the execution of existing community policies'.

2.3 There are twenty Commissioners appointed by mutual agreement of the member governments. Current practice is for the five larger countries to appoint two each (the maximum) and for the ten smaller countries to appoint one each. The five larger countries are the UK, France, Germany, Italy and Spain.

2.4 The Commission has a wide legislative function. It is responsible for drafting most Community legislation, and puts its proposals before the Council for enactment.

The Council of Ministers

2.5 The Council is the Community's decision-making body. It 'takes the final decision on most EC legislation, concludes agreements with foreign countries and, together with the Parliament, decides on the Community budget'.

2.6 The Council comprises representatives of the member states; each government sends a relevant minister as its delegate, depending on the business to be dealt with. Thus foreign ministers would attend most meetings on general matters, while ministers of agriculture or finance might attend meetings on their respective areas of policy.

2.7 Different voting arrangements apply in different situations. Sometimes a unanimous vote is required; more usually a 'qualified majority' will suffice. This involves the use of a weighted voting system, based on the relative population of member states, and requiring a minimum number of states to be in favour to prevent motions being carried by the five larger states. The UK has 10 votes out of a total of 81.

The European Parliament

2.8 The European Parliament is a directly elected body. There are 518 members, including 87 representing the UK. Members sit in political groupings rather than by country. The Parliament has consultative and advisory functions which are exercised through standing committees dealing with specialist topics. Its formal opinion is required on many proposals before they can be adopted by the Council.

The European Court of Justice

2.9 The Court is a court of first instance from which there is no appeal. The jurisdiction of the European Court falls under four main heads.

   (a) Legal matters arising from the acts or omissions of member states, such as failure of a member state to fulfil its treaty obligations.

   (b) Rulings on legal issues affecting persons which arise from EC law.

   (c) Actions brought against EC institutions by member states, individuals or companies.

   (d) Disputes between the Communities and their employees.

2.10   When an issue in category (b) comes before the Judicial Committee of the House of Lords, which is the final court of appeal in the UK, the Judicial Committee is obliged to refer it to the European Court for a ruling. Any lower court may also do so. Any such reference is merely to establish what is the meaning of the relevant part of EC law.

2.11   Thereafter the English court (duly instructed as to the meaning) must apply the rule to the case before it. This system has already begun to affect the development of English law. Over a period of years it may make a considerable impact.

2.12   The Court consists of fifteen judges appointed for six year periods on recommendation of member states from distinguished judges and legal experts. They are assisted by eight *Advocates-General* who submit reasoned argument on the issues before the Court. The Court gives a single judgment and dissenting opinions are not expressed.

Other institutions

2.13   The four institutions described above are the main European Community institutions. There are a number of other less important bodies (from the legal viewpoint) including the Economic and Social Committee, the European Investment Bank and the European Court of Human Rights.

3   EC LAW   *6/94, 12/94, 12/95, 6/96, 12/96, 6/97, 12/97, 12/98, 6/99*

3.1   The sources of Community Law may be described as primary or secondary. The *primary sources of law* are the foundation treaties themselves.

(a)   The Treaty of Paris 1951, which established the ECSC.
(b)   The First Treaty of Rome 1957, which established the EEC.
(c)   The Second Treaty of Rome 1957, which established EURATOM.

3.2   The Amsterdam Treaty took effect on 1 May 1999, revising the treaties on which European Union is founded. Existing articles have been renumbered: for example, key competition articles such as Articles 85 and 86 become Articles 81 and 82. The Treaty amends the Treaty on European Union and the Treaty establishing the European community in four significant areas:

(a)   Freedom, security and justice
(b)   The Union and the citizen
(c)   Effective and coherent external policy
(d)   Institutional reforms.

3.3   The EC treaties are self-executing, that is they do not require any other legal backing in order to become law in the member states. They become law on their ratification by the states. Treaties are therefore *directly applicable*. The normal procedure is for the heads of governments to indicate their agreement to a treaty by signing it, but that agreement needs to be ratified by national governments acting with their parliaments' authorities.

3.4   Each EC treaty is divided into numbered articles. Most articles of EC treaties have *direct effect*. EC law which itself creates rights which persons may enforce is said to have direct effect. Such rights must be protected by the courts in the states; there is no need to go to the ECJ to take legal action on the basis that EC legislation has direct effect. If the rights are against other persons, the law has horizontal effect. If the rights are against states, the law has vertical effect.

3.5   Some treaty articles do not have direct effect. This may be because they state that further legislation is required, or because they give states discretionary power on their application. In the latter case, their effect is subject to the exercise of that discretion.

Direct applicability and direct effect

3.6 To understand the importance of regulations, directives and decisions, it is necessary to appreciate the distinction between direct applicability and direct effect. Community law which is directly applicable in member states comes into force without any act of implementation by member states. Law has direct effect if it confers rights and imposes obligations directly on individuals. This should be clear once we have explained the three types of secondary legislation.

3.7 Secondary legislation takes three forms, with the Council and Commission empowered to do the following.

(a) Make regulations.
(b) Issues directives.
(c) Take decisions.

They may also make recommendations and deliver opinions although these are only persuasive in authority.

Regulations

3.8 *Regulations*, for example to implement Article 85 of the Treaty of Rome, may be issued. These are 'self-executing', they have the force of law in every EC state without need of national legislation. In this sense regulations are described as directly applicable. Their objective is to obtain uniformity of law throughout the EC.

3.9 Direct law making of this type is generally restricted to matters within the basic aims of the Treaty of Rome, such as the establishment of a single unrestricted market in the EC territory in manufactured goods. For example, certain types of agreement which would restrict competition are prohibited, and attract punishment by fine.

3.10 Acts of implementation are usually prohibited, in case a member state, intentionally or unintentionally, alters the scope of the regulation in question. Occasionally, national legislation is required.

EC Commission v United Kingdom (Re Tachographs) 1979
A regulation concerning tachographs in vehicles required states to enact national legislation. The United Kingdom did not incorporate the whole of the regulation in the UK legislation.

Held: states must not implement regulations in an incomplete or selective way. The UK had therefore not fulfilled its EC obligations.

Directives

3.11 *Directives* are issued to the governments of the EC member states requiring them within a specified period (usually two years) to alter the national laws of the state so that they conform to the directive. Thus the Financial Services Act 1986 embodies certain directives on company securities and the Companies Act 1989 gives force to the Eighth Directive. However, most directives are incorporated into UK law by statutory instruments.

3.12 Until a directive is given effect by a UK statute it does not usually affect legal rights and obligations of individuals. In exceptional situations the wording of a directive may be cited in legal proceedings, but generally statutory interpretation is a matter for the UK courts.

Van Duyn v Home Office 1974
Article 48 of the Treaty of Rome requires that nationals of EC member states should be free to take up employment anywhere in the EC area, subject to any restrictions imposed on grounds of 'public policy, public security or of public health'. The plaintiff, a Dutch national, was refused leave to enter the UK on the ground that she was intending to work for the Church of Scientology, a movement which the UK government saw as socially harmful. An EC directive required that any such restriction on the grounds of 'public policy or of public security shall be based exclusively on the personal conduct of the individual concerned'. She claimed that the refusal was not based on personal conduct, and challenged the decision of the Home Office to deny her entry to the UK entirely on the grounds of her membership of the Church of Scientology.

Held: a directive could be directly effective (if its wording was appropriate). But the plaintiff's membership of an organisation was 'personal conduct' and so the decision to exclude her was consistent with the directive.

3.13   Directives can only confer rights on individuals (as in *Van Duyn v Home Office 1974*). They cannot impose obligations on individuals in favour of the state.

Marshall v Southampton and South West Hampshire Area Health Authority 1986
The plaintiff was dismissed at the age of 62, although she wished to continue working until the age of 65. The defendant's policy was that normal retirement age for its employees was the age when a state pension becomes payable (in this instance 60: the policy had been waived in respect of the plaintiff for 2 years).

Held: a directive (on equal treatment) was to be interpreted as meaning that a policy, based on the qualifying age for a state pension, which under national legislation was different for men and women, constituted discrimination on the grounds of sex. The policy was therefore contrary to the directive, which could be relied on against a state authority in its capacity as employer.

3.14   Directives are the most significant and important means of importing continental law into the UK legal system since the EC has a wide-ranging programme of assimilating the laws of member states to a common EC model.

Decisions

3.15   Decisions of an administrative nature are made by the EC Commission in Brussels. Such decisions are immediately binding on the persons to whom they are addressed. A decision may be addressed to a state, person or a company and is binding only on the recipient.

Legislative procedure

3.16   Proposals for EC legislation are *initiated by the Commission*, usually in the form of draft directives. These drafts are referred to member states for comments. In the United Kingdom it is the normal practice for a committee of Parliament to examine each draft and for the appropriate ministry to consult trade associations and other bodies which would be affected by the proposals if implemented.

3.17   These preliminary consultations between the Commission and the member states may continue over a period of years and result in extensive alteration of the draft directive to meet national objections. The directives are also debated in the preparatory stage by the European Parliament. The final stage is the consideration of a directive by the Council of Ministers.

3.18   If the Council approves, it authorises the issue of the directive and the member states must then alter their law accordingly.

4 EC LAW IN THE UK

6/96

4.1 It is true that membership of the EC restricts the sovereignty of the UK Parliament (among other EC national legislatures). But the directives to which Parliament must ultimately conform are issued as a result of negotiation and often agreement between the UK government and the other governments of the EC.

4.2 The UK government in turn is dependent on the support of a majority of Members of Parliament to retain office. To that extent, Parliament has indirect influence on the EC law-making process. It is certainly true to say, however, that since 1973 the EC has had considerable impact on the law, and this is set to increase.

4.3 The House of Lords acknowledged the supremacy of EC law in the *Factortame* litigation, which appears to affect not only areas of actual conflict between UK and EC law, but also areas of potential conflict.

> *Factortame Ltd v Secretary of State for Transport (No 2) 1991*
> Article 52 of the Treaty of Rome prohibits discrimination against the nationals of another EC member state. The Merchant Shipping Act 1988 requires 75% of directors and shareholders in companies operating British-registered fishing vessels to be British. Certain UK companies controlled by Spanish nationals and fishing in British waters were unable to meet these conditions. They brought a claim against the UK government on the grounds that the Act was incompatible with EC law.
>
> *Held*: the House of Lords granted interim relief by suspending relevant provisions of the 1988 Act and referred the matter to the ECJ, which laid down that EC law must be fully and uniformly applied in all member states.

4.4 The words of Hoffmann J in *Stoke-on-Trent CC v B & Q plc 1991* sum up the current position. Here, B & Q regularly opened its store on a Sunday in breach of s 47 Shops Act 1950, contending that s 47 was in breach of Article 30 of the EC Treaty.

> 'The EEC Treaty is the supreme law of this country, taking precedence over Acts of Parliament. Our entry into the European Economic Community meant that (subject to our undoubted but probably theoretical right to withdraw from the Community altogether) Parliament surrendered its sovereign right to legislate contrary to the provisions of the Treaty on matters of social and economic policy which it regulated.'

4.5 As an example of EU law in action, the Human Rights Act 1998 received Royal Assent in November 1998, with the main provisions due to be implemented during 2000. The Act incorporates the European Convention for the Protection of Human Rights and Fundamental Freedoms into UK law. Where possible, domestic legislation must be given effect in a way that is compatible with the Convention. The Convention provides for the right to a fair trial without undue delay, a right to freedom of speech and respect for private and family life. Property rights are also protected under the Convention.

5 INTERPRETATION OF EC LAW

5.1 EC legislation is drafted in a different way from UK legislation. The legislation states the broad principles and leaves the judges to develop the detail and thereby assist the objectives of legislation. English techniques of interpretation are not well-suited to be applied to EC legislation. Additionally, EC legislation is deemed equally valid in any language in which it is originally published. The exact meaning of words used inevitably varies between versions. There is no intention that lawyers should be able to 'shop around' to find the version most favourable to their case.

5.2 Lord Denning, in *HP Bulmer Ltd v J Bollinger SA 1974*, has said the following.

> 'The draftsmen of our statutes have striven to express themselves with the utmost exactness. They have tried to foresee all possible circumstances that may arise and to provide for them. They have sacrificed style and simplicity. They have foregone brevity ....How different is

this treaty! It lays down general principles. It expresses aims and purposes ... It uses words and phrases without defining what they mean .... It is the European way.'

5.3   The English courts should therefore try to follow the approach of European courts when interpreting the legislation. To do otherwise would create differences in the way in which the law is interpreted and applied in different member states.

5.4   In *Iberion (UK) Ltd v BPB Industries plc and Another 1996* it was held that the courts should not interpret rules of procedure in a way that risked that they and institutions of the European Union would arrive at inconsistent results on EU competition issues.

5.5   In the matter of interpreting UK statutes, it is open to the UK courts to decide that a British statute should be interpreted according to British court rules. The interpretation of EC directives need not be taken into account: *Duke v Reliance Systems Ltd 1988.*

5.6   The European Communities Act 1972 does not enable directives to affect the validity or construction of domestic legislation: *R v Secretary of State for Employment ex parte Seymour-Smith 1997.*

Chapter roundup

- There are three individual European Communities. The European Coal and Steel Community was established by the Treaty of Paris 1951, the European Economic Community by the First Treaty of Rome 1957 and the European Atomic Energy Community by the Second Treaty of Rome 1957.

- The Treaties by which the European Community was founded also established four main Institutions. The European Commission is the executive and legislative body of the Community. The Council of Ministers is the Community's decision-making body. The European Parliament has a consultative role. The European Court of Justice is the judicial body of the Community.

- The sources of EC law may be described as primary or secondary. The primary sources of law are the Foundation treaties themselves. The secondary sources of law are legislation, which takes three forms. Regulations are self-executing. Directives require national legislation to be effective, usually within two years. Decisions are immediately binding on the person to whom they are addressed.

Test your knowledge

1   Which Community institution is the main legislative body? (see para 2.4)

2   What is the jurisdiction of the ECJ? (2.9)

3   What treaty established the EEC? (3.1)

4   What type of European Community legislation is directly applicable? (3.8)

5   What were the facts of *EC Commission v United Kingdom (re Tachographs) 1979*? (3.10)

Now try illustrative question 4 at the end of the Study Text

Part B
Introduction to property law

Chapter 5

THE NATURE OF PROPERTY

This chapter covers the following topics.

1 Legal and equitable rights of ownership

2 Types of property

3 Restrictions on rights

4 Transfer of property

5 Ownership and possession

Introduction

This short chapter provides an introduction to the law of property. It introduces a number of terms which may be new to you. You may find it helpful to refer from time to time to the diagram on the next page.

Property is anything that can be owned. Property is generally classified as tangible or intangible and within these categories there are a number of subdivisions. These and other distinctions are explained later. It is first necessary to consider *ownership*, as an understanding of the legal rights to property is core to any study of this area of the law.

In the next chapter we will examine some of the general principles of land law in a little more detail.

---

1   LEGAL AND EQUITABLE RIGHTS OF OWNERSHIP

Legal ownership

1.1   Legal ownership is a common law concept. As an example, suppose that Reg is entered in the register of members of a company as the holder of 100 shares. He has legal ownership and if his name is wrongly removed from the register without his consent - for example as a result of a forged transfer - he has a legal right to recover his property (called a right *in rem*) from anyone, even from an honest person who bought the shares in ignorance that the transfer to him was forged and even if that transferee's name has been entered in the register.

Equitable ownership

1.2   Equitable ownership is a creation of equity which recognises legal ownership but imposes obligations on the legal owner (as trustee) in favour of another person (termed the beneficiary). To vary the example above, suppose that Reg buys 100 shares and has them registered in the name of Jo who agrees to hold the shares for Reg (who therefore receives the dividends and may instruct Jo to sell them). Reg has no direct legal rights of ownership over the shares (those rights are Jo's), but Reg has a personal right (a right *in personam*) to call Jo to account. If Jo wrongly transfers the shares to Kim, who buys them in ignorance of Jo's default in her obligations to Reg, and Kim becomes the registered holder of the shares - he acquires legal ownership for value and in good faith - Reg cannot recover the shares from Kim. Reg's remedy is to claim the value (the price paid by Kim) from Jo as a personal liability of Jo. If Jo is by then insolvent Reg will suffer loss.

Exercise 1

From the above explanation you should now be able to describe and differentiate a right *in rem* and a right *in personam*.

Solution

The difference between these rights stems from the action required to recover real and personal property.

(a)   If dispossessed of real property the plaintiff has a right to get back the very thing he has lost. This is known as a right *in rem* (a right in the thing) and is enforced by a real action.

(b)   If dispossessed of anything else (including leasehold land) a person's only right is to monetary compensation from the person who has dispossessed him. This is known as a right *in personam* and is enforced by a personal action.

2   TYPES OF PROPERTY   *12/95, 6/96, 12/96, 12/97, 6/99*

2.1   For historical reasons English law distinguishes different types of property. Note that 'chose' is, in this context, the legal word for 'thing' (derived from the French).

2.2   Tangible and intangible property can be further analysed as shown in the diagram below

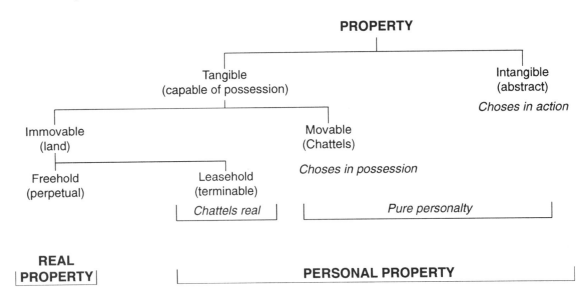

Land

2.3   Land includes buildings and anything else which is permanently attached to the land; a freehold or a leasehold may be owned.

Real property

2.4   Real property (also 'realty') is land owned in perpetuity (a 'fee simple absolute in possession'). The owner may change but the ownership continues. The mediaeval common law courts granted special remedies, ie the right of the dispossessed owner to have the land returned to him. For that historical reason land in freehold ownership is in a category (real property) of its own.

Leasehold property

2.5   Leasehold property ('chattels real'). The right of a tenant (or lessee) will come to an end either by expiry of a fixed period (which may be as much as 999 years) or by termination by notice (and in other more unlikely events). When it terminates the landlord (or lessor) resumes possession from the tenant. The landlord is therefore said to have a 'reversion' which becomes possession when the lease terminates. While the lease continues the tenant has possession but is usually required to pay a rent to the landlord. A lease is a form of contract; if granted for a term of more than three years it must generally be in the form of a deed. (In mediaeval terminology a lease was a 'chattel real' since it had something in common with real property - it was ownership of land - and something in common with chattels, since both are personal property).

Choses in possession

2.6 Moveable tangible property - generally called *chattels* or *choses in possession* - are literally those items of property of which ownership and possession can be transferred simply by delivery, such as furniture, books, jewellery, clothes etc.

Choses in action

2.7 The owner of intangible property such as patents, cannot enforce his rights by retaining or seeking possession as he could do with 'things in possession' which are moveable objects capable of being physically possessed. If his rights are disputed he enforces them by legal action in the courts. For example, a customer of a bank would sue the bank if it wrongly refused to pay his cheques. Transfer of choses in action is generally effected by a process called 'assignment'.

2.8 *Personal property* is anything which is not real property (freehold land). It is so called because the owner's claim could be satisfied by payment of the value instead of returning the property - his claim was against the wrongdoer personally and he could not automatically recover the property or thing. Personal property comprises (i) leasehold land and (ii) pure personalty (chattels and things in action). Banknotes and coins are 'things in action'.

2.9 These technical terms can be significant. For example a testator may by his will give his 'real estate' to A, his 'chattels' to B and his remaining personalty to C.

Exercise 2

Look back at the diagram on the previous page and add to it one example each of freehold property, leasehold property, a chose in possession and a chose in action.

Solution

A freehold property might be a factory owned by a company. A leasehold property might be a flat owned by an individual on a 999 year lease. A motor vehicle is an example of a chose in possession, and choses in action include patents.

---

3   RESTRICTIONS ON RIGHTS

3.1 All the above categories define the owner's rights over his property. But there are a number of restrictions on those rights.

Lease

3.2 This gives the leaseholder rights of possession over the land and buildings of the freeholder.

Servitude

3.3 Others may own rights which affect the enjoyment of land. Examples are as follows.

(a) Rights of way, rights of light and rights of support for building (*easements*).

(b) Right to take something, such as game or firewood, from another's land (*profits a prendre*).

Security

3.4 An owner may offer his property as security for a loan. This creates rights for the lender (such as the right to enforce sale if the debt is not repaid) which restricts those of the owner-borrower.

4   TRANSFER OF PROPERTY

4.1 When valuable property (for example a house) is transferred there is often a preliminary contract. Whether there is such a preliminary contract or not the actual transfer must be effected in the appropriate way.

(a) *Land* (including a lease) is transferred by deed.

(b) *Chattels* are transferred by mere delivery of possession if it is clear that the transferor intends to transfer ownership and not merely possession.

(c) *Choses in action* are transferred by assignment which is usually a written transfer.

4.2 Some forms of property such as land held under registered title, shares and debentures of companies, negotiable instruments, ships and policies of life assurance are subject to special requirements for transfer of ownership.

Transfer by deed

4.3 Apart from for a transfer of land, a deed is also required in some other contexts. For instance, when a person binds himself to a gratuitous promise, such as a covenant to make annual payments to a charity, he must execute a deed. This is a formal contract, which is written, signed, witnessed and delivered (delivered meaning 'put into effect'). Delivery is not necessarily a physical transfer of possession, but is conduct indicating that the person executing the deed intends to be bound by it.

Assignment

4.4 The standard method of assigning the ownership of a thing in action - 'statutory assignment' - is prescribed by s 136 Law of Property Act 1925.

(a) The assignment must be in writing and signed by the assignor.

(b) It must be 'absolute' - an unconditional assignment of the entire debt so that the assignor retains no interest in it.

(c) Written notice of the assignment must be given to the debtor so that he can make payment to the assignee. He would otherwise be able to discharge his debt by payment to the assignor as the original creditor.

4.5 Statutory assignment is based on common law rules and is confined to legal things in action. Equity provides a less formal procedure for assignment of equitable things in action and is able to give effect to informal assignment where the intention to assign is sufficiently clear but the statutory procedure has not been followed.

4.6 Assignments are made 'subject to equities'. This means that a person to whom a right is assigned takes it subject to any right of set-off against the original assignor. Thus if an assignee brings an action against a debtor, the debtor can set off any amounts owed to him by the assignor.

4.7 Certain types of assignment of choses in action are controlled by particular statutes. In such cases the specific statute overrides the prescriptions of the 1925 Act. Examples are given below.

(a) Bills of exchange are covered by the Bills of Exchange Act 1882.

(b) Shares in registered companies are covered by the Companies Act 1985.

Assignment by operation of law

4.8 Assignment by operation of law (involuntary assignment) occurs in the event of death (rights and liabilities to personal representatives) or bankruptcy (to trustee in bankruptcy).

5   OWNERSHIP AND POSSESSION

Ownership

5.1 The owner of property has various rights of ownership. He may usually do with his property what he pleases - use it or not use it, lend it, give it away or sell it, or offer it as security for a loan. Ownership is sometimes described as a bundle of legal rights since the owner may give up to someone else various rights over his property while remaining the owner. If, for example, A lends his property to B, A transfers possession (which is one of the normal rights of ownership) to B temporarily while the loan continues.

5.2 In the above example, B has possession of A's property. Possession gives B certain legal rights but does not make B the owner of what is still A's property. The essential elements of possession are *physical control of property with the intention of excluding others from interfering with it.*

(a) It is much wider than immediate physical control, though it includes this, for example a person who holds a book in his hand obviously has possession of it. But he also has possession of property in his house while he is away at work. A working farmer has possession of his land although he does not - and cannot - sit on every inch of it to keep out trespassers.

(b) It is possible to have physical control without possession - as when a porter at a railway station carries a passenger's luggage.

(c) It is possible to have possession of something on or under the surface of one's land even though one is unaware of its existence (for example buried treasure trove).

(d) One does not have possession of something lying unnoticed on land (such as in the public part of a shop) to which everyone has access.

5.3 The test is one of control and exclusion of others. Only property which is tangible can be possessed - there can be no possession of incorporeal property such as the rights to receive payment of a debt. That type of property is protected in other ways.

5.4 Ownership and possession are often combined.

(a) The owner of property is entitled to possession of it unless he gives up that right.

(b) A person in possession is likely to be the owner - possession is a sign of ownership until it is established that the possessor is not also the owner.

5.5 But as we have already seen, ownership and possession may be separated. The owner can assert his own rights as owner in a dispute with the person who has possession of his property.

Possession

5.6 Possession is the basis of a number of particular legal rights and obligations.

(a) In tort, a plaintiff who sues for trespass to land or goods must have or be entitled to possession as the basis of his action.

(b) When goods are delivered into the possession of another person (the bailee) for any particular purpose, there is a 'bailment' under which the bailee owes a duty to the bailor to take reasonable care of the goods. The bailment may be to the advantage of the bailor (for example when the owner of the goods leaves them with another person for safekeeping), or to the advantage of the bailee (for example when goods are supplied to a hirer under a hire purchase agreement).

(c) Possessory lien is a right to retain goods in the creditor's possession until he is paid what is owing by the owner/debtor. It arises by operation of law but continues only while the creditor has possession. In its simplest form a lien gives a creditor, for example a shoe repairer or a hotel-keeper, the right to retain possession of a debtor's property until he has paid his debt.

Legal and illegal possession

5.7 Possession may be obtained legally or illegally.

5.8 *Legal possession* occurs where property is passed from A to B by:

(a) contractual agreement;
(b) gift;
(c) inheritance;
(d) loan; or
(e) bailment.

5.9 *Illegal possession* may arise where B has obtained possession of A's property by:

(a) crime - as where he has stolen it; or

(b) tort - A may have the right to sue in the tort of conversion or he may be able to claim wrongful interference, which is an invasion of possession.

Chapter roundup

- In any study of property law, two categories of ownership should be distinguished. Legal ownership is a common law concept which gives a right *in rem*. Equitable ownership is, as its name suggests, a creation of equity. It gives a right *in personam*.

- Property may be tangible or intangible. Intangible property consists of *choses in action*. Tangible property may be moveable (chattels) or immoveable (land). Chattels are *choses in possession*. Land may be freehold (real property) or leasehold (chattels real).

- Whenever property is transferred, the transfer must be effected in the appropriate way. Typical methods of transfer are transfer by mere delivery of possession, transfer by deed and transfer by assignment.

- Ownership and possession are very different concepts. Ownership has been described as 'a bundle of legal rights'. Possession is physical control of property with the intention of excluding others from interfering with it.

Test your knowledge

1 What is real property? (see para 2.4)

2 What is a chose in possession? (2.6)

3 Give an example of a chose in action. (2.7)

4 What is a servitude? (3.3)

5 How are chattels transferred? (4.1)

6 How is a statutory assignment effected? (4.4)

7 Give two practical examples which distinguish ownership from possession (5.2)

Now try illustrative question 5 at the end of the Study Text

Chapter 6

LAND

This chapter covers the following topics.

1 Land law

2 Rights over land

3 Legal estates

4 Legal interests

5 Equitable interests

6 Unregistered and registered land

7 Mortgages of land

8 Remedies of mortgagees

Introduction

Chapter 5 gave a general introduction to the law of property. In this chapter we look in more detail at land law.

Land Law was overhauled and radically modernised in 1925 by a group of statutes of which the Law of Property Act 1925 (referred to as 'LPA') is referred to in this chapter unless otherwise stated. (The other major statute is the Land Registration Act 1925 'LRA'.)

---

1 LAND LAW

1.1 The term 'land' includes any building or structures on it and rights over land (including mining below the surface and to some extent the air above it). There are borderline categories.

   (a) Fixtures are things attached to land or to a building as part of it. Movable things (such as pictures hanging on a wall) are not fixtures. Land includes any fixtures attached to it.

   (b) Growing crops are usually not part of the land if they are to be severed from it in the course of harvesting.

1.2 There is a common law maxim which says that he who owns the surface owns everything up to the heavens and down to the depths of the earth. There are however a number of exceptions to this rule. Some mineral rights (for example over coal and petroleum) have been taken into public ownership (Coal Industry Nationalisation Act 1946) or are vested in the Crown (Petroleum (Production) Act 1934). Aircraft have a statutory right to fly over land at a safe height (Civil Aviation Act 1949).

1.3 The framework of land law is supported by a system of registers to which the public has access. The main elements are as follows.

Registered title

1.4   Some, but not yet all, land ownership in England is based on a system of entries in public registers maintained in District Land Registries at main centres (with a principal registry in London). A person who wishes to inspect an entry must usually obtain the prior consent of the owner of the land comprised in that entry. The right of inspection carries a right to have a copy (on payment of a fee).

Registered charges

1.5   Some, but not all, types of mortgage and other rights and encumbrances over land are protected by entry in a Land Charges Register at the Land Charges Registry. The standard procedure for investigating title to land requires that a search should be made in this register (usually by postal application and official certificate of search). If the land is owned by a registered company it may also be necessary to make a search at the Companies Registry. Most charges over company land require registration at that registry.

Local authority register

1.6   Local authorities (county councils, borough and district councils etc) have statutory powers to regulate and to promote land development, for example by means of planning restrictions. Orders and decisions of local authorities may affect particular areas or specific plots of land. The local authorities maintain registers in which these matters are recorded. It is part of the standard procedure in land transactions to apply to the local authorities of the area in which the land is situated for copies of entries in their registers (or answers to specific questions). In legal jargon these entries are called 'local searches'.

2   RIGHTS OVER LAND

2.1   For historical reasons land law relates to *rights over land* rather than to land itself. A person does not own land but rather owns an estate in land. For example, when a customer mortgages his freehold land to a bank as security, he encumbers (restricts) his freehold rights of ownership by giving to the bank rights over his land in the form of a legal or equitable mortgage. The land is still land but the rights over it have been altered and divided.

The distinction between legal and equitable rights

2.2   The law draws a most important distinction between rights which are legal and rights which are equitable. A legal right is *valid against anyone* (but priorities may depend on notice, as we shall see shortly). For instance, if a purchaser of land later discovers that someone has legal rights over the land of which he was previously unaware, he is bound by those rights. The person who has legal rights cannot (without his consent) be deprived of them (except by a public authority acting under an Act of Parliament, for example, a compulsory purchase order made by a local authority).

2.3   The reason for the distinction between legal and equitable rights is that by this means a purchaser of land can limit the expensive investigation of the seller's title to discovering whether there are legal rights over it. He can then strike a bargain with the persons who own those rights for their sale to him. As regards equitable rights, the purchaser makes searches in the register. If he thereby discovers rights which affect the land he can deal with them as he sees fit. But he need not make any further investigation to discover equitable rights since if there are any more of them and they are not registered or can be overreached they do not concern him. (This is a slightly simplified summary which suffices to bring out the main points.)

Legal rights

2.4 Legal rights over land are classified as legal estates and legal interests.

(a) A legal *estate* is that kind of right of ownership which carries an entitlement to possess - to occupy the land.

(b) A legal *interest* is a right over land given to a non-owner. But it is valid against everyone and gives a right to something less than possession.

2.5 For example, freehold ownership of land is a legal estate but a permanent 'right of way' over a neighbour's land is a legal interest. A person who has that legal interest may cross the land but may not take possession of it. Legal interests are discussed further later in this chapter.

Equitable rights

2.6 Equitable rights are valid against *anyone who has notice of them, actual or constructive, at the time of the relevant transaction.* A purchaser of land without notice of equitable rights over it usually acquires the land free of those rights. The person who has the equitable rights does of course have safeguards.

(a) In some cases he can *register* his rights at the Land Charges Registry and he thereby gives constructive notice to everyone who may thereafter have dealings with the land.

(b) In other cases, the equitable rights over land which is sold are transferred so as to become rights over the proceeds of sale which the seller receives and holds in trust for the persons with equitable rights. This system is called *overreaching* equitable rights.

Co-ownership

2.7 It is possible for more than one person to own land. If land is purchased or transferred to two or more persons, these persons become either 'joint tenants' or 'tenants in common'.

Joint tenancy

2.8 Joint tenancy arises where two or more people acquire land but no words of 'severance' are used. This means that the transfer does not state what share in the land each person has. The land is merely 'held by X and Y'. It is both legal and equitable co-ownership. *Joint tenancy* is a convenient way for a husband and wife to own the matrimonial home.

Tenants in common

2.9 Tenants in common have shares in the land. For instance, a conveyance may state that the land should go to 'P, Q and R equally' - each then owns one third part of the interest. It is equitable ownership.

2.10 The importance of the distinction is that if a joint tenant dies his interest lapses and the land is owned wholly by the survivor(s). He may not pass his interest on by will. The advantage is that only a limited number of interests can exist. The disadvantage is obviously the unfair fact that survival decides ownership. With tenants in common, each tenant can bequeath his interest which means that a house owned by tenants in common (A, B and C equally) will, if C dies and leaves his interest to D, E, F and G, be owned by A, B, (one third part each) D, E, F and G (one twelfth part each). Whilst being fairer, this can be cumbersome!

2.11 LPA achieved a compromise by providing that, where land is owned by two or more persons, no more than four of those persons hold the *legal* estate as joint tenants and trustees, for the benefit or *equitable* interest of themselves and other co-owners. Thus transfers can be effected by four signatures but the sale proceeds are subject to trusts so that all the owners get fair shares.

3   LEGAL ESTATES   *6/94, 6/97, 6/99*

3.1   LPA recognises only two legal estates in land (before the Law of Property Act 1925 was passed there were several more). Essentially the difference between them is how long they last (their 'tenure').

(a)   *Freehold ownership* is technically called 'fee simple absolute in possession'.
(b)   *Leasehold ownership* is known as 'term of years absolute'.

Freeholds

3.2   In freehold ownership, 'fee simple' means that the owner can transfer ownership at death to whomsoever he pleases. 'Absolute' means that there are no overriding conditions limiting the ownership. 'In possession' means that the owner has a right *now* to occupy the land or, if it is let to a tenant, to receive the rent.

Leaseholds

3.3   In leasehold ownership the expression 'term of years' is misleading. There can be very long leases, for example for 999 years, or for a very much shorter period such as a weekly tenancy. 'Term of years' simply indicates that it is an estate for a defined or terminable period. There are certain restrictions, so that for example a lease cannot be granted 'for a lifetime' or for a period beginning more than 21 years in the future. But these are not important distinctions here. Leaseholds are usually created by deed, but if the term is for less than three years, just a written or even an oral lease will suffice.

Exercise 1

What is the essential distinction between freehold and leasehold?

Solution

The essential distinction between freehold and leasehold rights of ownership is that a freehold continues for ever but a leasehold must end. Obviously the owner of freehold land may not continue in ownership of it for ever. If he is an individual he will die or perhaps sell or give away the land in his lifetime. But if this happens the perpetual right of ownership continues to exist and passes to the next owner - and so on.

3.4   Leasehold ownership is a complicated concept. Because land itself is indestructible, there must always be an owner of the perpetual freehold estate from which the leasehold estate has been carved out for a period of time. Even a lease for 999 years must come to an end when 999 years have passed. The land will then revert to the possession (it is already subject to the existing ownership) of the freeholder. The rights of a landlord (also called a 'lessor') of land let under a lease to a tenant (or 'lessee') are called rights 'in reversion' or reversionary interests because possession is due to revert to the landlord when the lease ends.

3.5   A lease may be defined as 'the grant of a right to the exclusive possession of land for a determinate term less than the grantor has himself in the land'. This definition may be expanded as follows.

(a)   *Exclusive possession* - in *Street v Mountford 1985* it was said that a tenant with exclusive possession is able to exercise the rights of an owner of land - he can keep out strangers and keep out the landlord. But even if he has exclusive possession, he is not a tenant unless he has been granted exclusive possession for a fixed or periodic term certain in consideration of a premium or periodical payments. With a lease it is still possible for the landlord to reserve the right to enter premises on certain occasions, to be exercised at reasonable hours and in a reasonable manner.

(b) *Determinate term* - a lease must last for a fixed period, though a 'periodic tenancy' may still qualify, and its commencement should be certain: *Lace v Chantler 1944*. To mitigate this requirement, a lease will often contain, for example, a term that it should be 'for n years subject to earlier termination on A's insolvency'.

3.6 The consideration given for a lease is normally rent (periodic payments) paid in money. However, a single premium will be sufficient consideration, and either rent or premiums may be paid in kind or through the performance of services.

Licences

3.7 A licence to use land creates a number of rights, none of which creates either an estate or an interest in land. A licensee does, however, have the authority to be present on land, so he cannot be a trespasser - he has permission, but no legal estate or interest. It is not normally easy to distinguish a licence from a lease, but it is often very important to do so since a licensee has no protection under the Rent Acts while a tenant does have considerable statutory protection. The most important difference is that a licensee does not have exclusive possession; the landlord may reserve the right to enter premises at any time and the licensee may have access restricted by the landlord: *Appah v Parncliffe Investments Ltd 1964*. If there is no exclusive possession then the agreement *cannot* be a lease.

Terms in leases

3.8 The owner of building land sometimes lets individual plots on long lease for, say, 99 years in return for a large initial premium and a small or even nominal rent (called a 'ground rent'). He also imposes a condition on the lease that the tenant shall build a house on this plot (this is a 'building lease'). The same general pattern can be adapted to letting flats in a block of flats or to disposing of numerous new houses built by the lessor in developing land under a building scheme. But commercial property such as lock-up shops may be let for comparatively short periods in return for an economic rent.

3.9 A lease is a contract made between lessor and original lessee. In principle the terms of the lease can be whatever they may agree upon. The lease will describe and define the property let (and any rights attached to it), state for how long it is to last (eg for a year or indefinitely until terminated by a month's notice), what rent is payable and at what intervals, and what obligations are imposed on lessor and lessee. In particular a lease may restrict the use to which the tenant may put the leasehold premises. This is particularly common in leases of commercial premises such as shops. The terms of leases are often varied or restricted by statutes, such as the Rent Act 1977 and the Protection from Eviction Act 1977 enacted to protect tenants.

Transfer

3.10 In general a leasehold is transferable on the basis that the new tenant is bound by the terms of the lease. The lease itself may give the lessor (or the later owner of the reversion if the original lessor has disposed of it) a limited right to withhold consent to any transfer (assignment) of the entire lease, and to any sub-letting.

3.11 A person to whom a lease is transferred is said to have 'privity of estate' with the lessor (or any person to whom the lessor on his part has transferred his reversionary rights). This expression means that although the present lessee was not a party to the lease when it was first made (as a contract) he does now own the legal estate (the lease) and this puts him into a direct relationship (rights and obligations) with the present owner of the reversion.

3.12 A lessee may sub-let all or part of the leasehold property for all or part of the unexpired period of the lease (subject to any veto retained by the lessor). It is usual then to call the lease granted by the freehold owner the 'head lease' and the sub-letting a 'sub-lease'. The lessee is also then a landlord or lessor (as regards the sub-lease).

Termination

3.13 A lease may come to an end in a number of ways.

(a) Expiry of a fixed period.

(b) Termination by notice (which must be in writing if the property is a dwelling).

(c) 'Forfeit' - where the lease's contractual terms are breached by default in payment of rent, bankruptcy, company liquidation or receivership.

3.14 Obviously if the lessor acquires the lessee's leasehold title or the lessee acquires the lessor's reversion, the freehold and leasehold are merged and the latter ceases to exist.

3.15 The Leasehold Reform Act 1967 gives a lessee who holds property under a lease granted for more than 21 years a right to purchase a lessor's reversion or to have it extended by 50 years. But this right applies only to house property, in respect of which the tenant must have satisfied certain rules governing occupancy.

Exercise 2

You may occupy or at some time have lived in rented accommodation. You probably had to sign a lease or a licence agreement. What are the main differences between a licence and a lease?

Solution

The principal differences are as follows. A lease is an interest in land; a licence is a contract between lessor and lessee. A lease grants a right to the exclusive possession of land; a licence does not. A licensee may have access restricted by the landlord, more usually the landlord will reserve the right to enter the premises at any time.

---

4   LEGAL INTERESTS   *6/95, 12/98, 6/99*

4.1 There are five legal interests in land recognised by LPA. Only the first two listed below have any practical importance nowadays.

(a) An easement, right or privilege over land of another person.

(b) A charge by way of legal mortgage.

(c) A rentcharge - a right (not arising from a lease) to receive an annual payment from the owner of land. (This type of legal interest is being extinguished over a long period of years by the Rentcharges Act 1977).

(d) A charge imposed on land by law.

(e) A right of entry - a right to resume possession given to a lessor of a lease or a person entitled to a rentcharge if there is default.

Easements

4.2 An easement is typically a right to do or to have something which restricts the rights of an owner of other land. As examples, one plot of land may carry a right of way over another, or a right of support (as when semi-detached houses share a party wall) or a right of light (which prohibits creating an obstruction to the passage of light to windows). It is also possible though less common that one piece of land gives to its owner a right to go on the land of another and remove something from it (fishing or shooting rights, or the right to collect firewood or to graze cattle). This right to take away something is called a *profit a prendre*.

Mortgages

4.3   The essential feature of a loan secured on land (other than a collateral security by guarantee) is that the borrower (called the 'mortgagor') gives to the lender (called the 'mortgagee') a right in priority to other creditors to resort to the land of the borrower to obtain repayment of the loan (and/or interest due on it) if (but only if) the borrower defaults, in which case the mortgagee may enforce his right by sale of the land.

4.4   In the normal case a mortgagor borrows money from the mortgagee, such as a bank, and undertakes to repay the loan at a specified date or on demand and to pay interest (at specified dates) until the principal is repaid. This is a loan contract. The mortgage is the security for the mortgagor's due performance of the contract. If the mortgagor duly performs his contract he is, under the terms of the contract, entitled to have his mortgage discharged by release of the land from the mortgagee's rights over it (with a legal mortgage those rights are a legal interest in the land). He is also freed from his personal obligations to the mortgagee.

Legal mortgages

4.5   A legal mortgage may (under s 85 LPA) be in one of the following forms. Either method gives to the mortgagee all the rights of a legal mortgagee, including in particular the power of sale. The mortgagor, however, remains the owner of the legal estate in the mortgaged property.

   (a)   Lease - the mortgagor grants to the mortgagee a lease of the land (rare nowadays).

   (b)   Legal charge - the mortgagor charges his land to the mortgagee by deed (discussed below).

4.6   In the context of a legal charge, 'charge' has the same meaning as 'mortgage' and gives the same rights and powers. The mortgagor grants to the mortgagee a charge over his land by way of legal mortgage. Such a charge must be created by deed and, following the Law of Property (Miscellaneous Provisions) Act 1989, be signed by the mortgagee as well as by the mortgagor.

4.7   There are two advantages to the use of this method. Most mortgagees therefore take a legal mortgage as their security by obtaining a legal charge from the borrower.

   (a)   If two or more properties, some freehold and some leasehold, are mortgaged by the same mortgagor, a single charge of this type can create mortgages over them all. Under the outdated lease method, freehold and leasehold land had to be mortgaged separately since the mortgage term (period of the lease) could not be the same for both.

   (b)   A mortgage of a leasehold by legal charge is not a subletting for which the lessor's consent may be required.

Equitable mortgages

4.8   In some circumstances it is not possible, or not convenient, to complete the formalities of a legal mortgage. The alternative is an equitable or informal mortgage, which may be created in either of the following ways.

   (a)   *Deposit of title deeds or land certificate* - there is a mortgage if the person who makes the deposit intends to hand over his document to the lender as security. But if the deposit is merely for safekeeping it does not create a mortgage. To remove any doubt the mortgagee usually insists on obtaining from the mortgagor a written *Memorandum of Deposit* which the latter signs (or sometimes executes as a deed) to express the intention and terms of the arrangement.

(b) *Equitable charge* - the mortgagor states in writing that, in consideration of the loan, specified property which he owns is to be security for the loan. If the bank needs to enforce the security, it must apply to the court for an order to sell.

4.9 When a mortgagee takes an equitable mortgage, it usually requires the mortgagor to sign its standard Memorandum of Deposit including an undertaking to execute a legal mortgage if called on to do so. At the same time the mortgagee obtains possession (if it does not already have it) of the title deeds etc.

4.10 An equitable mortgage is less safe and less easy to enforce than a legal mortgage. But an equitable mortgagee can usually sell the property with the sanction of a court order. An equitable mortgage is more convenient if the borrower requires only a short-term loan such as a 'bridging loan' to pay the price of a new house pending the sale soon afterwards of the borrower's old house. It is also less expensive in fees than a formal legal mortgage.

5 EQUITABLE INTERESTS *6/95, 12/98*

5.1 It is possible to have interests in land which are *equitable* - interests which are not legal estates or legal interests as described above. Equitable interests are valid against a purchaser of the land for value if he has notice of them (but if they arise from a trust and can be overreached the law does not permit him to be so affected by them). All equitable interests must exist behind a trust.

5.2 One example of an equitable interest is a restrictive covenant. This is a promise made by deed by which the covenantor promises not to do certain things on his land, such as keep pigs or trade as a business. For the most part, since covenants are made between two parties to a contract they may only be enforced by one against the other under the rule of privity of contract. A restrictive covenant may not usually be enforced against a subsequent purchaser.

5.3 In certain circumstances, equity will enforce a covenant against the current owner of the property. Where a purchaser acquires land with knowledge of the restrictive covenants he is bound to observe them. Such a covenant is said to 'run with the land' in equity.

> *Tulk v Moxhay 1848*
> A one-time owner of part of Leicester Square in London covenanted with the owner of adjacent property that the square would be maintained as a garden. When the land changed hands, the purchaser, believing he was not bound by the promise made by someone else, intended to build on the square.
>
> *Held*: the neighbour had an equitable right to enforce the covenant against the purchaser, since the latter had known of the promise when he bought the land.

5.4 This basic rule has been analysed in later cases so that it now states that a restrictive covenant may be binding on a later purchaser if the following conditions are satisfied.

(a) It is negative (a promise not to erect buildings in Leicester Square and to maintain a garden);

(b) The covenant had been made in favour of a person who, at the time, owned the land to be benefited.

(c) The promise had been intended to run with the land from inception.

(d) General equitable principles apply.

6 UNREGISTERED AND REGISTERED LAND *12/94*

6.1 There are two further categories of land of which you should be aware - unregistered and registered land. The system of registered title to land was introduced a hundred years ago on a limited scale. In recent years it has been progressively extended throughout the country, with priority for built-up areas. But even in an area of compulsory registration there may still be unregistered titles since registration becomes compulsory only on transfer of freeholds and some leaseholds. The intention is that eventually all land ownerships (other than short leases) shall be registered.

Unregistered land

6.2 Title to unregistered land is denoted by possession of title deeds (the owner will hold these unless the land is charged). Title deeds comprise the following documents.

   (a) Abstracts of title - prepared by a solicitor to indicate past transactions whose documentation is not included with the deeds.

   (b) Conveyances - documents conveying title to another person.

   (c) Mortgages - creating charges over the property.

   (d) Releases of mortgages - signifying that the charges are discharged.

   (e) Search certificates.

   (f) Assignments - transferring leasehold interests.

   (g) A schedule listing the documents included.

Registrable interests

6.3 To simplify the rules on notice it is provided that certain interests in land may be registered at the Land Charges Registry. These registrable interests include some legal interests and some equitable interests. If they are registered, the registration operates as constructive notice to everyone, whether or not he actually knows of them. If they are not registered these interests are void against a third party even if he actually knew of them. Accordingly it is standard procedure to search the registers at the Land Charges Registry when buying *unregistered land* only.

6.4 The registrable charges over land are divided in the Land Charges Registry register into classes. The most important classes are classes C, D and F.

   (a) Charges over land registrable in Class C of the Land Charges Register include *legal mortgages* if not protected by deposit of title deeds and general *equitable charges* such as an equitable mortgage (which is not, as mentioned above, a legal interest) and estate contracts, which are preliminary contracts for the sale of land or grant of a lease.

   (b) Charges over land registrable in Class D include charges for *inheritance tax, restrictive covenants* (a restriction on the use of land imposed after 1925 for the benefit of other land) and *equitable easements* created after 1925 (an easement which does not qualify as an overriding legal interest may nonetheless be protected by registration which gives notice of its existence).

   (c) Class F shows the right of a spouse to occupy a house owned by the other spouse - very important to a mortgagee since the mortgagee will wish to sell (if he sells) with vacant possession.

6.5 If a registrable charge is not registered, a purchaser of the land is generally not affected by it. A 'purchaser' includes a mortgagee such as a bank lending on security. But a Class D land charge and an estate contract (in Class C) will, if unregistered, be valid and binding on a purchaser unless he acquires a legal estate in the land.

Transfer of unregistered land

6.6 An owner of *freehold* land transfers his ownership by deed - by a written transfer. A transfer is usually a sale. Before he pays the price, the purchaser (and any mortgagee who is lending part of the price) investigates the seller's title and other matters affecting the land and its value.

6.7   The vendor is required by the contract to 'deduce' - demonstrate his title - by showing:

     (a)   that he is the owner of the land (to the extent described in the contract);

     (b)   how he acquired it from the previous owner; and

     (c)   what has been the sequence of previous dealings (including earlier changes of ownership) over a period of years.

6.8   If the sequence of documents (title deeds) raises no doubts (or if they can be removed), and no one is challenging the present owner's rights, the purchaser is reasonably safe in buying those rights of ownership from him.

6.9   The general sequence of action in transfer of unregistered *leasehold* land is broadly the same as for a transfer of unregistered freehold land. But here the vendor's title is the lease granted to him (or to his predecessor). He discloses the ownership and dealings with it for the previous 15 years. He must at completion assign the lease (by deed) and hand over the lease itself and the relevant earlier documents.

Registered land

6.10   The purpose of the system of registered title is to simplify the transfer of ownership of land. When unregistered title is converted to registered title, the title deeds are delivered to the District Land Registry for the area in which the land is situated. The Registry extracts and summarises the relevant particulars which are entered together in the register as follows.

     (a)   *Property Register.* This is a description of the land and the owner's rights supplemented by reference to a general map or filed plan which shows the boundaries and the position of the land in relation to adjoining properties.

     (b)   *Proprietorship Register.* This states:

         (i)   the class of title (described below);

         (ii)   the name, address etc of the registered proprietor - on each change of ownership the particulars of the new owners are inserted so that from the time of registration onwards the sequence of ownership is visible on the register (but this is not material - it is only the latest entry which counts);

         (iii)   any restrictions on the registered owner's right of disposal (say, because of bankruptcy proceedings).

     (c)   *Charges Register.* This gives particulars of mortgages, charges, leases and other encumbrances other than 'overriding interests' (explained below) and 'minor interests'. Occasionally it is necessary to supplement this data by retaining a copy of a document.

6.11   All these particulars can generally be typed on two sides of one large page in the register. An exact copy of the entries is issued to the registered proprietor as evidence of his title. This copy (authenticated by the Registry seal) is called the *Land Certificate.* The old title deeds are returned to the owner but are endorsed to the effect that the title has been registered (so that the deeds cannot be used in a fraudulent sale as an unregistered title).

Overriding interests

6.12   Overriding interests (in registered or unregistered land) are not registered but nonetheless bind anyone who acquires an interest in the land (for example, by purchase). Overriding interests (such as those of a spouse) can be discovered by enquiry of the occupier (and so the intending purchaser is expected to make this enquiry for himself). They include such interests as leases not exceeding 21 years, rights of persons in occupation, duties to repair and legal easements such as rights of way.

Hodgson v Marks 1971

H transferred her house into the name of her lodger (E) solely to prevent her nephew turning E out of the house. H remained in occupation. E sold the house to another person who mortgaged it to a building society.

Held: although H was not a party to the later transaction she was in 'actual occupation'. Her transfer to E had given her certain equitable rights against E (a resulting trust in her favour). These rights were an overriding interest and valid against the subsequent registered owner.

Classes of registered title

6.13   The Proprietorship Register describes the title of the registered owner as one of four categories.

(a)   *Absolute Title* - this is a state-guaranteed title limited only by:

(i)   what may appear from the register itself;
(ii)   any overriding interests; and
(iii)   any minor interests of which the person affected has notice.

(b)   *Possessory Title* - this is a provisional title which is not guaranteed. It is the category used in cases of doubt. But after 15 years a registered owner of freehold land held under possessory title may have it upgraded to absolute title. A leaseholder may similarly progress to good leasehold title after 10 years. Possessory title is a holding operation - the proprietor fails at the outset to establish his title beyond doubt but if time passes without challenge being made he achieves absolute title.

(c)   *Qualified Title* - this is rare. It is a registered title qualified by explicit limits or reservations on it.

(d)   *Good Leasehold Title* - this guarantees a leasehold title but it does not guarantee that the leasehold was granted out of a guaranteed freehold title. After 10 years, however, it may be upgraded to absolute title.

Transfer of registered land

6.14   The transferor completes a printed form of transfer as a deed. This transfer and the transferor's Land Certificate are delivered to the District Land Registry. The particulars of the transferee are entered in the Proprietorship Register. A new Land Certificate is then issued to the transferee as registered proprietor.

6.15   The main difference between transfer of registered and unregistered land is that the vendor proves his title merely by producing his Land Certificate. As the Land Certificate may not show entries made on the register since the Land Certificate was issued or last up-dated it is usual to send the Certificate in for updating when the sale is agreed or to apply to the Registry for a copy of the entries on the register (relating to the land to be sold). But in proving title, suitable evidence of what the register now contains is all which the vendor must produce and which the purchaser need concern himself with. There are of course complications to be kept in view, such as possible overriding interests. But in essentials registered title reduces to a minimum the task of extracting information about the rights and interests in the land of the registered proprietor and any third parties.

Exercise 3

Describe how an owner proves title to:

(a)   unregistered land; and
(b)   registered land.

Solution

(a)   Title to unregistered land is shown by possession of title deeds. The vendor must demonstrate title by showing a good 'root of title' going back at least 15 years.

(b) Title to registered land is shown by issue of a land certificate by the District Land Registry. Title deeds are endorsed to show that the land has been registered.

---

7 MORTGAGES OF LAND

Mortgages of unregistered land

7.1 The owner of unregistered land which is unencumbered by any mortgage has possession of the title deeds. This is one of the normal rights of ownership. If the owner creates a mortgage over his land the mortgagee requires him to hand over the title deeds which the mortgagee retains until the mortgage debt is discharged. The mortgagee obtains the title deeds to prevent the mortgagor from selling the land (for which the vendor must produce the deeds) or from creating another mortgage without giving notice of his mortgage (since the other mortgagee would demand the deeds).

7.2 If it is a legal mortgage then the mortgagor must execute a deed.

7.3 Since the owner of land subject to a mortgage is unable to produce his deeds, the fact that he does not have them operates as notice to any purchaser from him (or another mortgagee) that there is an existing mortgage. But if the owner is left in possession of his title deeds by a mortgagee, then the mortgagee has failed to give notice of his mortgage by the best available means and may on that account be held (it is not an automatic result) to have misled others about the existence of his mortgage. He is then ranked in priority behind a purchaser for value.

7.4 If a mortgagee has possession of the title deeds it is not required to register its mortgage (to give notice of it) because it effectually gives notice by taking possession of the deeds.

7.5 These general principles are applied and extended as follows.

(a) An *equitable mortgage* can be created merely by obtaining possession of the deeds without the formalities of a legal mortgage, but it will not be actionable unless it is in writing and signed by both parties.

(b) A *first mortgagee* in possession of title deeds should take precautions if he is asked to release them.

(c) An *intending purchaser or mortgagee* should always enquire at the outset whether the owner has possession of the deeds. If the enquiry is not made (and followed by delivery of the deeds on completion of the sale or mortgage) the purchaser or mortgagee is deemed to have notice of an existing mortgage and is bound by it.

(d) A *second mortgagee* cannot protect his mortgage by obtaining possession of the title deeds. He is therefore required to register his mortgage in order to give notice of it by registration at the Land Charges Registry as a Land Charge Class C. A legal second mortgage is registered as a *puisne* mortgage (since it is not protected by deposit of title deeds) and an equitable second mortgage as a general equitable charge. Both are Land Charges Class C.

Mortgages of registered land

7.6 The same general principles apply to the procedure for creating a *legal mortgage* of registered land. But the registration requirements are different because a registered title (Part C) itself records mortgages etc. Contrast this with a mortgage of unregistered land which is registered at a different registry (Land Charges Registry) in those cases where registration is a necessary safeguard.

7.7 The mortgagee (when it is a first *legal mortgage*) obtains possession of the mortgagor's Land Certificate and sends it with the executed mortgage deed to the District Land Registry for registration as a 'charge' on the land. The particulars of the mortgage are entered in the Charges Register part of the registered title. The Registry then issues a

Charge Certificate which comprises the contents of the former Land Certificate now enclosed in a different cover which is plainly labelled 'Charge Certificate', together with the new mortgage over the land.

7.8   By these means no one can be in doubt that he is dealing with a registered title which is subject to a registered charge. Unless it is registered in the Charges Register within two months it ceases to be a legal mortgage and become an equitable mortgage - the mortgagor has no legal right.

7.9   Registering a charge in this way:

(a)   gives the transferee good title, free of minor interests (unless they are overriding); and

(b)   determines priority, normally in the order of entry in the register subject to other agreement and some statutory charges.

7.10   An *equitable mortgage* of registered land is usually a deposit with the mortgagee of the mortgagor's Land Certificate with or without a suitable Memorandum of Deposit. It is not actionable unless it is in writing and signed by both parties.

7.11   An equitable mortgage is a 'minor interest' in registered land, unless it is protected on the register within two months of creation. So too is a legal mortgage which is not properly registered on the Charges Register. Failure to register and/or protect means that a purchaser or mortgagee can acquire title free of minor interests.

Second mortgages

7.12   A mortgagor is free to create a second or later mortgage which (if the holder of the first mortgage has taken the normal steps to protect his interests) ranks after the first or prior mortgages. In effect the mortgagor uses his equity of redemption (of the first mortgage) as security for further borrowing.

7.13   A second mortgage of *registered land* is registered at the Land Registry. The holder of a legal second mortgage obtains a Charge Certificate from the Registry (to show that his title is entered against the title in the Charges Register). An equitable second mortgagee lodges a 'caution' which is noted in the register.

Exercise 4

What do you think are the disadvantages inherent in the position of second mortgagees?

Solution

(a)   The security may be *inadequate in value*. The first mortgage may sell at a time when the market value has fallen to less than the aggregate of the two mortgage loans.

(b)   There is *no possession of title deeds* - but registration and notice to first mortgagee improve the second mortgagee's position.

8   REMEDIES OF MORTGAGEES

Remedies of a legal mortgagee

8.1   While a mortgage is still in force, the legal mortgagee has the following rights over the property.

(a)   *Documents of title* - the first mortgagee of unregistered land is entitled to hold these; with registered land he will have a Charge Certificate.

(b) *Possession* - this is immediate on the mortgage's creation - there need not be default. It is a risky right and seldom used.

(c) *Grant/surrender leases of less than 50 years* - only if there is possession.

(d) *Protection of property* - the mortgagee is impliedly or expressly allowed to restrain deliberate damage, insure against fire and perform necessary repairs.

(e) *Additional property* - such as added fixtures (for instance, a patio), a new lease or a freehold reversion on a leasehold, are included in the original mortgage.

8.2   If the mortgagor defaults, the legal mortgagee has five remedies and may pursue any of them at the same time or in sequence (but not so as to recover more than the full debt).

(a) *Action for debt.* This is an action against the debtor personally to enforce his obligation to pay. On obtaining judgment for his debt the creditor may enforce it by seizure of the debtor's property or by obtaining a court charging order on it. He may also go on to petition for bankruptcy of an individual debtor or compulsory winding up of a company. This remedy is available to unsecured as well as secured creditors. It has nothing to do with mortgage law.

(b) *Sale of the mortgaged property* (see below).

(c) *Appointment of a receiver* where the property generates income such as rent.

(d) *Foreclosure* - transfer of the mortgaged property by court order into the outright ownership of the mortgagee. Many conditions impede and restrict foreclosure. It is rarely used.

(e) *Taking possession* of the property. This is risky to the mortgagee. If he fails to obtain the maximum income from the property while in his possession he must account for the deficit. Again mortgagees rarely resort to this remedy.

Sale of the property

8.3   Any mortgage made by deed, whether legal or equitable, confers on the mortgagee a power to sell when the mortgage debt is due for payment and, in doing so, to transfer to the purchaser the entire estate and interest in the property of the mortgagor, free of the mortgage and any mortgages subsequent to it (but not free of mortgages (if any) which rank ahead of the mortgage under which the sale is made): s 101.

8.4   In arranging to sell the mortgaged property the mortgagee must:

(a) act in good faith (for instance he cannot buy the property himself);

(b) use reasonable care to realise the true value of the property - a professional valuation should be carried out by a chartered surveyor to ascertain the market value of the property.

Cuckmere Brick Co Ltd v Mutual Finance Ltd 1971
The mortgagee advertised the mortgaged property for sale but gave incomplete information of the available planning permission for erecting buildings on the land. The sale did not realise the full amount of the loan.

Held: the mortgagee had been negligent. Its claim to recover the balance of the loan failed because it had not obtained the full value of the mortgaged property although it had been in its power to do so.

8.5   On receipt of the proceeds of sale the mortgagee has a duty to apply the money as follows:

(a) to meet the costs of the sale; then
(b) to discharge the mortgage debt and interest; then
(c) to pay the residue to the person entitled.

Remedies of an equitable mortgagee

8.6   An equitable mortgagee has rights against the mortgagor if he defaults (he can sue for debt), but he has no legal interest in the land to enable him to sell it as mortgagee.

8.7   An equitable mortgagee can overcome this difficulty if he takes his mortgage in the form of a deed (s 101) or if he obtains from the mortgagor an *irrevocable power of attorney* which authorises him to sell the land as agent of the mortgagor or a *declaration of trust*. If these devices are used, the mortgagee sells as agent or as trustee and is not impeded by its lack (as equitable mortgagee) of power to sell arising from the mortgage.

8.8   If the equitable mortgage is not in the form of a deed (with the elements mentioned above) the equitable mortgagee may:

(a)   require the mortgagor to execute a legal mortgage if he has previously undertaken to do so; or

(b)   apply to the court for an order for sale.

But remember that no charge is actionable unless it was made in writing and signed by both parties.

Exercise 5

What are the benefits for a mortgagee of a legal mortgage compared with an equitable mortgage?

Solution

A legal mortgage is a better security than an equitable mortgage for two reasons.

(a)   It gives *greater security* - the mortgagee acquires a legal interest in the mortgaged land. That interest is valid against anyone to whom the borrower may sell or mortgage the land (provided that a legal mortgage not protected by deposit of title deeds is registered).

(b)   It provides *better remedies* - the legal interest of the mortgagee in the land gives him better remedies, in particular a power of sale. However that a legal mortgage does not take priority over an existing equitable mortgage if, at the time when the legal mortgage is created, the legal mortgagee has notice of the existence of an equitable mortgage.

Chapter roundup

- Land law is concerned with rights over land. A person does not own land but owns an estate in land. A key distinction is between legal rights, valid against anyone, and equitable rights, which are valid against anyone who has notice of them at the time of the relevant transaction.

- Under LPA 1925 there are two legal estates in land. Freehold ownership is also called 'fee simple absolute in possession'. Leasehold ownership is also called 'term of years absolute'.

- There are five legal interests in land, of which the two most important are the easement and the charge by way of legal mortgage. It is also possible to have an equitable interest in land, which is valid against a purchaser of the land for value if he has notice of it, for example a restrictive covenant.

- Land may be classified as registered or unregistered. Procedures for evidencing title and for transferring land depend on which category land is in.

- Under a mortgage, which is effectively security for performance of a loan contract, the borrower (mortgagor) gives to the lender (mortgagee) a right, in priority to other creditors, to resort to the land of the borrower to obtain repayment in the event of default.

- A mortgage may be legal or equitable. An equitable mortgage is less safe and less easy to enforce than a legal mortgage.

Test your knowledge

1   Describe a legal estate and a legal interest (see para 2.4)

2   What is the difference between joint tenancy and tenancy in common? (2.8, 2.9)

3   What is meant by 'fee simple absolute in possession'? (3.2)

4   Define a lease. (3.5)

5   How may a legal mortgage be created? (4.5)

6   What were the facts of *Tulk v Moxhay 1848*? (5.3)

7   What do title deeds consist of? (6.2)

8   What is shown in Class C of the Land Charges Register? (6.4)

9   What are the four classes of registered title? (6.13)

Now try illustrative question 6 at the end of the Study Text

Part C
Trusts

Chapter 7

TYPES OF TRUST

This chapter covers the following topics.

1   The nature of trusts

2   The uses of the trust

3   Classification of trusts

4   Express private trusts

5   Secret trusts

6   Charitable trusts

7   Trusts arising by operation of law

Introduction

The trust, or 'use' as it was formerly known, has evolved over several centuries and was originally used most frequently to avoid medieval feudal dues. If a tenant of land died leaving an infant heir, the lord of the manor could use the land for his own benefit during the infant's minority. Indeed, he could even select a spouse for the child and on the child's majority (21 years of age) he could exact half a year's profits of the land before transferring it.

These and other feudal dues could be avoided by the tenant, before his death, by conveying the land to his friends to hold for the use of his son. As the infant would not be the legal owner the lord of the manor was deprived of his rights. Whereas common law only recognised the legal owner of the property (the trustee and not the beneficiary) the courts of equity sought to protect the beneficiary by establishing duality of ownership. The trustee would hold the legal title and the beneficiary would hold an equitable title.

The Statute of Uses 1535 was an attempt to prevent the development of trusts. However, during the following centuries the courts of equity continued to develop rules covering equitable interests in property and the statute was finally repealed in 1925.

In this chapter we provide an introduction to trust law by examining the different types of trust which may be created. In Chapter 8, we will look at the conditions which must be satisfied for a trust to be created, including the three certainties of an express trust.

In Chapter 9 we will consider the rights of beneficiaries and the duties of trustees.

---

1   THE NATURE OF TRUSTS

6/96

1.1   Smith conveys Blackacre, a freehold farm, to Thomas, directing Thomas to hold it on trust for Brown. Smith is known as the settlor. Thomas is known as the trustee and Brown is known as the *beneficiary* or *cestui que trust* (he who trusts). Blackacre is known as the *trust property*. Trust property may be either real (freehold property) or personal (all other property).

1.2   The trustee has an *equitable obligation* to administer the property for the benefit of the beneficiary whose interest in the trust property is an *equitable interest*. Originally both obligation and interest were recognised only in the courts of equity.

1.3   No formal definition of a trust exists although the definition given by Sir Arthur Underhill is most commonly quoted. It states that a trust is: 'an equitable obligation, binding a person (who is called a trustee) to deal with property over which he has control (which is called the trust property), for the benefit of persons (who are called beneficiaries or *cestui que trust*), of whom he may himself be one, and any of whom may enforce the obligation. Any act or neglect on the part of a trustee which is not authorised or excused by the terms of the trust instrument, or by law, is called a breach of trust'.

This definition, however, ought to be extended to include charitable trusts (which might not have human beneficiaries), and certain valid but unenforceable trusts (trusts of imperfect obligation).

1.4   Note that whereas a contract is not as a general rule enforceable by third parties, a trust may be enforced by a beneficiary who is not a party to the instruments creating the trust.

1.5   Parliament has dealt with various aspects of trust law and a number of statutes have been enacted to address different areas of the law. Much of the law on the powers and duties of trustees is found in the Trustee Act 1925, the Trustee Investments Act 1961 and the Perpetuities and Accumulations Act 1964. The relevant sections of statutes are cited in the text where appropriate so that you may refer to them if necessary. With the exception of a few very important sections, you are not expected to memorise and cite section numbers in your written answer.

2   THE USES OF THE TRUST

2.1   A trust is a valuable mechanism which is flexible enough to be adapted to special uses, such as in connection with employees' pension funds and unit trusts. But its original use, with which this syllabus is concerned, is to permit wealthy settlors to provide for their relatives or other dependants by the transfer of property to trustees who administer it for the benefit of the designated beneficiaries.

2.2   The main practical advantages of this type of family trust are as follows.

Skilled management

2.3   The trustees are often professional people, such as accountants, chartered secretaries or solicitors, or 'executors and trustee companies' owned by the banks to provide services of this kind to customers.

Flexibility

2.4   Within limits, more especially of duration, a settlor can allocate the benefit of his trust fund as he wishes. In a simple case he may in his will provide that his widow is to receive the income of his estate during her lifetime and may at the trustees' discretion receive advances of capital, and the capital remaining is to be divided at her death between their children in whatever proportions he (in his will) or she (if he gives her the discretion) may determine, or in equal shares. Another very flexible arrangement is the discretionary trust under which the trustees decide how much of each year's trust income is to go to each beneficiary.

Tax saving

2.5   The essential feature of trust taxation is that if the settlor observes certain anti-avoidance rules, the capital and income of the trust are taxed independently and no longer form part of his or her capital and income. Instead they are taxed at the beneficiary's tax rate, which may be substantially lower (in a non-discretionary trust).

3   CLASSIFICATION OF TRUSTS   6/96, 6/99

3.1   The main classification can be illustrated by the diagram below.

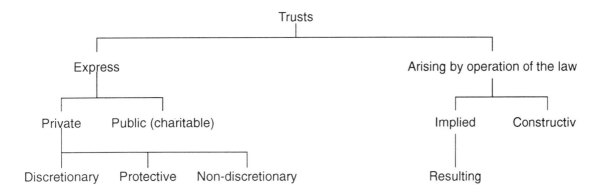

3.2   All express trust, except public (charitable) trusts, are private trusts whose object is to benefit private individuals.

3.3   Statutory trusts are trusts created by law as an automatic consequence of certain circumstances. If, for example, land is owned jointly by two or more persons, the first four named as owners hold the land in trust for themselves (and any additional joint owners) as beneficial owners. As another example, if a minor becomes entitled under the rules of intestacy to all or part of the estate of a deceased person, the personal representatives of the deceased hold the minor's property in trust for him until he is 18 years of age.

Terminology

3.4   Where an express trusts has been created, the terms *trust* and *settlement* have the same meaning and are used interchangeably.

3.5   A trust may be established by the settlor in his lifetime or he may create it (to take effect at his death) by his will. In the latter case it is called a *will trust*. The will must be valid under the legal rules on wills - it must be in writing, signed by the settlor/testator and witnessed. But if the will is valid a trust created by it is essentially similar to a lifetime (*inter vivos*) trust.

3.6   A trust is usually created by a written document, a deed or a will, and in certain cases it must be created in that way. Any document which creates a trust is referred to as the 'trust instrument'.

3.7   The expression *sui juris* applied to a beneficiary may be translated broadly as 'legally competent'. In many contexts the beneficiaries may only give a binding consent or exercise a legal power if they are sui juris. A minor lacks legal competence because he is under age. A person who is so mentally disordered that he does not understand legal transactions is also not *sui juris*.

3.8   A *life tenant* is the income beneficiary of the capital held in trust; he has no right in the capital itself. On his death, the capital becomes the *remainderman's*. A life tenant is said to have a *life interest*.

4   EXPRESS PRIVATE TRUSTS   12/95, 12/97

4.1   Express private trusts are usually made in writing or by deed to ensure certainty of the terms. They can, however, be created orally, with the following exceptions.

(a) Trusts of any property (real or personal) which are intended to arise on the settlor's death and can, therefore, be revoked until that event, must comply with s 9 Wills Act 1837. Such trusts must be in writing and signed by the testator with the signature witnessed and attested by two or more witnesses.

(b) Trusts of an equitable interest in property (real and personal) must be in writing and signed by the settlor (s 53 LPA). An example is where an income beneficiary (for example life tenant) of another trust creates a trust of his life interest.

(c) Trusts of land or any interest therein must be in writing and signed by the settlor (s 2 LP(MP)A).

4.2 The requirement for writing, when it exists, applies only to express trusts. It is not essential in implied, resulting or constructive trusts.

4.3 The statutory requirements for the creation of express private trusts were intended to prevent fraud and they must not be used as a cloak for fraud.

Bannister v Bannister 1948
A vendor sold a cottage for a reduced price on the verbal understanding that she could live there for life, rent free. Subsequently, the purchaser brought an action to recover possession of the cottage.

Held: although there was no evidence in writing, the vendor was allowed to prove the trust by oral evidence and could live in the cottage as long as she wished to do so. An automatic application of the statute would have had the unintended effect of allowing fraud by one party to succeed.

Discretionary and protective trusts

4.4 If you refer back to the diagram, you will see that a private trust (whether created in secret or expressly) may be discretionary, protective or non-discretionary. The vast majority of trusts are non-discretionary - the trustees have only to follow the wishes of the settlor. But discretionary and protective trusts are important. They are often created to protect beneficiaries from the probable consequences of their extravagance or other financial misfortune.

Discretionary trusts

4.5 Trustees have discretionary powers vested in them either by the trust instrument or by general law (for example which investments to hold, to maintain infant beneficiaries etc). In a discretionary trust the beneficiary has no right to receive any trust income but the trustees are given discretionary powers to pay or apply all or part of the trust income for his benefit, as they think fit. For example: property is left in trust 'for the benefit of Bernard and Carol at the absolute discretion of the trustees'.

4.6 A discretionary trust may be exhaustive or non-exhaustive.

(a) *Exhaustive* discretionary trusts require that all income arising must be distributed, but give trustees powers of discretion as to whom the income will be paid in a class of beneficiaries.

Re Locker's Settlement Trusts 1978
Although the trust deed required that the trustees 'shall distribute' income they failed to do so.

Held: the court directed the trustees to distribute the income and if they did not, new trustees would be appointed;

(b) *Non-exhaustive* discretionary trusts give the trustees discretionary powers:
(i) whether or not to make a distribution; and
(ii) to decide how the income will be distributed among a class of beneficiaries.

In this case the court will not override a decision of the trustees to accumulate all or part of the income since they are given a discretion on this point. But the legal restrictions on long-term accumulation have to be kept in mind.

4.7   The corresponding disadvantage is that the beneficiary can only hope that the trustees will exercise their discretion in his favour. If they decline to do so he gets nothing. Generally trustees (in accordance with their knowledge of the settlor's wishes) follow a consistent practice in allocating income from year to year between beneficiaries until some reason for a change arises. But they cannot be compelled to do this. The protective trust, as described below, gives to a beneficiary an assurance of a steady income while retaining the safeguard described at (b) above.

Protective trusts

4.8   The protective trust gives the beneficiary a life interest (or an interest for a shorter specified period) in the trust, which may end on his bankruptcy or on an attempt by him to dispose of his life interest (for example 'life interest to Albert until he becomes bankrupt or attempts to alienate his interest'). However it is sufficient and is normal practice simply to say in the trust instrument that the beneficiary is to have a life interest 'on protective trusts', since the law (s 33 TA) implies the details if those three words are used.

4.9   When the beneficiary becomes bankrupt or attempts to dispose of his interest he forfeits his life interest and a discretionary trust arises in favour of:

(a)   the same beneficiary (known as the principal beneficiary) and his spouse or issue; or

(b)   if there is no spouse or issue, the principal beneficiary and the persons who would be entitled if he were dead.

4.10   However, if the beneficiary surrenders his life interest for some reason (such as the avoidance of inheritance tax), not realising that a discretionary trust would thereby arise, the court may set aside the surrender: *Gibbon v Mitchell 1990*.

4.11   This discretionary trust will continue until the principal beneficiary dies (or the original period of his interest ends), when the original provisions of the trust resume. For example, if the trust is 'to Albert for life on protective trusts with the remainder to Albert's children in equal shares' and Albert becomes bankrupt, a discretionary trust would arise until his death and then the original trust 'to children in equal shares' takes effect.

4.12   In theory the trustees may exercise their discretion to pay trust income to the principal beneficiary after he has lost his entitlement to it as of right. In practice they do not do so since he is unlikely to make wise use of it and if he is an undischarged bankrupt his creditors may claim it. But if the trustees pay the income to some other person, such as the spouse of the principal beneficiary it is available for his maintenance.

Exercise

What are the advantages of the following types of express private trust?

(a)   A discretionary trust.
(b)   A protective trust.

Solution

(a)   Under inheritance tax the tax saving attainable by the use of discretionary trusts has been greatly reduced in recent years. But they are a useful type of trust because:

(i)   they are flexible - the trustees can take account of changing circumstances; and

(ii) the beneficiary has no rights which he may lose if he becomes bankrupt or improvidently attempts to sell his future rights to receive income for a capital sum. Hence discretionary trusts protect beneficiaries against misfortune or the consequences of extravagance.

(b) The advantage of a protective trust over the discretionary trust is that the beneficiary has a fixed entitlement to the trust income and can rely on it *until* his bankruptcy or attempted alienation (which may never occur and are avoidable by him if he is wise).

5   SECRET TRUSTS

5.1   The doctrine of secret trusts was originally evolved to prevent the fraudulent use of the statutory requirements for the creation of express trusts. Also, by his will (which is a public document and open to inspection by anyone), a testator (the person who made the will) might wish to provide for certain beneficiaries secretly, for example his mistress or illegitimate children. The doctrine is confined to trusts created by will. It has no application to a trust created by a settlor in his lifetime. The effect of a secret trust is that:

(a) the testator gives property, by the terms of his will, to a named person or persons; but

(b) there is a binding agreement, not fully disclosed in the will, by which the legatee holds the property in trust for someone else.

The legatee's obligation 'off the record' of the will is enforced because it would be unfair that he should be permitted to repudiate an arrangement made with the testator in the lifetime of the latter when he could still alter his will to cancel the legacy given on trust.

5.2   There are two types of secret trust.

(a)   Fully secret trusts.
(b)   Half secret trusts.

Fully secret trusts

5.3   Fully secret trusts occur where a will discloses neither the existence of the trust nor its terms ('I leave £20,000 to Albert' - where in fact Albert is trustee of a secret trust for the benefit of Marie.) The following essential elements must be proved for a fully secret trust to be enforceable.

(a)   The testator must communicate the terms of the trust to the legatee (Albert) *before the testator's death* (either before or after the will is made). If he does not, the legatee takes the property for himself since he does not know of the secret trust intention.

(b)   The legatee must accept the trust. If he refuses to accept the position of trustee, then on the testator's death he takes the property beneficially.

(c)   If the legatee accepts his position as trustee but is not told the identity of beneficiaries within the testator's lifetime, then he must hold the property on *resulting trust* for the testator's estate.

5.4   No formalities are required for a fully secret trust and communication may be oral or in writing.

5.5   A trustee of a secret trust (who may also be a beneficiary) may be required to carry out the terms of the trust by his (the trustee's) will, rather than during his lifetime.

Ottoway v Norman 1972
The defendant was left a house and its contents by T who informed her that it was his intention that she should leave them in her will to the plaintiff. The defendant agreed but did not, in fact, comply with T's wish. The plaintiff sued.

Held: the basis of the doctrine is the obligation imposed on the conscience of the primary donee and the machinery for carrying out the obligation is immaterial. The plaintiff's claim could succeed.

5.6 Property subject to a secret trust may be left to two or more persons in their capacity as trustees. Where the trustees are:

(a) *joint tenants* (eg £20,000 to Albert and Bernard) and the trust is communicated to and accepted by one trustee, then the trust is binding on all trustees;

(b) *tenants in common* (eg £20,000 to Albert and Bernard in equal shares), only the trustee who has been told of the trust and accepted the position is bound. In this case there are two gifts of £10,000 each to A and B.

Half secret trusts

5.7 *Half secret trusts* occur when a will discloses the existence of a trust but not the name of the beneficiary 'I leave £20,000 to Albert on the trusts I have told him'. The major advantage of the half secret trust is that the legatee is unable to claim the property for himself. The following conditions must be satisfied at or before the execution (making) of the will.

(a) The testator must communicate to the legatee that he is to hold the property on a trust.

(b) The testator must communicate to the legatee the identity of the beneficiary.

(c) The legatee must accept the trust.

> *Re Cooper 1939*
> A bequeathed £5,000 to B and C 'upon trusts I have already communicated to them', and B and C accepted before the will was executed. Later, A increased the legacy to £10,000 by a codicil (a clause inserted into an executed will) but did not communicate this to B and C.
>
> *Held:* The trust was effective as regards the £5,000 but failed in relation to the second £5,000 bequeathed by the codicil.
>
> *Re Bateman's Will Trusts 1970*
> The testator directed his trustees to pay the income out of part of his property 'to such persons as shall be stated by me in a sealed letter to my trustees.'
>
> *Held:* the words 'shall be' indicated that the testator was reserving the power to alter his will by naming a trustee and then making unwitnessed dispositions in the future. Such a direction contravened the Wills Act 1837 and the trustee must hold the property on resulting trust for the testator's estate. The secret trust failed.

5.8 However, it does appear that communication and acceptance of the trust property may be validly communicated by means of a sealed envelope given to the trustee before the will is executed, but with instructions for it 'not to be opened until after my death'. Such a communication is sufficient to create a half secret trust: *Re Keen 1937*.

5.9 A half secret trust is regarded as an express trust on the face of the will. Therefore, if the subject matter is land or an equitable interest, the communication must be in writing.

5.10 The trustees of a half secret trust cannot also be beneficiaries of the trust, and any evidence establishing a half secret trust is inadmissible if it contradicts the terms of the will.

5.11 A beneficiary under a secret trust will not lose his interest in the trust even if he:

(a) is a witness to the testator's will: *Re Young 1951*; or

(b) dies before the testator, provided he was alive at the date of communication of the trust to the trustee: *Re Gardner 1923*. (Note that if the trustee dies before the testator the gift to him will lapse and the trust will fail unless the court appoints new trustees.)

6   CHARITABLE TRUSTS
12/94, 12/97

6.1   A charitable trust must satisfy three requirements.

(a) It must be a trust whose purpose is charitable.
(b) It must be *wholly and exclusively* charitable.
(c) Its purpose must tend to promote a public benefit.

Each of these requirements needs some further brief explanation.

Charitable purposes

6.2   The following purposes are recognised as charitable, following the preamble in the Charitable Uses Act 1601 and much case law.

(a) The relief of poverty.

(b) The advancement of education.

(c) The advancement of religion.

(d) The provision of facilities for recreation etc if provided in the interests of social welfare: Recreational Charities Act 1958.

(e) Other purposes beneficial to the community.

6.3   To illustrate how these categories have been interpreted the examples below are modern cases in which a trust has been upheld as having a charitable purpose.

Re Glyn's Will Trusts 1950
There was a trust to build and endow cottages to be occupied rent-free by 'persons of the working class' aged 60 or more.

Held: this was a trust for the relief of poverty since elderly persons of this social class may be poor.

Royal Choral Society v IRC 1943
There was a trust to maintain a choir 'in order to promote the practice and performance of choral works'.

Held: this was a trust for an educational purpose although it did not involve classroom teaching.

Re Hetherington 1989
A lady left money in her will for the saying of masses for the repose of the souls of herself, her parents, husband and sister.

Held: this was held to be for the advancement of religion, since there was public benefit - in the edifying and improving effect on members of the public who attend the masses and in the promotion of stipends to priests who say them.

6.4   On the other hand a trust for the purpose of political education (*Re Hopkinson 1949*) or to promote or campaign against a change in the law (*National Anti-Vivisection Society v IRC 1948*) is not charitable.

Wholly and exclusively charitable

6.5   The second requirement is that the purpose of the trust shall be wholly and exclusively charitable.

Chichester Diocesan Fund v Simpson 1944
There was a gift 'for charitable or benevolent objectives', as the trustees might choose.

Held: this was not a charitable trust. The words *'or* benevolent' permitted the application of the fund to non-charitable purposes. If it had been a gift for 'charitable and benevolent purposes' applying a double test in each case, one test being charitable purpose, it would have been exclusively charitable. Ancilliary tests attached to a charitable purpose are permissible. This decision had widespread implications since many trusts had the fatal word 'or' between 'charitable' and other purposes. The Charitable Trusts (Validation) Act 1954 reversed the decision as regards trusts existing in 1952 in respect of their remaining funds. It does not validate a post-1952 trust if its wording is 'charitable or ...'

Public benefit

6.6   The requirement that a trust, to qualify as charitable, shall be for the public benefit means generally that the community or a substantial part of the community shall derive some benefit from the prescribed use of the charitable fund. If, for example, a trust which has a charitable purpose is restricted in its effect to a small group the trust is not 'charitable'.

Oppenheim v Tobacco Securities Trust 1951
A fund was established to provide for the education of children of employees of the British American Tobacco Co Ltd.

Held: although the purpose was the advancement of education, the range of persons who could benefit was too restricted to satisfy the 'public benefit' test. It was not an educational charity.

However, a trust for the relief of poverty may be charitable even though its potential benefit is restricted to aiding relatives of the settlor or some other narrowly defined group.

Differences between charitable and other trusts

6.7   The status of a charitable trust gives it important reliefs from taxation; for this reason many of the reported cases in this subject area are challenges by the Inland Revenue to a claim to charitable status.

6.8   There are also the following differences between charitable and other trusts.

(a)   A charitable trust need not have 'certainty of objects' though its purpose must be exclusively charitable.

(b)   The rule against perpetuities is modified in respect to gifts to charitable trusts. Property must vest within the perpetuity period but, once it has done so, it may continue in trust indefinitely.

(c)   Charitable trusts are subject to administrative supervision by the Charity Commissioners, who maintain a register. However, an unregistered trust may still be charitable.

(d)   If it is impossible or later becomes impossible to carry out the purpose of a charitable trust, the property given to the charity may be applied to a similar but different purpose under the *cy-pres* rule (see below).

Cy-pres doctrine

6.9   If a private trust cannot be put into effect or if it has surplus funds after fulfilling its tasks, there is a resulting trust of the remaining assets. However, if a charitable trust is either initially impossible to be put into operation or becomes so later, the court may order that the property of the trust shall be applied to some other charitable purposes which resembles the original purpose as far as possible. The court may also so order where there are remaining original purposes which could be fulfilled, but those purposes would not be charitable or would be contrary to the spirit of the gifts. The words *cy-pres* used for this principle mean 'as near' as possible.

6.10   The underlying principle of *cy-pres* is that the settlor intended the gift to be fully used for charitable purposes. The law should cooperate in carrying out his intentions as nearly as possible. The principle, which is of very ancient origin, is restated in the Charities Act 1960.

6.11   The most common case of 'impossibility' is where there is a gift, perhaps in a will made many years before the testator's death, to an institution such as a school or a hospital which no longer exists at the time of death.

> *Re Faraker 1912*
> A gift by will to 'Mrs Bailey's Charity, Rotherhithe'. There had been a charity called 'Hannah Bayly's Charity' which existed at the time of the will but had merged with other charities before the testator's death.
>
> *Held:* the other charities should take the gift under a *cy-pres* scheme.

6.12   If the gift cannot be applied to the specific purpose when the gift takes effect, it will only be re-directed on *cy-pres* principles if the court is satisfied that the donor had a *general* charitable intention and did not intend to restrict the benefit to one person and no other.

7   TRUSTS ARISING BY OPERATION OF LAW   6/94, 12/96

Implied and resulting trusts

7.1   *An implied trust is a non-express trust based on the presumed or inferred intentions of the settlor.* Apart from mutual wills, implied trusts are also resulting trusts, the beneficial interest in the property coming back (resulting) to the settlor or to his estate.

7.2   The main types of implied trust arise on the following.

(a)   The failure of the trust to take effect.
(b)   The failure to dispose of the whole beneficial interest.
(c)   Purchases in the name of another.
(d)   Making mutual wills.

Failure of the trust to take effect

7.3   An implied trust may arise when a condition laid down for the use of property has not been fulfilled.

> *Barclays Bank Ltd v Quistclose Investments Ltd 1968*
> Rolls Razor Ltd was in financial difficulties and owed its bank nearly £500,000. The company obtained a loan of £210,000 from Quistclose on the condition that it was used to pay a dividend and this money was put into a separate account. A month later the company went into liquidation before the dividend was paid and the bank sought to offset the bank overdraft against the loan from Quistclose.
>
> *Held:* Rolls Razor Ltd was under a contractual duty to repay the loan to Quistclose and, as the only purpose of the loan had failed, the money was subject to a resulting trust for Quistclose. Since the bank knew of the purpose of the loan it became a trustee of the money for Quistclose. The bank did not have the right of set-off and had to repay £210,000 to Quistclose.

Failure to dispose of the whole beneficial interest

7.4   A resulting trust in favour of the donor (or his representatives) will arise in two situations.

   (a)   Where the settlor does not declare how absolute interests are to be distributed.

      Re Abbott Fund Trusts 1900
      A fund was created to maintain two handicapped ladies, but no provision was made for its disposal on their deaths.

      Held: the fund was held on a resulting trust for the benefit of the subscribers to the fund.

   (b)   Where the purpose of the fund fails to exhaust the trust property.

      Re Gillingham Bus Disaster Fund 1958
      A bus, out of control, killed 42 Royal Marine cadets and injured others. A fund for funeral expenses and care of the injured was set up but £7,000 remained undisposed of.

      Held: the trust was not a charitable trust to which a different solution could apply. The gifts had been made for a particular purpose which had failed and so the surplus was to be held on resulting trusts for the donors, even if they were untraceable. The trustees had to pay the fund into court to await claims by donors.

7.5   A more practical solution in such cases would be to assume that untraceable donors intended to make their gifts absolutely, regardless of whether the original intention of the trust could be carried out or not. As the case below illustrates, this intention to make an outright non- returnable gift is readily inferred when money is obtained by street collectors, proceeds of public events etc, in which the donors must know that their identity can never be traced. In such cases the balance goes to the state as unclaimed property (*bona vacantia*).

   Re West Sussex Constabulary's Widows, Children's and Benevolent (1930) Fund Trusts 1971
   A fund was set up in 1930 which, owing to the reorganisation of police forces became redundant in 1969.

   Held: that part of the fund which arose out of collecting box donations should go to the Crown *bona vacantia*, the unidentified donors being taken to have intended to part with their money absolutely.

Re West Sussex has not settled the problem however, and many experts feel that distinguishing between identified and unidentified donors is an artificial exercise.

Purchases in the name of another

7.6   An implied trust arises were Albert buys property from Bernard but directs Bernard to convey the property to Carol. Since Albert has provided the money, Carol must hold the property on resulting trust for Albert: *Dyer v Dyer 1788*. But this is again a matter of presumed intention (of Albert) and may be overridden by evidence that he had no such intention.

7.7   An implied trust of this type also arises if X and Y contribute to the purchase price of property which is then transferred into the name of X only. X holds the property as trustee for himself and for Y in the proportions in which they contributed to the price.

7.8   The presumed intention of the purchaser can be rebutted by showing that he had some other intention, usually to make an outright gift to the person to whom the property is transferred. This may occur in either of the following circumstances:

(a) if there is sufficient evidence that a gift to the transferee was intended by the purchaser; or

(b) if the relationship between the purchaser and the transferee is either husband (purchaser) and wife (transferee) or father (purchaser) and child (transferee). In these cases it is presumed, unless the contrary intention is established by evidence, that in paying for the property to be transferred to his wife or child the purchaser intended to make an outright gift. This presumption is called the 'presumption of advancement'.

7.9 Note that there is no presumption of advancement where a wife pays for the property transferred to her husband or where a child does this for a parent. 'Child' includes a child of any age and also a person other than a child for whom the purchaser has assumed parental obligations, eg the support of an orphaned grandchild. The presumption of advancement, when applicable, may be rebutted by evidence that the purchaser:

(a) treated the property as his own, say by retaining the title deeds or collecting the income from it; or

(b) resorted to purchase in the name of a wife or child merely to conceal his own identity as the owner.

Mutual wills

7.10 Mutual wills arise when two persons agree to particular irrevocable provisions in each of their wills. On the death of one, any property passing under these provisions to the survivor is held on trust by him to carry out his part of the agreement. This implied trust is binding on the survivor and on his personal representatives: *Dufour v Pereira 1769.*

> *Re Green 1951*
> By their respective wills, husband and wife each bequeathed his/her estate to the other. But if the other died first, half the survivor's estate (increased by inheritance from the first spouse to die) went to a particular person. The wife died first.
>
> *Held:* half the husband's estate on his death was held on trust for the beneficiary named in the mutual wills. The husband could not make contrary dispositions of half his estate by a new will made after his first wife's death.

Note that an implied trust arising from mutual wills is not also a resulting trust - the benefit goes to a third party and not back to the estate of the deceased person who provided it.

Resulting trusts arising from express trusts

7.11 In addition to the circumstances outlined above, resulting trusts will also arise when:

(a) an express trust becomes void through uncertainty, impossibility, illegality, or by offending the rule against perpetuities; or

(b) the trust instrument expressly provides that the property is to revert back to the settlor in due course.

Constructive trusts

7.12 A constructive trust arises by operation of the law, either because of the implied intentions of the parties or because it would be inequitable not to impose a trust. In such cases someone who acquires property must hold it as trustee for someone else.

Profits from trust

7.13   It is a strict rule of equity that a trustee or other person in a fiduciary position is not entitled to make a secret profit from his trust: his first step should be to disclose it. Even if he does disclose it, a profit from an unfair transaction must be held by him on constructive trust.

> *Keech v Sandford 1726*
> A lease, held on trust for an infant, expired. The trustee renewed the lease in his own name as the lessor refused to grant a new lease to the infant.
>
> *Held:* the trustee held the new lease on a constructive trust for the benefit of the infant and must account for any profits made since the renewal.

7.14   This rule has developed to cover:

(a)   *leases:* when a part-owner of a lease renews it in his own name, he holds the lease on constructive trust for himself and the other persons who held the original lease (eg a partner renewing a partnership lease in his own name);

(b)   *a general concept of constructive trusts* - in the relationship between a professional adviser such as a solicitor or accountant and his client, if such an adviser holds his client's money and earns interest on it, he is regarded as a constructive trustee of such profits.

Directors of a company

7.15   Directors owe a fiduciary duty to the company and are sometimes compared with trustees. Directors do not own the company's property and their duties of care are different, but they must account for secret profits made.

> *Industrial Development Consultants v Cooley 1972*
> The defendant, an architect employed by IDC as managing director, failed to secure a lucrative building contract for IDC from the Eastern Gas Board. Resigning from IDC on grounds of ill health, he obtained the building contract for himself.
>
> *Held:* the defendant had obtained information and this opportunity *because* of his directorship; the information properly belonged to the company and so he could not use it to make a profit for himself. He had acted in breach of his fiduciary duty to IDC and was, therefore, accountable to IDC for any profits made.

7.16   A director of a company is required by s 317 Companies Act 1985 to give notice of his interest in a contract with the company to the board of directors. If he fails to do so, or gives notice only to a committee of the board, he holds any sums received as a constructive trustee for the company: *Guinness plc v Saunders and Another 1990.*

Other constructive trusts

7.17   Constructive trusts may also arise in the following circumstances.

(a)   Where a mortgagee exercises his power of sale, he may recoup the outstanding capital and interest owing to him; any surplus money is held on trust for the mortgagor (s 105 LPA).

(b)   A person who fraudulently acquires property is a constructive trustee of that property for the persons injured by his actions: *Sellack v Harris 1708.* A knowing participant in a fraud (including one who is ignorant of the fraud because he fails to make enquiries which an honest person would make) is likewise a constructive trustee, and property may be traced into his hands. This rule could apply, for example, to an accountant who transmits money which has been fraudulently obtained: *AGIP (Africa) v Jackson 1989.*

(c)   A trustee may transfer trust property to another person in breach of trust; if the transferee knew that it was trust property and that it came to him in breach of trust, he holds the property on constructive trust for the real beneficiary: *Nelson v Larholt 1948*.

(d) Where a person with no authority to act takes upon himself to deal with trust property, he makes himself a *trustee de son tort* (of his own wrongdoing) and is held to be a constructive trustee.

(e) A spouse or partner may be given a share of the house in which he or she has lived with his or her spouse or partner; even if the property is not held in joint names and the person has not made any financial contribution, a constructive trust may exist.

> *Eves v Eves 1975*
> The parties lived together, intending to marry. A house was purchased in the man's name, he told the plaintiff it was their house. She made no financial contribution but did a lot of work to the house and garden 'much more than many wives would do'. The couple split up.
>
> *Held:* (by a majority) there was an enforceable bargain in which the plaintiff contributed labour towards improvement of the property in which she was to have some beneficial interest. Lord Denning reached the same decision by a different route. He imposed a constructive trust because it would be inequitable for the defendant to deny the plaintiff a share in the property.

7.18 In addition to the situations dealt with above, it is clear that the courts will use the principle of constructive trusts in any circumstances where it may be necessary to redress a wrong - it is, after all, an equitable principle. However, a person who acts as agent for a trustee and innocently assists in the commission of a breach of trust does not automatically become a constructive trustee: *Barnes v Addy 1874*. In this case the dictum included the following.

'It is equally important to maintain the doctrine of trusts which is established in this court, and not to strain it by unreasonable construction beyond its due and proper limits. There would be no better mode of undermining the sound doctrines of equity than to make unreasonable and inequitable applications of them.'

Chapter roundup

- Trusts may be express or they may arise by operation of the law. All express trusts, except public (charitable) trusts, are private trusts whose object is to benefit private individuals.

- Express private trusts are usually made in writing or by deed to ensure certainty of the terms. They can, with three exceptions, be created orally.

- Private trusts may be discretionary, protective or non-discretionary. The majority of trusts are non-discretionary. In certain circumstances there are advantages to discretionary or protective trusts.

- Under a secret trust, a testator gives property under a will to a named person, but there is a binding agreement, not fully disclosed in the will, by which the legatee holds the property in trust for someone else. Such trusts may be fully secret or half secret.

- A charitable trust must satisfy three requirements. It must be a trust whose purpose is charitable. It must be wholly and exclusively charitable. Its purpose must tend to promote a public benefit.

- An implied trust is a non express trust based on the presumed or inferred intentions of the settlor. Most implied trusts are also resulting trusts, under which the beneficial interest in the property comes back to the settlor or to his estate.

- A constructive trust arises by operation of law, either because of the implied intentions of the parties or because it would be inequitable not to impose a trust.

Test your knowledge

1   Give a definition of a trust (see para 1.3)

2   Why are trusts set up? (2.1)

3   What are the three categories of private trust? (3.1)

4   Give three exceptions to the principle that express private trusts need not be in writing (4.1)

5   Distinguish between an exhaustive discretionary trust and a non-exhaustive discretionary trust (4.6)

6   What three conditions must be satisfied for a half secret trust? (5.7)

7   Give five examples of purposes recognised as charitable. (6.2)

8   What is the *cy-pres* doctrine? (6.9)

9   Give three examples of implied trusts (7.2)

10   What were the fact of *Industrial Development Consultants v Cooley 1972*? (7.15)

Now try illustrative question 7 at the end of the Study Text

Chapter 8

CREATION OF TRUSTS

This chapter covers the following topics.

1   Capacity to create a trust

2   The three certainties of an express trust

3   Creation of charitable trusts

4   Completely constituted trusts

5   The rule against perpetuities

6   The rule against accumulations

7   Other causes of failure

Introduction

Now that we have seen the different types of trust which may be created, we will examine the conditions necessary for creation of a trust.

---

1   CAPACITY TO CREATE A TRUST

6/96

1.1   Virtually anyone who is able to hold a legal or equitable title to property may create a trust, but the following cases are worth consideration.

Minors

1.2   A minor may settle personal property and equitable interests in land (a beneficial interest in land under another trust) but the settlement is voidable by him during minority or shortly after. A minor must be old enough to appreciate the nature of his act otherwise the act is void. If a property has been transferred the transferee must then hold it upon a resulting trust for the minor. A minor cannot, of course, hold a legal estate in land and so cannot create a trust of a legal estate in land.

Persons of unsound mind

1.3   A person of unsound mind who is incapable of managing his affairs and whose estate is being administered by a receiver appointed under the Mental Health Act 1983, cannot make a valid disposition of his property. Any such trust is void. If a receiver has not been appointed, the trust may be set aside where it can be shown that the settlor did not understand the meaning of his actions.

Companies

1.4   Companies incorporated under the Companies Act 1985 may settle property on trust. For instance, where a company issues debenture stock secured by trust deeds, property is assigned to trustees for the benefit of the debenture holders.

2   THE THREE CERTAINTIES OF AN EXPRESS TRUST

2.1   An express trust will only be valid if the three certainties as laid down by Lord Langdale in *Knight v Knight 1840* are present. They are as follows.

(a) Certainty of words.
(b) Certainty of subject matter.
(c) Certainty of objects.

Certainty of words

2.2   The words used to declare a trust need not be formal - indeed there is no obligation for a settlor to use the word trust. However, the word must be imperative and show that a trust was intended. The problems which arise normally do so when trusts or wills have been drafted without professional advice and use *precatory* words such as 'in the hope', 'requesting', 'beseeching', rather than leaving property 'on trust'.

> *Re Adams and Kensington Vestry 1884*
> The testator gave all his property to his wife absolutely 'in full confidence that she will do whatever is right as to the disposal thereof between my children'.
>
> *Held:* the wife took the property free from any trust as the precatory words 'in full confidence' were insufficient indication of the intention to create a trust.

2.3   Since this case it has become accepted that precatory words will not create a trust unless, on the consideration of all words employed, the court comes to the conclusion that the intention was to create a trust.

> *Re Steele's Will Trust 1948*
> The testatrix left a diamond necklace to her son, grandson and remoter descendants requesting her son 'to do all in his power...to give effect to this my wish'.
>
> *Held:* it is necessary to consider the intention of the testatrix deduced from the words used. If in a borderline case like this the words used have in the past been held sufficient to impose a binding obligation the court will be more readily disposed to interpret the intention of those words as again imposing a binding trust. There was therefore a binding trust in this case.

2.4   The expression 'precatory trust' is something of a contradiction in itself. It means that words of request etc can (in cases such as *Steele's will* above) be interpreted to impose a binding obligation although that is not what they say. But (as the *Kensington Vestry* case shows) the courts are not easily persuaded to apply that interpretation to such words. If there is no sufficient indication of intention to create a binding trust the donee takes the property beneficially.

Certainty of subject matter

2.5   This requires that

(a) the property which is the subject of the trust, and
(b) the interests of the beneficiaries in that property

must be ascertainable.

Property

2.6   The property held on trust must be certain.

> *Palmer v Simmonds 1854*
> The testatrix left the residue of her estate to H 'for his own use and benefit, as I have full confidence in him, that if he should die without lawful issue he will leave the bulk of my residuary estate unto X and Y.'

Held: the 'bulk of my estate' was too vague. H took the gift of residue for himself absolutely without obligation to X and Y.

Beneficial interests

2.7 Each beneficiary's interest in the trust property must also be certain. If the beneficial interest is clearly vested in a beneficiary, but he is directed to apply unascertained parts of it for the benefit of others, the principal beneficiary takes all, the others being disregarded.

> *Curtis v Rippon 1820*
> The testator left all his property to his wife, 'trusting that she would, in fear of God and in love of the children committed to her care, make such use of it as should be for her own and their temporal good, remembering always, according to circumstances, the Church of God and the poor'.

> *Held:* the wife took the entirety as the Church and the poor were given unascertained rights out of the bequest to her - she did not hold it on trust for them as their shares were not defined.

2.8 If all the beneficial interests are uncertain (eg 'all my shares in trust, some for Albert and the rest for Bernard') then the property may be held on resulting trust for the settlor's estate. More probably, however, the maxim 'equality is equity' will apply and there will be an equal division between the beneficiaries: *Doyle v Attorney General 1735*.

> *Re Steel 1978*
> The testator gave £25, £50, £100, £200 and £250 to relatives and friends with the residue of his estate 'to be divided between those beneficiaries who have only received small amounts'.

> *Held:* the gift of the whole residue was not uncertain and was to be divided equally between the beneficiaries.

2.9 If beneficial interests are contingent upon one beneficiary choosing his interest, the trust may fail for uncertainty.

> *Boyce v Boyce 1849*
> The testator left two houses on trust, instructing that 'whichever she may think proper to choose or select' be conveyed to M, and the other to C. M predeceased the testator.

> *Held:* C had no claim as the trust was uncertain as to what was her beneficial interest.

Certainty of objects

2.10 The 'objects' of a trust are the actual beneficiaries who benefit from it. 'Certainty of objects' means that the settlor must identify or supply the means of identifying the persons whom the trustees are to recognise as the beneficiaries of the trust. Two different kinds of problem may arise.

Non-discretionary trusts

2.11 If the trust is not discretionary and the settlor provides that the beneficiaries are to have pre-determined fixed interests, such as equal shares, in the trust fund, but fails to identify the beneficiaries, the trust fails and the property is held on a resulting trust for the settlor or, if he is dead, for his estate.

> *Sale v Moore 1827*
> The testator left property to his wife recommending her 'to consider my nearest relations'.

Held: even if the words could be construed as creating a trust, it would not be a binding trust as the 'near relation' could not be ascertained with reasonable certainty. So also a gift 'to my dependants' failed for uncertainty: *Re Ball 1947*.

Discretionary trusts

2.12 If the trust gives to the trustees a discretion to allocate benefits to members of a class, it is sufficient if the trust instrument enables the trustees to decide whether or not an individual is a member of the class.

> *McPhail v Doulton 1970*
> The issue before the House of Lords was whether the following clause in a deed constituted a trust and if so, whether it was void for uncertainty: 'The trustees shall apply the net income of the fund in making at their absolute discretion grants to or for the benefit of any officers and employees or ex-officers and ex-employees of the company or to any relatives or dependants of any such persons in such amounts at such times and on such conditions (if any) as they think fit'.
>
> *Held*: the clause was mandatory and constituted a trust, and the trust was valid and not void for uncertainty of objects. The trustees had an adequate definition to use in dealing with each case before them.

The beneficiary principle

2.13 The basic rule of the beneficiary principle is that, with the exception of charitable trusts, 'a trust to be valid must be for the benefit of individuals'. It cannot be just for a purpose or an object since then its validity would depend on the whim of the trustee, and the courts could neither enforce nor control the trust. But trusts set up for the purpose of, for example, providing a sports ground may still be valid since the court will identify persons who will be interested in the disposal - effectively the people who will use the ground.

2.14 There are other exceptions to this rule, known as 'unenforceable' trusts, 'trusts of imperfect obligation' or 'private purpose trusts'. The court can enforce them by obtaining an agreement from the trustee, or even the residuary legatees, that they should be carried out. These are trusts for the following.

(a) The erection or maintenance of monuments or graves.

(b) The saying of non-charitable masses.

(c) The maintenance or benefit of animals in general, or of a class of animal (a charitable purpose).

(d) The benefit of unincorporated associations.

(e) Miscellaneous cases - such as a legacy to A to be applied to the furtherance of fox-hunting: *Re Thompson 1934*.

3   CREATION OF CHARITABLE TRUSTS

3.1 Among the 'three certainties' required in an express private trust is certainty of objects - the beneficiaries must be identified or at least identifiable as individuals with rights (certainty of subject matter) to benefit from the trust. The underlying assumption is that if the trustees do not discharge their duties under the trust the beneficiaries will complain to the court. In considering the complaint the court decides whether the claimant is really an 'object' of the trust. So the existence of beneficiaries is essential to a private trust and provides the means of enforcing it.

3.2 However, the law also enforces charitable trusts which have no human 'objects'. To put it another way, a charitable trust is not required to satisfy a test of 'certainty of objects'. Instead a charitable trust must satisfy a test of certainty of charitable purpose. If the trustees fail to apply trust income or capital to this purpose, the Attorney General may bring the trustees before the court to enforce the trust.

3.3   Payments by a charitable trust, such as scholarships provided from an educational charity or a grant made from a trust for the relief of poverty, do benefit individuals who receive them, but no individual is the identifiable 'object' or intended beneficiary of the trust who can claim a benefit from the trust.

4   COMPLETELY CONSTITUTED TRUSTS

4.1   A trust becomes completely constituted when the legal title to the trust property is effectively vested in the trustees. Once a settlor has done everything required of him by law to transfer the property comprised in the settlement to the trustees, the trust becomes completely constituted and is irrevocable, unless there is an express power of revocation in the trust.

4.2   There are two main ways of completely constituting a trust.

(a)   Conveyance of the trust property by the settlor to the trustees in the manner required by law to make the trustees the legal owners of the property.

(i)   Land, by conveyance, under seal.

(ii)   Personal chattels capable of delivery, by deed or delivery (physical delivery may not be necessary).

(iii)   Registered shares and other choses in action, by proper form of transfer.

(iv)   Equitable interests by assignment in writing.

(b)   Declaration by the settlor that he himself will hold the property on trust for the beneficiaries. As he is already owner of the property there is no need for any transfer and the trust is completely constituted on its declaration, which must be in writing in the case of land or an equitable interest. An imperfect transfer which does not satisfy (a) will not however be treated as a declaration of trust with the settlor and trustee: *Richards v Delbridge 1874*.

Incompletely constituted trusts

4.3   An incompletely constituted trust is one which requires some further action by the settlor and arises where the property is not properly conveyed, or when the settlor covenants to settle property in the future but fails to do so.

4.4   Whereas a completely constituted trust can be enforced by any beneficiary (whether he gives value or not) and is binding on all persons, an incompletely constituted trust can only be enforced by a beneficiary who has given value. A trust is by its nature usually an indirect gift by the settlor to the beneficiaries and so a beneficiary rarely gives value to secure the benefit of a trust. If he has not given value he is called a 'volunteer'.

4.5   A beneficiary may give value (and therefore not be a volunteer):

(a)   by giving valuable consideration such as money or money's worth to the settlor for the promise to create a trust in his favour; or

(b)   by giving consideration in the form of marriage. Settlements made before and in contemplation of marriage have the marriage as valuable consideration, and the parties to the marriage, their children and remoter issue can enforce an incompletely constituted trust.

4.6   This situation is most likely to occur when a settlor establishes a marriage settlement and covenants to bring into the settlement property which he expects to acquire but does not yet own ('after acquired property') - for example, an inheritance from a parent. The parties to the marriage or their descendants can compel the settlor, or if he is dead, his executors to complete the transfer to the trustees of the after acquired property:

Pullan v Coe 1913. But if the parties to the marriage die without leaving issue, the next of kin, entitled in those circumstances to the trust property under the terms of the trust instrument, are mere volunteers (not 'within the marriage consideration') and cannot enforce the transfer: *Re Plumptre's Settlement 1910*. Children of a previous marriage of one spouse are not 'issue of the marriage' of the two spouses and so they rank as volunteers: *Re Cook's Settlement 1965*.

4.7   There are some other minor exceptions to the principle that an incompletely constituted trust cannot be enforced by a volunteer as follows.

(a)   As an infant cannot hold a legal estate in land, a purported conveyance (transfer) of land to an infant is treated as an agreement for value - a binding contract to hold the land in trust for the infant: s 27 SLA.

(b)   Land law requires that there shall be two separate deeds to create a trust of land. If the settlor attempts to combine the two requirements in a single deed, the law imposes an obligation to regularise the situation and complete the trust by a second deed: s 9 SLA.

(c)   Property may pass to the trustee by operation of the law. For example, Albert appoints Bernard as trustee but does not convey any property to him. If Albert also appoints Bernard as his executor, then on Albert's death the title to the trust property passes to Bernard as executor by operation of law. This is known as the rule in *Strong v Bird 1874,* and will apply even if Albert has left no valid will but Bernard is appointed his administrator: *Re James 1935*.

(d)   *A donatio mortis causa* (gift made in contemplation of death) is enforceable on death even though the legal formalities of conveyance have not been observed. A *donatio* exists if the gift was made in contemplation of death and is conditional on it (for example, the gift is revocable until death) and delivery of the property or something representing it (such as keys to a safe) is made to the donee by the donor in his lifetime. But note that a *donatio mortis causa* cannot be made of real property because such a transfer must be in writing: *Sen v Headley 1989*.

4.8   A completely constituted express trust may be either executed or executory, depending on its construction at the time of creation.

(a)   An *executed trust* is one where no further document or instrument is necessary to define the duties of the trustees and the rights of the beneficiaries (as when Albert vests property in trustees Xavier and Yvonne on trust for Bernard for life and on Bernard's death, for Carol absolutely).

(b)   An *executory trust* is one where the trust is expressed in general terms and a further instrument is required to carry out the intentions expressed in the first trust instrument (as when Albert, in his will, bequeaths £10,000 to Xavier and Yvonne on trust to buy land and settle it on Albert's son Bernard and Bernard's children). In such trusts, the court may have considerable scope to construe the real intention of the settlor.

5   THE RULE AGAINST PERPETUITIES

5.1   The rule against perpetuities aims to prevent the settlor tying up property for ever. The rule does not apply to charitable trusts.

The rule

5.2   Where there is a possibility that a future interest in property will vest outside the 'perpetuity period', the interest is void. Apart from the effect of the Perpetuities and Accumulations Act 1964 (P & AA), the perpetuity period is the period of a life or any number of lives in being at the time when the instrument creating the interest becomes effective, plus a period of 21 years, plus any period of gestation.

5.3   A person is a 'life in being' if he is born or *en ventre sa mère* (in the womb) at the date of the instrument under which a lifetime disposition is made, or, in the case of a disposition by will, at the date of the testator's death.

Vested interest

5.4   When a person has a vested interest in property he has an immediate fixed right to present or future enjoyment of that property. For example, the clause 'I leave my freehold house to my wife for life and then to my son absolutely' confers vested interests on both beneficiaries, the widow having an interest in possession while the son's interest is postponed until the widow's death.

Contingent interest

5.5   A contingent interest is one where the right to enjoyment of the property is subject to the occurrence of a future event which may or may not happen.

5.6   For the purposes of the rule against perpetuities, a bequest becomes vested when it ceases to be contingent.

The Perpetuities and Accumulations Act 1964

5.7   S 3 P & AA established the 'wait and see' rule whereby an interest which may vest outside the perpetuity period will not be void from the outset. It is now possible to wait and see whether the property will vest within the perpetuity period and if it does, the trust is good.

5.8   S 1 P & AA provides that a settlor can specify, in the trust instrument, a perpetuity period not exceeding 80 years, if he so wishes. If no time is mentioned in the instrument, the normal rule applies.

Example: the perpetuity period

5.9   Albert settles property on trust for the eldest child (as yet unborn) of Bernard, provided that the eldest son reaches 21 years of age. Is the interest valid?

Solution

5.10   Unless the trust instrument specifies some other person(s) as the life in being, Bernard is taken to be the life in being. Before he dies, Bernard must have a child (born or conceived) if he is to have one at all. His eldest child will reach 21 years (if he reaches that age at all) within the perpetuity period (Bernard's life + 21 years + any period of gestation, if relevant). Therefore, under the rule the interest is valid, as the property will vest (if it vests at all) within the perpetuity period.

Exercise

Albert settles property on trust for the eldest child (as yet unborn) of Bernard provided that the eldest child becomes a qualified chartered secretary. Is the interest valid?

Solution

In this case there is a possibility that the property will vest outside the perpetuity period. Bernard's eldest child might qualify as a chartered secretary, say, 25 years after Bernard's death, which is outside the perpetuity period. (Prior to the amendment of the rule by the Perpetuities and Accumulations Act 1964 such a trust would have been void from the beginning, the property resulting back to Albert, or to his estate if he is dead.) The interest is a contingent interest.

The trust would become void if Bernard did not have any children, or if his eldest child did not become a chartered secretary within 21 years (plus any period of gestation, if relevant) after Bernard's death.

The class closing rules

5.11   Property is sometimes given in trust for a member of a class, for example 'the children of A who reach the age of 21'. It is usually provided that each member of the class takes an equal share.

5.12   The share of any member of the class could be altered by the admission to the class of more members or the elimination of a member of the class. If, for example, a gift is made to the children of A at 21 in equal shares and A then has three children, aged 23, 18, and 16 there are two possibilities to consider.

(a)   More children may be born to A.

(b)   The children who do not yet qualify, being aged 18 and 16, may or may not live to the age of 21 to take a vested interest at that age.

The eldest child, aged 23, has an indefeasible vested interest but, even if A has no more children, the prospective share of the eldest child may be reduced from all the fund to half (in three years time) and then to one third (in five years time).

5.13   Under the rule in *Andrews v Partington 1791* a class closes and no new member can be admitted to it even on a contingent basis as soon as one member of the class has an indefeasible vested interest. In the above example, the following consequences would ensue.

(a)   The perpetuity period (unless the donor has expressly provided, for example, an 80 year period) is the lives of A and his three children plus 21 years from the date of the last of the four to die. The shares in the entire trust fund must vest within that period.

(b)   The class (the children of A) entitled to a share of the fund closes immediately the gift is made since the eldest child aged 23 already has a vested interest. If A later has another child, that child will not be entitled to a share, even at the age of 21, since the class is already closed.

(c)   The eldest child begins with a vested interest in a minimum of one third of the trust fund since there are only two other members of the class. His share will increase if either or both the younger children die before reaching 21.

(d)   The two younger children have contingent interests which will vest if they reach 21. If either or both dies before reaching 21 the trust fund is shared by those who do acquire a vested interest. If for example the second child dies at 20 but the third reaches 21, the eldest and the youngest take one half each.

(e)   The shares in the entire trust fund will vest within five years at most, when the child now aged 16 will, if alive, reach 21. This is well within the perpetuity period.

6   THE RULE AGAINST ACCUMULATIONS

6.1   The rule against long accumulations of income limits the period during which income from trust property may be accumulated by the trustees and added to capital instead of being paid to beneficiaries. This is a rule which applies to income each year and not to the period over which it may be held in the trust. If for example the trust runs for 80 years and income of year 1 is accumulated, it may be retained for the full 80 years and will then be shared out as capital. But if the rule limits the accumulation period to 21 years (see below) all the income of year 22 and any later year must be distributed as income and may not be retained as an addition to the capital of the trust fund.

6.2 No person may settle property so that the income is accumulated for a longer period than specified by s 164 LPA and s 13 P & AA. The maximum alternative periods are set out below.

(a) The life of the settlor.

(b) 21 years from the death of the settlor.

(c) The minority of any persons, living or conceived at the death of the settlor. For example an instruction to accumulate income during the minority of a child aged 3 at the time of the settlor's death gives a maximum accumulation period of 15 years.

(d) The minority of any persons who if of full age would be entitled to the income. For example, in a trust for grandchildren accumulation of income may continue during the minority of the first grandchild, then another and another and so on, even if the subsequent grandchildren are not even conceived at the settlor's death. If no grandchild is yet born at the settlor's death, the trust income will be held on a resulting trust for his estate, accumulation commencing only when the first grandchild is born.

(e) 21 years from the date of the settlement.

(f) The minority of any persons living or conceived at the date of the settlement.

6.3 The age of majority is 18 years. If the settlor fails to select a period of accumulation from the alternatives available the trust instrument will be examined to determine which is most appropriate.

6.4 Where the trust instrument directs accumulation of income for a period in excess of the statutory periods, then the court will select the appropriate period of accumulation which could have been used. The accumulation is void only in respect of the excess period: income may be accumulated during the selected period.

6.5 If an accumulation of income were to last longer than the perpetuity period, the rule against perpetuities would be violated.

6.6 The rule against accumulations does not apply to directions to trustees to accumulate trust income:

(a) for the payment of debts;

(b) to raise portions (capital sums by way of endowment) for children or remoter issue of a life tenant.

6.7 The rule against accumulations applies both to trusts by which the trustees are directed to accumulate income and to trusts in which the trustees have a discretion to accumulate income if they deem this to be preferable to distributing it.

7 OTHER CAUSES OF FAILURE

7.1 A trust may be voidable or void.

(a) It is *voidable* where it is created as a result of ignorance, fraud, mistake or duress. Such a trust may be cancelled or rectified in certain circumstances.

(b) It is *void* where it is illegal, immoral or against public policy. Such a trust will not be enforced.

Bankruptcy

7.2 Any transfer of property at undervalue made with the purpose of putting assets beyond the reach of the creditors or otherwise prejudicing them is voidable at the instance of the person who is thereby prejudiced or of a trustee in bankruptcy or a supervisor of a voluntary arrangement.

7.3 This rule is not subject to any limit on the length of time between the conveyance and the later avoidance of it nor is it necessary that the transferor should have been made bankrupt. But it is necessary to establish that there was intent to prejudice creditors.

7.4 If a transferor of property at undervalue becomes bankrupt then even without proof of intent to prejudice creditors, the transfer will be voidable:

(a) if made within two years of the bankruptcy; or

(b) if made more than two years but within five years of the bankruptcy, if it is shown that the transferor was insolvent immediately before the transfer, or becomes insolvent as a consequence of it. Such insolvency is presumed (unless the contrary is shown) where the transaction is with an associate of the transferor.

Mistake and fraud

7.5 Trusts executed in ignorance or by mistake, or which are procured by fraud or undue influence may be set aside (or possibly amended) provided that:

(a) the parties involved can be reinstated to their original positions; and
(b) the settlor has not accepted the settlement on being informed of its legal effect.

Trusts contrary to public policy

7.6 A trust may be void, or in some cases only voidable, if it is for a purpose deemed contrary to public policy. For example a trust to provide money for the payment of fines imposed as a punishment for criminal offences would be void: *Thrupp v Collett 1854*.

7.7 Much of the case law reflects the public policy of upholding marriage and family life. A trust which seeks to impose a *total* restraint on marriage, for example 'to pay the income to A provided that she does not marry' will fail and the beneficiary will be entitled to the income whether or not she marries.

7.8 However a partial restraint on marriage, such as 'to A, provided that she does not marry X' or 'to A, provided that she does not marry without her parents' consent', is valid and binding. So also is a trust to provide income for a beneficiary until marriage, unless it is considered that the real purpose is to restrain the beneficiary from marriage altogether.

7.9 A trust to induce husband and wife to live apart, for example 'to H so long as he does not live with his wife', is void. So also is a trust designed to separate parents from their children, for example 'to B provided that he does not continue in the custody of his father'. However, a trust to provide for a spouse where separation has already been decided on is valid.

7.10 A person who applies for maintenance from his or her spouse may ask the court to set aside a previous disposition of property by the spouse made with a view to defeating the maintenance claim. A spouse or other dependant may make a similar application in seeking to obtain provisions from the estate of a deceased person.

Chapter roundup

- A trust may be created by anyone who is able to hold a legal or equitable title to property. The rules relating to minors and persons of unsound mind are of importance.

- An express trust will only be valid if the three certainties laid down by Lord Langdale in *Knight v Knight 1840* are present. They are certainty of words, certainty of subject matter and certainty of objects.

- It could be said that a charitable trust is not required to satisfy the test of certainty of objects. The trust will not fail for want of certainty of objects where there is a clear intention to give property for charitable purposes.

- A trust becomes completely constituted when the legal title to the trust property is effectively vested in the trustees. There are two primary ways in which a trust may become completely constituted.

- The rule against perpetuities aims to prevent the settlor tying up property for ever. The rule does not apply to charitable trusts

- The rule against accumulations limits the period during which income from trust property may be accumulated by the trustees and added to capital instead of being paid to beneficiaries.

Test your knowledge

1   Explain the legal rules governing the creation of trusts by minors (1.2)

2   What were the facts of *Re Adams and Kensington Vestry 1884?* (2.2)

3   What are the two factors to consider under certainty of subject matter ?(2.5)

4   Give four exceptions to the beneficiary principle. (2.14)

5   Describe the two ways in which a trust becomes completely constituted. (4.2)

6   Describe and distinguish between an executed trust and an executory trust (4.8)

7   What is the rule against perpetuities ?(5.2)

8   Distinguish between a void trust and a voidable trust. (7.1)

9   Give an example of a trust which is void as contrary to public policy (7.6)

Now try illustrative question 8 at the end of the Study Text

Chapter 9

THE ROLE AND DUTIES OF TRUSTEES

This chapter covers the following topics.

1   The appointment of trustees

2   Termination of appointment

3   The vesting of property in trustees

4   The duties of trustees

5   Powers of trustees

6   The rights of beneficiaries

7   Breach of trust

Introduction

The role of trustee is a very important one. In this chapter we look at appointment and retirement or removal of trustees and at the duties of a trustee.

---

1   THE APPOINTMENT OF TRUSTEES   *6/95, 6/98*

Who may be appointed as a trustee?

1.1   Any person capable of holding property may act as trustee, but certain persons (bankrupts, criminals etc) may be regarded as undesirable and the court may remove them. The following situations should be noted.

Minors

1.2   A minor cannot be expressly appointed as a trustee but can be a trustee under an implied or constructive trust: *Re Vinogradoff 1935.*

Corporations

1.3   A corporation may be appointed. It is usually advantageous if it is a trust corporation. A trust corporation is normally a body corporate which fulfils three basic conditions.

    (a)   The company is registered and constituted under the law of any member state of the EC and has a place of business within the EC.

    (b)   The memorandum authorises it to undertake the business of acting as a trustee and of acting as a personal representative.

    (c)   The company must have an issued capital of not less than £250,000 of which not less than £100,000 must have been paid up in cash (or equivalent amounts for other EC corporations).

Other persons

1.4   Certain other persons are also granted the status of trust corporation. They are:

(a) any company appointed by the court;
(b) certain charities;
(c) certain public officers (eg The Public Trustee);
(d) certain local and public authorities.

1.5   Some persons may not be appointed trustees by the court, although they may be appointed by the settlor. These include bankrupts, persons resident abroad and beneficiaries (or their spouses or solicitors).

Appointment

1.6   In creating a settlement the settlor appoints the first trustees and they are usually parties to the trust deed to signify their acceptance of the appointment. Where there is no formal appointment, say in a trust created by operation of law, the person(s) in whom the trust property is vested is or are the first trustee(s).

1.7   The first trustees of a will trust are the personal representatives - the executors of the deceased. When they have completed their duties in winding up the estate they automatically become trustees of any trust created by the will, unless the will nominates other trustees. It is sometimes necessary for the executors to execute a formal vesting assent constituting themselves trustees instead of executors, but this is generally confined to cases where they are to hold land as trustees: *Re King's Will Trust 1964*. The transition from executorship to trusteeship may arise, for example, if the will provides that the testator's widow is to have a life interest in the estate. As soon as matters incidental to the testator's death (called the 'administration of the estate') have been dealt with, the executors hold the estate as trustees with the widow receiving income as beneficiary.

1.8   The trust instrument may also provide for the appointment of replacement trustees when the need arises. A will may, for example, give to the testator's widow the power of appointing trustees of his estate in her lifetime. If however there is no such express power, or if it cannot be exercised, for example because the person concerned is now dead, the statutory power of appointment is available.

1.9   It is a maxim that 'equity never wants for a trustee' - a trust is never allowed to fail for lack of a person to perform the duties of trustee. There is therefore a statutory power (s 36 TA) to appoint a trustee as replacement for another who:

(a) dies, retires, or is removed;
(b) remains out of the UK for more than 12 months;
(c) refuses to act;
(d) is physically or mentally incapable of acting;
(e) is a minor;
(f) is a corporation which is dissolved.

1.10 The replacement trustee may be appointed, in writing, by:

(a) persons named in the trust instrument; or, if none (or none willing to act)

(b) other trustees, or personal representatives of the last trustee if he is dead (they may appoint themselves in an emergency, for example, when there is only one trustee and two are required to sell land).

1.11 The court may appoint trustees under s 41 TA, whenever it is inexpedient, difficult or impracticable to appoint trustees without the assistance of the court, whether or not there are remaining trustees. The beneficiaries or the trustee may apply to the court for an appointment to be made (s 58 TA) and the desires of the beneficiaries will be taken into account. However, the court will not exercise this power of appointment to interfere with appointments made by others entitled to do so.

1.12 After appointing the first trustees the settlor has no power to appoint replacement or additional trustees unless the trust instrument reserves that power to him. A person who has the statutory power of appointment may appoint himself as a replacement trustee but not as an additional trustee. In selecting a person for appointment as trustee he should do what is conducive to the interests of the trust. It is undesirable though not absolutely prohibited to appoint as trustee a person who is a beneficiary of the trust, since there may be a conflict of interest. A sole beneficiary could not be a sole trustee, as then he would hold all interests in the property and there would be no trust.

1.13 A beneficiary has no inherent power to appoint trustees nor any right to be consulted about appointments: *Re Brockbank 1948*. But in certain circumstances he may be able to terminate or reconstitute the trust.

1.14 If all beneficiaries are *sui juris* and absolutely entitled to the trust property, then acting together they may terminate the trust (*Saunders v Vautier 1841*) and:

(a) require the trustees to hand over the trust property to whomsoever they may direct; or

(b) require the trustees to settle the property on fresh trusts by:

(i) transferring it to new trustees to hold on new trusts; or
(ii) continuing to hold it subject to new trusts.

1.15 Additional trustees (not replacing retiring trustees) may be appointed under s 36(6) TA subject to the following limitations.

(a) The number of trustees may not be increased above four.

(b) No additional trustees may be appointed if the existing trustees include a trust corporation.

(c) The appointor may not appoint himself: *Re Power's Settlement Trusts 1951*.

1.16 A trustee is appointed in writing (except where he becomes trustee by operation of law) and it is standard procedure to make the appointment by deed in order to effect an automatic transfer to the trustee of trust property. As an example suppose that A, B and C are the present trustees, C wishes to retire and X, to whom is given the power of appointment, proposes to appoint D as a new trustee. X, A, B, C and D will join in the deed of appointment by which X appoints D to replace C. C retires, D accepts the appointment and A and B agree to continue as trustees jointly with D.

1.17 No one can be compelled to accept appointment as trustee, which may be a burdensome office. A prospective trustee is invited to be a party to the deed of appointment so that it is clear that he has accepted office. If he refuses he is said to disclaim, for which no formality is legally necessary. A disclaimer may be:

(a) in writing, such as a letter of refusal, or by deed;
(b) orally;
(c) merely by not acting as a trustee.

However it is normal practice to execute a deed of disclaimer. If the matter is left in doubt and the designated person interferes with the trust property in any way, he risks being deemed to have accepted office by his conduct in acting as trustee. Once he has accepted a trusteeship he cannot relinquish it except by retirement.

The number of trustees

1.18 There is no general maximum or minimum number, but if the trust property includes land, the maximum number of trustees is four (s 34 TA), and:

(a) if the trust instrument names more than four trustees, the first four named take office;

(b) additional trustees may only be appointed to fill a vacancy.

1.19 Unless the trust instrument expressly requires a minimum of two trustees, a single trustee is sufficient to administer a trust. But if the trust property includes land and the single trustee (other than a trust corporation) wishes to sell it he alone cannot give a valid receipt for the proceeds of the sale: s 14 TA. Any purchaser would insist on obtaining a valid receipt and so in practice a trust which includes land should have at least two trustees, or a trust corporation.

1.20 The rules which require a minimum of two trustees in certain situations apply only to individual *trustees*. One trust corporation as sole trustee can do anything for which a minimum of two individual trustees is required.

2   TERMINATION OF APPOINTMENT   6/98

Retirement

2.1   A trustee may retire from his office:

(a)   under a provision in the trust instrument;

(b)   with the consent of the court;

(c)   with the consent of all the beneficiaries, being sui juris and absolutely entitled;

(d)   under s 36 TA, on appointment of a new trustee; or

(e)   under s 39 TA, without a new appointment, provided that:

  (i)   the request to retire is by deed;

  (ii)   he obtains the consent of the other trustees by deed;

  (iii)   he obtains the consent by deed of anyone named in the trust instrument as having power to appoint new trustees; and

  (iv)   there will remain at least two trustees or a trust corporation, either already in office or appointed on his retirement.

Removal

2.2   A trustee may be *removed* from his office:

(a)   under a power contained in the trust deed;

(b)   by the court under s 41 TA for any reason if for the benefit of the beneficiaries (for example, if a trustee becomes bankrupt);

(c)   under s 36 TA where the trustee has remained out of the UK for more than 12 months, or refuses to act or is unfit or incapable of acting.

3   THE VESTING OF PROPERTY IN TRUSTEES

3.1 The settlor must vest the property in the first trustees, otherwise the trust may be incompletely constituted.

3.2   Property vests automatically in the trustees where the appointment of a new trustee is by deed (s 40 TA), except for the following property:

(a)   mortgages of land (where trustees have *lent* money on the security of land, the mortgage must be transferred into the names of the new trustees);

(b)   leasehold land held under a covenant not to assign without consent (which must be assigned, or transferred and registered);

(c)   stocks and shares (must be transferred and the new owners registered).

4   THE DUTIES OF TRUSTEES   *12/98*

4.1   A trustee's duties are imposed by the trust instrument and the general law and the trustee must carry out his duties *with the utmost diligence*. There are matters where the trustee can use his discretion (such as investing in particular securities) and in these he must act honestly and with the care that a prudent man of business would exercise in the management of his own affairs.

4.2   The primary duties of a trustee are

(a)   to carry out the *instructions* of the trust instrument and, subject to that,
(b)   to place the trust property in a state of *security and control*.

If any property is not automatically vested in a newly appointed trustee under s 40 TA he must take steps to ensure the legal property is properly transferred to him or to the joint trustees (if there are two or more).

4.3   Trustees are not liable for property stolen from them provided they had taken reasonable care, but any documents relating to the trust or the trust property (particularly deeds to freeholds) should be deposited for safekeeping with a bank: s 21 TA. They should collect trust income and capital without delay - for example, allowing rents to fall into arrears is a breach of trust: *Tebbs v Carpenter 1816*.

4.4   Further duties of trustees can be classified as follows.

(a)   Duties of investment.
(b)   Duty to keep accounts.
(c)   Duty not to take secret, undisclosed personal advantage.
(d)   Duty of personal action.
(e)   Duty of unanimous action.
(f)   Duty to hand over trust property.

Duties of investment

4.5   In the investment of trust funds, a trustee has two general duties.

(a)   He must invest only in investments which are authorised for this trust. The authorised investments are defined either by the trust instrument or by the Trustees Investment Act 1961.

(b)   He must select authorised investments in a proper manner, as defined by case law and by s 6 TA.

4.6   The trustee's duty of care in selecting authorised investments was summed up in *Learoyd v Whiteley 1887* as:

(a)   showing the same care as 'a man of *ordinary prudence* would exercise in the management of his own private affairs'; *but*

(b)   avoiding investments of a 'speculative character' - a trustee may not put *trust money* at risk even though he would be willing to accept the risk for his own money.

4.7   Case law imposes two additional duties regarding investment on trustees.

(a)   The trustee must act *impartially* in the interests of all the beneficiaries. In particular, he should strike a balance, in the choice of investments, between those which yield high income (to the advantage of a life tenant) and those which offer a prospect of long-term increase of value (to the advantage of a remainderman). If a single investment inclines to one or another advantage the trustee should strike a balance between investments of different types.

(b)   The trustee has a *duty to convert* (often referred to as the rule in *Howe v Earl of Dartmouth 1902*). This means that a trustee of a will trust with property other than freehold land who finds there is property which is 'wasting', which does not give rise to income or which is risky should sell that property and reinvest the proceeds.

4.8   It is not proper for the trustees to permit their personal opinions of a non-financial character to affect their choice: *Cowan v Scargill 1984* (a case involving the National Union of Miners pension fund - Arthur Scargill disapproved of investment overseas in sources of energy other than coal).

Accounts

4.9   Trustees have the duty to keep true and accurate accounts of all transactions for which they are responsible as trustees. No particular form is required by law for trust accounts, but they must include all receipts and payments, together with the substantiating vouchers. The beneficiaries are entitled to examine the accounts and the trustees must have them ready for inspection at any time.

4.10   The accounts *may* be audited at the cost of the trust estate but, except in special circumstances, not more than once in every three years. In his bill, the auditor should distinguish between fees relating to capital and those relating to income. However the trustees have complete discretion as to the proportion to be charged to capital or income: s 22(4) TA.

4.11   A trustee or beneficiary has the right to apply to the Public Trustee to have the accounts investigated and audited, but in doing so he must give reasons for the request. The Public Trustee may refuse the application which, in any case, may not be made within 12 months of a prior audit.

4.12   A beneficiary also has the right to inspect 'trust documents' such as title deeds, share certificates etc relating to trust property. But he is not entitled to an explanation from the trustees of their reasons for exercising their discretion as they have done, nor may he see letters of advice, minutes of trustee meetings etc. relating to their decision: *Re Londonderry's Settlement 1965*.

Personal advantage

4.13   A trustee may not secure any secret, undisclosed personal advantage ('profit') from his position as trustee. *A trustee should avoid any situation or transaction where his personal interest and his duty of disinterested service may conflict, and he is under a duty to disclose, and make fair bargains in relation to, any transaction involving conflict.* If he does secure an illicit profit, he either holds it in trust for the original trust or, in certain cases, the transaction is voidable.

4.14   This duty of disinterested service may conveniently be divided into three categories.

(a)   Trustee's remuneration for services.
(b)   Purchase of trust property by a trustee.
(c)   Profit obtained by a trustee from his position.

Remuneration

4.15   In principle a trustee is not remunerated for his services. But the principle is so impractical that there are numerous exceptions to it. He may have remuneration in the following circumstances.

(a)   Where the trust deed authorises it: *Webb v Earl of Shaftesbury 1802*.

(b)   By order of the court if the trust is more onerous than the trustee reasonably expected when he had accepted appointment: *Re Duke of Norfolk's Settlement Trusts 1981*.

(c)   By consent of all the beneficiaries who must be sui juris and absolutely entitled.

(d)   The Public Trustee and custodian trustee have a statutory right to remuneration.

(e)   A solicitor trustee may charge for work done in contentious business on behalf of all trustees.

(f)   A trust corporation appointed by the court may charge a fee if the court so authorises.

(g)   Where the trust property is situated abroad, the foreign law permits payment and the payment was received without the trustees' volition.

Purchase of trust property

4.16   If a trustee purchases trust property any beneficiary may, within a reasonable time after becoming aware of the purchase, apply to the court for an order to set aside the sale - it is voidable. The trustee must then return the property but must be repaid the purchase price with interest.

4.17   The objection is to the conflict of interest. Accordingly the purchase is voidable even if:

(a)   there are other trustees whose decision to sell was entirely disinterested; or

(b)   the price paid was based on an independent valuation or can otherwise be shown to be a fair price; or

(c)   the sale is advantageous to the trust - for example because it needed to raise money for other purposes.

4.18   The trustee may not evade the rule by sale to his own nominee or to his partner. Any of the following circumstances will be closely investigated and the sale *may* be set aside if the court concludes that there has been deliberate evasion.

(a)   Purchase by the trustee's spouse.
(b)   Purchase by a company of which the trustee is a member.
(c)   Sale to a third party followed by resale to a trustee.

4.19   Purchase of trust property by a trustee will be valid and binding in the following cases:

(a)   If the trust instrument authorises it.

(b)   If the beneficiaries, being *sui juris*, give their consent or lose their right of objection by failing to object within a reasonable time, provided that the underlying transaction itself was fair.

(c)   If the trustee obtains leave of the court - though the court is likely to withhold approval until attempts to sell the property to another buyer have proved unsuccessful.

(d)   If the trustee retires from his trusteeship and a long interval ensues (12 years in *Re Boles and British Land Company's Contract 1902*) before the purchase is arranged;

(e)   If, before the beneficiaries intervene, the trustee has re-sold the property to a third party who was unaware of the breach of trust - but the beneficiaries may be able to recover from the trustee his profit on re-sale.

(f)   If the purchaser is a life-tenant of settled land who holds the legal estate on trust for all the beneficiaries: s 68 SLA.

4.20   A trustee may purchase from a beneficiary the latter's interest in the trust. But the trustee should disclose all the material facts to the beneficiary (*Hill v Langley 1988*) and also pay a fair price. A trustee is in a better position if the beneficiary has taken the initiative in proposing the purchase: *Coles v Trecothick 1804*. If the trustee takes unfair advantage of his position, the sale may be voidable.

4.21   A trustee is entitled to be reimbursed out of the trust estate for any out-of-pocket expenses properly incurred in the execution of his duties: s 30(2) TA. He also has the right to a personal indemnity for his expenses from a beneficiary who is *sui juris* and absolutely entitled.

Hardoon v Belilios 1901
At the request of X, who was *sui juris*, Y held partly paid shares as trustee for X.

Held: X must indemnify Y against Y's liability for calls on the share.

4.22   The rule that a trustee cannot act in a position where his interest and his duty conflict does not apply if he has been put in that position by the settlor. Thus trustees of land held on trust for sale who are also tenants of that land do not have to vacate the land in order to increase its value: *Sergeant v National Westminster Bank 1990*.

Personal action

4.23   Except for the provisions below, a trustee cannot delegate his duties unless he is given authority by the trust instrument to do so.

4.24   By s 23 TA *trustees may employ and pay an agent* (for example, a solicitor or a stockbroker) to transact any business or do any act required in the execution of a trust including the receipt and payment of money. The agent, who need not necessarily be a professional person, is unable to make the basic decisions required of a trustee but may implement those decisions. The trustees must, however, select the agent themselves (*Re Weall 1889*), and the agent must be acting within his usual business: *Fry v Tapson 1884*.

4.25   Trustees are entitled to be paid charges and expenses incurred in employing an agent. They are not responsible for the default of any agent employed in good faith as a trustee is only answerable for his own acts or negligence and not for those of any other person with whom any trust money may be deposited or for any other loss 'unless the same happens through his own wilful default': s 30(1) TA.

Re Vickery 1931
A solicitor was employed by the executor of a will to wind up an estate. One of the beneficiaries informed the executor that the solicitor had at one time been suspended from practice, although he had subsequently been allowed to practise again. The solicitor absconded with part of the trust funds. The beneficiary sued the executor.

Held: the executor appointed the agent in good faith and was therefore not liable for the agent's default. This decision has been much criticised but it still stands. It seems to exonerate a trustee from the consequences of mere negligence in the choice of an unsuitable agent.

4.26   By s 25 TA, as amended by s 9 Powers of Attorney Act 1971, *a trustee may delegate all or any of his discretionary powers by power of attorney*, but:

(a)   this is the only occasion on which he may delegate his discretionary powers;

(b)   the delegation cannot be for a period exceeding 12 months;

(c)   the trustee must give written notice of the delegation within seven days to each of the other trustees, and to any other person who has power to appoint new trustees;

(d)   the trustee may not delegate to a sole co-trustee unless it is a trust corporation;

(e)   the trustee is liable for every act or default of his delegate.

Unanimous action by trustees

4.27   As a general principle, trustees are required to exercise their powers jointly. Hence they must act unanimously and a majority decision is not binding (except in the case of charitable trusts, or where the trust instrument authorises majority decisions). But if the trustees take a joint and unanimous decision, for example to instruct a stockbroker to sell trust investments, they may authorise one trustee to carry out their decision by writing a suitable letter.

4.28 Difficulties may arise from a disagreement among the trustees as to what they should do.

   (a) If the matter at issue is a duty, for example to distribute all the income of an exhaustive discretionary trust, the court will if necessary order the trustees to perform that duty even against a dissenting majority.

   (b) If, however, the trustees have a discretionary power, for example to make advances of capital to beneficiaries, the court will not overrule a minority of trustees who object. The power cannot then be exercised.

   (c) If the trustees are at loggerheads or in dispute over their legal position the majority may apply to the court for an order to pay the trust moneys into court so that the trustees' responsibility is ended: s 63(3) TA.

Handing over trust property

4.29 Trustees have a duty to hand over trust property to beneficiaries in accordance with the terms of the trust. If they pay the wrong people, they will only avoid liability to pay again (to the right people) if they paid to an apparent beneficiary on the face of the trust document without notice of any facts or documents which might indicate that some other person was entitled. If in doubt, they should apply to the court for directions.

4.30 A wrongful recipient will have to return assets given to him under a mistake of fact, but not assets given to him under a mistake of law.

4.31 Trustees and personal representatives may avoid personal liability for unknown claims by advertising under s 27 TA that they are about to make a distribution. The procedure is as follows.

   (a) Trustees must advertise their intention to make a distribution in the *London Gazette* and in newspapers local to the area where any land is situated.

   (b) The advertisement must require interested persons to submit their claims within a stipulated time of not less than two months.

   (c) At the end of the stipulated time the trustees may distribute the trust property after providing for all known claims.

   (d) A subsequent claimant may follow the property into the hands of any person other than a purchaser but he has no claim against the trustees.

4.32 Without this safeguard, trustees might feel obliged in their own interest to withhold a substantial sum for a period of years as a reserve against claims. By following the s 27 procedure they are able to distribute the entire trust fund at the appropriate time.

4.33 When a trust is wound up, the trustees can ask for, but may not be given, a discharge under seal by the beneficiaries. If they do not obtain such a release, they may apply to the court for their accounts to be approved.

5   POWERS OF TRUSTEES

5.1 In order to be able to perform his duties, a trustee must obviously be given powers. Powers and duties go hand-in-hand; misuse of the former may also be breach of the latter, and together they may constitute breach of trust.

5.2 The details of a trustee's powers are beyond the scope of your syllabus, but you should know in outline what they are. They include powers:

   (a) to choose investments;

   (b) to advertise for claimants;

   (c) to delegate (subject to restrictions discussed above);

   (d) to sell trust property (provided a fair market price is obtained);

(e)   to pay or compound debts;

(f)   to insure property (up to 75% of its value, unless the trust instrument forbids it, or the beneficiary may request that the property be conveyed to him; premiums are payable out of income but receipts are treated as capital);

(g)   to maintain minor beneficiaries - it is expressed as the power to pay for 'maintenance, education or benefit' out of income;

(h)   to advance *capital money* to any beneficiary with a vested or contingent interest, with the purpose of establishing a beneficiary for life (for example, to buy a house);

(i)   to ask for discharge - when the trust is finally distributed the trustee presents his accounts to the beneficiaries and asks for a discharge by deed. Once this is given (under court supervision if necessary) no further claims may be made against the trustees.

6   THE RIGHTS OF BENEFICIARIES

6.1   The essential purpose of a trust is to give to the trustees control of trust property with adequately defined duties and powers. As a general rule the beneficiaries cannot intervene in the management of the trust and the court will not interfere. But there are some exceptions, in particular when the trustees appear not to be performing their functions in a proper way. There can also be situations in which the trustees and/or the beneficiaries apply to the court for its assistance in resolving difficulties which have arisen.

The beneficiaries and the trustees

6.2   The beneficiaries are entitled to information from the trustees as to the state of the trust and the calculation of their benefits from it. Remember that beneficiaries have no right to information on the advice received and discussion between trustees in reaching their decisions (the *Londonderry* case).

6.3   The beneficiaries have no right to interfere, or even be consulted, on such matters as:

(a)   the trustees' exercise of their power to appoint new trustees: *Re Brockbank 1948*;

(b)   the investment of trust funds, provided always that the trustees exercise their powers in a proper way;

(c)   the trustees' decision whether to exercise the discretionary power to advance capital - if they refuse a beneficiary's application he must accept their decision;

(d)   the allocation of income between beneficiaries of a discretionary settlement or the trustees' decision whether to distribute all the income or to accumulate all or part of it - provided in this case that the trust is non-exhaustive.

6.4   The best course of action for beneficiaries who are dissatisfied with the trustees' decisions but cannot show that they are in breach of trust is to join in winding up the trust, or transferring it to new trustees. However under the rule in *Saunders v Vautier 1841*, the beneficiaries may only require the trustees to pay over the entire capital if all the beneficiaries have vested rights and are *sui juris*. Where the beneficiaries do have this right it prevails over any directions in the trust instrument requiring that the trust shall continue.

6.5   Where there are several beneficiaries any one of them who has an absolute vested right to a defined share of the trust property may require the trustees to transfer his share to him: *Re Marshall 1914*. He may also apply to the court for an order to the trustees to sell land and pay over to him his share of the proceeds: s 30 LPA.

6.6   In any case where a beneficiary has a justifiable cause for complaint against the trustees his remedy is to apply to the court for:

(a) an order or an injunction to be issued to the trustees;

(b) their removal from office by the court;

(c) recovery of damages for breach of trust; or

(d) recovery of trust property by tracing (as described later).

The court and the trustees

6.7   Unless some breach of trust is established the court will not usually interfere with the trustees' exercise of their discretion.

6.8   The ground of complaint is sometimes that the trustees have *failed to exercise their discretion at all*, for example, to distribute income of an exhaustive discretionary trust. In such cases the court usually orders them to do so: *Re Locker's Settlement 1978*. But much depends on the reasons for the trustees' delay.

> *Re Gulbenkian's Settlement Trusts (no 2) 1969*
> In 1957 the trustees of a settlement worth many millions of pounds became aware of a court decision which raised doubt over the validity of certain provisions of the trust. For 10 years they retained the trust income until the legal point was resolved. They then took a decision to distribute income in a manner to which a beneficiary objected. He applied to the court for an order to vary the distribution alleging that by their long delay the trustees had lost their discretionary power.
>
> *Held:* in the circumstances the trustees had acted reasonably and retained their discretionary power.
>
> *Re Allen-Meyrick's Will Trust 1966*
> The trustees applied to the court to accept a surrender to the court of their discretion to apply income for the benefit of a bankrupt beneficiary as they could not agree among themselves.
>
> *Held:* the court would give directions over the accumulated income but it would not relieve the trustees of their discretionary power over future income.

6.9   The allegations against the trustees, especially if they are professional trustees, may be want of care, say in exercising the power of advancement without taking proper care to ensure that the money advanced did in fact go to the benefit of the beneficiary: *Re Pauling's Settlement Trust 1964* (the money went to pay the debts of the beneficiary's mother). This is a breach of trust for which the trustees may be liable to compensate the trust.

6.10 More often the trustees themselves will apply to the court to get a decision on a problem they could not resolve amongst themselves (as in the *Allen-Meyrick* case above). The court may confer on them the power:

(a) to effect any transaction for the 'management or administration of the trust property' (s 57 TA);

(b) to deal with trust property for maintenance etc (s 53 TA); and

(c) to deal with settled land.

Variation of trusts

6.11 But the most important way in which the court can intervene is in allowing a variation of beneficial interests. The Variation of Trusts Act 1958 confers wide powers on the court to *approve* variations in management, administration and beneficial interests on behalf of certain beneficiaries. The categories of beneficiaries on whose behalf the court can approve the new arrangement are:

(a) a beneficiary who cannot consent by reason of minority or incapacity (eg insanity);

(b) a beneficiary yet unborn;

(c) a potential adult beneficiary with a contingent interest;

(d) a person who has a discretionary interest under a protective trust, so long as the principal beneficiary's interest has not yet failed or determined.

The court will not approve a variation on behalf of anyone in categories (a), (b) or (c) unless it is for their benefit.

6.12 Although the Act does not define the 'benefits' for which trusts may be varied, decided cases since the Act suggest that these benefits include:

(a) tax avoidance;

(b) postponement of the vesting of trust property in an irresponsible minor on his attaining majority;

(c) prevention of family dissent; and

(d) alteration of investment clauses.

Special trustees

6.13 On application by a settlor, trustee or beneficiary the court may appoint, at its discretion, any fit or proper person as a *judicial trustee*. This procedure may be useful where the administration of the trust has broken down. The judicial trustee is under the control of the court and although he has all the normal powers of any other trustee, he may be given specific directions as to the administration of the trust (Judicial Trustees Act 1896 and Judicial Trustee Rules 1986).

6.14 *A custodian trustee* is one in whom property is vested for greater security, but with the administration of the trust being carried on by the ordinary trustees. The Treasury Solicitor, trust corporations and (in certain cases) local authorities may be custodian trustees.

6.15 On application by a trustee or beneficiary, the court may appoint the Public Trustee (a public official) as:

(a) ordinary trustee - replacement or additional;
(b) judicial trustee;
(c) custodian trustee; or
(d) personal representative.

7 BREACH OF TRUST   6/97

7.1 A breach of trust occurs when a trustee fails to carry out any of the duties imposed on him by the trust deed or by law, or when he exercises his discretionary powers improperly.

7.2 A trustee is always responsible for his own acts or defaults, but is not liable for acts, deceits, neglects or other defaults of any bankers, brokers or other persons with whom any trust monies or securities are deposited, unless it happens through the trustee's own wilful default (s 30 TA).

7.3 A trustee is guilty of wilful default only if he knows that he is committing and intends to commit a breach of trust, or commits a breach by acting recklessly, not caring whether it is a breach or not: *Re City Equitable Fire Insurance Co 1925*.

7.4 A trustee is not responsible for the acts or defaults of his co-trustees unless his own neglect or wilful default contributed to the breach - for example, where his co-trustees are allowed to hold funds for an unreasonable length of time without any enquiry as to their actions.

Hamburg v Kirkland 1829

There were three trustees but two of them accepted without further enquiry the statement of the third trustee that there was a favourable opportunity of investing trust money as mortgage security. Trust investments were sold and the money handed to the third trustee in whose hands the other two left the whole transaction. He absconded with the money.

Held: the two innocent trustees were, by their failure to make enquiries or to participate in the transaction, guilty of breach of trust, for which they must compensate the trust fund.

7.5   A new trustee is not liable for past breaches of trust but should try to persuade the other trustees to make good a prior breach. A retiring trustee is not liable for future breaches unless he retired to enable them to be committed: *Head v Gould 1898.*

Defences of trustees

7.6   A trustee may be excused, either in whole or in part, for a breach of trust if he has acted *honestly and reasonably* and ought fairly to be excused: s 61 TA. Paid professional trustees would rarely be excused as they must exercise the degree of diligence and skill required from a specialist in trust administration: *Re Pauling's Settlement Trust 1964.*

7.7   Under s 62 TA the court may order a beneficiary to indemnify the trustee for a breach of trust when the beneficiary has requested or consented to the breach in writing. The trustee must establish that the beneficiary knew all the facts regarding the trustee's proposed actions and was fully aware that they constituted a breach of trust.

7.8   If all the beneficiaries, being *sui juris* and fully entitled, agree to the trustee's acts (whether in concurrence in or waiver of the breach), there is no breach of trust.

7.9   A trustee is usually protected against personal liability for a breach of trust by lapse of time - the period prescribed by the Limitation Act 1980 being six years from the date at which the right of action against the trustee accrued (12 years in the case of an action to recover land). This period of limitation will not apply where:

(a)   the trustee has been party or privy to any fraud or fraudulent breach of trust;

(b)   the trustee is in possession of the trust property, or the proceeds thereof, or has converted trust property to his own use, even though innocently.

The starting date for the period is normally the date of the breach of trust.

7.10   Where two or more trustees are liable for a breach of trust, their liability is *joint* and *several* and a beneficiary may bring an action against one or all of the trustees. If one trustee has to pay the damages arising, he has the right of:

(a)   contribution from the other trustees, so they all share the damages equally;

(b)   indemnity for the *whole* amount of the damages if he is an innocent trustee and another co- trustee has committed the breach and:

   (i)   has got the money into his hands and made use of it;

   (ii)   is a solicitor and the breach was committed in consequence of his advice and control; and

   (iii)   is also a beneficiary (indemnity is limited to the beneficial interest of the beneficiary-trustee).

Following and tracing property

7.11   If trustees are unable to compensate the trust (say because of insolvency) a beneficiary may use the remedy of following or tracing the trust property.

7.12 A beneficiary may *follow* the trust property and claim it back from the present holder, provided:

(a) the property remains clearly identifiable either in its original form or as property into which it has been converted, for example when trust money is used to buy property or trust property is sold and the proceeds deposited in a separate bank account;

(b) the present holder is not a purchaser in good faith and for value; and

(c) the beneficiary's right of action exists against the trustee personally. It does not exist, for example, where the beneficiary has consented to the breach in writing.

7.13 *Tracing* is resorted to when the trust property has become mixed with other property, but means of identification exists. The following equitable rules have evolved.

(a) Where a trustee purchases property with trust money and his own, the beneficiaries will have a first charge on the property purchased: *Re Oatway 1903*.

(b) Where a trustee mixes trust money with his own in a single bank account, the beneficiaries have a first charge on the mixed fund. When withdrawals are made by the trustee after mixing, he is deemed to be using his own money first: *Re Hallett's Estate 1880*.

(c) If the trustee draws on the mixed bank account so that it is shown he has used trust money, he will not be deemed to be replacing it if he subsequently pays in his own money: *Roscoe Ltd v Winder 1915*.

(d) Where a trustee mixes the funds of two separate trusts and withdraws money for private purposes, the presumption is that the first money paid into the account is the first drawn out: *Clayton's case 1816*. Where the funds of two trusts are mixed in other ways (not in an active bank account) the two sets of beneficiaries share the proceeds on the same basis as a beneficiary and an innocent volunteer.

7.14 A beneficiary may trace and recover property from the hands of third parties, but may not recover from a *bona fide* purchaser for value who had no knowledge of the breach of trust.

7.15 Where a beneficiary is able to trace property to a third party and that property is now part of a mixed fund, then the beneficiary and the third party are entitled to share in the mixed fund in proportion to their respective contributions. For example, where £12,000 of trust money and £4,000 of the third party's money are paid into an account, then if only £8,000 is in the account at the relevant time, the beneficiary is able to recover £6,000 (three quarters of the mixed fund).

Chapter roundup

- Any person capable of holding property may act as a trustee, but it may be undesirable for certain person to do so. The rules relating to minors and corporations are of interest.

- The first trustees are usually appointed by the settlor. Acceptance of the appointment is indicated by their being parties to the trust deed. Equity never wants for a trustee and there are statutory powers to appoint replacement trustees.

- The appointment of a trustee may be terminated upon retirement of the trustee or upon his removal from office.

- A trustee must carry out his duties with the utmost diligence. His primary duties are to carry out the instructions of the trust instrument and, subject to that, to place the trust property in a state of security and control.

- As a general rule the trustees are in control of the trust property and the beneficiaries cannot intervene. However in certain circumstances, particularly where the trustees do not appear to be carrying out their role in a proper way, the beneficiaries may exercise certain rights.

- A breach of trust occurs when a trustee fails to carry out any of the duties imposed on him by the trust deed or by law, or when he exercises his discretionary powers improperly.

Test your knowledge

1   What three conditions must a body corporate fulfil to be appointed as a trust corporation? (see para 1.3)

2   What are the three rules limiting the appointment of additional trustees? (1.15)

3   Give four ways in which a trustee may retire. (2.1)

4   What are the two primary duties of trustees? (4.2)

5   What are the two general duties of investment imposed on a trustee? (4.5)

6   Give two exceptions to the duty of personal action. (4.23 - 4.26)

7   List six powers of trustees. (5.2)

8   What is meant by variation of trusts? (6.11)

9   What are the rules on following of trust property? (7.12)

10 What are the rules on tracing of trust property? (7.13)

Now try illustrative question 9 at the end of the Study Text

Part D
Business associations

Chapter 10

BUSINESS ASSOCIATIONS

This chapter covers the following topics.

1   The concept of legal personality

2   Incorporation and limited liability

3   Types of company

4   Registration procedures and documentation

5   The veil of incorporation

6   Partnership

7   Differences between companies and partnerships

Introduction

The Companies Act 1985 regulates the activities of companies in the UK. In this chapter we examine the different types of company, in particular the limited company. We also consider the other types of organisations which may carry on a business, notably the partnership.

---

1   THE CONCEPT OF LEGAL PERSONALITY   *12/97*

1.1   A person possesses legal rights and is subject to legal obligations. In law, the term person is used to denote two categories of legal person. An individual human being is a *natural person*; the law also recognises *artificial persons* in the form of corporations.

1.2   A legal person is a being recognised by the law as having rights and obligations. The owner of property or a party to a contract is necessarily a person. A corporation is an artificial person which is recognised in law as a *separate legal entity*, provided that the legal formalities for its creation have been complied with.

1.3   A corporation, such as a limited company, must be distinguished from an unincorporated association. An *unincorporated association* is not a separate legal entity; it does not have a legal identity separate from that of its members. A typical example of an unincorporated association is a partnership.

1.4   Some types of person have only limited legal capacity. A company, unlike an individual, cannot marry or make a will. The legal capacity to enter into contracts is limited in the case of companies, minors (individuals under the age of eighteen) and individuals who are mentally incapacitated.

1.5   All individuals are natural persons in the eyes of the law, although some have limited capacity.

Minors

1.6   Minors are a special case of natural person. The position of minors is as follows.

(a)   They cannot vote at general or local elections.

(b) They usually take the nationality and domicile of their father.

(c) They can marry at 16, but must have parental consent if under 18.

(d) They cannot be held liable in criminal law if under 10 years of age.

(e) They cannot own a legal estate in land.

(f) They cannot make a valid will, except in very restricted circumstances (privileged wills).

(g) They have limited contractual capacity.

(h) There are many other rules concerning, for example, driving, employment and drinking.

Mental incapacity

1.7 A person is presumed to be sane until the contrary is proved - that he either did not know what he was doing or did not know that it was wrong. Insanity is mainly significant as a defence or mitigating factor in trials on criminal charges. It may also restrict capacity to enter into a binding contract.

Artificial persons

1.8 A corporation is a legal entity separate from the natural persons connected with it, for example as members. Corporations are classified in one of the following categories.

(a) *Corporations sole.* A corporation sole is an official position which is filled by one person who is replaced from time to time. The Public Trustee and the Treasury Solicitor are corporations sole.

(b) *Chartered corporations.* These are usually charities or bodies such as the Institute of Chartered Secretaries and Administrators.

(c) *Statutory corporations.* Statutory corporations are those corporations formed by special Acts of Parliament. This method is little used now, as it is slow and expensive. It was used in the nineteenth century to form railway and canal companies and to constitute local authorities. Its advantage is that the Act can confer on the particular corporation any special legal powers which it may need, such as the power to make compulsory acquisitions of land.

(d) *Registered companies.* Registration under the Companies Act 1985 is the normal method of incorporating a commercial concern. Any body of this type is properly called a company. (The term 'firm', sometimes used to describe this type of undertaking, is best reserved for partnerships, which are unincorporated.) Registered companies are usually companies limited by shares, although a small number are unlimited companies or companies limited by guarantee.

Unincorporated associations

1.9 Besides partnerships (dealt with later) and companies, persons may form other sorts of aggregate (usually non-profit-making) which are known as unincorporated associations. These may be sports or social clubs, amateur dramatics societies, trade associations etc. But they have no separate, independent personality and hence title to property remains with the members.

1.10 As there is no legal personality, any person who enters into a contract 'on behalf of' such an association is personally liable on that contract - although all the members may ratify it afterwards.

1.11 No member may buy goods on credit or borrow unless he has the consent of all the members. This is essentially because it is the members' credit which is pledged, not the club's. To operate a bank account for instance a bank will usually be given a mandate signed by the club's secretary and chairman, stating that a meeting of members agreed to open an account and certain members were authorised to operate the account.

1.12   Members have rights over the association's property when it is dissolved, but not when it is actually functioning. The rules, which form a contract between members, normally give them other rights (such as voting) which they may enforce in the courts.

1.13   If a person wishes to sue an association, it is usually impractical to sue all the members, since there may be thousands of them. There are two alternatives in such a case.

(a)   Only those members who are liable are sued.

(b)   A representative action is taken against some members. If it is successful, these latter pay out and are then indemnified by the association or by other members if there are insufficient funds.

2   INCORPORATION AND LIMITED LIABILITY

2.1   The most important consequence of registration is that a company becomes *a legal person distinct from its owners*. The owners of a company are its members, or shareholders. The case which clearly established the separate legal personality of the company is of great significance to any study of company law, and is therefore set out in some detail below.

> *Salomon v Salomon & Co Ltd 1897*
> The plaintiff had for some years carried on business as a leather merchant and boot manufacturer. He decided to form a limited company to purchase the business, he and six members of his family each subscribing for one share. The company then purchased the business for £38,782, the purchase price being payable to the plaintiff by way of the issue of 20,000 £1 shares, the issue of debentures for £10,000 (effectively making Salomon a secured creditor) and the payment of £8,782 in cash. The company did not prosper and was wound up a year later, at which point its liabilities exceeded its assets. The liquidator, representing unsecured trade creditors of the company, claimed that the company's business was in effect still the plaintiff's (he owned 20,001 of 20,007 shares) and that he should bear liability for its debts and that payment of the debenture debt to him should be postponed until the company's trade creditors were paid.
>
> *Held:* at first instance, and in the Court of Appeal, that the other shareholders were 'mere puppets' and that the company had been incorporated for an unlawful purpose. Salomon should indemnify the company against its liabilities. The House of Lords unanimously reversed the earlier decision and held that the business was owned by, and it debts the liability of, the company. The plaintiff was under no liability to the company or its creditors, his debentures were validly issued and the security created by them over the company's assets was effective.

The principle of separate legal personality has been confirmed by more recent cases:

> *Lee v Lee's Air Farming Ltd 1960*
> Mr Lee, who owned the majority of the shares of an aerial crop-spraying business, and was the sole working director of the company, was killed while piloting the aircraft.
>
> *Held:* although he was the majority shareholder and sole working director of the company, he and the company were separate legal persons and therefore he could also be an employee with rights against it when killed in an accident in the course of his employment.

Characteristics of a company

2.2   A company has a number of other characteristics in consequence of being a legal entity separate from its members.

Limited liability

2.3   One of the principal advantages of trading as a limited company is that the liability of the members of the company is limited. This is important: it is not the liability of the *company* which is limited, but that of its *members*. The company is liable without limit for its own debts.

2.4   A company obtains its capital from and distributes its profits to its members. It may be - and usually is - formed on the basis of limited liability of members: it is then known as a limited company. In that case if the company becomes insolvent the members cannot be required to contribute more than the amount outstanding (if any) on their shares, or, if it is a company limited by guarantee, the amount of their guarantee. This is because a shareholder's liability to contribute towards payment of the company's debts is measured by the nominal value of the shares he holds. As soon as he has paid that nominal value plus any premium agreed at the time of issue of the shares, he is no longer liable to contribute any further amounts towards the company's debts.

2.5   It is important to note that a shareholder is liable to *contribute* to the payment of the company's debts; he is not liable to *pay* the debts himself. This means that he cannot be sued by a creditor who wishes to obtain repayment of a debt, even if there is still an amount unpaid in respect of his shares. The procedure is for the creditor to petition the court to wind up the company and a liquidator to be appointed. The liquidator realises the company's assets and, if this does not produce enough to meet the company's liabilities, he will call on the shareholders to the extent of the balance of capital unpaid on their shares.

Transferable shares

2.6   The interest of a member, as proprietor of the company, is a form of property (measured in 'shares') which he can transfer to another person, subject to any restrictions imposed by the constitution of the company.

Perpetual succession

2.7   A change of membership or the death of a member is not a change in the company itself. It is a separate person which continues unaffected by changes among its members.

Assets, rights and liabilities

2.8   The assets and liabilities, rights and obligations incidental to the company's activities are assets of the company and not of its members.

> *Macaura v Northern Assurance Co Ltd 1925*
> The plaintiff, a landowner, sold the timber on his estate to a company of which he was the sole owner and a major creditor. Before the sale to the company, he had insured the timber in his own name. He did not transfer the insurance policy to the company name. Two weeks later almost all the timber was destroyed by fire. He claimed for the loss under his policy but the insurers denied liability on the grounds that he personally did not have, as insurance law requires, an insurable interest in the timber.
>
> *Held:* the claim must fail as 'the debt was not exposed to fire and nor were the shares ... his relation was to the company, not to its goods'. Thus since it was the company which owned the timber, the plaintiff merely owning shares in the company, the timber was not effectively covered by his individual policy.

Capital

2.9   The sums paid to the company by its members in return for their shares form the company's capital. If it is a company with limited liability it may not ordinarily distribute capital to the members but must retain it as a fund to meet its own debts.

Supervision

2.10 A company is created by the legal process of incorporation, being registration under the Companies Act 1985. It exists as an artificial person under the Act until it is formally dissolved by removal of its name from the register at the Companies Registry. While it exists it is subject to detailed regulation; for instance, it must prepare and, unless it is an unlimited company, deliver to the registry *annual accounts and an annual return* (a summary of its situation).

2.11 The Registrar of Companies, the Department of Trade and Industry (of which the Registrar is part) and the courts all have power of regulation and investigation over companies. The public has a legal right of access to the records at the Companies Registry and to other sources of information.

Management

2.12 A company cannot, as an artificial person, manage itself. It must therefore have managers, called directors. Together with the company secretary they are the *officers* of the company. Directors may be appointed and removed by a simple majority vote of the members: s 303. Since they are in a position of trust where they control large sums of other people's money, and it is relatively easy to abuse this trust, directors are subject to a wide variety of statutory and non-statutory rules. The members as members, have no claim to be directors though they usually have power to appoint the directors and may so appoint themselves.

2.13 This distinction between members (proprietors) and directors (managers) is extended to require that:

(a) the *directors as a body* (the *board of directors*) shall have defined powers of management delegated to them by the company; and

(b) the *members as a body* shall meet as a general meeting of the company to decide those matters (including the appointment and removal of directors) which are to delegated to the directors.

These two elements are known as the *'organs'* of the company.

Written constitution

2.14 A company has no mind of its own to decide what to do. The structure of divided control between directors and members must be clearly defined. A company therefore has a written constitution. On the creation of a company, the promoters must file certain documents with the Registrar of Companies. These include the Articles of Association and the Memorandum of Association. The Articles contain details of how the company will be run from day to day, for example the duties of directors, the rights of each class of shares, and procedure at meetings. The Memorandum lays down the constitution of the company, for example its name, authorised capital and objects.

3   TYPES OF COMPANY   *6/95, 12/98*

Public and private companies

3.1 A company may be registered as public or private. Public companies must:

(a) be registered as public companies;
(b) have at least two members; and
(c) state in their constitutions that they are public companies.

3.2   Private companies are limited companies having a minimum of one member, and which are not registered as public companies - a company is private unless it is specifically registered as public. The main reason for distinguishing between public and private companies is that private companies are generally small enterprises in which some if not all shareholders are also directors and *vice versa*. Ownership and management are thus combined in the same individuals. In that situation, it is unnecessary to impose on the directors complicated restrictions to safeguard the interests of members and so the whole structure of the company can be simplified.

3.3   The main differences between public and private companies are as follows.

(a) *Purpose*. Public and private companies fulfil different economic purposes. The purpose of a public company is usually to raise capital from the public to run the enterprise.

(b) *Issue of capital*. A private company may not raise capital by issuing its securities to the public. There is no restriction on the offer of securities by a public company.

(c) *Transferability of shares*. The shares of a public company are freely transferable (in the case of listed companies, on the Stock Exchange). A private company will, in contrast, wish to remain under the control of the 'family' or 'partners' concerned.

(d) *Minimum share capital*. A public company must have a minimum allotted share capital of £50,000. A private company has no minimum share capital.

(e) *Company name*. The name of a public company must end with the words 'Public Limited Company' which may be abbreviated to 'PLC' or 'plc'. A private company's name must end with 'limited'. This may be abbreviated to 'ltd'.

(f) *The memorandum*. A public company's memorandum must state that 'the company is to be a public company'.

(g) *Payment for shares*. There are a number of differences in the rules relating to the consideration given in return for shares. For example, if a public company issues shares in return for the transfer of a non-cash asset, that asset must be independently valued.

(h) *Dividends*. There are detailed rules which differentiate between the ability of public and private companies to distribute their profits as dividends.

(i) *Directors*. A public company must have at least two directors but a private company only one. The rules on loans to directors are much more stringent in their application to public companies and their subsidiaries than to private companies.

(j) *Accounts*. A public company has seven months from the end of its accounting reference period in which to produce its statutory audited accounts. A private company has ten months. A private company may, if qualified by size, have partial exemption from various accounting provisions.

(k) *Commencement of business*. A private company can commence business as soon as it is incorporated. A public company, if incorporated as such, must first obtain from the Registrar of Companies a trading certificate.

3.4   A public company has to meet much more stringent rules on disclosures, accounts and loans to directors, as well as formalities in documentation. For example, a public company must produce its statutory audited accounts within 7 months from the end of its accounting referencing period whereas a private company has 10 months and some private companies will be exempted from various accounting provisions on account of size.

Limited and unlimited companies   *6/98*

Limited liability companies

3.5   Liability is usually limited by *shares*. This is the position when a company which has share capital states in its memorandum of association that 'the liability of members is limited'. When such a company allots shares it fixes a price which the allottee agrees to pay in money or money's worth at or soon after the time of allotment.

3.6 Part payments may be made by *instalments*, whereby the contract of allotment states that payment of the unpaid balance shall be made on specific dates. This was the approach adopted in a number of privatisation issues in the UK.

3.7 A company may alternatively be limited by *guarantee*. Its memorandum of association then states the amount which each member undertakes to contribute in the event of a liquidation. As with a company limited by shares, a creditor has no direct claim against a member under his guarantee, nor in this case can the company require a member to pay up under his guarantee until the company goes into liquidation.

3.8 Companies limited by guarantee are appropriate to non-commercial activities, such as a charity or a trade association, which aims to keep income and expenditure in balance but also have their members' guarantees to fall back on in the event of insolvency.

Unlimited liability companies

3.9 A company may also be formed with unlimited liability. Its memorandum of association makes no reference to the liability of members. If the company goes into liquidation, the liquidator (but not the creditors) of the company can require members to contribute as much as may be necessary to enable the company to pay its debts in full. An unlimited company can only be a private company, since a public company is by definition always limited.

3.10 The main advantage of operating as an unlimited company is that the company need not file a copy of its annual accounts and reports with the Registrar of Companies, unless during the relevant accounting period:

(a) it is (to its knowledge) a subsidiary of a limited company;
(b) it is the parent company of a limited company;
(c) it is the promoter of a trading stamp scheme.

It may also without formality purchase its own shares from its own shareholders.

3.11 The unlimited company can be a useful vehicle. It provides a separate legal entity which can conveniently hold assets to which liabilities do not attach. Partners in a professional firm, for whom a limited company is not an available option, may find an unlimited company a useful medium through which to carry on some of their activities. The main advantage is the maintenance of privacy about the financial position which cannot be obtained by a limited company, whose accounts must be available for inspection at the Companies Registry.

4   REGISTRATION PROCEDURES AND DOCUMENTATION   *12/98*

4.1 Incorporation of a company may be achieved in a number of ways. The most important method is incorporation under the Companies Act 1985. The legal person will then be a company with either limited or unlimited liability of its members. If there is limited liability this may be limited by guarantee or by shares. Companies can also be formed by Royal Charter, Royal Prerogative, Act of Parliament or by delegated legislation.

4.2 Under the Companies Act, the following *documents* should be prepared and delivered to the Companies Registry to obtain registration of a company limited by shares:

(i)   the *memorandum of association*;

(ii) the *articles of association* (a note may be added to the memorandum stating that the company will adopt Table A (1985 edition) as its articles);

(iii) *particulars* of the company's first directors and secretary (with their signed consent to act) and of the address of the registered office;

(iv) a *statutory declaration* by one of the persons named as directors or secretary or by a solicitor that there has been compliance with the requirements of the Companies Act 1985 on company formation; and

(v)   a *registration fee*.

4.3   Once these have been checked and found to be in order by the Registrar of Companies, a *certificate of incorporation* is issued. This is conclusive evidence that the formalities of registration have been complied with.

4.4   The *articles of association* set out the internal regulations and procedures for the daily running of the company. The *memorandum of association* sets out the company's basic constitution and its relationship with the outside world. It must contain the company's *name and registered office address*, the *objects* of the company (which define the company's contractual capacity to act), the *authorised share capital* and a clause stating that, where this is the case, the *liability* of the members is limited. If the company is limited by guarantee rather than by shares, the amount guaranteed by the members will be stated.

4.5   In the event of any inconsistency between the memorandum and articles, the memorandum prevails.

5   THE VEIL OF INCORPORATION   *6/99*

5.1   The veil of incorporation means simply that a company is to be distinguished as a separate person from its members. It is in many ways an inappropriate expression since there is no concealment of the members whose identity is revealed by the register of members which any member of the public may inspect: s 356. There are also many rules which require that information about a company shall be available to the public, for example the register of directors and the filing of accounts at the Companies Registry.

5.2   Exceptions are made (called lifting the veil of incorporation) in some specific situations. The effect of so doing is either:

(a)   to *identify the company with other persons*, that is its members or directors, or;

(b)   to treat a group of companies as a *single commercial entity*.

There is no consistent principle applied in making these exceptions, each of which has to be considered separately, but their general purpose is:

(a)   to enforce rules of company law;

(b)   to prevent fraud or other evasion of legal obligations by the use of companies; or

(c)   to recognise that in economic reality the enterprise is the group and not the individual companies within it.

The main instances of lifting the veil are explained below.

Lifting the veil by statute to enforce the law

Liability of a sole member for a company's debts

5.3   Every public company must have a minimum membership of at least two members: s 1. If therefore a public company has two members and one dies or transfers his shares to the other, the rule is broken. To enforce its observance so that a second member is introduced when necessary, the one surviving member is made liable (with the company) for its debts if:

(a)   *the company carries on business after six months* from the time when the membership is reduced to one, and

(b)   *the surviving member knows* that it is carrying on business with himself as sole member.

5.4   The member's liability is not retrospective and extends only to debts of the company incurred after the six months have expired: s 24. The rule is not often applied since the sole surviving member can easily remedy the situation by transferring one of his own shares to another person who becomes the second member. This rule no longer applies to private companies.

Fraudulent trading

5.5   If, when a company is wound up, it appears that its business has been carried on with intent to defraud creditors or others the court may decide that the persons (usually the directors) who were knowingly parties to the fraud shall be *personally responsible* for debts and other liabilities of the company: s 213 Insolvency Act 1986. This is a restraint on directors who might otherwise permit their company to continue trading fraudulently when they know that it can no longer pay its debts. Even in the absence of fraud, s 214 Insolvency Act 1986 (wrongful trading) may apply.

Liability for trading without trading certificate

5.6   A public company must, under s 117, obtain a certificate from the Registrar before it may commence to trade. Failure to do so leads to *personal liability* for the directors for any loss or damage suffered by a third party to a transaction entered into by the company in contravention of s 117.

Disqualified directors

5.7   Directors who participate in the management of a company in contravention of an order under the Company Directors Disqualification Act 1986 will be jointly or severally liable along with the company for the company's debts.

Abuse of company names

5.8   There have been a large number of instances where directors of a company which went into insolvent liquidation formed another company with an identical or similar name, which bought the original company's business and assets from its liquidator.

5.9   S 216 Insolvency Act 1986 now prevents a director or shadow director of a company that goes into insolvent liquidation being involved for the next five years with the directing, managing or promoting of a business which has an identical name to the original company, or a name similar enough to suggest a connection. Breach of the rules is an offence of strict liability and proof of intent is not required (*R v Cole and Other 1997*).

Liability for use of company name in incorrect form

5.10   A company is identified by its name which distinguishes it from other companies. Every company is required to *exhibit its name in its correct form* outside every place of business, on its seal (if it has one) and on its business letters and other documents such as bills of exchange. If the rule is broken an officer of the company responsible for the default may be fined and, as regards business documents, he is *personally liable* to the creditor if the company fails to pay the debt: s 349.

> *Penrose v Martyr 1858*
> A company secretary accepted a bill of exchange drawn on the company on which its name was incorrectly written by omitting the word 'limited' from the name. The company defaulted.
>
> *Held:* the secretary was personally liable on the bill.
>
> *Durham Fancy Goods Ltd v Michael Jackson (Fancy Goods) Ltd 1968*
> A creditor drew a bill on the company and wrote on it a form of acceptance which did not state the correct name of the company (it used 'M Jackson' instead of 'Michael Jackson' in full). The defendant signed the acceptance for the company.
>
> *Held:* the defendant was not liable since the error had been introduced by the plaintiff. But for that fact he would have been liable.

5.11   The fact that a company name is incorrect does not make the document ineffective, provided that it is clear that it was intended to name that company: *Bird (London) Ltd v Thomas Cook & Son (Bakers) Ltd 1937.*

5.12   Until recently, when a company's name was given wrongly on a cheque or other financial instrument, this was a mistake and it was unfortunate for the officer responsible that the creditor could proceed against him personally. This applied even to trifling errors in the company's name: *Hendon v Adelman 1973.*

5.13   However, more recently the High Court gave an interpretation of s 349 which is more generous to company directors and other officers.

> *Jenice Ltd and Others v Dan 1993*
> Mr Dan was a director of a company called Primekeen Ltd. The bank incorrectly printed the company's cheques in the name of 'Primkeen Ltd'. Mr Dan signed several of these. They were dishonoured and returned by the various plaintiffs including Jenice. Primekeen Ltd then went into creditors' voluntary winding up and the various plaintiffs sued Mr Dan as personally liable on the cheques because of s 349(4).
>
> *Held:* Mr Dan was not liable. The purpose of s 349(4) was to ensure that outsiders knew they were dealing with a company and that the liability of its members was limited. There was no doubt that in this case outsiders would have known that they were dealing with a limited company, so no mischief had been done.

Identification of a company and its members

Evasion of obligations imposed by law

5.14   A company may be identified with those who control it, for instance to determine its residence for tax purposes. The courts may also ignore the distinction between a company and its members and managers if the latter use that distinction to evade their legal obligations.

> *Gilford Motor Co Ltd v Horne 1933*
> The defendant had been employed by the plaintiff company under a contract which forbade him to solicit its customers after leaving its service. After the termination of his employment he formed a company of which his wife and an employee were the sole directors and shareholders. He managed the company and through it evaded the covenant by which he himself was prevented from soliciting customers of his former employer.
>
> *Held:* an injunction requiring observance of the covenant would be made both against the defendant and the company which he had formed as a 'a mere cloak or sham'.

> *Jones v Lipman 1962*
> A vendor of land wished to evade an order of specific performance of a contract for sale of land. He purchased the share capital of a company formed by third parties, registered the shares in the name of himself and a nominee, and had himself and the nominee appointed as directors. He conveyed the land to the company.
>
> *Held:* the acquisition of the company and the conveyance of the land to it was a mere cloak or sham for the evasion of the contract. Specific performance was ordered against the company.

Public interest

5.15   In time of war it is not permitted to trade with 'enemy aliens'. The courts may draw aside the veil if, despite a company being registered in the UK, it is suspected that it is controlled by aliens. The court may then determine the owners' nationality.

Daimler Co Ltd v Continental Tyre and Rubber Co Ltd 1916
The defendant, a UK incorporated company, was owned by 5 individuals and a company incorporated in Germany. Only one individual was British and he held one share.

Held: the plaintiffs need not discharge a debt to the defendants since effective control of the latter was in enemy hands and hence to do so would be to trade with the enemy.

5.16 The question of nationality may also arise in peacetime, where it is convenient for a foreign entity to have a British facade on its operations.

Re F G Films Ltd 1953
An English company was formed by an American company to 'make' a film which would obtain certain marketing and other advantages from being called a British film. Staff and finance were American and there were neither premises nor employees in England; the film itself was produced in India.

Held: The British company was the American company's agent and so the film did not qualify as British. Effectively, the corporate entity of the British company was swept away and it was exposed as a 'sham' company.

Evasion of liabilities

5.17 The veil of incorporation may also be lifted where directors themselves ignore the separate legal personality of two companies and transfer assets from one to the other in disregard of their duties in order to avoid a contingent liability.

Creasey v Breachwood Motors Ltd 1992
Breachwood Welwyn Ltd ('Welwyn') had dismissed the plaintiff from his position as manager in 1988. He issued a writ against Welwyn alleging wrongful dismissal. Welwyn then ceased to trade and transferred its assets to the defendants. The plaintiff obtained judgment against Welwyn which by then had no assets. Welwyn was dissolved in 1991.

Held: where a company with a contingent liability (in this case to the plaintiff), transferred its assets to another company which continued its business under the same trade name, then the court would lift the veil of incorporation in order to allow the plaintiff to proceed against the new company.

Re H and Others 1996
The facts: the court was asked to rule that various companies within a group, together with the minority shareholders, should be treated as one entity in order to restrain assets prior to trial.

Held: the order was granted. The court thought there was evidence that the companies had been used for the fraudulent evasion of excise duty.

Evasion of taxation

5.18 The court may lift the veil of incorporation where it is being used to conceal the nationality of the company.

Unit Construction Co Ltd v Bullock 1960
Three companies, wholly owned by a UK company, were registered in Kenya. Although the companies' constitutions required board meetings to be held in Kenya, all three were in fact managed entirely by the holding company.

Held: the companies were resident in the UK and liable to UK tax. The Kenyan connection was a sham, the question being not where they ought to have been managed, but where they were managed.

Quasi-partnership

5.19 An application to wind up a company on the 'just and equitable' ground under s 122(1)(g) Insolvency Act 1986 may involve the court piercing the veil to reveal the company as a quasi- partnership. This may happen where individuals who have operated contentedly as a company for years fall out, and one seeks to remove the other: The courts are willing in such cases to consider the central relationship between directors rather than to look at the 'bare bones' of the company.

> *Ebrahimi v Westbourne Galleries Ltd 1973*
> The plaintiff and N carried on business together for 25 years, originally as partners and for the last 10 years through a company in which each originally had 500 shares. They were the first directors and shared the profits as directors' remuneration; no dividends were paid. When N's son joined the business he became a third director and the plaintiff and N each transferred 100 shares to N's son. Eventually there were disputes; N and his son used their voting control in general meeting (600 votes against 400) to remove the plaintiff from his directorship under the power of removal given by s 303 Companies Act 1985 (removal by ordinary resolution).
>
> *Held:* the company should be wound up. N and his son were within their legal rights in removing the plaintiff from his directorship, but the past relationship made it 'unjust or inequitable' to insist on legal rights and the court could intervene on equitable principles to order liquidation.

Groups of companies

5.20 The principle of the veil of incorporation extends to the holding company/subsidiary relationship. Although holding companies and subsidiaries are part of a group under company law, they retain their separate legal personalities.

5.21 However, this has proved a particularly controversial area of company law. The most important recent case comprehensively reviewed the issues involved.

> *Adams v Cape Industries plc 1990*
> *The facts:* Cape, an English company, headed a group which included many wholly-owned subsidiaries. Some of these mined asbestos in South Africa, and others marketed the asbestos in various countries including the USA. Several hundred plaintiffs had been awarded damages by a Texas court for personal injuries suffered as a result of exposure to asbestos dust. The defendants in Texas included one of Cape's subsidiaries, NAAC. The courts also considered the position of AMC, another subsidiary, and CPC, a company linked to Cape Industries, though not actually a subsidiary.
>
> *Held:* the judgement would not be enforced against the English holding company, Cape, either on the basis that Cape had been 'present' in the US through its local subsidiaries (an argument which would have involved lifting the veil) or because it had carried on business in the US through the agency of NAAC. Slade LJ commented in giving the judgement that English law 'for better or worse recognises the creation of subsidiary companies ... which would fall to be treated as separate legal entities, with all the rights and liabilities which would normally be attached to separate legal entities'. Whether desirable or not, English law allowed a group structure to be used so that legal liability falls on an individual member of a group rather than the group as a whole.

5.22 As regards liability, there is no general rule that the commercial activities of a subsidiary are to be treated as acts of the holding company merely because of the relationship of holding company and subsidiary. The Court of Appeal in the *Cape Industries* case specifically stated that it could not ignore Salomon 'merely because it considers that justice so requires'.

5.23   In the *Cape Industries* case, three reasons were put forward for identifying the companies as one, and lifting the veil of incorporation:

(a)   where the subsidiary is acting as *agent* for the holding company;
(b)   where the group is to be treated as a *single economic entity*;
(c)   where the *corporate structure* is being used as a *facade* to conceal the truth.

There points are examined below.

Subsidiary as agent

5.24   The Firestone case used the agency argument to identify the subsidiary with the holding company.

> *Firestone Tyre & Rubber Co Ltd v Lewellin 1937*
> An American company obtained orders from customers in Europe and arranged for the goods to be made by its UK subsidiary and shipped directly to the customers who paid the American holding company. The latter, to avoid UK tax on its profits, reimbursed the UK subsidiary its costs plus 5%.
>
> *Held:* the subsidiary acted as agent of the American holding company which was liable to UK tax on profits made in one and the same enterprise.

5.25   However the judgement in *Adams v Cape Industries* appears to have restricted the use of this exception. The court held that there were a number of indicators that NAAC was carrying on business on its own. It leased premises, carried on various activities on its own account, and earned and paid tax on profits. In addition NAAC's creditors and debtors were its own and not Cape Industries'. The court also held that the agency argument was even weaker against CPC because not only did it carry on business on its own account, but it was also wholly owned by its managing director.

Group as single economic entity

5.26   Case law is somewhat confused as to whether a holding and subsidiary company can be regarded as a single entity if they are carrying on what amounts to a single business.

> *DHN Food Distributors Ltd v Tower Hamlets LBC 1976*
> DHN carried on business as grocers from premises owned by a subsidiary of DHN. The subsidiary itself had no business activities. Both companies had the same directors. The local authority (the defendant) acquired the premises compulsorily but refused to pay compensation for disturbance of the business since the subsidiary which owned the premises did not also carry on the business.
>
> *Held:* the Court of Appeal upheld the claim. Denning LJ said that holding company and subsidiary should be regarded as an 'economic entity'. Accordingly there was a valid claim for disturbance since ownership of the premises and business activity were in the hands of a single group.

5.27   However in *Woolfson v Strathclyde Regional Council 1978*, the facts of which were similar to the DHN case, the House of Lords upheld a decision of the Scottish courts which did not follow the English case.

5.28   The judges in the *Cape Industries* case accepted that the wording of a statute or document might justify the court treating a holding company and subsidiary as one unit. However as a general principle company law recognised subsidiaries as being separate legal entities and the court could not disregard this point.

5.29   In addition, the courts are reluctant to extend the principle of identification too far beyond the area of commercial activities.

Dimbleby and Sons Ltd v National Union of Journalists 1984

The NUJ instructed its members not to provide copy for Dimbleby Newspapers, which were to be printed by TBF (Printers) Ltd. The NUJ were in dispute with T Bailey Forman Ltd, an associated company of TBF, and were 'blacking' the Dimbleby Newspaper copy in order to bring pressure to bear on Forman. There was no dispute between the NUJ and Dimbleby. The NUJ sought to argue that TBF and Forman were an entity, so that industrial action taken against TBF would enjoy the same immunities in tort as if it were action taken against Forman.

Held: (by the House of Lords) - the court would not extend the immunity given in clear terms by the Employment Act 1980 to trade union action against an associated company (as therein defined). It would be wrong to apply principles of company law to treat associated companies of any kind as an entity in this context of industrial relations legislation.

Corporate structure as facade

5.30   There are no direct cases in this point. The *Gilford* case may indicate this argument could be used.

5.31   In the *Cape Industries* case the court held that AMC was a facade as AMC was not only a wholly-owned subsidiary, but also merely a corporate name which Cape and its subsidiaries used on their invoices. However this point was irrelevant to the main judgement since AMC was not carrying on any business in the United States.

5.32   However, the court also held that companies could use subsidiaries (or other structures) as a means of directing where limited liability should fall. 'We do not accept as a matter of law that the court is entitled to lift the corporate veil ... merely because the corporate structure has been used to ensure that the legal liability in respect of particular future activities of the group will fall on another member of the group rather than the defendant company'.

Summary of the effect of the Cape Industries case

5.33   The Cape case then has reinforced the basic principles of Salomon that a company is a distinct legal entity. Any identification of group members as one entity is likely to be exceptional. In *Re Polly Peck International plc (in administration) 1996* the High Court rejected the argument that the various companies within a group should be identified as one. The judge stated that identifying the group companies as one entity could mean creating an exception to Salomon additional to those given in the *Cape Industries* case and that he could not do this.

Liability for insolvent subsidiaries

5.34   In general the courts have taken a strict view, and only imposed liability on a holding company if it has promised to *support* a subsidiary in future.

5.35   In *Kleinwort Benson Ltd v Malaysian Mining Corporation Berhad 1989* the holding company made the statement that 'it is our policy to ensure that the business is at all times in a position to met its liabilities to you'. The court held that this statement was a representation of fact and not a promise of future support, and hence not enforceable on the holding company.

Restructuring

5.36   It has been ruled that damages for misrepresentation and breach of warranty cannot be claimed from another group company after a restructuring.

Ord v Belhaven Pubs 1998
A subsidiary company had warranted the turnover and profitability of a pub that the claimants had bought (the pub was not, in fact, a going concern). The claimants wanted to claim damages from the parent company because they were concerned that Belhaven (the subsidiary) would not have the resources to meet any judgement against it. Substituting the parent company as defendant was initially allowed by the High Court.
Held: The Court of Appeal reversed this, and would not draw aside the veil of incorporation to regard the companies in the group as one entity. The restructuring (during which the establishments owned by Belhaven were transferred to the parent) was held to have been the ordinary trading of a group of companies as a response to a recession, which the group was entitled to do. The *Salomon* principle could not be ignored.

6   PARTNERSHIP   *6/94, 12/94*

6.1   Partnership is the normal organisation in the professions but is less common is commerce. This is because most professions prohibit their members from carrying on practice through limited companies. Businessmen are not so restricted and generally prefer to trade through a limited company so that, if it becomes insolvent, they are not liable for its debts. A partner is personally liable for all the debts of the firm (incurred while he is a partner and sometimes even after he has ceased to be a partner).

6.2   The word 'firm' is correctly used to denote a partnership. It is not correct to apply it to a registered company (though the newspapers often do so). The word 'company' may form part of the name of a partnership firm, eg 'Smith & Company'. But 'limited company' or 'registered company' is only applied to a company incorporated under the Companies Act 1985. You are advised to avoid using the word 'company' in connection with a partnership (and you should never use the words 'limited company' in that connection) as it may suggest that you are unable to distinguish a partnership from a registered company.

Definition of partnership

6.3   In most cases there is no doubt about the existence of a partnership. The partners declare their intention by such steps as signing a written partnership agreement and adopting a firm name. But these outward and visible signs of the existence of a partnership are not essential - a partnership can exist without them. The main consequence of a partnership is that there is no separate legal person as distinct from its members. A partnership exists whenever the facts satisfy the statutory definition (s 1 Partnership Act 1890), which is as follows.

'Partnership is the relation which subsists between persons carrying on a business in common with a view of profit'.

The relation which subsists between persons

6.4   Partnership is *the relation which subsists between persons*. 'Person' includes a corporation such as a registered company as well as an individual living person.

6.5   There must be at least two partners. If, therefore, two men are in partnership, one dies and the survivor carries on the business he is a sole trader - there is no longer a partnership.

6.6   The standard maximum number of partners permitted by law is 20: s 716 Companies Act 1985. The intention of this rule is that if more than 20 persons wish to carry on a commercial business they should form a registered company for that purpose.

6.7   As professional practice cannot usually be carried on by a registered company, solicitors, chartered surveyors and many other professions are permitted to form partnerships with any number of partners; the limit of 20 only applies to commercial, not professional partnerships.

Carrying on a business

6.8   The next point in the statutory definition of a partnership is that the persons concerned are *carrying on a business*. Business is defined to include 'every trade, occupation or profession': s 45. But three points should be noted.

    (a)   A business is a *form of activity*. If two or more persons are merely the passive joint owners of revenue-producing property, such as investments or rented houses, that fact of itself does not make them partners: s 2(1).

    (b)   A business can consist of a *single transaction*. These situations are often described as 'joint ventures' - the partners associate solely for the purpose of completing one deal, such as a joint speculation in buying potatoes wholesale for resale: *Mann v Darcy 1968*.

    (c)   Carrying on a business must have a *beginning and an end*. A partnership begins when the partners begin their business activity: it does not make any difference if they entered into a formal partnership agreement with effect from some earlier or later date. Similarity, statements that the individuals involved are partners does not establish a business. Courts will decide whether a business is being carried on in common by reviewing the facts: *Kahn and Others v Miah and Others 1997*.

    (d)   Making preparations to carry on a partnership, such as obtaining finance, is *not* the same as carrying it on. Thus in the *Kahn v Miah* case partnership could not commence until the Indian restaurant the partnership was set up to run had actually opened.

In common

6.9   To constitute a partnership the partners must also carry on business *in common*. Broadly this phrase means that the partners must be associated in the business as joint proprietors. The evidence that this is so is found in their taking a share of the profits.

A view of profit

6.10   The persons must have a *view of profit*. If persons enter into a partnership with a view to making profits but they actually suffer losses, it is still a partnership. The test to be applied is one of intention.

Liability of the partners

6.11   Every partner is liable *without limit* for the debts of the partnership. It is possible to register a limited partnership in which sole partners have limited liability, but the limited partners may not take part in the management of the business: Limited Partnerships Act 1907.

Changes of membership

Death of a partner

6.12   The death of a partner may itself dissolve the partnership (s 33 so provides unless otherwise agreed). This is usually avoided by expressly agreeing that so long as there are two or more surviving partners the partnership shall continue. The estate of a deceased partner is only liable for debts of the partnership incurred *before* his death.

Retirement of a partner

6.13   The effect of retirement is that the partner who retires:

(a) is still liable for any outstanding debts incurred while he was a partner unless the creditor has agreed to release him from liability; and

(b) is also liable for debts of the firm incurred after his retirement if the creditor knew him to be a partner (before retirement) and has not had notice of his retirement. This is due to the principle that a person who was previously known to be a partner continues to be an 'apparent member' of the partnership and liable for all its debts until notice is given that he is no longer a partner; s 36.

6.14 To avoid being still an 'apparent member' of the firm after his retirement the retiring partner should give notice of his retirement.

(a) To creditors who had dealings with the firm while he was a partner, he should give actual notice of his retirement. This need not be an express notice. If for example the firm reprints its letterhead to omit him from the list of partners and writes a letter on the new letterhead to a creditor that is sufficient notice to the creditor of the change.

(b) To persons who may have known that he is a partner (before his retirement) but who begin to have dealings with the firm for the first time after his retirement, the retired partner cannot easily give actual notice since he does not know (at his retirement) who they may prove to be. But sufficient notice is given to them if he advertises the fact of his retirement in the London Gazette: s 36(2). They are then deemed to have notice even if they have not read the advertisement.

New partner

6.15 A new partner admitted to an existing firm is liable for debts incurred only after he becomes a partner. He is not liable for debts incurred before he was a partner unless he agrees to become liable.

Partnership property

6.16 The initial property of the partnership is that which the partners expressly or impliedly agreed shall be partnership property. It is quite possible that property used in the business is not partnership property but is the sole property of one of the partners; it depends entirely on the intention of the partners.

A partner's authority as agent of the firm

6.17 The Partnership Act 1890 defines the apparent authority of a partner to make contracts as follows.

'Every partner is an agent of the firm and his other partners for the purpose of the business of the partnership; and the acts of every partner who does any act for carrying on in the usual way business of the kind carried on by the firm of which he is a member bind the firm and his partners, unless the partner so acting has in fact no authority to act for the firm in the particular matter, and the person with whom he is dealing either knows that he has no authority, or does not know or believe him to be a partner': s 5.

The Act also states that the partnership is only bound by acts done by a partner in the firm's name and not apparently for the partners personally: ss 6 and 7.

6.18 Sometimes a single partner enters into a transaction which the other partners wish to repudiate on the ground that it is outside the limits of the *business of the kind carried on by the firm*. It is indeed usual to specify in a partnership agreement what is the nature of the firm's business. But unless the person with whom a partner deals is aware of the agreed limits he may hold the firm bound by a transaction which would appear to him (and other outsiders) to be the kind of business which such a firm ordinarily carries on.

Mercantile Credit v Garrod 1962
P and the defendant entered into partnership to let lock-up garages and repair cars. P ran the business and the defendant was a sleeping partner. Their partnership

agreement provided expressly that the firm would not buy and sell cars. But P sold a car which the firm did not own to a finance company (the plaintiff) so that it might be let on hire purchase to a customer. The plaintiff sued the defendant to recover the £700 which it had paid P for the car. The defendant denied liability on the ground that P in selling the car had been acting outside the agreed limits of the firm's business and so P had no actual or apparent authority from him. Evidence was given that other garage businesses of the type carried on by P and the defendant did deal in cars.

Held: the test of what is the firm's business is not what the partners agreed it should be but 'what it appeared to the outside world' to be (established by the practice of 'businesses of a like kind'). By that test P appeared to the plaintiff to be carrying on business of the kind carried on by such a firm. Buying and selling the firm's goods is within the authority of a single partner.

6.19   The second test of s 5 is that a partner is agent of the firm in carrying on the firm's business *in the usual way*. What is usual in any particular business must always depend partly on the general practice of businesses of a similar type and size. In particular a distinction is made between commercial firms which trade in buying and selling goods and non-commercial firms (including of course professional partnerships) which do not do so. A single partner of a commercial firm (acting on behalf of the firm and within the apparent limits of its kind of business) is deemed to have the authority of the other partners to engage in any of the following transactions.

(a)   To buy and sell goods in the course of the firm's business (including the purchase of fixed assets for use in the business such as a typewriter or a delivery van).

(b)   To receive payment of debts owed to the firm and to issue receipts.

(c)   To engage employees to work in the firm's business.

(d)   To sign cheques drawn on the firm's bank account.

(e)   To sign bills of exchange as drawer acceptor or endorser.

(f)   To borrow money and to give security by pledging the firm's goods or by deposit of title deeds etc relating to the firm's land and buildings.

6.20   The following transactions are not within the apparent authority of a single partner in any kind of partnership.

(a)   To execute a deed such as a legal mortgage of property; for this he requires a power of attorney executed by all the partners.

(b)   To give a guarantee of another person's debt unless it is the custom in the firm's trade to do so.

(c)   To submit a dispute to arbitration.

(d)   To accept property, eg fully-paid shares of a company, in satisfaction of a debt owed to the firm.

The partnership agreement

6.21   There is no legal requirement for a written partnership agreement. A partnership may be established without formality by oral agreement or even by conduct. But in practice there are advantages in setting down in writing (signed by the partners) the terms of their association. This is called a 'partnership agreement' or 'articles of partnership'.

(a)   It fills in the details which the law would not imply - the nature of the firm's business, the firm name, and the bank at which the firm will maintain its bank account.

(b)   A written agreement serves to override terms otherwise implied by the Partnership Act 1890 which are inappropriate to the partnership. The Act for example implies (unless otherwise agreed) that partners share profits equally. But in many firms the older partners take a larger profit share than the younger ones.

Terms implied by the Partnership Act 1890

6.22 The partnership agreement is often used as a way of codifying the relationship and can exclude terms implied by the Partnership Act 1890. Some of the more important areas covered by this Act are as follows.

(a) *Freedom of variation.* Under s 19 Partnership Act 1890, the partnership agreement may be varied with the consent of all the partners. This may be formal or informal.

(b) Good faith. There is a duty of utmost good faith once the partnership is established, although the contract of partnership is not itself *uberrimae fidei* ('of the utmost good faith').

(c) *Profits and losses.* These are shared equally in the absence of contrary agreement. However, if the partnership agreement states that profits are to be shared in certain proportions then, prima facie, losses are to be shared in the same proportions: s 24.

(d) *Interest on capital.* None is paid on capital except by agreement. However, a partner is entitled to 5% interest on advances beyond his original capital: s 24.

(e) *Indemnity.* The firm must indemnify any partner against liabilities incurred in the ordinary and proper conduct of the partnership business or in doing anything necessarily done for the preservation of the partnership property or business: s 24.

(f) *Management.* Every partner is entitled to take part in managing the firm's business; ordinary management decisions can be made by a majority of partners: s 24.

(g) *Change in business.* Any decision on changing the nature of the partnership's business must be unanimous: s 24.

(h) *Remuneration.* No partner is entitled to remuneration such as salary for acting in the partnership business: s 24.

(i) *Records and accounts.* These must be kept at the main place of business, and must be open to inspection by all partners: s 24.

(j) *New partners.* New partners must only be introduced with the consent of all existing partners: s 24.

(k) *Expulsion.* A partner may only be expelled by a majority of votes when the partnership agreement allows; even then, the power must only be used in good faith and for good reason: s 25.

(l) *Misrepresentation.* When a partner is induced to enter into a partnership by misrepresentation he remains liable to creditors for obligations incurred whilst a partner, but he has several remedies against the maker of the statement including, for example, rescission and/or damages.

(m) *Dissolution.* The authority of the partners after dissolution continues so far as is necessary to wind up the partnership affairs and complete transactions already begun. On dissolution, any partner can insist on realisation of the firm's assets (including goodwill), payment of the firm's debts and distribution of the surplus, subject to any contrary agreement.

(n) *Capital deficiency.* A distinction is made between a loss (including a capital loss such as the sale of a fixed asset for less than its book value) and a capital deficiency. It can happen that as a result of normal losses a partner's capital is exhausted and in addition he becomes (by reason of his share of the losses) a debtor to the firm. If in those circumstances he is unable to pay what he owes to the firm, there is a capital deficiency. If there are two or more solvent partners with credit balances on capital account the assets (less the irrecoverable sum owed by the insolvent partner) will be less than the aggregate of those balances. They share the deficiency not as a loss but in ratio to the amounts of capital which they originally contributed to the firm. This is the rule in *Garner v Murray 1904*.

Dissolution

6.23 Dissolution of a partnership occurs in the following situations.

(a) By *passing of time*, if the partnership was entered into for a fixed term.

(b) By *termination of the venture*, if entered into for a single venture.

(c) By the *death or bankruptcy* of a partner, unless the partnership agreement otherwise provides.

(d) By *subsequent illegality*, such as an event which makes it unlawful to continue the business.

(e) By *notice* given by a partner if it is a partnership of indefinite duration.

(f) By *order of the court* granted to a partner, for one or several reasons - for example the permanent incapacity of a partner or because it is just and equitable to order dissolution.

Supervision

6.24 There is no formal statutory supervision of partnerships. Their accounts need not be in prescribed form nor is an audit necessary. The public has no means or legal right of inspection of the firm's accounts or other information such as companies must provide.

6.25 If, however, the partners carry on business under a firm name which is not the surnames of them all, say, 'Smith, Jones & Co', they are required to disclose the names of the partners on their letterheads and at their places of business. Business Names Act ss 1 and 4. They are required to make a return of their profits for income tax and usually to register for VAT.

Other matters

6.26 Other matters relevant to partnerships are as follows.

(a) There are no equivalent restrictions on *distribution of capital* to those contained in companies legislation. The assets transferred as capital are the partners'; there is no exchange for shares.

(b) A partnership, unlike a company, cannot create a *floating charge* over its assets - such as stock in trade or book debts - as security for a loan.

7 DIFFERENCES BETWEEN COMPANIES AND PARTNERSHIPS
6/94, 12/94, 6/95, 6/96, 12/96, 6/97

7.1 The owners of a small business have a choice whether to trade as a partnership or as a company although, as noted above, some professions, including solicitors, do not permit their members to practise as companies. The choice is often determined by the amount of tax likely to be paid under one alternative or the other. There are however a number of other factors of comparison.

7.2 The crucial factors (apart from tax) which often swing a decision as to whether to incorporate or to remain a partnership are *limited liability* and *privacy*. The former is clearly an advantage for anyone seeking to invest money or who wishes to protect himself against further outlay. The lack of privacy, however, may be offputting; even a small company must prepare annual accounts, have them audited and (usually) lay them before a general meeting. This is often expensive, and is particularly burdensome on small, proprietor-run companies. Since August 1994, small companies (now most of those with a turnover below £350,000) are exempt from the requirement for an annual audit.

7.3 The principal differences between companies and partnerships can be summarised under the following headings.

(a) Legal entity.
(b) Liability of members/partners.
(c) Perpetual succession.
(d) Transferability of interest.

(e) Ownership of assets.
(f) Repayment of capital.
(g) Management.
(h) Written constitution.
(i) Accounts and audit.
(j) Security/charges.

Review of liability for partnerships

7.4 Proposals have been put forward by the DTI for limited liability partnerships in the UK in the wake of Jersey law reform. Such partnerships will have the benefit of separate legal personality and limited liability. Price Waterhouse and Ernst & Young, two of the major accountancy firms, announced in 1996 that they intend to registered as limited liability partnerships in Jersey. You should keep an eye on the press for further developments in this area.

Exercise

Using the above headings, draw up a table which sets out the differences between companies and partnerships.

Solution

	Company	*Partnership*
(a)	Separate entity	No separate entity
(b)	Members' liability may be limited	Partners' liability usually unlimited
(c)	Perpetual succession - no cessation by change of member ship	A change of partners is a termination of the old firm and the beginning of a new one
(d)	Members own transferable shares	A partner can assign his interest but the assignee does not become a partner
(e)	Company (not members) own assets	Partners jointly own partnership property
(f)	Capital subscribed by shareholders may only be repaid to them under certain rules	Partners may (by mutual agreement) withdraw capital as they wish
(g)	A company must have one or more directors. A member has no involvement in management	Partners are entitled to participate in management and are agents of the firm
(h)	A company always has a written constitution	A partnership may exist without any written partnership agreement
(i)	Usually, a company must deliver annual accounts, annual returns and other notices to Registrar of Companies	A partnership must disclose the names of the partners. But no one except a partner has any right to inspect accounts
(j)	A company may offer security by way of floating charge over its assets	Partners cannot usually provide security by a floating charge on goods

Chapter roundup

- In legal terms the word 'person' is used to denote both individual human beings (natural persons) and other bodies. The law attaches rights to a person and imposes legal obligations on him. Legal persons include natural persons and artificial legal persons (for example corporate bodies and local authorities).

- Because it is a separate legal entity a company has the following features.

   o Limited liability of its *members,* not of the company itself.

   o Transferable shares in its ownership.

   o Perpetual succession.

   o Ownership of a company's assets, rights and liabilities is vested in the company.

   o Capital provided by members whose liability for the company's debts is limited to that amount.

   o Companies are subject to detailed supervision.

   o Management is effected by directors

   o A written constitution is necessary.

- Companies may be distinguished as to whether they are public or private companies or as to whether they have limited or unlimited liability of members.

- A public company has to meet much more stringent rules on disclosures, accounts and loans to directors, as well as formalities in documentation.

- Partnership is defined as 'the relation which subsists between persons carrying on a business in common with a view of profit'. A partnership is not a separate legal person distinct from its members - it is merely a 'relation' between persons. Each partner (there must be at least two) is personally liable for all the debts of the firm. A partnership may exist without any formal documentation or procedure (although many firms do have such a formal agreement).

- In the absence of express terms in a partnership agreement, the 1890 Act implies a number of terms into the relationship.

- Each partner is an agent of the firm when he acts in carrying on in the usual way business of the kind carried on by the firm, although his authority may be restricted by the other partners. The authority of an individual partner varies depending on whether the firm is commercial or non-commercial.

Test your knowledge

1   What are the four categories into which corporations may be classified? (see para 1.8)

2   Outline the facts of *Salomon v Salomon & Co Ltd 1897* (2.1)

3   Explain the concept of limited liability (2.3)

4   What is the written constitution of a company? (2.14)

5   List eight differences between public and private companies. (3.3)

6   What is a company limited by guarantee? (3.6)

7   What documents should be delivered to the Registrar of Companies when a company is registered? (4.2)

8   When might the veil of incorporation be lifted? (5.2)

9   What are the facts of *Gilford Motor Co Ltd v Horne 1933*? (5.14)

10   Give an example of the lifting of the veil when this is in the public interest. (5.15, 5.16).

11   How can a retiring partner avoid becoming an 'apparent member' of a partnership? (6.14)

Now try illustrative question 10 at the end of the Study Text

Part E
Contract

Chapter 11

INTRODUCTION TO THE LAW OF CONTRACT

This chapter covers the following topics.

1   Definitions of contract

2   Factors affecting the modern contract

3   The essentials of a contract

Introduction

This chapter introduces the topic of the law of contract. The essential elements for the formation of a contract are discussed in detail in Chapters 12 to 14 and the concept of contractual capacity is examined in chapter 15.

The nineteenth century saw English contract law develop into a form which is recognisable today. One important influence came from France. In Pothier's *Treatise on the Law of Obligations,* translated into English in 1806, the author wrote that contract depended on 'a concurrence of intention in two parties, one of who promises something to the other, who on his part accepts such promise'. In 1879, Anson wrote in *Principles of the English Law of Contract* that 'we may regard contract as a combination of the two ideas of agreement and obligation'. He was influenced by a second Frenchman, Savigny.

If continental legal principles formed one influence on English contract law, a second influence was nineteenth century economic theory, particularly the belief that individualism was a hallmark of a civilised society. However, the individual's freedom of contract, a concept which originated in the work of Adam Smith, was not fully compatible with a desire to protect the disadvantaged, particularly in their dealings with large or monopolistic organisations. Restrictions have therefore been imposed on freedom of contract by Parliament, in the form of statute.

The coverage of the law of contract in this part (chapters 11-16) of this Study Text addresses the requirements of the syllabus for the *Introduction to English and European Community Law* examination paper . The syllabus is designed to provide an introduction to the law of contract and provides coverage of binding agreements with reference to the doctrines of privity and formalities.

A greater understanding of the law of contract developed through further study of the subject area will inevitably be to the student's advantage. In Part G of the study text we provide additional material on the law of contract to extend your knowledge of this subject area. You will study these areas in greater depth in the pre-professional examination in *Business Law.*

1   DEFINITIONS OF CONTRACT

1.1   A contract may be defined as an *agreement which legally binds the parties.* A party to a contract is bound because he has agreed to be bound. The underlying theory, then, is that a contract is the outcome of 'consenting minds'. However, this is in itself misleading; no court can discover the *intent* of a party to a contract. Parties are not judged by what is in their minds, but by what they have said, written or done. It is often said that English law adopts an objective test of agreement.

1.2   Contracts are sometimes referred to as *enforceable agreements.* This too is somewhat misleading. English law will not usually allow one party to force the other to fulfil his part of the bargain. He will usually be restricted to the remedy of damages.

2 FACTORS AFFECTING THE MODERN CONTRACT

2.1 Many principles of modern contract law are strongly influenced by the events and important cases of the nineteenth century. However, a number of developments in the twentieth century should be brought into consideration.

Inequality of bargaining power

2.2 It is almost invariably the case that the two parties to a contract bring with them differing levels of bargaining power. Many contracts are made between experts and ordinary consumers. It may be said that there is a stronger party and a weaker party in many cases. The law will intervene only where the former takes *unfair* advantage of his position.

The standard form contract

2.3 Mass production and nationalisation have led to the standard form contract. The standard form contract is a standard document prepared by many large organisations and setting out the terms on which they contact with their customers. The individual must usually take it or leave it - he does not really 'agree' to it. For example, a customer has to accept his supply of electricity on the electricity board's terms - he is not likely to succeed in negotiating special terms, unless he represents a large consumer of electricity, such as a factory.

2.4 In *Schroeder Music Publishing Co Ltd v Macaulay 1974* Lord Diplock described the situation as follows.

> 'The terms of this kind of standard form of contract have not been the subject of negotiation between the parties to it, or approved by any organisation representing the interests of the weaker party. They have been dictated by that party whose bargaining power, either exercised alone or in conjunction with others providing similar goods or services, enables him to say "If you want these goods or services at all, these are the only terms on which they are obtainable. Take it or leave it." '

Consumer protection

2.5 In the second half of the twentieth century, there has been a surge of interest in consumer matters. In 1961, the Molony Committee on Consumer Protection reported a 'growing tendency for manufacturers to appeal directly to the public by forceful national advertising'. This new method of doing business arrived together with the further influence of 'the development of a mass market for extremely complex mechanical and electrical goods ... [whose] performance cannot in some cases be accurately established by a short trial; ... inherent faults may only come to light when the article breaks down after a period of use'. These developments were identified as leading to a greater need for consumer protection. The consumer could no longer rely on his own judgement when buying sophisticated goods or services.

2.6 Consumer interests are now served by:

(a) *consumer protection agencies*, which include government departments (the Office of Fair Trading) and independent bodies (the Consumers Association); and

(b) *legislation*.

2.7 *Public policy* sometimes requires that the freedom of contract should be modified. For example, the Consumer Credit Act 1974, the Unfair Contract Terms Act 1977 and the Unfair Terms in Consumer Contracts Regulations 1994 all regulate the extent to which contracts can contain certain terms, the former in consumer credit agreements specifically and the latter in contracts generally. The consumer is further protected by the law of tort (covered in Part G) and consumer protection legislation such as the Consumer Protection Act 1987.

3   THE ESSENTIALS OF A CONTRACT   *6/98*

3.1   The courts will usually look for the evidence of three elements in any contract. The essential elements of a contract are as follows.

(a)   There is an agreement made by *offer and acceptance*.

(b)   The parties must have an *intention to create legal relations* between themselves.

(c)   There is a bargain by which the obligations assumed by each party are supported by *consideration* (value) given by the other.

3.2   Even if these essential elements can be shown, a contract may not necessarily be valid. The validity of a contract may also be affected by any of the following factors.

(a)   *Capacity*. Some persons have only restricted capacity to enter into contracts and are not bound by agreements made outside those limits.

(b)   *Form*. Some contracts (not all) must be made in a particular form or supported by written evidence.

(c)   *Content*. In general the parties may enter into a contract on whatever terms they choose. But a contract can only be enforced if it is sufficiently complete and precise in its terms. Some terms which the parties do not express may be implied and some terms which the parties do express are overridden by statutory rules.

(d)   *Genuine consent*. A misrepresentation or mistake made by one party to the contract may affect the validity of a contract.

(e)   *Legality*. The courts will not enforce a contract which is deemed to be illegal or contrary to public policy.

3.3   A contract which does not satisfy the relevant tests may be either void, voidable or unenforceable.

3.4   A *void* contract is treated as being no contract at all. The parties have no rights or obligations arising under a void contract, and property transferred under it will be recoverable.

3.5   The law will declare a contract void, for example, where there is a *common mistake* as to some fundamental term (such as the subject matter) and no legal consequences will attach to it. Thus in *Couturier v Hastie 1852*, a contract for the sale of a cargo of corn was declared void since, unknown to both parties, the cargo had already been sold by the master of the ship. Similarly where it turns out that property contracted to be purchased in fact already belongs to the purchaser, the contract for sale and purchase will be void (*Cochrane v Willis 1865*).

3.6   Another example of a void contract may be where it is declared *illegal* or *contrary to public policy*. Some contracts may be declared void by *statute*, for example restrictive trading agreements, resale price maintenance agreements, and cartel agreements.

3.7   Some may be void at common law on the grounds of public policy such as contracts in restraint of trade or agreements to commit crime or to promote sexual immorality or other corruption.

3.8   In certain cases it may be possible to treat separately those parts of a contract which are void and those which are valid. In such cases, the valid part may remain valid and enforceable.

3.9   A *voidable* contract is one which one of the parties may avoid and terminate at his option. The contract remains valid unless and until the innocent party chooses to terminate it. Property transferred before avoidance is usually irrecoverable from a third party who acted in good faith.

3.10   Voidable contracts include those which have been induced by *misrepresentation, duress* or *undue influence*. Thus in *Car & Universal Finance Co Ltd v Caldwell 1965*, a car was sold to a rogue who fraudulently misrepresented that his cheque would be honoured. The contract was voidable and the seller's election to rescind the contract, by informing the police and the AA of the fraud, was held to be effective.

3.11 When a third party has acquired rights which would be prejudiced by rescission of the contract, then the contract with the third party is valid.

Lewis v Averay 1972
Lewis sold his car to a rogue who misrepresented his identity. The rogue then sold the car on to Averay, who took the car in good faith. The cheque paid to Lewis bounced, and Lewis sought to recover the car from Averay.

Held: The contract between Lewis and the rogue was voidable for misrepresentation but the sale to Averay took place before Lewis tried to rescind and so Averay could keep the car.

3.12 In addition, contracts entered into by a *minor* where he acquires some sort of continuing interest will be voidable by the minor during his minority and within a reasonable time after attaining his majority. These contracts include those concerning land, purchases of shares, partnership agreements and marriage settlements.

3.13 An *unenforceable* contract is a valid contract but one where it is not in the form required by law. For example, written evidence of its terms may be required by law (such as in a contract for the sale of land) but these may not be available. Property transferred under an unenforceable contract cannot be recovered, even from the other party to the contract. If either party refuses to perform his part of the contract, the other party cannot compel him to do so. Thus a contract of guarantee will be unenforceable where there is no written evidence of its terms, as is required by law.

3.14 You will find it easier to grasp these general principles after you have studied their application in particular areas of the law contract.

Exercise

What are the essential elements of a binding contract?

Solution

There must be an intention to create legal relations. There must be an agreement made by offer and acceptance. There must be consideration.

Chapter roundup

- A valid contract is a legally binding agreement, formed by the mutual consent of two parties. The law seeks to protect the idea of 'freedom of contract', although contractual terms may be regulated by statute, particularly where the parties are of unequal bargaining strength. The three essential elements of a contract are offer and acceptance, consideration and intention to enter into legal relations.

- There are a number of vitiating factors which may affect the validity of a contract. For a contract to be binding it must also satisfy various tests relating to legality, the form of the agreement, content of the agreement, genuineness of consent and the capacity of the parties to contract.

- A contract which does not satisfy the relevant tests above may be void (neither party is bound because no genuine agreement has been reached), voidable (the contract is binding unless and until one party chooses to repudiate or avoid it), or unenforceable (the contract is valid but its terms cannot be enforced in a legal sense (although it may be ratified)).

Test your knowledge

1   What is a standard form contract? (see para 2.3)

2   Give two examples of legislation which protects the consumer who enters into a commercial contract (2.7)

3   List five factors which may affect the validity of a contract (3.2)

4   Distinguish void, voidable and unenforceable contracts (3.4-3.13)

Now try illustrative question 11 at the end of the Study Text

Chapter 12

OFFER AND ACCEPTANCE

This chapter covers the following topics.

1 Offer

2 Acceptance

3 Communication of acceptance

4 Termination of offer

5 Agreement without offer and acceptance

Introduction

In Chapter 11 we introduced the general principles of the law of contract. In this chapter we consider one of the three essential elements of a contract.

The first essential element of a binding contract is agreement. To determine whether or not an agreement has been reached, the courts will consider whether one party has made a firm offer which the other party has accepted.

In most contracts, offer and acceptance may be made orally or in writing, or they may be implied by the conduct of the parties. The person making an offer is the *offeror* and the person to whom an offer is made is the *offeree*.

The particular significance of offer and acceptance is that a binding contract is thereby formed, so new terms cannot thereafter be introduced into the contract unless both parties agree. From this moment on the terms of the contract appear from the offer and acceptance rather than from the unexpressed intentions of the parties. As we will see in Chapter 16, though, there are circumstances in which additional terms may be *implied* into a contract by law.

---

1 OFFER *6/94, 12/94, 6/95, 12/95, 6/96, 6/99*

1.1 An offer is a definite promise to be bound on specific terms. It cannot be vague. However, if an apparently vague offer can be made certain by reference to the parties' previous dealing or the customs of the trade, then it will be regarded as certain.

> *Gunthing v Lynn 1831*
> The offeror offered to pay a further sum for a horse if it was 'lucky'.
>
> *Held:* the offer was too vague and no contract could be formed by any purported acceptance.

> *Hillas & Co Ltd v Arcos Ltd 1932*
> The plaintiffs agreed to purchase from the defendants '22,000 standards of softwood goods of fair specification over the season 1930'. The agreement contained an option to buy a further 100,000 standards in 1931, without terms as to the kind or size of timber being specified. The 1930 transaction took place, in spite of the vague specification used, but the sellers sought to prevent the buyers from exercising the option. They refused to supply any wood in 1931, saying that the agreement was too vague to bind the parties.

Held: the missing terms of the agreement could be ascertained by reference to previous transactions between the parties. The wording used, and the previous transactions, showed a sufficient intention to be bound.

1.2 A definite offer does not have to be made to a particular person. It may be made to a class of persons or to the world at large. (The principles in the last three defences raised in the case below will be considered further later.)

> *Carlill v Carbolic Smoke Ball Co 1893*
> The manufacturers of a patent medicine published an advertisement by which they undertook to pay '£100 reward .... to any person who contracts .... influenza .... after having used the smoke ball three times daily for two weeks'. The advertisement added that £1,000 had been deposited at a bank 'showing our sincerity in this matter'. The plaintiff read the advertisement, purchased the smoke ball and used it as directed. She contracted influenza and claimed her £100 reward. In their defence the manufacturers argued a number of defences.

(a) The offer was so vague that it could not form the basis of a contract as no time limit was specified.

(b) It was not an offer which could be accepted since it was offered to the whole world.

(c) The plaintiff had not communicated to them her acceptance of the offer.

(d) The plaintiff had not supplied any consideration.

(e) The offer was mere sales 'puff' not intended to create legal relations.

> *Held*: the court considered each defence as follows:

(a) The smoke ball must protect the user during the period of use - the offer was not vague.

(b) Such an offer was possible, by comparison with so called 'reward cases'. The court took the view that the advertisement was an offer to the whole world; not an attempt to contract with the whole world but only with that limited portion of the public who came forward and claimed on the basis of the offer. This is similar to a situation where a reward is offered.

(c) Communication was not necessary, again a comparison was drawn with reward cases.

(d) The act of sniffing the smoke ball was consideration (the purchase price was consideration for a contract with the retailer).

(e) The deposit of £1,000 indicated an intention to create legal relations.

1.3 An offer must be distinguished from:

(a) the mere supply of information; and
(b) an invitation to treat.

The mere supply of information

1.4 Only an offer in the proper sense (made with the intention that it shall become binding when accepted) may be accepted so as to form a binding contract.

> *Harvey v Facey 1893*
> The plaintiff telegraphed to the defendant 'Will you sell us Bumper Hall Pen? Telegraph lowest cash price'. The defendant telegraphed in reply 'Lowest price for Bumper Hall Pen, £900'. The plaintiff telegraphed to accept what he regarded as an offer; the defendant made no further reply.
>
> *Held*: The defendant's telegram was merely a statement of his minimum price if a sale were to be agreed. It was not an offer which the plaintiff could accept. No contract had been made.

1.5   But if, in the course of negotiations for a sale, the vendor states the price at which he will sell, that statement may be an offer which can be accepted. Where 'the parties would regard themselves at the end of the correspondence, quite correctly, as having struck a bargain for the sale and purchase of the property', they are held to have made a contract.

> *Bigg v Boyd Gibbons 1971*
> In the course of correspondence the defendant rejected an offer of £20,000 by the plaintiff and added 'for a quick sale I would accept £26,000 .... if you are not interested in this price would you please let me know immediately' (so that the he might open negotiations with another potential purchaser). The plaintiff accepted this price of £26,000 and the defendant acknowledged his acceptance, stating that he had given instructions for the sale to his solicitor.
>
> *Held*: in this context the defendant must be treated as making an offer (at £26,000) which the plaintiff had accepted.

1.6   Reference to a more detailed document will not necessarily protect one party. A 'promise' which makes such reference may be construed as an offer which creates a legal obligation.

> *Bowerman and Another v Association of British Travel Agents Ltd 1996*
> The case arose out of the insolvency in 1991 of a tour operator through whom a school party (including Emma Bowermann) had booked a holiday. The party claimed a full refund under the ABTA scheme of protection, which did not however cover the holiday insurance premium. This was explained in ABTA's handbook, to which customers were referred, but had not been seen by the teacher booking the holiday. The plaintiff argued that the 'ABTA promise' (widely advertised in the press) constituted an offer to the public at large, and that offer was accepted when the holiday was booked with the relevant tour operator. ABTA counter-argued that it was not so or that, if the 'promise' was intended to create contractual relations, it did so only on the basis of an offer on the terms of the ABTA handbook ie excluding reimbursement of the insurance premium.
>
> *Held:* the public had been encouraged by ABTA to read the written 'ABTA promise' as creating a legally binding obligation to reimburse all the expenses of the holiday. Hobhouse, LJ stated: 'A contracting party cannot escape liability by saying that he had his fingers crossed behind his back!' The court found that the plaintiff was entitled to full reimbursement.

A statement of intention

1.7   Advertising that an event such as an auction will take place is not an offer to sell which may be accepted; potential buyers may not sue the auctioneer for having made an offer if the auction does not take place: *Harris v Nickerson 1873*. This is categorised as a *statement of intention*, which is not actionable.

1.8   Similarly, a sign on private land stating that unauthorised vehicles will be wheel-clamped cannot be construed as an offer (which is accepted by a driver who parks on that land). Both of these are examples of statements of intention, which are not actionable.

An invitation to treat

1.9   Where a party is initiating negotiations, or inviting another party to make an offer, he is said to have made an invitation to treat. An invitation to treat is not an offer in itself and cannot be converted into a contract by acceptance.

1.10   There are four types of invitation to treat.

(a)   Auction sales.
(b)   Advertisements (for example price lists or newspaper advertisements).
(c)   Exhibition of goods for sale.
(d)   An invitation for tenders.

Auction sales

1.11   An auctioneer's request for bids is not a definite offer to sell to the highest bidder, it is rather an invitation to treat. The bid itself is the offer, which the auctioneer is then free to accept or reject: *Payne v Cave 1789*.

Advertisements

1.12   An advertisement of goods for sale is an attempt to induce offers and is therefore classified as an invitation to treat.

> *Partridge v Crittenden 1968*
> Mr Partridge placed an advertisement in Cage and Aviary Birds magazine's 'classified' columns containing the words 'Bramblefinch cocks, bramblefinch hens, 25s each'. One person who, in response to the advertisement, purchased a bird, reported Partridge to the RSPCA, who brought a prosecution against him for offering for sale a protected species in contravention of the Protection of Birds Act 1954. The justices, satisfied that the bird in question was a wild bird which had been trapped, convicted Partridge. He appealed.
>
> *Held*: the conviction was quashed. Although there had been a sale in contravention of the Act, the prosecution could not rely on the offence of 'offering for sale', as the advertisement constituted an invitation to treat.

1.13   The circulation of a price list is also an invitation to treat: *Grainger v Gough 1896*. In this case, Lord Herschell explained why it could not be an offer.

> 'The transmission of such a price-list does not amount to an offer to supply an unlimited quality of the wine described at the price named, so that as soon as an order is given there is a binding contract to supply that quantity. If it were so, the merchant might find himself involved in any number of contractual obligations to supply wine of a particular description which he would be quite unable to carry out, his stock of wine of that description being necessarily limited'.

Exhibition of goods for sale

1.14   Displaying goods in a shop window or on the open shelves of a self service shop (with a price tag), or advertising goods for sale is to invite customers to make offers to purchase, or an 'invitation to treat'. It is *not* an offer to sell.

> *Fisher v Bell 1961*
> A shopkeeper was prosecuted for offering for sale an offensive weapon by exhibiting a flick knife in his shop window.
>
> *Held*: 'according to the ordinary law of contract, the display of an article with a price on it in a shop window is merely an invitation to treat. It is in no sense an offer for sale the acceptance of which constitutes a contract.'
>
> *Pharmaceutical Society of Great Britain v Boots Cash Chemists (Southern) 1952*
> Certain drugs containing poisons could only be sold 'under the supervision of a registered pharmacist.' The plaintiff claimed this rule had been broken by Boots who put supplies of these drugs on open shelves in a self-service shop. Boots, however, contended that there was no sale until a customer brought the goods which he had selected to the cash desk at the exit and offered to buy them. A registered pharmacist was stationed at this point.
>
> *Held*: The court found for the defendant and commented that if it were true that a customer accepted an offer to sell by removing goods from the shelf he could not then change his mind and put them back as this would constitute breach of contract. Plainly neither Boots nor their customers intended such an absurd result.

Invitation for tenders

1.15 A tender is an estimate submitted in response to a prior request. When a person tenders for a contract he is making an offer to the person who has advertised a contract as being available. An invitation for tenders does not amount to an offer to contract with the person quoting the lowest price.

2   ACCEPTANCE   *6/94, 12/94, 6/95, 12/95, 6/96, 12/98*

2.1 Acceptance may be by express words or by action (as in *Carlill's* case). It may also be inferred from conduct.

> *Brogden v Metropolitan Railway Co 1877*
> For many years the plaintiff supplied coal to the defendant. He suggested that they should enter into a written agreement and the defendant's agent sent a draft to him for consideration. The plaintiff added the name of an arbitrator in a space left for the purpose and, having marked it 'approved', returned the amended draft to the defendant's agent. The agent took no further action on it. The plaintiff continued to supply coal and the parties applied to their dealings the terms of the draft agreement, but they never signed a final version of it. The plaintiff later denied that there was any agreement between him and the defendant.
>
> *Held*: the return of the draft was not an acceptance of the company's offer, since the plaintiff had added a new term which the company had not accepted or rejected. However, the subsequent conduct of the parties was only explicable on the assumption that they both agreed to the terms of the draft. The draft agreement became a binding contract as soon as the defendant ordered and the plaintiff supplied coal after the return of the draft to the agent.

Silence

2.2 There must, however, be some act on the part of the offeree to indicate his acceptance. Mere passive inaction is not acceptance.

> *Felthouse v Bindley 1862*
> The plaintiff wrote to his nephew offering to buy the nephew's horse for £30.15s, adding 'If I hear no more about him, I consider the horse mine at that price'. The nephew intended to accept his uncle's offer but did not reply. He instructed the defendant, an auctioneer, in whose possession the horse was at the time, not to sell the horse by auction. Owing to a misunderstanding the horse was sold to someone else. The uncle sued the auctioneer in conversion (a tort alleging wrongful disposal of another's property).
>
> *Held*: the action failed. There could be no acceptance by silence in these circumstances - the offeror cannot impose acceptance merely because the offeree does not reject the offer. The plaintiff had no title to the horse and could not sue in conversion.

2.3 Goods which are sent or services which are rendered to a person who did not request them are not 'accepted' merely because he does not return them to the sender. His silence is not acceptance of them, even if the sender includes a statement that he is deemed to have agreed to buy and/or pay unless he rejects them: Unsolicited Goods and Services Act 1971.

2.4 Indeed, provided the goods were sent with a view to his acquiring them otherwise than for a trade or business, and he has not agreed to pay for or to return them, the recipient may treat them as an unsolicited gift. However if, within six months, the sender tries to repossess them or the recipient unreasonably prevents repossession the goods are not deemed to be his.

Counter-offer

2.5 Acceptance must be unqualified agreement to the terms of the offer. *Acceptance which introduces any new terms is a counter-offer.* A counter-offer is a final rejection of the original offer. If a counter-offer is made, the original offeror may accept it, but if he rejects it his original offer is no longer available for acceptance.

> *Hyde v Wrench 1840*
> The defendant offered to sell property to the plaintiff for £1,000 on 6 June. Two days later, the plaintiff made a counter-offer of £950 which the defendant rejected on 27 June. The plaintiff then informed the defendant on 29 June that he accepted the original offer of £1,000.
>
> *Held:* the original offer of £1,000 had been terminated by the counter-offer of £950 made on 8 June; it could not therefore be revived by the plaintiff changing his mind and tendering a subsequent acceptance.

2.6 A counter-offer may be accepted by the original offeror; this will have the effect of creating a binding contract.

> *Butler Machine Tool Co v Ex-cell-O Corp (England) 1979*
> The plaintiff offered to sell tools to the defendant. Their quotation included details of their standard terms and conditions of sale. The defendant 'accepted' the offer, enclosing their own standard terms, which differed from those of the plaintiff. The plaintiff acknowledged acceptance by return a tear-off slip from the order form.
>
> *Held:* the defendant's order was really a counter-offer. The plaintiff had accepted this by returning the tear-off slip.

Request for information

2.7 It is possible, however, to respond to an offer without accepting or rejecting it by making a *request for information*. Such a request may be a request as to whether or not other terms would be acceptable. This does not necessarily amount to an acceptance on these terms.

> *Stevenson v McLean 1880*
> The defendant offered to sell iron at '40s nett cash per ton, open till Monday'. The plaintiff enquired whether he would agree to a contract, at the same price, by which delivery would be spread over two months. The defendant did not reply and (within the time limit fixed by the offer), the plaintiff then sent a letter accepting the offer as made originally. Meanwhile the defendant had sold the iron to a third party, arguing that Stevenson's query was a counter-offer.
>
> *Held:* there was a contract since the plaintiff had merely enquired as to a variation of terms which was not a counter-offer. The offer was still open when it was accepted by the plaintiff.

Acceptance 'subject to contract'

2.8 Acceptance '*subject to contract*' is neither acceptance, rejection by counter-offer nor a request for information. It means that the offeree is agreeable to the terms of the offer but proposes that the parties should negotiate a formal (usually written) contract on the basis of the offer.

2.9 Neither party is bound until the formal contract is signed. Agreements for the sale of land in England are usually made 'subject to contract'. This gives the buyer protection, as he has time to investigate title and carry out a survey, but may also act to his detriment where market conditions lead to the practice of gazumping.

2.10   Acceptance 'subject to contract' must be distinguished from outright and immediate acceptance, made on the understanding that the parties wish to replace the preliminary contract later with another, more elaborate one. Even if the immediate contract is described as 'provisional', it takes effect at once.

> *Branca v Cobarro 1947*
> A vendor agreed to sell a mushroom farm under a contract which was declared to be 'a provisional agreement until a fully legalised agreement, drawn up by a solicitor and embodying all the conditions herewith stated, is signed'.
>
> *Held*: by the use of the word 'provisional', the parties had intended their agreement to be binding from the outset. They were bound by their provisional contract until, by mutual agreement, they made another to replace it.

Letters of intent

2.11   A *letter of intent* is a means by which one party gives a strong indication to another that he is likely to place a contract with him. Thus a building contractor tendering for a large construction contract may need to sub-contract certain (specialist) aspects of the work. The sub-contractor will be asked to provide an estimate so that the main contractor can finalise his own tender.

2.12   Usually, a letter of intent is worded so as not to create any legal obligation. However in some cases it may be phrased so that it includes an invitation to commence preliminary work. In such circumstances, it creates an obligation to pay for that work.

> *British Steel Corpn v Cleveland Bridge and Engineering Co Ltd 1984*
> The defendants were sub-contractors on a contract to build a bank in Saudi Arabia. They approached the plaintiffs with a view to engaging them to supply nodes for a complex steel lattice-work frame. They sent the plaintiffs a letter of intent, stating their intention to place an order on the defendants' standard terms. The plaintiffs stated that they were unwilling to contract on such terms, but started work, and eventually completed and delivered all the nodes. They sued for the value of the nodes and the defendants counter-claimed for damages for late delivery.
>
> *Held*: since the parties had not reached agreement over such matters as progress payments or late delivery, there was no contract, and so there could be no question of damages for late delivery. However, since the plaintiffs had undertaken work at the request of the defendants and the defendants had accepted this work, the plaintiffs were entitled to payment on a *quantum meruit* basis. (*Quantum meruit* is a reasonable remuneration for services rendered.)

Acceptance of a tender

2.13   As we saw earlier, an invitation for tenders is an invitation to treat. It follows that a person who makes a tender is making an offer to the person who advertised the contract as being available. There are two distinct types of tender.

(a)   A 'tender' to perform one task, such as building a new hospital, is an offer which can be accepted. Acceptance of the tender creates a legal obligation.

(b)   A 'tender' to supply or perform a series of things, up to a maximum amount, such as the supply of vegetables daily to a restaurant, is not accepted until an order is placed. It is a *standing offer*. Acceptance of the tender does not create a binding contract. Each order placed by the offeree is an individual act of acceptance creating a separate contract. He is not bound to place any orders unless he has expressly undertaken to do so.

2.14   The successful tender is regarded as a standing offer which the other party converts into a series of contracts by placing specific orders (which are acceptances). Until orders are placed there is no contract and the tenderer can terminate his standing offer.

Great Northern Railways v Witham 1873
The defendant tendered successfully for the supply of stores to the plaintiff over a period of one year. In his tender he undertook 'to supply ... such quantities as the company may order from time to time'. After making some deliveries he refused to fulfil an order which the plaintiff had given.

Held: he was in breach of contract in refusing to fulfil the order given but might revoke his tender and need not then fulfil any future orders within the remainder of the 12 month period.

2.15   An *invitation for tenders* does not amount to an offer to contract with the person quoting the lowest/best price, except where the person inviting tenders makes it clear that he is in fact making an offer, for example by the use of words such as 'we confirm that if the offer made by you is the highest offer received by us, we bind ourselves to accept such offer provided that such offer complies with the terms of this telex': *Harvela Investments Ltd v Royal Trust Co of Canada Ltd 1985*

3   COMMUNICATION OF ACCEPTANCE

3.1   The general rule is that acceptance must be communicated to the offeror and is *not effective until this has been done*.

Waiver of communication

3.2   As noted above, silence cannot constitute acceptance: *Felthouse v Bindley 1862*. But the offeror may, by his offer, dispense with the need for communication of acceptance. Such a waiver may be express or may be inferred from the circumstances. In *Carlill v Carbolic Smoke Ball Co 1893*, it was held that it was sufficient for the plaintiff to act on the offer without previously notifying her acceptance of it. This was an example of a unilateral contract, where the offer takes the form of a promise to pay money in return for an act. Similarly, acceptance by conduct will suffice in reward cases.

Prescribed mode of communication

3.3   The offeror may call for acceptance by specified means. Unless he stipulates that this is the only method of acceptance which suffices, then acceptance by some other means equally expeditious would constitute a valid acceptance: *Tinn v Hoffmann 1873* Thus a telegram or even a verbal message could be sufficient acceptance of an offer inviting acceptance 'by return of post'. This would probably apply also to acceptance by fax machine. The offeror would have to use very precise wording if a specified means of communication is to be treated as mandatory.

Yates Building Co v R J Pulleyn & Sons (York) 1975
The offer called for acceptance by registered or recorded delivery letter. The offeree sent an ordinary letter which arrived without delay.

Held: the offeror had suffered no disadvantage and had not stipulated that acceptance must be made in this way only. The acceptance was valid.

No mode of communication prescribed

3.4   As noted above, the general rule is that acceptance must be communicated to the offeror. Thus if the offeror makes an offer over the telephone, the offeree must ensure that his acceptance is understood. If interference on the line prevents the offeror from hearing the reply, no contract is formed and the offeree must repeat his acceptance. This applies to any instantaneous method of communication.

The postal rule

3.5   The offeror may expressly or by implication indicate that he expects acceptance by means of a letter sent through the post. The postal rule states that, where the use of the post is within the contemplation of both the parties, the acceptance is complete and effective as soon as a letter (if it is correctly addressed and stamped and actually put in the post) is *posted*, even though it may be delayed or even lost altogether in the post.

> *Adams v Lindsell 1818*
> The defendants made an offer by letter to the plaintiff on 2 September 1817 requiring an answer 'in course of post'. The letter of offer was misdirected and somewhat delayed in the post. It reached the plaintiffs on 5 September; they immediately posted a letter of acceptance, which reached the defendants on 9 September. If the original offer had been properly addressed, the defendants could have expected a reply by 7 September, and they assumed that the absence of a reply within the expected period indicated non-acceptance and sold the goods to another buyer on 8 September.
>
> *Held*: the acceptance was made 'in course of post' (no time limit was imposed) and was effective when posted. The contract was made on 5 September, when the acceptance was posted.

3.6   The intention to use the post for communication of acceptance may be deduced from the circumstances - for example, if the offer is made by post - without express statement to that effect.

> *Household Fire and Carriage Accident Insurance Co v Grant 1879*
> The defendant handed a letter of application for shares to the plaintiff company's agent in Swansea with the intention that it should be posted (as it was) to the company in London. The company posted an acceptance (letter of allotment) which was lost in the post, and never arrived. The defendant was called upon to pay the amount outstanding on his shares.
>
> *Held*: the defendant had to pay. The contract between the company and him had been formed when the letter of allotment was posted, regardless of the fact that it was lost in the post.

3.7   Under the postal rule, the offeror may be unaware that a contract has been made by acceptance of his offer. If that possibility is clearly inconsistent with the nature of the transaction the postal rule is excluded and the letter of acceptance takes effect only when received. In particular, if the offer stipulates a particular mode of communication, the postal rule may not apply.

> *Holwell Securities v Hughes 1974*
> Hughes granted to the plaintiff an option to purchase land to be exercised 'by notice in writing'. A letter giving notice of the exercise of the option was lost in the post.
>
> *Held*: the words 'notice in writing' must mean notice actually received by the vendor; hence notice had not been given to accept the offer (the option).

3.8   Acceptance of an offer may only be made by a person authorised to do so. This will usually be the offeree or his authorised agents.

> *Powell v Lee 1908*
> The plaintiff applied for a post as a headmaster and after a series of interviews the school management passed a resolution appointing him; however, no decision was made as to how the appointment was to be communicated. Without authorisation, the plaintiff was informed of the appointment by one of the managers. Later, it was decided to give the post to someone else. The plaintiff sued for breach of contract.
>
> *Held*: he failed in his action for breach of contract. Since communication of acceptance was unauthorised, there was no valid agreement and hence no contract.

Exercise

Under the postal rule, acceptance made by letter is complete and effective as soon as the letter is posted. Do you think that the offeree can subsequently withdraw his acceptance before the letter reaches the offeror?

Solution

Any such attempt should fail, as a binding contract is formed when the letter is posted. This view is supported by decisions in New Zealand and South Africa, but has not actually been tested in the UK courts.

3.9   It is likely that the postal rule applies in the case of communication by fax and email, although the point has not yet been tested (See Chapter 16).

Cross-offers

3.10   If two offers, identical in terms, cross in the post, there is no contract: *Tinn v Hoffmann 1873*. If A offers to sell his car to B for £1,000 and B offers to buy A's car for £1,000, there is no contract, as there is no acceptance. This phenomenon is known as *cross-offers*. In the *Tinn v Hoffmann* case, the key case on this point, it was held by a majority that no contract had been concluded. Blackburn J said the following.

> 'When a contract is made between two parties, there is a promise by one in consideration of the promise made by the other; there are two assenting minds, the parties agreeing in opinion and one having promised in consideration of the promise made by the other - there is an exchange of promises. But I do not think exchanging offers would, upon principle, be at all the same thing ... The promise or offer being made on each side in ignorance of the promise or offer made on the other side, neither of them can be construed as an acceptance of the other.'

Reward cases

3.11   The question arises as to whether contractual obligations arise if a party, in ignorance of an offer, performs an act which fulfils the terms of the offer. If A offers a *reward* to anyone who finds and returns his lost property and B, in ignorance of the offer, does in fact return it to him, is B entitled to the promised reward? There is agreement by conduct, but B is not accepting A's offer since he is unaware of it. In fact there is no contract by which A is obliged to pay the reward to B.

R v Clarke 1927
A reward of £1,000 was offered for information leading to the arrest and conviction of a murderer. If the information was provided by an accomplice, he would receive a free pardon. C saw the offer and later gave the necessary information. He claimed the reward, admitting that he had acted to save his own skin and that all thought of the reward had passed out his mind.

Held: his claim failed. Although he had seen the offer, it was not present in his mind when he acted. There could not be acceptance without knowledge of the offer.

3.12   However, acceptance may still be valid even if the offer was not the sole reason for the action.

Williams v Carwardine 1833
A reward was offered to bring criminals to book. The plaintiff, an accomplice in the crime, supplied the information, with knowledge of the reward but moved primarily by remorse at her own part in the crime.

Held: as the information was given with knowledge, the acceptance was related to the offer despite the fact that remorse was the prime motive.

4   TERMINATION OF OFFER

4.1   An offer may only be accepted (so as to form a binding contract) while the offer is still open. An offer is terminated (and can no longer be accepted) in any of the following circumstances.

   (a)   Rejection.
   (b)   Lapse of time.
   (c)   Revocation by the offeror.
   (d)   Failure of a condition to which the offer was subject.
   (e)   Death of one of the parties.

Rejection

4.2   As noted earlier, outright rejection terminates an offer. A counter-offer also terminates the original offer: *Hyde v Wrench 1840*.

Lapse of time

4.3   An offer may be expressed to last for a *specified time*. It then expires at the end of that time. If, however, there is no express time limit set, it expires after a *reasonable time*. What is reasonable depends on the circumstances of the case, on what is usual and to be expected.

> *Ramsgate Victoria Hotel Co v Montefiore 1866*
> The defendant applied to the company in June for shares and paid a deposit to the company's bank. At the end of November the company sent him an acceptance by issue of a letter of allotment and requested payment of the balance due. The defendant contended that his offer had expired and could no longer be accepted.
>
> *Held:* the offer was for a reasonable time only and five months was much more than that. It was an excessive interval. The offer had lapsed.

Revocation of an offer

4.4   The offeror may revoke his offer at any time before acceptance: *Payne v Cave 1789*.

4.5   If he undertakes that his offer shall remain open for acceptance for a specified time he may nonetheless revoke it within that time, unless by a separate contract (an option agreement) he has bound himself to keep it open for the whole of the specified time.

> *Routledge v Grant 1828*
> The defendant offered to buy the plaintiff's house for a fixed sum, requiring acceptance within six weeks. Within the six weeks specified, he withdrew his offer.
>
> *Held*: the defendant could revoke his offer at any time before acceptance, even though the time limit had not expired. The plaintiff could only have held him to his offer if there had been a separate option agreement (for which consideration must be given).

4.6   Revocation may be an express statement to that effect or may be an act of the offeror indicating that he no longer regards the offer as in force. But however he revokes it, his revocation does not take effect (and the offer continues to be available for acceptance) *until the revocation is communicated to the offeree*. This raises two important points.

4.7   While posting a letter is a sufficient act of acceptance, it is not a sufficient act of revocation of offer.

> *Byrne v Van Tienhoven 1880*
> The defendants were in Cardiff; the plaintiffs in New York. The sequence of events was as follows.

1 October   Letter posted in Cardiff, offering to sell 1,000 boxes of tinplates.
8 October   Letter of revocation of offer posted in Cardiff.
11 October   Letter of offer received in New York and telegram of acceptance sent.
15 October   Letter confirming acceptance posted in New York.
20 October   Letter of revocation received in New York. The offeree had meanwhile resold the contract goods.

Held: the letter of revocation could not take effect until received (20 October); it could not revoke the contract made by the telegram acceptance of the offer on 11 October. Simply posting a letter does not revoke the offer until it is received.

4.8   While acceptance must be communicated by the offeree or his authorised agent, revocation of offer may be communicated by any third party who is a sufficiently reliable informant.

> *Dickinson v Dodds 1876*
> The defendant, on 10 June, wrote to the plaintiff to offer property for sale at £800, adding 'this offer to be left open until Friday 12 June, 9.00 am.' On 11 June the defendant sold the property to another buyer, A. B, who had been an intermediary between Dickinson and Dodds, informed Dickinson that the defendant had sold to someone else. On Friday 12 June, before 9.00 am, the plaintiff handed to the defendant a formal letter of acceptance.
>
> *Held*: the defendant was free to revoke his offer and had done so by sale to a third party; the plaintiff could not accept the offer after he had learnt from a reliable informant of the revocation of the offer to him. His purported acceptance was too late.

Failure of a condition

4.9   An offer may be conditional. If the condition is not satisfied, the offer is not capable of acceptance.

> *Financings Ltd v Stimson 1962*
> The defendant wished to purchase a car, and on 16 March signed a hire-purchase form. The form, issued by the plaintiffs, stated that the agreement would be binding only upon signature by them. On 20 March the defendant, not satisfied with the car, returned it to the motor dealer. On 24 March the car was stolen from the premises of the dealer, and was recovered badly damaged. On 25 March the plaintiffs signed the form. They sued the defendant for breach of contract.
>
> *Held*: the defendant was not bound to take the car. His signing of the agreement was actually an offer to contract with the plaintiff. There was an implied condition in this offer that the car would be in substantially the same condition when the offer was accepted as when it was made.

Termination by death

4.10   The death of the *offeree* terminates the offer. Unless an offer is made to the world at large, it assumes the continued existence of the offeree.

4.11   The *offeror's* death terminates the offer unless the offeree accepts it in ignorance of the offeror's death, and the offer is not of a personal nature.

> *Bradbury v Morgan 1862*
> X offered to guarantee payment (up to £100) by Y in respect of goods to be supplied by the plaintiff on credit to Y. X died and the plaintiff, in ignorance of his death, continued to supply goods to Y. The plaintiff then sued X's executors on the guarantee.
>
> *Held:* X's offer was a continuing commercial offer which the plaintiff had accepted by supply of goods after X's death. The guarantee stood.

5   AGREEMENT WITHOUT OFFER AND ACCEPTANCE

5.1   The rules applied by the courts to establish the existence of a contract are based on the assumption that there is agreement between the parties. Because the courts cannot ascertain the intentions of the parties, they must rely on what the parties say or do when considering whether or not there is agreement. In certain cases they may go beyond what can be inferred from the words and actions of the parties and *construct* a contract where the usual formalities of offer and acceptance have not taken place.

> *Clarke v Dunraven 1897*
> The owners of two yachts entered them for a regatta. Each undertook in a letter to the Club Secretary to obey the Club's rules, which included an obligation to pay 'all damages' caused by fouling. While they were manoeuvring before the start of the regatta, the defendant's yacht fouled the plaintiff's yacht, which sank. The plaintiff sued for damages. The defendant argued that his only liability was under the Merchant Shipping Act 1862 and was therefore limited to £8 per ton.
>
> *Held*: a contract had been created between the parties when they entered their yachts for the regatta, at which point they had accepted the club's rules as being binding upon each other. The defendant was liable for 'all damages'.

Collateral contracts

5.2   A collateral contract is a contract the consideration for which is the making of some other contract. If there are two separate contracts by offer and acceptance between on the one hand A and B and on the other hand A and C, on terms which involve some concerted action between B and C, there may be a contract between B and C. In contracting with A, both B and C look forward to the possible relationship between them (B and C) which will result, and are deemed to offer and accept the terms of the relationship - there is a contract between B and C despite the absence of direct communication between them.

> *Shanklin Pier Ltd v Detel Products 1951*
> The defendants gave assurances to the plaintiffs, the owners of a pier, that paint manufactured by them (the defendants) would be satisfactory and durable if used in repainting the plaintiff's pier. The plaintiffs in their contract with X and Co for the repainting of the pier, specified that X and Co should use this paint. The paint proved very unsatisfactory and the remedial work cost £4,127. The plaintiffs sued the defendants for breach of undertaking. The defendants argued that there was no contract between the plaintiffs and themselves.
>
> *Held*: the contract between the plaintiffs and X and Co requiring the use of the defendant's paint (to be purchased and supplied by X and Co) was the consideration for a contract between the plaintiffs and the defendant, by which the latter guaranteed that their paint was of the quality described.

No coincidence of offer and acceptance

5.3   An interesting Court of Appeal case (not involving collateral contracts) looks as if it might have re-opened a debate on whether there must be a matching offer and acceptance.

> *G Percy Trentham Ltd v Archital Luxfer Ltd 1993*
> The plaintiffs were main contractors on a building contract. They entered into negotiations with the defendants for supply and installation of doors and windows. When the work was completed and paid for, they tried to recover a contribution towards a penalty which they had to pay under the main contract. The defendants denied that any binding contract had ever been formed. Although there had been exchanges of letters and telephone calls, there was no matching offer and acceptance and no clear agreement as to whose standard terms governed the contract.
>
> *Held*: there was a valid and binding contract. This was a case of acceptance by conduct (following *Brogden*) evidenced by the defendant's carrying out the work in

acceptance of the plaintiff's offer. The fact that the contract was executed (performance had taken place) rather than executory was of significance: 'a contract came into existence during performance even if it cannot be precisely analysed in terms of offer and acceptance.' (Note that the issue here was simply whether a contract had come into existence and not the time at which it arose or the terms on which it arose. These are added complications which future cases might address.)

Chapter roundup

- The first essential element of a binding contract is agreement. This is usually evidenced by offer and acceptance. An offer is a definite promise to be bound on specific terms, and must be distinguished from the mere supply of information and from an invitation to treat.

- Acceptance must be unqualified agreement to all the terms of the offer. It may be by express words or inferred from conduct. Inaction does not imply acceptance. A counter-offer is a rejection of the original offer.

- Acceptance is not effective until communicated to the offeror, with two exceptions. The offeror may waive the need for communication of acceptance by making an offer to the entire world, or may indicate that he expects acceptance through the post. In the latter case, the 'postal rule' applies: acceptance is complete and effective as soon as notice of it is posted.

- An offer is terminated, and no longer open for acceptance, in the following circumstances.
  - Rejection by the offeree.
  - Lapse of time
  - Revocation by the offeror.
  - Failure of a condition to which the offer was subject.
  - Death of one of the parties

- In certain circumstances, the courts may infer the existence of a contract without the formalities of offer and acceptance.

Test your knowledge

1   Give the names of a case in which an offer was made to the world at large. (see para 1.2)

2   What is an invitation to treat? (1.9)

3   When do offer and acceptance take place at an auction sale? (1.11)

4   How is the circulation of a price list categorised in the law of contract? (1.13)

5   Outline the facts of *Pharmaceutical Society of Great Britain v Boots Cash Chemists (Southern) 1952* (1.14)

6   What is a counter-offer and what is its effect at law? (2.5)

7   What is the effect of acceptance 'subject to contract'? (2.8)

8   Explain the 'postal rule'. (3.5)

9   What is a cross-offer and what is its effect at law? (3.10)

10   How can an offeree ensure that the offeror does not revoke his offer before acceptance? (4.5)

11   What is a collateral contract? (5.2)

Now try illustrative question 12 at the end of the Study Text.

Chapter 13

INTENTION TO CREATE LEGAL RELATIONS

> ## This chapter covers the following topics.
>
> 1 Domestic arrangements
>
> 2 Commercial agreements
>
> ### Introduction
>
> In Chapter 11 we introduced the general principles of the law of contract. In this chapter we consider the second of the three essential elements of a contract.
>
> An agreement is not a binding contract unless the parties intend thereby to create legal relations. This is true even if the other essential elements of a contract are present. Intention to create legal relations is thus an essential element of a binding contract. Where the parties have not expressly denied such intention, what matters is not what the parties have in their minds, but the inferences that reasonable people would draw from their words or conduct. It is an objective test. In *Carlill v Carbolic Smoke Ball Co 1893*, the defendants' deposit of £1,000 with their bankers 'to show their sincerity' was held to be clear evidence that they had contemplated legal liability and intended to create legal relations.
>
> Where there is no express statement as to whether or not legal relations are intended, as may be said to be true of the majority of contracts, the courts apply one of two presumptions to a case. *Social, domestic and family arrangements* are not usually intended to be binding. *Commercial agreements* are usually intended by the parties involved to be legally binding. This intention must be rebutted by the party seeking to deny it.

1 DOMESTIC ARRANGEMENTS   *6/97*

1.1 In most agreements no intention is expressly stated. If it is a domestic agreement between husband and wife, relatives or friends it is presumed that there is no intention to create legal relations unless the circumstances point to the opposite conclusion.

Husband and wife

1.2 Where a husband pays an allowance to his wife for her personal expenditure, it would not normally be expected that either party contemplated legal relations. *However, the fact that the parties are husband and wife does not mean that they cannot enter into a binding contract with one another.*

> *Balfour v Balfour 1919*
> The defendant was employed in Ceylon. He and his wife returned to the UK on leave but it was agreed that for health reasons she would not return to Ceylon with him. He promised to pay her £30 a month as maintenance. Later the marriage ended in divorce and the wife sued for the monthly allowance which the husband no longer paid.
>
> *Held*: an informal agreement of indefinite duration made between husband and wife whose marriage had not at the time broken up was not intended to be legally binding.

Merritt v Merritt 1970
The husband had left the matrimonial home, which was owned in the joint names of husband and wife, to live with another woman. The spouses met and held a discussion in the husband's car, in the course of which he agreed to pay her £40 a month out of which she agreed to keep up the mortgage payments on the house. The wife refused to leave the car until the husband signed a note of these agreed terms and an undertaking to transfer the house into her sole name when the mortgage had been paid off. The wife paid off the mortgage but the husband refused to transfer the house to her.

Held: in the circumstances, an intention to create legal relations was to be inferred and the wife could sue for breach of contract.

1.3   Where agreements between husband and wife or other relatives relate to *property matters* the courts are very ready to impute an intention to create legal relations.

Relatives

1.4   Agreements between other family members may also be examined by the courts.

Jones v Padavatton 1969
The plaintiff wanted her daughter to move from the USA to England in order to train as a barrister and offered to pay her a monthly allowance while she read for the Bar. The daughter did so in 1962. The allowance was never paid, but in 1964 the plaintiff bought a house in London for her daughter to use; part of the house was occupied by the daughter, rent free, and part let to tenants whose rent was collected by the daughter to cover the maintenance. In 1967 the plaintiff and her daughter quarrelled and the plaintiff issued a summons reclaiming the house. The daughter demanded the arrears of allowance.

Held: there were two agreements to consider: the daughter's agreement to read for the bar in exchange for a monthly allowance, and the agreement by which the daughter lived in her mother's house and the rent from tenants covered the maintenance. Neither agreement was intended to create legal relations. They were family arrangements which depended on the good faith of the promises made, and were not intended to be binding.

Other domestic arrangements

1.5   Domestic arrangements extend to those between people who are not related but who have a close relationship of some form. The nature of the agreement itself may lead to the conclusion that legal relations were intended.

Simpkins v Pays 1955
The defendant, her granddaughter and the plaintiff, a paying boarder, took part together each week in a competition organised by a Sunday newspaper. The arrangements over postage and other expenses were informal and the entries were made in the grandmother's name. One week they won £750; the paying boarder claimed a third share, but the defendant refused to pay on the grounds that there was no intention to create legal relations.

Held: there was a 'mutuality in the arrangements between the parties', amounting to a joint enterprise. As such it was not a 'friendly adventure' as the defendant claimed, but a contract.

2   COMMERCIAL AGREEMENTS   6/97

2.1   When businessmen enter into *commercial agreements* it is presumed that there is an intention to enter into legal relations unless this is expressly disclaimed or the circumstances (such as difficulty in enforcement) displace that presumption. Any express statement by the parties of their intention *not* to make a binding contract is conclusive.

> *Rose and Frank v Crompton 1923*
> A commercial agreement by which the defendants (a British manufacturer) appointed the plaintiff (a New York firm) to be its distributor in the USA contained a clause described as 'the Honourable Pledge Clause' which expressly stated that the arrangement was 'not subject to legal jurisdiction' in either country. The defendants terminated the agreement without giving notice as required, and refused to deliver goods ordered by the plaintiffs although they had accepted these orders when placed.

> *Held*: the general agreement was not legally binding as there was no obligation to stand by any clause in it. However the orders for goods were separate and binding contracts. The claim for damages for breach of the agreement failed, but the claim for damages for non-delivery of goods ordered succeeded.

2.2 The words relied on by a party to a commercial agreement to show that legal relations are not intended are not always clear. In such cases, the burden of proof is on the party seeking to escape liability.

> *Edwards v Skyways Ltd 1964*
> In negotiations over the terms for making the plaintiff redundant, the defendants gave him the choice either of withdrawing his total contributions from their contributory pension fund or of receiving a paid-up pension. It was agreed that if he chose the first option, the defendants would make an *ex gratia* payment to him. He chose the first option; his contributions were refunded but the *ex gratia* payment was not made. He sued for breach of contract.

> *Held*: although the defendants argued that the use of the phrase *ex gratia* showed no intention to create legal relations, this was a commercial arrangement and the burden of rebutting the presumption of legal relations had not been discharged by the defendants.

Statutory provisions

2.3 *Procedural agreements* between employers and trade unions for the settlement of disputes are not intended to give rise to legal relations in spite of their elaborate and very legal contents: s 179 Trade Union and Labour Relations (Consolidation) Act 1992.

Letters of comfort

2.4 The presumption that commercial agreements are legally binding needs to be expressly rebutted. However, for many years, holding companies have given '*letters of comfort*' to creditors of subsidiaries which purport to give some comfort as to the ability of the subsidiary to pay its debts. Such letters have always been *presumed in the past not to be legally binding*, and the decision in the case below gives the reasons for such a presumption.

> *Kleinwort Benson Ltd v Malaysia Mining Corpn Bhd 1989*
> The plaintiffs lent money to the defendant's subsidiary, having received a letter from the defendant stating 'it is our policy to ensure that the business is at all times in a position to meet its liabilities to you.' The defendant had refused to provide a full guarantee, and the bank had accepted the 'letter of comfort', charging a higher rate of interest as a result. On the collapse of the International Tin Council the subsidiary went into liquidation, and the bank claimed against the holding company, MMC, for the outstanding indebtedness.

> *Held:* the letter of comfort was a statement of existing policy and not a promise that the policy would continue in the future. Such a promise could not be implied where it was not expressly stated. Because both parties were well aware that in business parlance a 'letter of comfort' imposed moral and not legal responsibilities,

it was held not to have been given with the intention of creating legal relations. The defendant's breach of moral responsibility was of no concern to the court.

Transactions binding in honour only

2.5   If the parties state that an agreement is 'binding in honour only', this amounts to an express denial of intention to create legal relations.

> *Jones v Vernons Pools 1938*
> The plaintiff argued that he had sent to the defendant a football pools coupon on which his predictions entitled him to a dividend. The defendants denied having received the coupon. A clause on the coupon stated that the transaction should not 'give rise to any legal relationship ... but ... be binding in honour only'.
>
> *Held*: this clause was a bar to an action in court.

2.6   Oral agreements made during the course of negotiations are not binding.

> *Walford v Miles 1991*
> The defendants were negotiating the sale of a business to the plaintiffs. The plaintiffs agreed not to withdraw from negotiations and the defendants agreed to break off negotiations with a third party. The defendants, however, continued to negotiate with the third party and sold the business to the third party.
>
> *Held*: the oral agreement to withdraw from negotiations with the third party (a 'lock-out' agreement) was in effect simply an agreement to continue to negotiate and was not legally enforceable. An agreement to negotiate is not enforceable in English law. A lock-out agreement may in principle be valid, providing a time limit is specified (none was specified here) and that there is consideration (as there was here).

Exercise

Under s 1 Law Reform (Miscellaneous Provisions) Act 1970, a contract of engagement, which is in effect an agreement to marry, is not enforceable at law. Under s 29 Post Office Act 1969, acceptance by the Post Office of letters and packets for transmission and delivery does not give rise to a contract between the sender and the Post Office. What legal principle is demonstrated by these rules?

Solution

Like the provision in s 179 TULRCA 1992, these rules are examples of statutory provisions which create a statutory presumption that, in the situations described, there is no intention to create legal relations.

Chapter roundup

- Both parties to a contract must intend the agreement to give rise to legal obligations. Their intentions as to this point may be express - ' this agreement is not subject to legal jurisdiction' - or may be inferred from the circumstances.

- Social, domestic and family arrangements are assumed not to be legally binding unless the contrary is clearly shown.

- Commercial agreements are assumed to be legally binding unless the contrary is clearly demonstrated.

Test your knowledge

1 What presumption do the courts apply to domestic arrangements? (see para 1.1)

2 Outline the facts of *Simpkins v Pays 1955*. (1.5)

3 What presumption do the courts apply to commercial agreements? (2.1)

4 What is a letter of comfort? (2.4)

Now try illustrative question 13 at the end of the Study Text

Chapter 14

CONSIDERATION

This chapter covers the following topics.

1 Definitions of consideration

2 Executory, executed and past consideration

3 Consideration must move from the promisee

4 Adequacy of consideration

5 Sufficiency of consideration

6 Promissory estoppel

7 Privity of contract

Introduction

In Chapter 11 we introduced the general principles of the law of contract. In this chapter we consider the third of the three essential elements of a contract.

Imagine that a window-cleaner telephones you and tells you that, as a special promotion, he will clean your windows free of charge on the following day. If he then fails to turn up, you cannot sue him for breach of contract, because there is no contract. You have not provided any consideration. In distinguishing the characteristics of a contract, the law looks for an element of a bargain; a contractual promise is one which is not purely gratuitous.

Consideration has been an important feature of English contract law since the sixteenth century. As a general rule, it may be said that the law will not enforce a gratuitous promise. The promise which a plaintiff seeks to enforce must be shown to be part of a *bargain* to which the plaintiff has himself contributed. Consideration is what the promisee must give in exchange for the promise to him.

A promise given by a promisor to a promisee in a contract is only binding on the promisor if it is supported by consideration or the promise is in the form of a deed. (We look at deeds in Chapter 16.)

---

1 DEFINITIONS OF CONSIDERATION

12/94, 6/95, 12/95, 12/97

1.1 There have been a number of case law definitions of consideration, for example from *Currie v Misa 1875*.

> 'A valuable consideration in the sense of the law may consist either in some right, interest, profit or benefit accruing to one party, or some forbearance, detriment, loss or responsibility given, suffered or undertaken by the other'.

1.2 Another definition of consideration was given by the House of Lords in *Dunlop v Selfridge 1915*.

> 'An act or forbearance of one party, or the promise thereof, is the price for which the promise of the other is bought, and the promise thus given for value is enforceable.'

1.3 Using the language of purchase and sale, it could be said that one party must know that he has bought the other party's promises either by performing some *act* of his own or by offering a *promise* of his own.

2   EXECUTORY, EXECUTED AND PAST CONSIDERATION

2.1   It is sometimes said that consideration may be *executed* or *executory*, but it *cannot be past*. These terms are explained below.

Executed consideration

2.2   *Executed* consideration is a performed, or executed, act in return for a promise. If, for example, A offers a reward for the return of lost property, his promise becomes binding when B performs the act of returning A's property to him. A is not bound to pay anything to anyone until the prescribed act is done. C's act in Carlill's case in response to the smoke ball company's promise of reward was thus executed consideration.

Executory consideration

2.3   *Executory* consideration is a promise given for a promise. If, for example, a customer orders goods which a shopkeeper undertakes to obtain from the manufacturer, the shopkeeper promises to supply the goods and the customer promises to accept and pay for them. Neither has yet done anything but each has given a promise to obtain the promise of the other. It would be breach of contract if either withdrew without the consent of the other.

Past consideration

2.4   Both executed and executory consideration are provided at the time when the promise is given. Anything which has already been done *before* a promise in return is given is past consideration which, as a general rule, is not sufficient to make the promise binding. In such a case the promisor may by his promise recognise a moral obligation (which is not consideration), but he is not obtaining anything in exchange for his promise (as he already has it before the promise is made).

> *Re McArdle 1951*
> Under a will the testator's children were entitled to a house after their mother's death. In the mother's lifetime one of the children and his wife lived in the house with the mother. The wife made improvements to the house. The children later agreed in writing to repay to the wife the sum of £488 'in consideration of your carrying out certain alterations and improvements' to the property, in settlement of the amount spent on such improvements. But at the mother's death they refused to do so.
>
> *Held:* the work on the house had all been completed before the documents were signed. At the time of the promise the improvements were past consideration and so the promise was not binding.

2.5   If there is an existing contract and one party makes a further promise subsequent to that transaction, no contract will arise. Even if such a promise is directly related to the previous bargain, it will be held to have been made upon past consideration.

> *Roscorla v Thomas 1842*
> The plaintiff agreed to buy a horse from the defendant at a given price. When negotiations were over and the contract was formed, the defendant told the plaintiff that the horse was 'sound and free from vice'. The horse turned out to be vicious and the plaintiff brought an action on the warranty.
>
> *Held:* the express promise was made after the sale was over and was unsupported by fresh consideration. The plaintiff could show nothing but 'past' consideration and his action failed.

2.6   In three cases past consideration for a promise *does* suffice to make the promise binding.

(a) Past consideration is sufficient to create liability on a *bill of exchange* (such as a cheque) under s 27 Bills of Exchange Act 1882. Most cheques are issued to pay existing debts.

(b) After six (or in some cases twelve) years the right to sue for recovery of a debt becomes statute barred by the *Limitation Act 1980*. If, after that period, the debtor makes written acknowledgement of the creditor's claim, the claim is again enforceable at law. The debt, although past consideration, suffices.

(c) When a request is made for a service this *request may imply a promise* to pay for it. If, after the service has been rendered, the person who made the request promises a specific reward, this is treated as fixing the amount to be paid under the previous implied promise, rather than as a new promise.

> *Lampleigh v Braithwait 1615*
> The defendant had killed a man and had asked the plaintiff to obtain for him a royal pardon. The plaintiff did so, 'riding and journeying to and from London and Newmarket' at his own expense. The defendant then promised to pay him £100. He failed to pay it and was sued.
>
> *Held:* the defendant's request was regarded as containing an implied promise to pay, and the subsequent promise merely fixed the amount.

2.7 The third exception above has been somewhat revised by the courts, so that both parties must have assumed throughout their negotiations that the services were ultimately to be paid for.

> *Re Casey's Patents, Stewart v Casey 1892*
> A and B, joint owners of patent rights, asked their employee, C, as an extra task (additional to his normal duties) to find licensees to work the patents. After C had done so, A and B agreed to reward him for his past services with one third of the patent rights. A died and his executors denied that the promise made was binding.
>
> *Held:* the promise to C was binding since it merely fixed the 'reasonable remuneration' which A and B by implication promised to pay before the service was given.

3 CONSIDERATION MUST MOVE FROM THE PROMISEE

3.1 This maxim means that *only the person who has paid the price of a contract can sue on it.* As consideration is the price of a promise, the price must be paid by the person who seeks to enforce the promise (the promisee). If, for example, A promises B that (for a consideration provided by B) A will confer a benefit on C, then C cannot as a general rule enforce A's promise since C has given no consideration for it.

> *Tweddle v Atkinson 1861*
> The plaintiff married the daughter of G. On the occasion of the marriage, the plaintiff's father and G exchanged promises that they would each pay a sum of money to the plaintiff. The agreement between the two fathers expressly provided that the plaintiff should have enforceable rights against them. G died without making the promised payment and the plaintiff sued G's executor for the specified amount.
>
> *Held*: the plaintiff had provided no consideration for G's promise. In spite of the express terms of the agreement he had no enforceable rights under it.

3.2 It is not essential that the promisor should receive any benefit from the promisee. In *Tweddle's* case each father as promisee gave consideration by his promise to the other but the plaintiff was to be the beneficiary of each promise. Each father could have sued the other but the plaintiff could not sue.

3.3 The rule that consideration must move from the promisee overlaps with the rule that only a party to a contract can enforce it. Together these rules are known as the principles of privity of contract. This principle is discussed later in this chapter.

4 ADEQUACY OF CONSIDERATION

4.1 As well as determining whether consideration is valid on the grounds of being executed or executory, the court will also seek to ensure that a particular act or promise can actually be deemed to be consideration. Two overlapping rules have evolved.

(a) Consideration *need not be adequate* (that is, equal in value to the consideration received in return). There is no remedy at law for someone who simply makes a poor bargain.

(b) Consideration must be *sufficient*. It must be capable in law of being regarded as consideration.

4.2 The courts will not enquire into the adequacy of consideration. It is presumed that each party is capable of serving his own interests, and the courts will not seek to weigh up the comparative value of the promises or acts exchanged.

> *Thomas v Thomas 1842*
> By his will the plaintiff's husband expressed the wish that his widow should have the use of his house during her life. The decedents, his executors, allowed the widow to occupy the house (a) in accordance with her husband's wishes and (b) in return for her undertaking to pay a rent of £1 per annum. They later said that their promise to let her occupy the house was not supported by consideration.
>
> *Held*: compliance with the husband's wishes was not valuable consideration (no economic value attached to it), but the nominal rent was sufficient consideration, even though inadequate as a rent.

5 SUFFICIENCY OF CONSIDERATION   *6/99*

5.1 Consideration is *sufficient if it has some identifiable value*. The value may however be nominal, such as 50p in consideration of a promise worth £1 million, or it may be very subjective. The law only requires an element of bargain, not that it shall be a good bargain.

> *Chappell & Co v Nestle Co 1960*
> As a sales promotion scheme, the defendant offered to supply a record of the dance tune *Rockin' Shoes* to anyone who sent in a postal order for 1s.6d and three wrappers from 6d bars of chocolate made by them. The plaintiffs owned the copyright of the tune and sued for infringement of copyright. In the ensuing dispute over royalties the issue was whether the wrappers, which were thrown away when received, were part of the consideration for the promise to supply the record (which the defendants obtained in bulk for 4d each from the recording company). The defendants offered to pay a royalty based on the price of 1s.6d per record, but the plaintiffs rejected this, claiming that the wrappers also represented part of the consideration.
>
> *Held*: the plaintiff had required that wrappers be sent (for obvious commercial reasons). It was immaterial that the wrappers when received were of no economic value to them. The wrappers were part of the consideration as they had commercial value.

5.2 As stated earlier, forbearance or the promise of it may be sufficient consideration if it has some value or amounts to giving up something of value. A party does not need to surrender a legal right, but the *claim* to a legal right. If the claim is in fact without foundation, this does not matter, even though it may appear that the claimant has got something for nothing. The plaintiff relying on such a waiver to support a contract must show that:

(a) the claim is a reasonable one;
(b) he has an honest belief in its chances of success; and
(c) he has withheld no information which might affect the validity of the claim.

Horton v Horton 1961
Under a separation agreement, the defendant agreed to pay his wife (the plaintiff) £30 per month. Under the deed this amount was to have been a net payment, after deduction of income tax; for nine months the husband paid it without any deduction, obliging his wife to pay income tax on the £30 herself. He then signed a document agreeing to pay such amount as 'after the deduction of income tax should amount to the clear sum of £30'. He paid this for three years, then stopped, pleading that the later agreement was not supported by consideration.

Held: the later agreement *was* supported by consideration: the wife could have sued to have the original agreement rectified, but did not.

5.3   A *promise not to pursue* a genuine but disputed claim may therefore be consideration. Even forbearance without any promise to forbear may suffice.

Alliance Bank v Broom 1864
A customer who had an overdraft at his bank promised to provide security. The bank did not enforce immediate repayment of the overdraft. The customer failed to provide the agreed security and the bank sued on the promise.

Held: the bank's forbearance in not enforcing its rights was consideration for the customer's promise; the promise was enforceable.

Performance of existing contractual duties

5.4   Performance of an *existing obligation* imposed by statute is *no consideration* for a promise of reward.

Collins v Godefroy 1831
The plaintiff had been subpoena'd to give evidence on behalf of the defendant in another case. He alleged that the defendant had promised to pay him six guineas [£6.30] for appearing.

Held: there was no consideration for this promise.

5.5   But if some *extra service* is given that is *sufficient consideration*.

Glasbrook Bros v Glamorgan CC 1925
At a time of industrial unrest, colliery owners, rejecting the view of the police that a mobile force was enough, asked for and agreed to pay for a special stationary guard on the mine. Later they repudiated liability saying that the police had done no more than perform their public duty of maintaining order, and that no consideration was given.

Held: the police had done more than perform their general duties. The *extra* services given, beyond what the police in their discretion deemed necessary, were consideration for the promise to pay. If the judgment of the police authorities had been that a stationary guard was necessary, they would not have been entitled to charge for it.

5.6   In the *Glasbrook* case, neither party could call off the strike, and so the threat to law and order was not caused, directly or indirectly, by them. Where one party's actions lead to the need for heightened police presence, and the police deem this presence necessary, they may also be entitled to payment.

Harris v Sheffield United F.C. Ltd 1988
The defendants argued that they did not have to pay for a large police presence at their home matches.

Held: they had voluntarily decided to hold matches on Saturday afternoons when large attendances were likely, increasing the risk of disorder. (An important point here is that the police were required to be inside the football club's premises.)

5.7   If there is already a contract between A and B, and B promises additional reward to A if he (A) will perform his existing duties, there is no consideration from A to make that promise binding; A assumes no extra obligation and B obtains no extra rights or benefits.

Stilk v Myrick 1809
Two members of the crew of a ship deserted in a foreign port. The master was unable to recruit substitutes and promised the rest of the crew that they should share the wages of the deserters if they would complete the voyage home short-handed. The shipowners however repudiated the promise.

Held: in performing their existing contractual duties the crew gave no consideration for the promise of extra pay and the promise was not binding.

5.8   If a plaintiff does more than perform an existing contractual duty, this may amount to consideration.

Hartley v Ponsonby 1857
17 men out of a crew of 36 deserted. The remainder were promised an extra £40 each to work the ship to Bombay. The plaintiff, one of the remaining crew-members, sued to recover this amount.

Held: the large number of desertions made the voyage exceptionally hazardous, and this had the effect of discharging the original contract. The plaintiff had therefore been left free to enter into a new contract, under which his promise to complete the voyage formed consideration for the promise to pay an additional £40.

5.9   However, the courts appear to be taking a slightly different line recently on the payment of additional consideration. The line seems to be that the principles of consideration will not be applied if the dispute before the court can be dealt with on an alternative basis. However, the principles of *Foakes v Beer 1884* described below, must not be forgotten.

Williams v Roffey Bros & Nicholls (Contractors) Ltd 1990
The plaintiffs agreed to do carpentry work for the defendants, who were engaged as contractors to refurbish a block of flats, at a fixed price of £20,000. The work ran late and so the defendants, concerned that the job might not be finished on time and that they would in that event have to pay money under a penalty clause in the main contract, agreed to pay the plaintiffs an extra £10,300 to ensure the work was completed on time. They later refused to pay the extra amount.

Held: the fact that there was no apparent consideration for the promise to pay the extra was not held to be important, and in the court's view both parties derived benefit from the promise. The telling point was that the defendants' promise had not been extracted by duress or fraud: it was therefore binding.

Re Selectmove 1994
A company which was the subject of a winding-up order offered to settle its outstanding debts by instalment. An Inland Revenue inspector agreed to this proposal. The company tried to enforce it.

Held: despite the verdict in *Williams v Roffey Bros & Nicholls*, the court followed *Foakes v Beer* in holding that an agreement to pay in instalments is unenforceable. Even though the creditor might obtain some practical benefit, this is not adequate consideration to render the agreement legally binding.

Performance of existing contractual duty to a third party

5.10 If A promises B a reward if B will perform his existing contract with C, there is consideration for A's promise since he obtains a benefit to which he previously had no right, and B assumes new obligations.

> *Shadwell v Shadwell 1860*
> The plaintiff, a barrister, was engaged to marry E (an engagement to marry was at this time a binding contract). His uncle promised the plaintiff that if he (the nephew) married E (as he did), the uncle would during their joint lives pay to his nephew £150 p.a. until such time as the nephew was earning 600 guineas p.a. at the bar (which never transpired). The uncle died after eighteen years owing six annual payments. The plaintiff claimed the arrears from his uncle's executors, who denied that there was consideration for the promise.
>
> *Held:* the nephew had provided consideration as he was initially under a duty only to his fiancee, but by entering into the agreement he had put himself under obligation to the uncle too.

Waiver of existing rights

5.11 We saw earlier that *forbearance* may amount to consideration (*Horton v Horton*). Particular complications arise over sufficiency of consideration for promises to *waive existing rights*, especially regarding rights to common law debts.

5.12 If X owes Y £100 but Y agrees to accept a lesser sum, say £80, in full settlement of Y's claim, that is a promise by Y to waive his entitlement to the balance of £20. The promise, like any other, should be supported by consideration. Payment on the day that a debt is due of less than the full amount of the debt is not necessarily consideration for a promise to release the balance.

> *Foakes v Beer 1884*
> The defendant had obtained judgment against the plaintiff for the sum of £2,091. Judgment debts bear interest from the date of the judgment. By a written agreement the defendant agreed to accept payment by instalments of the sum of £2,091, no mention being made of the interest. Once the plaintiff had paid the amount of the debt in full, the defendant claimed interest, claiming that the agreement was not supported by consideration.
>
> *Held*: she was entitled to the debt with interest. No consideration had been given by the plaintiff for waiver of any part of her rights against him.

5.13 There are, however, exceptions to the rule that the debtor (denoted by 'X' in the following paragraphs) must give consideration if the waiver is to be binding. These exceptions concern variation of the original contract terms.

(a) If X offers and Y accepts anything to which Y is not already entitled, the extra thing will be sufficient consideration for the waiver. This may be for example

   (i) goods instead of cash: *Anon 1495*; or
   (ii) payment before the date payment is due: *Pinnel's Case 1602*.

(b) If X arranges with a number of creditors that they will each accept part payment in full settlement, that is a bargain between the creditors. X has given no consideration but he can hold the creditors individually to the agreed terms: *Wood v Robarts 1818*.

(c) If a third party (Z) offers part payment and Y agrees to release X from Y's claim to the balance, Y has received consideration from Z against whom he had no previous claim: *Welby v Drake 1825*.

(d) The principle of *promissory estoppel* may prevent Y from retracting his promise with retrospective effect.

6   PROMISSORY ESTOPPEL

6.1   If a creditor (Y) makes a promise (unsupported by consideration) to the debtor (X) that Y will not insist on the full discharge of the debt (or other obligation), *and the promise is made with the intention that X should act on it and he does so* (by more than just making part payment), Y is estopped (prohibited) from retracting his promise, unless X can be restored to his original position. This last point will prevent Y from retracting his waiver with retrospective effect, though it may permit him to insist on his full rights in the future.

> *Central London Property Trust v High Trees House 1947*
> In September 1939, the plaintiffs let a block of flats to the defendants at an annual rent of £2,500 p.a. It was difficult to let the individual flats in wartime, so in January 1940, the plaintiffs agreed in writing to accept a reduced rent of £1,250 p.a. No time limit was set on the arrangement but it was clearly related to wartime conditions. The reduced rent was paid from 1940 to 1945 and the defendants sublet flats during the period on the basis of their expected liability to pay rent under the head lease at £1,250 only. In 1945 the flats were fully let. The plaintiffs demanded a full rent of £2,500 p.a., both retrospectively and for the future. They tested this claim by suing for rent at the full rate for the last two quarters of 1945.
>
> *Held:* the agreement of January 1940 was a temporary expedient only and had ceased to operate early in 1945. The claim was upheld. However, had the plaintiffs sued for arrears for the period 1940-1945, the 1940 agreement would have served to defeat the claim.

6.2   In the *High Trees* case, if the *defendants* had sued on the promise, they would have failed for want of consideration. The principle is 'a shield not a sword', ie it is a defence, which does not create new rights.

> *Combe v Combe 1951*
> A wife obtained a divorce decree *nisi* against her husband. He then promised her that he would make maintenance payments of £100 per annum. The wife did not apply to the court for an order for maintenance but this forbearance was not at the husband's request. The decree was made absolute; the husband paid no maintenance; the wife sued him on his promise. In the High Court the wife obtained judgment on the basis of the principle of promissory estoppel.
>
> *Held:* (in the Court of Appeal) promissory estoppel 'does not create new causes of action where none existed before. It only prevents a party from insisting on his strict legal rights when it would be unjust to allow him to enforce them'. The wife's claim failed.

6.3   From this it can be seen that *promissory estoppel applies only to a voluntary waiver of existing rights*. A promise which creates new obligations is not binding unless supported by consideration in the usual way.

> *D and C Builders v Rees 1966*
> The defendants owed £482 to the plaintiffs (a small firm of builders). The plaintiffs, who were in acute financial difficulties, reluctantly agreed to accept £300 in full settlement (in order to obtain the money quickly). They later claimed the balance.
>
> *Held:* the debt must be paid in full. Promissory estoppel only applies to a promise voluntarily given. The defendants had been aware of and had exploited the plaintiffs' difficulties ('he was held to ransom' said Lord Denning). In this important case it was also held that payment by cheque (instead of in cash) is normal and gives no extra advantage which could be treated as consideration for the waiver under the rule in *Pinnel's Case*.

Exercise

In 1495, Chief Justice Brian said the following. 'The action is brought for £20, and the concord is that he shall pay £10, which appears to be no satisfaction for the £20; for payment of £10 cannot be payment of £20. But if it was a horse which was to be paid according to the concord, this would be good satisfaction, for it does not appear that the horse be more or less than the sum in demand'. What rule of law is illustrated by this statement?

Solution

This statement was made in *Anon 1495*. It is the basis for the rule that a waiver of existing rights by a creditor need not be supported by consideration if the debtor offers, and the creditor accepts, goods instead of cash. (Many of the earliest recorded cases concerned purchase or sale of horses.)

7   PRIVITY OF CONTRACT   6/97

7.1   We saw earlier in this chapter the illustration of the rule that consideration must move from the promisee. A related rule was developed in the nineteenth century: that no-one may be entitled to or bound by the terms of a contract to which he is not an original party: *Price v Easton 1833*.

7.2   These two rules together are the basis of the doctrine of privity of contract. As a general rule, only a person who is a party to a contract has enforceable rights or obligations under it. The following is the leading case in this area:

Dunlop v Selfridge 1915
The plaintiff, a tyre manufacturer, supplied tyres to X, a distributor, on terms that X would not re-sell the tyres at less than the prescribed retail price. If X sold the tyres wholesale to trade customers, X must impose a similar condition on those buyers to observe minimum retail prices (such clauses were legal at the time though prohibited since 1964 by the Resale Prices Act). X resold tyres on these conditions to the defendant. Under the terms of the contract between X and Selfridge, Selfridge was to pay to the plaintiff a sum of £5 per tyre if it sold tyres to customers below the minimum retail price. They sold tyres to two customers at less than the minimum price. The plaintiff sued to recover £5 per tyre as liquidated damages

Held: the plaintiff could not recover damages under a contract (between X and Selfridge) to which it was not a party. Third parties who are not privy to a contract generally have no right of action. This is true even if they receive benefits under it.

7.3   In these circumstances the party to the contract who imposes the condition or obtains a promise of a benefit for a third party can usually enforce it, but damages cannot be recovered on the third party's behalf unless the contracting party is suing an agent or trustee, since a plaintiff can only recover damages for a loss he has suffered. Thus only nominal damages can be given if the contract was only for a third party's benefit. Other remedies may be sought however.

Beswick v Beswick 1968
X transferred his business to the defendant, his nephew, in consideration for a pension of £6.10s per week and, after his death, a weekly annuity to X's widow. Only one such annuity payment was made. The widow brought an action against the nephew, asking for an order of specific performance. She sued both as administratrix of her husband's estate and in her personal capacity as recipient.

Held: as her husband's representative, the widow was successful in enforcing the contract for a third party's (her own) benefit. In her personal capacity she could derive no right of action.

7.4   Where the contract is one which provides something for the enjoyment of both the contracting party and third parties - such as a family holiday - the contracting party may be entitled to recover damages for *his* loss of the benefit: *Jackson v Horizon Holidays Ltd*

1975. If the contract is broken and the plaintiff, being a party to the contract, seeks damages on the other peoples' behalf he can also recover for the loss suffered by those other people: *Woodar Investment Development Ltd v Wimpey Construction (UK) Ltd 1980.*

Exceptions

7.5.   There are a number of real or apparent exceptions to the general rule of privity of contract.

Implied trusts

7.6   Equity may hold that an implied trust has been created.

> *Gregory and Parker v Williams 1817*
> P owed money to G and W. He agreed with W to transfer his property to W if W would pay his (P's) debt to G. The property was transferred, but W refused to pay G. G could not sue on the contract between P and W.
>
> *Held:* P could be regarded as a trustee for G, and G would therefore bring an action jointly with P.

Statutory exceptions

7.7   There are statutory exceptions which permit a person injured in a road accident to claim against the *motorist's insurers* (Road Traffic Act 1972) and which permit husband or wife to *insure his or her own life* for the benefit of the other under a trust which the beneficiary can enforce (Married Woman's Property Act 1882).

7.8   The Landlord and Tenant (Covenants) Act 1996 abolished privity of contract in relation to leases entered into after 1 January 1996. This means that the original lessee no longer takes responsibility for obligations under the lease when an assignee fails to comply.

Agency

7.9   In normal circumstances the agent discloses to a third party with whom he contracts that he (the agent) is acting for a principal whose identity is also disclosed. The contract, when made, is between the principal and the third party. The agent has no liability under the contract and no right to enforce it.

7.10   If a person enters into a contract apparently on his own account as principal but in fact as agent on behalf of a principal, the doctrine of the undisclosed principal determines the position of the parties. An undisclosed principal may adopt a contract made for him by an agent. The undisclosed principal will usually intervene and enforce the contract on his own behalf against the other party since it is really his contract, not the agent's. Until such time as the principal takes this action, the agent himself may sue the third party (since he is treated as the other party to the contract).

Covenants

7.11   A restrictive covenant may run with the land.

> *Tulk v Moxhay 1848*
> The plaintiff owned several plots of land in Leicester Square. He sold one to X, who agreed not to build on it, but to preserve it in its existing condition. It was sold on, eventually being purchased by the defendant, who, although he was aware of the restriction, proposed to build on it. The plaintiff sought an injunction.
>
> *Held:* the injunction was granted.

Collateral contracts

7.12   A *collateral contract* is a contract the consideration for which is the making of some other contract. If there are two separate contracts by offer and acceptance between, on the one hand A and B and on the other hand A and C, on terms which involve some concerted action between B and C, there may be a contract between B and C. In contracting with A, both B and C look forward to the possible relationship between them (B and C) which will result, and are deemed to offer and accept the terms of the relationship - there is a contract between B and C despite the absence of direct communication between them: *Shanklin Pier Ltd v Detel Products 1951.*

Assignment

7.13   A party to a contract can *assign* or transfer to another person (the assignee) the *rights* contained in the contract, subject to the rules stated below. But he cannot, without the consent of the other party, assign the burden of his contractual *obligations*.

7.14   A legal assignment must be absolute, it must be in writing, and notice must be given to the other party: s 136 Law of Property Act 1925. The assignee has no better rights under the contract than the assignor had. It is not possible to assign:

(a)   a *right of action*, which is a claim for unliquidated (an unspecified amount of) damages for breach of contract; or

(b)   *rights which are so personal* to the original parties to the contract that assignment to another would alter them.

> *Kemp v Baerselman 1906*
> The defendant contracted to supply to the plaintiff, a cake manufacturer, all the eggs which the latter might require over a period of a year. During the year the manufacturer sold his business to a much larger concern (the National Bakery Company) and purported as part of the sale to assign the benefit of the egg supply agreement.
>
> *Held:* the assignment was invalid since the assignee's requirements were much larger and the supplier's right to supply all the assignor's requirements (he would no longer have any) became valueless.

7.15   Although a party to a contract cannot escape from his contractual obligations by assignment, he may (unless the contract requires personal performance by him) delegate performance to another person. But he remains liable if his substitute's performance is a breach of contract.

The Contracts (Rights of Third Parties) Bill

7.16   The Contracts (Rights of Third Parties) Bill which is currently before Parliament seeks to enable rights to be conferred upon someone not party to a contract if the contract expressly provides that he may, or it does *not* appear that the parties to the contract did *not* intend the term to be enforceable by the third party.

Chapter roundup

- 'A valuable consideration in the sense of the law may consist either in some right, interest, profit or benefit accruing to one party, or some forbearance, detriment, loss or responsibility given, suffered or undertaken by the other'. This definition of consideration, the third essential element of a binding contract, was given in *Currie v Misa 1875*.

- Consideration may be executed (an act in return for a promise) or executory (a promise in return for a promise). It may not be past, unless one of three recognised exceptions applies.

- Consideration need not be adequate, but it must be sufficient. This means that what is tendered as consideration must be capable in law of being regarded as consideration, but need not necessarily be equal in value to the consideration received in return (for example a peppercorn rent).

- The principle of promissory estoppel was developed in *Central London Property Trust v High Trees House 1947*.

- As a general rule, only a person who is a party to a contract has enforceable rights or obligations under it. This is the doctrine of privity of contract, as demonstrated in *Dunlop v Selfridge 1915*.

Test your knowledge

1   What is executed consideration? (see para 2.2)

2   What is past consideration? (2.4)

3   Give three situations where past consideration may make a promise binding. (2.6)

4   Give the name of a case which illustrates the rule that consideration must move from the promisee. (3.1)

5   What point of law is illustrated by *Chappell & Co v Nestle Co 1960?* (5.1)

6   Summarise the facts of *Stilk v Myrick 1890* and *Hartley v Ponsonby 1857,* showing the distinction between them. (5.7, 5.8)

7   List two situations in which a debtor need not give consideration for a creditor who promises to accept a lesser sum in full settlement of a debt to be bound by his promise. (5.13)

8   What is the doctrine of promissory estoppel? (6.1)

Now try illustrative question 14 at the end of the Study Text

Chapter 15

CAPACITY

This chapter covers the following topics.

1 Minors

2 Companies

3 Mental incapacity

Introduction

In Chapter 11 we saw how the validity of a contract might be affected by one of a number of vitiating factors. In this chapter we consider contractual capacity.

It is a prerequisite for forming a binding agreement that both parties should have the capacity to enter into it. In restricted circumstances certain types of legal person do not have that capacity, namely minors, limited companies and persons suffering from mental incapacity.

---

1   MINORS

1.1   The legal capacity of minors (persons under the age of 18) is determined by the Minors' Contracts Act 1987. A contract between a minor and another party may be of one of three types.

(a)   A *valid* contract is binding in the usual way.

(b)   A *voidable* contract is binding unless and until the minor rescinds the contract.

(c)   An *unenforceable* contract is unenforceable against the minor unless he ratifies (adopts) it - but the other party is bound.

Valid contracts of a minor

1.2   Two sorts of contract are valid and binding on a minor.

(a)   Contracts for the supply of goods or services which are *necessaries*.
(b)   A *service contract* for the minor's benefit.

Necessaries

1.3   If goods or services which are necessaries are delivered to a minor under a contract made by him, he is bound to pay a reasonable price (not the contract price if that is excessive) for them: s 3 Sale of Goods Act 1979. Necessaries are defined in s 3 Sale of Goods Act 1979 as goods suitable to the condition in life of the minor and to his actual requirements at the time of sale and delivery. Services may also be necessaries. The goods (or services) must therefore satisfy a double test - *suitability* and *need* - if they are to be necessaries.

1.4   *Suitability* is measured by the living standards of the minor. Things which are in ordinary use may be necessaries even though they are luxurious in quality, if that is what the minor ordinarily uses. Food, clothing, professional advice and even a gold watch have been held to be necessaries. However, in some cases it is clear that a broad definition of necessaries has been adopted, not for the benefit of the minor, but to protect traders who gave credit to young men from wealthy families. It has been said that an item of 'mere luxury' cannot be a necessary, for example a racehorse, but that a luxurious item of utility such as an expensive car may be a necessary. Expensive items bought as gifts are not usually necessaries, but an engagement ring to a fiancee can be.

1.5   The second test is whether the minor requires the goods for the personal *needs* of himself (or his wife or child if any). Goods required for use in a trade are not necessaries, nor are goods of any kind if the minor is already well supplied with them and so does not need any more.

> *Nash v Inman 1908*
> N was a Savile Row tailor who had solicited orders from I, a Cambridge undergraduate of extravagant tastes. N sued I on bills totalling £145 for clothes, including eleven fancy waistcoats, supplied over a period of nine months. It was conceded that the clothes were suitable for I but it was shown that he was already amply supplied with clothing.
>
> *Held:* the clothes were not necessaries since, although quite suitable for his use, the minor had no *need* of them. It was immaterial that N was unaware that I was already well supplied.

> *Mercantile Union Guarantee Corporation v Ball 1937*
> A minor obtained a lorry on hire purchase terms for use in his road haulage business.
>
> *Held:* this was not a contract for necessaries since the lorry was required for business, not personal use. Under the hire purchase contract the owner could recover the lorry as still his property, but could not enforce payment of the hire purchase instalments.

1.6   If a minor uses borrowed money to pay for necessaries the lender can stand in the shoes of the supplier who has been paid with the lender's money, and the lender may recover so much of his loan as corresponds with a reasonable price for the necessaries.

Service contracts

1.7   A service contract for the minor's benefit is the other type of contract which is binding on a minor.

> *Doyle v White City Stadium 1935*
> D, who was a minor, obtained a licence to compete as a professional boxer. Under his licence (which was treated as a contract of apprenticeship or vocation) he agreed to be bound by rules under which the British Boxing Board of Control could withhold his prize money if he was disqualified for a foul blow (as in fact happened). He asserted that the licence was a void contract since it was not for his benefit.
>
> *Held:* the licence enabled him to pursue a lucrative occupation. Despite the penal clause, it was beneficial as a whole.

1.8   Apart from the test of benefit, the contract must relate to education or training, or relate to some occupation or vocation, such as training as a dancer or as a professional snooker player.

> *Chaplin v Leslie Frewin (Publishers) Ltd 1966*
> The plaintiff, a son of Charlie Chaplin, was a minor. He contracted with the defendants to give them, for an advance of £600, exclusive rights to his autobiography. He later claimed that the completed work, written by two journalists based on information furnished by him, contained libellous matter and attributed to him views which he did not hold. He sought to repudiate the contract.

Held: the contract was binding; it was on the whole, beneficial to him as it would enable him to make a start as an author.

Voidable contracts of a minor

1.9   A minor may enter into a contract by which he acquires an interest of a continuing nature. Such contracts are voidable by the minor during his minority and within a reasonable time after attaining his majority. Until he rescinds (avoids) the contract it is binding. If he rescinds it before his majority, he may withdraw his rescission within a reasonable time afterwards. If he rescinds it, he is relieved of any future obligations. There are four categories of these voidable contracts.

(a)   Contracts concerning land - for example, leases.
(b)   Purchases of shares in a company.
(c)   Partnership agreements.
(d)   Marriage settlements.

1.10   A contract of this type does not require any kind of ratification by the minor on his majority. It remains binding unless he repudiates it within a *reasonable time*.

> *Edwards v Carter 1893*
> A marriage settlement was made under which the father of the husband to be agreed to pay £1,500 per annum to the trustees. The husband to be, who was a minor at the time of the settlement, executed a deed under which all property which he might receive under his father's will would also be vested in the trustees. He attained his majority one month later; three and a half years later his father died. A year after this, he repudiated the agreement, arguing that, when he signed the agreement he did not realise the extent of his obligations and that he could only reach a decision once he knew the details of the will.
>
> *Held:* the repudiation was too late and was ineffective

1.11   The effect of repudiation is to relieve the minor (or former minor) of any contractual obligations arising after the repudiation. There are conflicting decisions as to whether repudiation relieves the minor of obligations which arose *before* the repudiation. (For example, if a minor repudiates a lease of land, is he liable for rent which has already fallen due?)

1.12   A minor cannot recover money paid unless there is a total failure of consideration.

> *Steinberg v Scala (Leeds) Ltd 1923*
> The plaintiff, a minor, applied for and was allotted shares in a company. She paid the amounts due on allotment and on the first call. She received no dividends and eighteen months after allotment (while still a minor), she sought to repudiate the contract and recover the monies paid.
>
> *Held:* she could repudiate the contract and avoid liability for future calls, but she could not recover what she had paid because she had received the consideration due, which was the allotted shares.

Unenforceable contracts of a minor

1.13   All other contracts entered into by a minor are described as unenforceable - the minor is not bound (though he may ratify or 'adopt' it) but the other party is bound. If he is to be bound the minor must ratify the contract within a reasonable time after his majority. Once ratified the contract is valid and is enforceable both by and against the ex-minor.

1.14   Where a contract is voidable and is rescinded by the minor, or where it is unenforceable and is not ratified by the minor, any guarantee of the contract given by a capable person is still valid. In addition, a minor may be required to return property which he acquired under a rescinded or unenforceable contract.

1.15 A minor is generally liable for his torts. He will not, however, be liable if he commits a tort in procuring a contract which is not binding on him. If he were liable, the other party would effectively be able to enforce such a contract by means of an action in tort.

> *R Leslie Ltd v Sheill 1914*
> An infant obtained a loan of £400 by means of a fraudulent misstatement of his age.
>
> *Held:* he could not be compelled to repay it, as this would constitute enforcement of the contract.

2 COMPANIES

6/98

2.1 Companies and other 'artificial' legal persons, such as local authorities, do not have the same unlimited capacity as a healthy human being. Often they are limited in what they can do by their constitutions, which only give them certain powers. Actions done outside those powers are said to be *ultra vires* - literally, 'beyond the powers'. *Ultra vires* contracts are void, so neither party can enforce their terms.

2.2 The *ultra vires* rule as it applies to companies is now of very limited effect following the Companies Act 1989, which amended relevant sections of the Companies Act 1985.

(a) Companies can adopt a general clause in their constitutions which enable them to act as a 'general commercial company', so they are not restricted to certain types of activity.

(b) The validity of an act done by a company cannot be questioned on the ground that the company lacked capacity; in addition, the power of the company's directors to bind it are deemed to be free of limitation, *provided* that the third party dealing with the company acted in good faith.

3 MENTAL INCAPACITY

3.1 If a person who is temporarily insane, under the influence of drugs or drunk enters into a contract it is binding on him unless:

(a) he is at the time incapable of understanding the nature of the contract; *and*
(b) the other party knows or ought to know of his disability.

3.2 When necessaries are supplied (not as a gift but with the intention of obtaining payment) to a person under such disability, he must pay a reasonable price for them in any event (s 3 Sale of Goods Act 1979). The rules are similar to those applicable to minors.

Chapter roundup

- The legal capacity of minors is determined by the Minors' Contracts Act 1987. There are two types of contract which are valid and therefore binding on a minor, other contracts may be voidable or unenforceable.

- Companies have a limited legal capacity. The powers of a company are laid down in the company's constitution.

- Special rules also apply to persons suffering from mental incapacity.

Test your knowledge

1   What piece of legislation governs the legal capacity of minors? (see para 1.1)

2   In a contract with a minor, what is meant by necessaries? (1.3)

3   What were the facts of *Nash v Inman* 1908? (1.5)

4   What is the second type of contract binding on a minor? (1.7)

5   Give two examples of voidable contracts of a minor. (1.9)

6   What is the effect of the companies Act 1989 on the *ultra vires* rule? (2.2)

7   When is a person who is insane not bound by a contract which he enters into? (3.1)

Now try illustrative question 15 at the end of the Study Text

Chapter 16

THE CONTENTS OF A CONTRACT

This chapter covers the following topics.

1 The form of a contract

2 Implied contract terms

3 Custom

4 The courts

5 Statute

Introduction

Finally in this part of the syllabus we take a look at the form of a contract and at implied contract terms.

---

1 THE FORM OF A CONTRACT

1.1 One of the most widely held misapprehensions about contracts is that they have to be in writing and signed by both parties. A binding contract does not need to be in writing. As a general rule, a contract may be made in any form. It may be written, or oral, or inferred from the conduct of the parties.

For example, a customer in a self-service shop may take his selected goods to the cash desk, pay for them and walk out without saying a word. The three essential elements of a contract are present and a contract of sale has been formed. The printed till receipt is merely evidence of payment and is not essential to the contract.

1.2 Writing makes it easier to prove the contents of the contract, but it is not usually necessary. To the general rule there are three exceptions.

(a) Some contracts must be *by deed* ('specialty' contract).
(b) Some contracts must be *in writing*.
(c) Some contracts must be *evidenced in writing*.

Contracts by deed

1.3 Some rights and obligations are required to be in the form of a deed and are not binding if they are not in that form.

1.4 Under s 1 Law of Property (Miscellaneous Provisions) Act 1989 contracts relating to the transfer of land must be by deed, *in writing, signed and witnessed*. Delivery must take place. This need not be a physical transfer of possession. Delivery is conduct indicating that the person executing the deed intends to be bound by it.

1.5 Contracts which must be by deed include:

(a) *leases* for three years or more;

(b) a *conveyance* or transfer of a legal estate in land (including a mortgage);

(c)   a *promise not supported by consideration* (such as a covenant to make annual payments to a charity.

Contracts which must be in writing

1.6   Some types of contract (mainly *commercial*) are required to be in the form of a written document, usually signed by at least one of the parties, and are usually void if not in that form. Contracts which must be in writing include:

(a)   a transfer of shares in a limited company;
(b)   the sale or disposition of an interest in land;
(c)   bills of exchange and cheques; and
(d)   consumer credit contracts.

1.7   A contract for the sale or disposition of land must be distinguished from the actual document which transfers the title to that land. The document which transfers title is the conveyance (unregistered land) or transfer (registered land). A contract for the sale or disposition of land promises to transfer title at a future date (usually four weeks hence) and must be in writing. The conveyance or transfer must, as noted above, be by deed and will therefore also be in writing. A contract promising to grant a lease must be in writing but the lease itself, if it is for three years or more must be by deed.

1.8   In the case of consumer credit transactions, the effect of non-compliance by the seller (failure to make a regulated consumer credit agreement in the prescribed form) is to make the agreement unenforceable against the debtor unless the creditor obtains a court order.

Contracts which must be evidenced in writing

1.9   Certain contracts may be made orally, but are not enforceable in a court of law unless there is written evidence of their terms. The most important contract of this type is the contract of guarantee.

1.10   A signed note of the material terms of the contract is sufficient. It must be signed by the guarantor and include material terms such as the names or identification of the parties and a description of the subject matter.

The electronic contract

1.11   English law has been concerned with formulating the rules for oral and written contracts for centuries, and cases decided in the 1800s continue to be valid today. However, business conducted on-line creates a new category of contract: the electronic contract.

1.12   This is a potentially wide ranging topic and the law is still in its infancy. Below is a summary of the issues which may need to be considered.

(a)   *In writing?* There are two main reasons why contracts need to be in writing.

(i)   A written contract provides evidence of the terms of the contract.

(ii)   The requirement of formality allows a weaker party to 'think twice' before entering into a transaction.

An electronic contract meets the reasoning behind the requirement for writing, and can thus be said to be in writing.

(b)   *Signed?* In early 1999 the UK government unveiled a new legal framework for electronic commerce, designed to boost consumer confidence in using the Internet. Among other proposals, the courts are to be allowed to recognise electronic signatures as legally binding, removing discrimination between electronic and traditional ways of doing business. A draft EU directive is also currently addressing online conclusion of contracts and trying to harmonise the approach of member states.

(c) *Timing of acceptance*. A contract comes into existence when an offer is accepted; in the case of acceptance by letter, this is when the letter is posted not when it is received. Internet e-mail shares many of the qualities of conventional mail - it is not usually instantaneous and may be subject to delay. Therefore the postal rule, with any problems arising from it, probably applies, although the point has not been tested.

(d) *Consideration*. Difficulties with credit card payments have slowed the growth of electronic commerce. The Internet is largely insecure, and this may cause problems when it comes to payment.

1.13 As the electronic contract has not been tested in the Courts, the best approach to take should it come up in the exam is to combine what you know of the principles of ordinary contract law with logic and common sense. You will gain marks for a reasoned answer.

2   IMPLIED CONTRACT TERMS

2.1 We saw in the chapter on offer and acceptance that an acceptance is an unqualified agreement to the terms of the offer. Under normal circumstances, then, the terms of a contract are fixed by this process of offer and acceptance. The terms which are agreed upon in this way are referred to as express terms.

2.2 Some terms, however, may be *implied* into a contract by law. These are terms which are not necessarily expressed, or indeed not even thought of, by the parties to the contract in their process of offer and acceptance, but which, for various reasons, are treated as being contract terms.

2.3 The terms of a contract are not included on the syllabus for this examination. You will study them in detail when you take the Pre-Professional *Business Law* paper. However, the June 1994 exam paper for *Introduction to English and European Community Law* included a question on implied contract terms. For this reason, we include in this chapter a discussion of implied terms. Other aspects of contract terms are dealt with in Chapter 20 of this Study Text for those who would like to read further on this topic.

Implied terms

2.4 As a general principle, the parties to a contract may by their offer and acceptance include in their contract whatever terms they prefer. However the law may in appropriate circumstances modify these express terms in a number of ways.

2.5 An implied term may be defined as a term deemed to form part of a contract even though not expressly mentioned by the parties. Some such terms may be implied:

(a) by *custom*, following trade practice in that type of business;
(b) by the *courts* as necessary to give effect to the presumed intentions of the parties;
(c) by *statute*, for example, the Sale of Goods Act.

3   CUSTOM

3.1 The parties may be considered to enter into a contract subject to a custom or practice of their trade.

> *Hutton v Warren 1836*
> The defendant landlord gave the plaintiff, a tenant farmer, notice to quit the farm. He insisted that the tenant should continue to farm the land during the period of notice. The tenant asked for 'a fair allowance' for seeds and labour from which he received no benefit (as he left before harvest time).

Held: by custom, he was bound to farm the land until the end of the tenancy; he was also entitled to a fair allowance for seeds and labour.

3.2   But any express term overrides a term which might be implied by custom.

> *Les Affreteurs v Walford 1919*
> A charter of a ship provided expressly for a 3% commission payment to be made 'on signing the charter'. There was a trade custom that it should only be paid at a later stage. The ship was requisitioned by the French government before the charterparty began, and so no hire was earned.
>
> *Held:* an express term prevails over a term otherwise implied by custom. The commission was payable on hire.

3.3   A more recent example demonstrates that this is still relevant.

> *British Crane Hire v Ipswich Plant Hire 1974*
> Both firms were in the business of hiring out cranes and heavy plant. IPH hired a crane from BCH for use on marshy ground. BCH sent IPH a copy of their standard conditions, which were similar to those used throughout the trade and which provided that the hirer would be liable for all expenses arising out of the crane's use. Before these were signed, the crane sank into the marshy ground and BCH claimed from IPH the expenses which it (BCH) incurred in recovering the crane.
>
> *Held:* The claim succeeded because:
>
> (a)   both parties were in the same trade;
>
> (b)   they had equal bargaining power; and
>
> (c)   there was evidence that they both understood that BCH's standard conditions would apply.

4   THE COURTS

4.1   Terms may be implied if the court concludes that the parties intended those terms to apply and did not mention them because they were taken for granted, or because they were inadvertently omitted. The court may then supply a further term to prevent the failure of the agreement and to implement the manifested intention of the parties. The contract is given 'business efficacy'.

> *The Moorcock 1889*
> The owners of a wharf agreed that a ship should be moored alongside to unload its cargo. It was well known to both wharfingers and shipowners that at low water the ship would ground on the mud at the bottom. At ebb tide the ship settled on a ridge concealed beneath the mud and suffered damage.
>
> *Held:* it was an implied term, though not expressed, that the ground alongside the wharf (which did not belong to the wharfingers) was safe at low tide since both parties knew that the ship must rest on it.

4.2   '*Prima facie* that which in any contract is left to be implied and need not be expressed is something so obvious that it goes without saying; so that, if while the parties were making their bargain an officious bystander were to suggest some express provision for it in their agreement they would testily suppress him with "Oh, of course" ': *Shirlaw v Southern Foundries 1939*. This is known as the 'officious bystander' test, and this type of implied term is sometimes referred to as a term *implied in fact*.

4.3   The court may also imply terms to maintain a standard of behaviour, even though the parties may not have intended them to be included. This is sometimes referred to as a term *implied in law*.

Liverpool City Council v Irwin 1977
The defendants were tenants of a maisonette in a tower block owned by the plaintiffs. There was no formal tenancy agreement. The defendants withheld rent, alleging that the plaintiffs had breached implied terms because *inter alia* the lifts did not work and the stairs were unlit. The council argued that there were no implied terms.

Held: it was necessary to consider the obligations which 'the nature of the contract itself implicitly requires'. Tenants could only occupy the building with access to stairs and/or lifts, so terms needed to be implied on these matters. A term was implied that the landlord would keep these parts reasonably safe.

5 STATUTE

5.1 Terms may be implied by statute. In some cases the statute permits the parties to contract out of the statutory terms (for instance the terms of partnership implied by the Partnership Act 1890 may be excluded). In other cases the statutory terms are obligatory: the protection given by the Sale of Goods Act 1979 to a consumer who buys goods from a trader cannot be taken away from him.

5.2 The terms implied by Sale of Goods Act 1979 represent one of the most important examples of terms being implied into a contract by statute. A sale of goods may be subject to statutory rules on the following.

(a) The effect of delay in performance (s 10).
(b) Title, or the sellers' right to sell the goods (s 12).
(c) Description of the goods (s 13).
(d) Quality of the goods (s 14(2)).
(e) Fitness of the goods for the purpose for which they are supplied (s 14(3)).
(f) Sale by sample (s 15).

5.3 The Unfair Contract Terms Act 1977 prohibits or restricts the possibility of modifying these statutory rules (other than those on time) by the use of exclusion clauses as follows. It is not possible to exclude or restrict:

(a) the statutory terms on the seller's title - his right to sell - in any circumstances; nor

(b) the statutory terms relating to contract description or sample, quality or fitness for a purpose (ss 13-15) when the buyer is dealing as consumer. In a contract under which the buyer is *not* dealing as a consumer, that is when seller and buyer are both engaging in the transaction in the course of business, ss 13-15 may be excluded or restricted, but only if the exclusion or restriction satisfies a requirement of *reasonableness*.

Chapter roundup

- Although most contracts may be made in any form, some must be made in a particular form. In particular, a number of commercial contracts must be made in writing.

- There is as yet no case law regarding business conducted on line, but it may be expected that the principles of ordinary contract law will apply.

- The law may complement or replace terms by implying terms into a contract. Terms may be implied by the courts, by statute or by custom.

Test your knowledge

1 Give an example of a contract which must be made by deed (see para 1.5)

2 Give three examples of contracts which must be in writing (1.6)

3 Outline the facts of *British Crane Hire v Ipswich Plant Hire 1974.* (3.3)

4 Outline the facts of *The Moorcock 1889.* (4.1)

Now try illustrative question 16 at the end of the Study Text

Part F
Further studies of the law of contract

Chapter 17

THE TERMS OF THE CONTRACT

This chapter covers the following topics.

1   The contents of the contract

2   Express terms

3   Terms and representations

4   Conditions and warranties

5   Implied terms

6   Exclusion clauses

7   Incorporation of exclusion clauses

8   Interpretation of exclusion clauses

9   The Unfair Contract Terms Act 1977

10 The Unfair Terms in Consumer Contracts Regulations 1994

Introduction

The coverage of the law of contract in Chapters 11 to 16 (Part E) of this Study Text addresses the requirements of the syllabus for the *Introduction to English and European Community Law* examination paper. The syllabus is designed to provide an introduction to the law of contract and provides coverage of binding agreements with reference to the doctrines of privity and formalities.

A greater understanding of the law of contract developed through further study of the subject area will inevitably be to the student's advantage. In this part of the Study Text we provide additional material on the law of contract to extend your knowledge of this subject area. You will study these areas in greater depth in the pre-professional examination *Business Law*.

In this chapter we look at the terms of the contract, considering in particular what constitutes a term, how terms are ascertained and what terms can be included in a contract. You may remember that we introduced the topic of implied terms in Chapter 16.

In Chapter 18 we introduce three factors which may affect the validity of contract terms: mistake, misrepresentation and illegality.

In Chapter 19 we describe the ways in which a contract may be discharged and in Chapter 20 we look at the remedies for breach of contract.

1   THE CONTENTS OF THE CONTRACT

1.1   As a general principle the parties may by their offer and acceptance include in their contract whatever terms they prefer. But the law may modify these express terms in various ways.

(a)   The terms must be sufficiently complete and precise to produce an agreement which can be binding. If they are vague there may be no contract. These *express terms* are considered in section 2.

(b)   Statements made in the pre-contract negotiations may become *terms* of the contract or remain as *representations*, to which different rules attach. The distinction is explained in section 3.

(c) The terms of the contract are usually classified as *conditions* or as *warranties* according to their importance. This classification is described in section 4.

(d) In addition to the express terms of the agreement, additional terms may be implied by law. We review implied terms briefly in section 5.

(e) To be enforceable, terms must be validly incorporated into the contract. Incorporation is considered in section 7. We look at this topic in the context of *exclusion clauses*, because most court decisions about valid incorporation of contract terms are made in respect of exclusion clauses.

(f) Terms which exclude or restrict liability for breach of contract (*exemption* or *exclusion clauses*) are restricted in their effect or are overridden by common law or statute. Exclusion clauses are discussed in sections 6-8.

2 EXPRESS TERMS 12/95

2.1 A legally binding agreement must be complete in its terms, otherwise there is no contract since the parties are still at the stage of negotiating the necessary terms and exclusion clauses.

> *Scammell v Ouston 1941*
> The defendants wished to buy a new motor-van from the plaintiffs on hire-purchase terms. They placed an order 'on the understanding that the balance of purchase price can be had on hire-purchase terms over a period of two years'. The hire-purchase terms were never specified. Hire-purchase terms may vary considerably.
>
> *Held*: there was no contract. The 'language used was so obscure and so incapable of any definite or precise meaning' that the court was unable to identify a contract which they could uphold.

2.2 However *it is always possible for the parties to leave an essential term to be settled by specified means outside the contract.* For example, it may be agreed to sell at the ruling open market price (if there is a market) on the day of delivery, or to invite an arbitrator to determine a fair price. The price may even be determined by the course of dealing between the parties.

> *Malcolm v University of Oxford 1990*
> An employee of the defendant (with authority) stated to an author that the defendant was 'committed' to publishing his book and that it would pay 'a fair royalty'. Terms on print run and royalty levels had not been agreed. The plaintiff sought to enforce the contract.
>
> *Held*: a contract had been entered into.

2.3 *Express*, in the context of contract law, means that which is specifically stated, as opposed to that which is implied from the circumstances. If the parties expressly agree to defer some essential term for later negotiation there is no binding agreement; this is described a an "*agreement to agree*" which is void because the parties may subsequently fail to agree.

Oral evidence of contract terms

2.4 Often there is no written evidence of the terms of a contract. The court is then unable to look to written documents. It must ascertain as a question of fact exactly what was said.

> *Smith v Hughes 1871*
> The plaintiff bought oats from the defendant, believing them to be old oats, which are more valuable than new oats. They were new oats. The plaintiff refused to complete the sale. The court had to ascertain whether the vendor had described them as 'good oats' or 'good old oats'.

Held: the contract was for the sale of 'good oats' and the buyer's mistake did not render the contract void.

2.5 If the contract is in writing, and all the necessary terms are present, the courts will interpret the terms of the contract by reference to the written document. *They will not admit oral evidence to add to, vary or contradict written terms.* This supports the principle that the courts are not usually concerned with the actual intention of the parties but with their manifested intention.

Hawrish v Bank of Montreal 1969
A solicitor gave to a company's bank a personal guarantee 'of all present and future debts' of the company. He later sought to give evidence to show that the guarantee applied only to a particular overdraft existing when the guarantee was given.

Held: such evidence was inadmissible.

2.6 There are the following exceptions to the rule.

(a) Oral evidence may be given of trade practice or custom: *Hutton v Warren 1836*.

(b) Evidence may be given to show that the parties agreed orally that their written consent should not take effect until a *condition precedent* had been satisfied, for example a written contract to buy a house subject to a verbal agreement that it would take effect only if the purchaser's surveyor gave a satisfactory report: *Pym v Campbell 1856*.

(c) Oral evidence may be given as an addition to a written contract if it can be shown that the document, such as printed conditions of sale, was not intended to comprise all the agreed terms. But the presumption is that a contract document is the entire contract until the contrary is proved. *SS Ardennes (Cargo Owners) v SS Ardennes (Owners) 1951*.

(d) Oral evidence may be adduced to correct a written agreement drawn up subsequently which contains a *mistake*.

3 TERMS AND REPRESENTATIONS

3.1 Once it has been established exactly what the parties to a contract have said or written, it is necessary to decide whether their words actually amount to contract terms. Statements may be classified as terms or as 'mere representations'.

A representation is something which induces the formation of a contract but which does not become a term of the contract. The importance of the distinction is that different remedies are available depending on whether a term is broken or a representation turns out to be untrue.

3.2 *If something said in pre-contract negotiations proves to be untrue, the party misled can only claim for breach of contract if the statement became a term of the contract.* Otherwise his remedy is for misrepresentation only.

3.3 Such factors as a significant interval of time between the statement and the formation of the contract, or the use of a written contract making no reference to the verbal statement, suggest that it is not a term of the contract.

3.4 The court will consider when the representation was made to assess whether it was designed as a contract term or merely as an *incidental statement* in the preliminary negotiations.

Bannerman v White 1861
In negotiations for the sale of hops the buyer emphasised that it was essential to him that the hops should not have been treated with sulphur adding that, if they had, he would not even bother to ask the price. The seller replied explicitly that no sulphur had been used. It was later discovered that a small proportion of the hops

(5 acres out of 300) had been treated with sulphur. The buyer refused to pay the price. The seller contended that the conversation was merely preliminary to the contract.

Held: the representation as to the absence of sulphur was intended to be a term of the contract, as the whole deal revolved around it. This contrasts with the next case:

Routledge v McKay 1954
The defendant, in discussing he possible sale of his motorcycle to the plaintiff, said on 23rd October that the cycle was a 1942 model; he took this information from the registration document. On 30 October the parties made a written contract which did not refer to the year of the model. The actual date was 1930.

Held: the buyer's claim for damages failed. The reference to a 1942 model was a representation made prior to the contract, and the deal did not depend on the model of the cycle.

3.5   If the party who makes the statement speaks with special knowledge of the subject, a statement is more likely to be treated as a contract term.

Dick Bentley Productions v Arnold Smith Motors 1965
The plaintiffs approached the defendants saying that they were looking for a 'well-vetted car'. The defendants sold them a car which they stated to have done only 20,000 miles since a replacement engine and gear-box had been fitted. In fact the car had covered 100,000 miles since then and was unsatisfactory.

Held: the defendants' statement was a term of the contract and the plaintiffs were entitled to damages.

Oscar Chess v Williams 1957
The defendant, a private motorist, negotiated the sale of an old Morris car to motor dealers in part exchange for a new Hillman Minx. The seller stated (as the registration book showed) that his car was a 1948 model and the dealers valued it at £280 in the transaction. In fact it was a 1939 model, worth only £175, and the registration book had been altered by a previous owner.

Held: the statement was a mere representation. The seller was not an expert and the buyer had better means of discovering the truth.

4   CONDITIONS AND WARRANTIES

4.1   Once it has been decided that something said or written is a contract term, a further distinction can be made. The obligations created by a contract are not all of equal importance. The terms of the contract are usually classified by their *relative importance* as *conditions* or *warranties*.

(a)   *A condition is a vital term*, going to the root of the contract, breach of which entitles the party not in breach to treat the contract as discharged and to claim damages.

(b)   *A warranty is a term subsidiary* to the main purpose of the contract, breach of which only entitles the injured party to claim damages.

Poussard v Spiers 1876
Mme Poussard agreed to sing in an opera throughout a series of performances. Owing to illness she was unable to appear on the opening night and the next few days. The producer engaged a substitute who insisted that she should be engaged for the whole run. When Mme Poussard recovered, the producer declined to accept her services for the remaining performances.

Held: failure to sing on the opening night was a breach of condition which entitled the producer to treat the contract for the remaining performances as discharged.

Bettini v Gye 1876

An opera singer was engaged for a series of performances under a contract by which he had to be in London for rehearsals six days before the opening performance. Owing to illness he did not arrive until the third day before the opening. The defendant refused to accept his services, treating the contract as discharged.

Held: the rehearsal clause was subsidiary to the main purpose of the contract. Breach of the clause must be treated as breach of warranty, so the defendant had no right to treat the contract as discharged and must compensate the plaintiff. He could however claim damages (if he could prove any loss) for failure to arrive in time for six days' rehearsals.

Schuler v Wickham Machine Tool Sales 1973

The plaintiffs entered into a four-year contract with the defendants giving them the sole right to sell panel presses in England. A clause of the contract provided that it should be a condition of the agreement that the defendants' representative should visit six named firms each week to solicit orders. The defendants' representative failed on a few occasions to do so and the plaintiffs claimed to be entitled to repudiate the agreement on the basis that a single failure was a breach of condition giving them an absolute right to treat the contract as at an end.

Held: such minor breaches by the defendants did not entitle the plaintiffs to repudiate. The House of Lords construed the clause on the basis that it was so unreasonable that the parties could not have intended it as a condition (giving Schuler a right of repudiation) but rather as a warranty.

Innominate terms

4.2   Determining whether a contractual term is a condition or a warranty is clearly very important. The court will only construe a broken term as a condition or warranty if the parties' intentions when the contract was formed *are very clear*. These terms should either be expressed in the contract or be ascertainable by inference from the nature, purpose and circumstances of the contract.

4.3   Where the term broken was not clearly intended to be a condition, and neither statute nor case law define it as such, it cannot necessarily be assumed that the term is a warranty. Instead, the contract must be interpreted; only if it is clear that in no circumstances did the parties intend the contract to be terminated by breach of that particular term can it be classed as a warranty. Such intention may be express or be implied from surrounding circumstances. Where it is not clear what the effect of breach of the term was intended to be, it will be classified by the court as *innominate*, intermediate or indeterminate (the three are synonymous).

4.4   The consequence of a term being classified as innominate is that the court must decide what is the *actual effect of its breach*. If the nature and effect of the breach is such as to deprive the injured party of substantially the whole benefit which it was intended he should obtain under the contract then it will be treated as a breached condition - so the injured party may terminate the contract and claim damages.

Hong Kong Fir Shipping Co Ltd v Kawasaki Kisa Kaisha Ltd 1962

The defendants chartered a ship from the plaintiffs for a period of 24 months. A term in the contract stated that the plaintiffs would provide a ship which was 'in every way fitted for ordinary cargo service'. They were in breach of this since the ship required a competent engine room crew which they did not provide. Because of the engine's age and the crew's lack of competence the ship's first voyage, from Liverpool to Osaka, was delayed for 5 weeks and further repairs were required at the end of it, resulting in the loss of a further 15 weeks. The defendants purported to terminate the contract, so the plaintiffs sued for breach of contract on the grounds that the defendants had no right to terminate; the defendants claimed that the plaintiffs were in breach of a contractual condition.

Held: the term was innominate and could not automatically be construed as either a condition or a warranty. The obligation of 'seaworthiness' embodied in many charterparty agreements was too complex to be fitted into one of the two categories. The term would be construed in the light of the actual consequences of the actual breach. The ship was still available for 17 out of 24 months. The consequences of the breach were not so serious that the defendants could be justified in terminating the contract as a result. The defendants were in breach of contract for terminating it when they did.

Exercise 1

To what is the injured party to a contract entitled in the event of:

(a)   breach of a condition by the other party; and
(b)   breach of a warranty by the other party?

Solution

(a)   He may treat the contract as discharged and rescind or terminate the contract, or alternatively he may go on with it and sue for damages.

(b)   He may claim damages only.

---

5   IMPLIED TERMS   6/94

5.1   There are occasions where certain terms are not expressly adopted by the parties, but may be imported from the context of the contract. Additional terms of a contract may be implied by custom, by statute or by the courts. You should be familiar with this from your reading of Chapter 16. The material is summarised here because it complements the discussion of express terms, above.

Terms implied by custom

5.2   The parties may be considered to enter into a contract subject to a custom or practice of their trade. But any express term overrides a term which might be implied by custom.

> *Les Affreteurs v Walford 1919*
> A charter of a ship provided expressly for a 3% commission payment to be made 'on signing the charter'. There was a trade custom that it should only be paid at a later stage. The ship was requisitioned by the French government before the charterparty began, and so no hire was earned.
>
> *Held*: an express term prevails over a term otherwise implied by custom. The commission was payable on hire.

Terms implied by statute

5.3   Terms may be implied by statute. In some cases the statute permits the parties to contract out of the statutory terms (for instance the terms of partnership implied by the Partnership Act 1890 may be excluded). In other cases the statutory terms are obligatory: the protection given by the Sale of Goods Act 1979 to a consumer who buys goods from a trader cannot be taken away from him.

Terms implied by the courts

5.4   Terms may be implied if the court concludes that the parties intended those terms to apply and did not mention them because they were taken for granted, or because they were inadvertently omitted. The court may then supply a further term to prevent the failure of the agreement and to implement the manifested intention of the parties. The contract is given 'business efficacy'.

The Moorcock 1889

The owners of a wharf agreed that a ship should be moored alongside to unload its cargo. It was well known to both wharfingers and shipowners that at low water the ship would ground on the mud at the bottom. At ebb tide the ship settled on a ridge concealed beneath the mud and suffered damage.

Held: it was an implied term, though not expressed, that the ground alongside the wharf (which did not belong to the wharfingers) was safe at low tide since both parties knew that the ship must rest on it.

5.5 The court may also imply terms to maintain a standard of behaviour even though the parties may not have intended them to be included.

Liverpool City Council v Irwin 1977

The defendants were tenants of the maisonettes in a tower block owned by the plaintiffs. There was no formal tenancy agreement. The defendants withheld rent, alleging that the plaintiffs had breached implied terms because *inter alia* the lifts did not work and the stairs were unlit. The council argued that there were no implied terms.

Held: it was necessary to consider to consider the obligations which 'the nature of the contract itself implicitly requires. Tenants could only occupy the building with access to stairs and/or lifts, so terms needed to be implied that the landlord would keep these parts reasonably safe.

5.6 '*Prima facie* that which in any contract is left to be implied and need not be expressed is something so obvious that it goes without saying; so that, if while the parties were making their bargain an officious bystander were to suggest some express provision for it in their agreement they would testily suppress him with a common "Oh, of course" ': *Shirlaw v Southern Foundries 1939.*

6 EXCLUSION CLAUSES

12/96, 12/98

6.1 If the parties negotiate their contract from positions of more or less equal bargaining strength and expertise, neither the courts nor Parliament have usually interfered. But there has been strong criticism of the use of exclusion (or exemption) clauses in contracts made between manufacturers or sellers of goods or services and private citizens as consumers. In such cases there may be great inequality. The seller puts forward standard conditions of sale which the buyer may not understand, but which he must accept if he wishes to buy. In those conditions the seller may try to exclude entirely or limit his liability for failure to perform as promised, for breach of contract or for negligence - or he may try to offer a 'guarantee' which in fact reduces the buyer's rights.

6.2 For many years the courts demonstrated the hostility of the common law to exclusion and limitation clauses by developing various rules of case law designed to restrain their effect. To these must now be added the considerable statutory safeguards provided by the Unfair Contract Terms Act 1977 (UCTA). But the statutory rules do permit exclusion and limitation clauses to continue in some circumstances (in many cases if they are 'reasonable'). Hence it is necessary to consider both the older case law and the newer statutory rules.

6.3 The courts have generally sought to protect consumers from the harsher effects of exclusion clauses in two ways.

(a) An exclusion clause must be properly *incorporated* into a contract before it has any legal effect.

(b) Exclusion clauses are *interpreted* strictly; this may prevent the application of the clause.

6.4   In addition to these common law rules, there are two other sources of regulation of contract terms.

(a)   The Unfair Contract Terms Act 1977 is examined in section 8 of this chapter.

(b)   The Unfair Terms in Consumer Contracts Regulations 1994 are discussed in section 9.

6.5   If an exclusion clause is made void by statute it is unnecessary to consider how other legal rules might affect it. It is simply void.

7   INCORPORATION OF EXCLUSION CLAUSES

7.1   Uncertainty often arises over which terms have actually been incorporated into a contract. It is not enough for one party to claim that he possesses a set of draft terms; it must be shown that any such terms were incorporated into the agreement between the parties when the agreement was formed. These rules apply to any contract terms and not just to exclusion clauses although it is convenient to discuss them here, as many do concern exclusion clauses.

(a)   The document containing notice of the exclusion clause must be an integral part of the contract.

(b)   If the document is an integral part of the contract, a term may not usually be disputed if it is included in a document which a party has signed.

(c)   The term cannot be part of the contract unless put forward *before* the contract is made.

(d)   It is not a binding term unless the person whose rights it restricts was made sufficiently aware of it at the time of agreeing to it.

(e)   Onerous terms must be sufficiently highlighted.

Contractual documents

7.2   A term will not be treated as part of the contract unless the party affected by it was adequately informed of it when he accepted it. The term must be put forward in a document which gives reasonable notice that conditions are proposed by it. It must be shown that this document is an integral part of the contract and is one which could be expected to contain terms.

> *Chapelton v Barry UDC 1940*
> There was a pile of deck chairs and a notice stating 'Hire of chairs 2d per session of three hours'. The plaintiff took two chairs, paid for them and received two tickets which he put in his pocket. One of the chairs collapsed and he was injured. The defendant council relied on a notice on the back of the tickets by which it disclaimed liability for injury.

> *Held*: the notice advertising chairs for hire gave no warning of limiting conditions and it was not reasonable to communicate them on a receipt. The disclaimer of liability was not binding on the plaintiff.

> *Thompson v LMS Railway 1930*
> An elderly lady who could not read asked her niece to buy her a railway excursion ticket on which was printed 'Excursion: for conditions see back'. On the back it was stated that the ticket was issued subject to conditions contained in the company's timetables. These conditions excluded liability for injury.

> *Held*: the conditions had been adequately communicated and therefore had been accepted.

7.3   In the *Chapelton* case, the ticket was a mere receipt showing only the time of hire and acknowledging the payment of a fee. In the *Thompson* case, it should have been obvious to a reasonable person that the ticket had contractual effect, as tickets of that kind generally contain contract terms and are more than a mere receipt for payment.

Signed contracts

7.4   If a person signs a document containing a term he is held to have agreed to the term even if he had not read the document. But this is not so if the party who puts forward the document for signature gives a misleading explanation of the term's legal effect.

> *L'Estrange v Graucob 1934*
> The defendant sold to the plaintiff, a shopkeeper, a slot machine under conditions which excluded the plaintiff's normal rights under the Sale of Goods Act 1893. The plaintiff signed the document described as a 'Sales Agreement' and including clauses in 'legible, but regrettably small print', without reading the relevant condition.
>
> *Held*: the conditions were binding on the plaintiff since she had signed them. It was not material that the defendant had given her no information of their terms nor called her attention to them. (Under the law as it now stands some rights under the Sale of Goods Act 1979, which replaced the 1893 Act, may not be excluded.)

> *Curtis v Chemical Cleaning Co 1951*
> The plaintiff took her wedding dress to be cleaned. She was asked to sign a receipt on which there were conditions. Before signing she enquired what was the effect of the document and was told that it restricted the cleaner's liability in certain ways and in particular placed on the plaintiff the risk of damage to beads and sequins on the dress. The document in fact contained a clause 'that the company is not liable for any damage however caused'. The dress was badly stained in the course of cleaning.
>
> *Held*: the cleaners could not rely on their disclaimer since they had misled the plaintiff as to the effect of the document which she signed. She was entitled to assume that she was running the risk of damage to beads and sequins only.

Prior information on terms

7.5   Since the terms of the contract are fixed at the moment of acceptance of the offer, *a term cannot be introduced thereafter except by mutual consent*. Each party must be aware of the contract's terms at the time of entering into the agreement if they are to be binding.

> *Olley v Marlborough Court 1949*
> A husband and wife arrived at a hotel and paid for a room in advance. On reaching their bedroom they saw a notice on the wall by which the hotel disclaimed liability for loss of valuables unless handed to the management for safe keeping. The wife locked the room and handed the key in at the reception desk. A thief obtained the key and stole the wife's furs from the bedroom.
>
> *Held*: the hotel could not rely on the notice disclaiming liability since the contract had been made previously (when the room was booked and paid for) and the disclaimer was too late.

7.6   An exception to the rule that there should be prior notice of the terms is where the parties have had consistent dealings with each other in the past, and the documents used then contained similar terms.

> *J Spurling Ltd v Bradshaw 1956*
> Having dealt with a company of warehousemen for many years, the defendant gave it eight barrels of orange juice for storage. A document he received a few days later acknowledged receipt and contained a clause excluding liability for damage caused by negligence. When he collected the barrels they were empty and he refused to pay.

Held: it was a valid clause as it had also been present in the course of previous dealings, even though he had never read it.

Onerous terms

7.7 Where a term is particularly unusual and onerous it should be highlighted so that the attention of the other party is drawn to it when the contract is being formed. Failure to do so may mean that it does not become incorporated into the contract.

> *Interfoto Picture Library Ltd v Stiletto Visual Programmes Ltd 1988*
> 47 photographic transparencies were delivered to the defendant together with a delivery note with conditions on the back. Included in small type was a clause stating that for every day late each transparency was held a 'holding fee' of £5 plus VAT would be charged. They were returned 14 days late. The plaintiffs sued for the full amount of £3,783.50.
>
> *Held*: the term was onerous and had not been sufficiently brought to the attention of the defendant. The court reduced the fee to 50p per transparency per day (one tenth of the contractual figure) to reflect more fairly the loss caused to the plaintiffs by the delay.

8 INTERPRETATION OF EXCLUSION CLAUSES

8.1 In deciding what an exclusion clause means, the courts interpret any ambiguity against the person at fault who relies on the exclusion. This is known as the *contra proferentem* rule ('against the person relying on it'). Liability can only be excluded or restricted by clear words. In particular, if the clause gives exclusion in unspecific terms it is unlikely to be interpreted as covering negligence - want of proper care - on his part unless that is the only reasonable interpretation.

> *Hollier v Rambler Motors 1972*
> A garage disputed liability for fire damage (caused by negligence of its employees) to the plaintiff's car on the basis of a contractual term which stated that the company was not liable for damage caused by fire to customers' cars on the premises.
>
> *Held*: the term was not incorporated into the contract; the defendants argued that as a matter of *interpretation* the disclaimer of liability could only be interpreted to apply to fire damage by negligence as this was the only possible cause of action in the first place. However the court held that it could be read simply as a warning about liability for fire damage caused in many way, including by negligence. Because of this possibility even if the term had formed part of the contract it would be construed against the garage. (In fact this case was decided on the matter of incorporation, not interpretation.)

The 'main purpose' rule

8.2 When construing an exclusion clause the court will also consider the 'main purpose' rule. By this, the court presumes that the clause was *not* intended to defeat the main purpose of the contract, although of course the presumption may be rebutted. In order to rebut the presumption the party relying on the clause will have to show that its wording is sufficiently precise and relevant. In the context of a clause in a supplier's standard term contract which allows the supplier to render performance in a substantially different manner, the 'main purpose' rule is supplemented by s 3 UCTA which provides that such a term must be 'reasonable'.

Fundamental breach

8.3 For more than twenty years there were conflicting judicial *dicta* on how far an exclusion clause can exclude liability in a case where the breach of contract was a failure to perform the contract altogether - that is, a fundamental breach. In the case given below the House of Lords overruled some earlier decisions of the Court of Appeal and so the legal position is now reasonably clear.

Photo Productions v Securicor Transport 1980
The defendants agreed to guard the plaintiffs' factory under a contract by which the defendant were excluded from liability for damage caused by any of their employees. One of the guards deliberately started a small fire which got out of hand and destroyed the factory and contents, worth about £615,000. It was contended (on the authority of earlier decisions of the Court of Appeal) that Securicor had entirely failed to perform their contract since they had not guarded the factory and so they could not rely on any exclusion clause in the contract.

Held: there is no principle that total failure to perform a contract deprives the party at fault of any exclusion from liability provided by the contract. It is a question of interpretation of the exclusion clause whether it is widely enough expressed to cover total failure to perform. In this case the exclusion clause was drawn widely enough to cover the damage which had happened

As the fire occurred before the UCTA was in force the Act could not apply here. If it had done it would have been necessary to consider whether the exclusion clause was reasonable.

9   THE UNFAIR CONTRACT TERMS ACT 1977   *12/98*

9.1   When considering the validity of exclusion clauses the courts have had to strike a balance between:

(a)   the principle that parties should have *complete freedom* to contract on whatever terms they wish; and

(b)   the need to *protect the public* from unfair exclusion clauses in standard form contracts used by large companies.

9.2   The use of exclusion clauses by large organisations to abuse their bargaining power is clearly indefensible. Nevertheless, exclusion clauses do have a proper place in business. They can be used to *allocate contractual risk*, and thus to determine in advance who is to insure against that risk. They also make it possible for a contracting party to quote different rates according to the risk borne by him.

9.3   Thus between businessmen with similar bargaining power exclusion clauses are a legitimate device, but limitations on their use have been necessary in contracts involving the public. The main limitations are now contained in the Unfair Contract Terms Act 1977, which applies to clauses excluding or limiting *business liability*, in contract or tort.

9.4   Before we consider the specific terms of UCTA, it is necessary to describe how its scope is restricted.

(a)   In general the Act only applies to clauses inserted into agreements by *commercial concerns or businesses*. In principle *private persons* may restrict liability as much as they wish.

(b)   The Act does not apply to:

   (i)   contracts relating to the creation or transfer of patents;
   (ii)   contracts of insurance;
   (iii)   contracts relating to the creation or transfer of an interest in land;
   (iv)   contracts relating to company formation or dissolution.

9.5   The Act uses two techniques for controlling exclusion clauses - some types of clauses are void, whereas others are subject to a *test of reasonableness*. The main provisions of the Act are contained in Sections 2, 3, 6 and 7.

Avoidance of liability for negligence (s 2)

9.6 A person acting in the course of a business cannot, by reference to any contract term, restrict his liability for death or personal injury resulting from negligence. In the case of other loss or damage, a person cannot restrict his liability for negligence unless the term is *reasonable*. Negligence covers breach of contractual obligations of skill and care, the common law duty of skill and care, and the common duty of occupiers of premises under the Occupiers' Liability Acts 1957 and 1984.

Avoidance of liability for breach of contract (s 3)

9.7 This section deals with two distinct types of contract. The person who imposes a contract on his own standard terms of business, and the person who deals with a consumer, cannot, *unless the term is reasonable* restrict liability for their own breach or fundamental breach or claim to be entitled to render substantially different performance or no performance at all.

> *George Mitchell Ltd v Finney Lock Seeds Ltd 1983*
> The plaintiff, a farmer, ordered 30 pounds of Dutch winter cabbage seeds from the defendants, who were seed merchants. The purchase price was £201.60. The defendant's standard term contract limited their liability to a refund of the amount paid by the plaintiff. The wrong type of cabbage seed was delivered. The seed was planted over 63 acres, but when the crop came up it was not fit for human consumption. The plaintiff claimed £61,500 damages plus £30,000 interest.
>
> *Held*: at common law the exclusion clause would have protected the defendant, but the court decided in favour of the plaintiff, relying exclusively on the statutory ground of reasonableness.

The statutory definition of consumer (s 12)

9.8 A person deals as a consumer if:

(a) he neither makes the contract in the course of a business, nor holds himself out as doing so:

(b) the other party does make the contract in the course of a business; and

(c) the goods are of a type ordinarily supplied for private use or consumption.

9.9 Where a business engages in an activity which is merely incidental to the business, the activity will not be in the course of the business unless it is an integral part of it and it will not be an integral part of it unless it is carried on with a degree of regularity.

> *R & B Customs Brokers Ltd v United Dominions Trust Ltd 1988*
> The plaintiffs, a company owned by Mr and Mrs Bell and operating as a shipping broker, bought a second-hand Colt Shogun. The car was to be used partly for business and partly for private use.
>
> *Held:* this was a consumer sale, since the company was not in the business of buying cars.

Avoidance of liability arising from the sale and supply of goods (ss 6-7)

9.10 Any contract for the sale or hire purchase of goods cannot exclude the implied condition that the seller has a right to sell or transfer ownership of the goods.

9.11 A *consumer* contract for the sale of goods, hire purchase, supply of work or materials or exchange of goods cannot exclude or restrict liability for breach of the conditions relating to description, quality, fitness and sample implied by the Sale of Goods Act 1979 and the Supply of Goods and Services Act 1982. In a non-consumer contract these implied conditions may be excluded only if the exclusion clause is *reasonable*.

The statutory test of reasonableness (s 11)

9.12   The term must be fair and reasonable having regard to all the circumstances which were, or which ought to have been, known to the parties when the contract was made. The burden of proving reasonableness lies on the person seeking to rely on the clause (*contra proferentem*). Statutory guidelines have been included in the Act to assist the determination of reasonableness, although the court has discretion to take account of all factors. For instance, the court will consider in relation to contracts for the sale and supply of goods the following factors.

(a)   The relative strength of the parties' bargaining positions and in particular whether the customer could have satisfied his requirements from another source.

(b)   Whether any inducement (eg a reduced price) was offered to the customer to persuade him to accept limitation of his rights.

(c)   Whether the customer knew or ought to have known of the existence and extent of the exclusion clause.

(d)   If failure to comply with a condition (eg failure to give notice of a defect within a short period) excludes or restricts the customer's rights, whether it was reasonable to expect when the contract was made that compliance with the condition would be practicable.

(e)   Whether the goods were made, processed or adapted to the special order of the customer (UCTA Sch 2).

> *Smith v Eric S Bush 1989*
> A surveyor prepared a report on a property which contained a clause disclaiming liability for the accuracy and validity of the report. In fact the survey was negligently done and the plaintiff had to make good a lot of defects once the property was purchased.
>
> *Held:* in the absence of special difficulties, it was unreasonable for the surveyor to disclaim liability given the cost of the report, his profession of skill and care and his knowledge that it would be relied upon to make a major purchase.
>
> *St Albans City and District Council v International Computers Ltd 1994*
> The defendants had been hired to assess population figures on which to base community charges (local government taxation). Their standard contract contained a clause restricting liability to £100,000. The database which they supplied to the plaintiffs was seriously inaccurate and the latter sustained a loss of £1.3 million.
>
> *Held:* the clause was unreasonable. The defendants could not justify this limitation, which was very low in relation to the potential loss. In addition, they had aggregate insurance of £50 million. The defendants had to pay full damages.

Exercise 2

The Unfair Contract Terms Act 1977 limits the extent to which it is possible to exclude or restrict *business liability*. What do you understand by the phrase business liability?

Solution

Business liability is liability, in tort or contract, which arises from things done or to be done in the course of a business or from the occupation of premises used for business purposes of the occupier. Business includes a profession and the activities of any government department or public or local authority.

10   THE UNFAIR TERMS IN CONSUMER CONTRACTS REGULATIONS 1994

10.1   These regulations, which came into effect on 1 July 1995, implement an EC directive on unfair contract terms. UCTA 1977 continues to apply. Companies supplying goods and services to consumers and non-consumers will have to have regard to both laws, as no consolidation has yet taken place. There are now *three layers* of relevant legislation.

(a) The *common law*, which applies to all contracts, regardless of whether or not one party is a consumer.

(b) *UCTA 1977*, which applies to all contracts and which has specific provisions for consumer contracts.

(c) *The Regulations*, which only apply to consumer contracts and to terms which have not been individually negotiated.

10.2 The new regulations apply to contracts for the supply of goods or services.

(a) They apply to *terms in consumer contracts*. A consumer is defined as 'a natural person who, in making a contract to which these regulations apply, is acting for purposes which are outside his business'.

(b) They apply to contractual terms which *have not been individually negotiated*, ie they have been drafted in advance and the consumer has not been able to influence their substance.

(c) There are a number of *exceptions* including contracts relating to family law or to the incorporation or organisation of companies and partnerships and employment contracts.

10.3 A key aspect of the regulations is the definition of an unfair term. This is:

'any term which contrary to the requirement of good faith causes a significant imbalance in the parties' rights and obligations under the contract to the detriment of the consumer.'

10.4 In making an assessment of good faith, the courts will have regard to the following. (The first three of these are very similar to UCTA terms on reasonableness.)

(a) The strength of the bargaining positions of the parties.

(b) Whether the consumer had an inducement to agree to the term.

(c) Whether the goods or services were sold or supplied to the special order of the consumer.

(d) The extent to which the seller or supplier has dealt fairly and equitably with the consumer.

10.5 The effect of the regulations is to render certain terms in consumer contracts unfair, for example:

(a) excluding or limiting liability of the seller when the consumer dies or is injured, where this results from an act or omission of the seller (UCTA 1977 covers only *negligent* acts or omissions);

(b) excluding or limiting liability where there is partial or incomplete performance of a contract by the seller (as in UCTA 1977); and

(c) making a contract binding on the consumer where the seller can still avoid performing the contract.

10.6 Terms should be written in plain, intelligible language; where they are unclear, they will be construed against the seller.

10.7 Two forms of redress are available.

(a) A consumer who has concluded a contract containing an unfair term can ask the court to find that the *unfair term should not be binding*. The remainder of the contract will remain valid if it can continue in existence without the unfair term.

(b) A complaint, for example by an individual, a consumer group or a trading standards department can be made to the *Director General of Fair Trading*, who is empowered to seek injunctions against unfair terms. He can bring an action against, besides sellers and suppliers, manufacturers, franchisors and trade associations.

Chapter roundup

- As a general rule, the parties to a contract may include in the agreement whatever terms they choose. This is the principle of freedom of contract. A legally binding agreement must be complete in its terms, though the parties may leave an essential term to be settled by specified means outside the contract.

- Statements made by the parties may be classified as terms or representations. Different remedies attach to breach of a term and to misrepresentation respectively.

- Statements which are classified as contract terms may be further categorised as conditions or warranties. A condition is a vital term going to the root of the contract, while a warranty is a term subsidiary to the main purpose of the contract. The remedies available for breach are different in each case. It may not be possible to determine whether a term is a condition or a warranty; such terms are classified by the courts as innominate terms.

- The law may complement or replace terms by implying terms into a contract. Terms may be implied by the courts, by statute or by custom.

- An exclusion (or exemption) clause may attempt to restrict one party's liability for breach of contract or for negligence. Because of inequality of bargaining power, the Unfair Contract Terms Act 1977 renders void certain exclusion clauses in sale of goods or supply of services contracts and any clause which purports to exclude liability for death or personal injury resulting from negligence.

- The courts protect customers from the harsher effects of exclusion clauses by ensuring that they are properly *incorporated* into a contract and then by *interpreting* them strictly.

- The application of UCTA 1977 depends to a great extent upon whether there is a consumer sale. A contract between business operations is considerably less affected by the Act. Both types have often to satisfy a statutory test of reasonableness.

Test your knowledge

1. How may an essential term of a contract be settled when it has not been included in the contract? (see para 2.2)

2. What is a representation? (3.1)

3. Distinguish between a condition and a warranty. (4.1)

4. What is an innominate term? (4.3)

5. What is the 'officious bystander' test? (5.6)

6. Outline the facts of *Chapelton v Barry UDC 1940* (7.2)

7. When might the terms of an exclusion clause be incorporated into a contract even though a party has no prior notice of the terms? (7.6)

8. What is the *contra proferentem* rule? (8.1)

9. When may a party to a contract restrict his liability for negligence? (9.6)

10. How is a consumer defined under the Unfair Contract Terms Act 1977? (9.8)

Chapter 18

MISTAKE, MISREPRESENTATION AND ILLEGALITY

This chapter covers the following topics.

1 The nature of mistake

2 Types of mistake

3 Equitable reliefs for mistake

4 The nature of misrepresentation

5 Types of misrepresentation

6 Remedies for misrepresentation

7 Illegality

Introduction

The coverage of the law of contract in Chapters 11 to 16 (Part E) of this Study Text addresses the requirements of the syllabus for the *Introduction to English and European Union Law* examination paper. The syllabus is designed to provide an introduction to the law of contract and provides coverage of binding agreements with reference to the doctrines of privity and formalities.

A greater understanding of the law of contract developed through further study of the subject area will inevitably be to the student's advantage. In this part of the Study Text we provide additional material on the law of contract to extend your knowledge of this subject area. You will study these areas in greater depth in the pre-professional examination in *Business Law*.

In Chapter 17 we examined the terms of contract. Even if there is certainty as to terms, the validity of a contract may be affected by mistake, misrepresentation or illegality. These vitiating factors are analysed in this chapter.

1   THE NATURE OF MISTAKE

1.1   The general rule is that a party to a contract is not discharged from his obligations because he is mistaken as to the terms of the contract or the relevant circumstances. The terms of the contract are established by offer and acceptance; what the parties may think or intend should not override those terms or render the contract void. There are, however, exceptional and limited categories of 'operative mistake' which render the contract void.

1.2   Operative mistake is usually classified as follows.

(a) *Common mistake* - there is complete agreement between the parties but both are equally mistaken as to some fundamental point. Both parties make the same mistake.

(b) *Mutual mistake* - the parties are at cross-purposes but each believes that the other agrees with him and does not realise that there is a misunderstanding.

(c) *Unilateral mistake* - one party is mistaken and the other (who may have induced the mistake) is aware of it.

2   TYPES OF MISTAKE

Common mistake

2.1   Common mistake does not render a contract void unless the parties make a contract relating to subject matter which, unknown to them both, does not exist or has ceased to exist; there is then no contract between them.

> *Couturier v Hastie 1852*
> A contract was made in London was for the sale of a cargo of corn thought to have been shipped from Salonika. Unknown to the parties the cargo had already been sold by the master of the ship at Tunis since it had begun to rot. The London purchaser repudiated the contract and the agent who had sold the corn to him was sued (as a *del credere* agent he had indemnified his principal against any losses arising from such a repudiation).
>
> *Held:* the claim against him failed. The corn was not really in existence when the contract was made. The contract presupposed that it was; the contract related to non-existent subject matter and was void.

2.2   The rule on non existent subject matter (*res extincta*) has been extended to the infrequent cases where a person buys what already belongs to him (*res sua*). In such cases the contract cannot be performed because there is nothing to buy.

> *Cochrane v Willis 1865*
> Under a family settlement A would inherit property on the death of his brother B. B had become bankrupt in Calcutta and, to save the property from sale to a third party, A agreed with B's trustee in bankruptcy in England, to purchase the property from B's bankrupt estate. Unknown to A and B's trustee, B had already died in Calcutta and so the property had passed to A by inheritance before he bought it.
>
> *Held:* the contract was void and A was not liable to pay the agreed contract price.

Mutual mistake

2.3   If the parties are at cross purposes without either realising it, the terms of the contract usually resolve the misunderstanding in favour of one or the other.

> *Tamplin v James 1880*
> J went to an auction to bid for a public house. J believed that the property for sale included a field which had been occupied by the publican. But the sale particulars, which J did not inspect, made it clear that the field was not included. J was the successful bidder but when he realised his mistake refused to proceed with the purchase. The auctioneer had been unaware of J's mistake.
>
> *Held:* J was bound to pay the price which he had bid for the property described in the particulars of sale. The contract was quite clear and his mistake did not invalidate it.

2.4   The parties may, however, have failed to reach any agreement at all if the terms of the contract fail to identify the subject matter. Such a mistake renders the contract void.

> *Raffles v Wichelhaus 1864*
> A and B agreed in London on the sale from A to B of a cargo of cotton to arrive 'Ex Peerless from Bombay'. There were in fact two ships named Peerless with a cargo of cotton from Bombay; one sailed in October and the other in December. B intended the contract to refer to the October sailing and A to the December one.
>
> *Held:* as a preliminary point B could show that there was an ambiguity and that he intended to refer to the October shipment. If the case had gone further (there is no record that it did) the contract would have been void.

2.5   Where the parties genuinely misunderstand each other the court will determine whether a contract was intended to come into existence by applying the standard of the reasonable third party.

> *Scriven Bros v Hindley & Co 1913*
> At an auction a buyer bid for two lots believing both to be hemp. In fact one lot was a mixed batch of hemp and tow. It was not normal practice to sell hemp and tow together and the sale particulars were confusing. The auctioneer was unaware of the buyer's mistake and had not said anything which induced it.
>
> *Held:* in the circumstances there was no agreement by which the buyer was bound to accept the mixed hemp and tow. The contract was therefore not binding.

Unilateral mistake

2.6   A unilateral mistake is usually the result of misrepresentation by one party. The party misled is entitled to rescind the contract for misrepresentation but it may then be too late to recover the goods. Title to the goods passes to the dishonest party under a contract which is voidable and he may resell them to an innocent third party who is entitled to retain them (since the rogue still had title at the time of the resale to him). If, on the other hand, the contract is void for mistake at the outset, no title passes to the dishonest party and it may be possible for the party misled to recover his goods. *The difference between a voidable and a void contract determines which of two innocent persons is to bear the loss caused by fraud.*

2.7   Most of the case law on this type of mistake is concerned with mistake of identity. A contract is only void for mistake by the seller about the buyer's identity if the seller intended to sell to someone different from the actual buyer. If that is the position the seller never intends to sell to the actual buyer and the contract with him is void. In any other case the contract is valid when made, though it may later be rescinded since it may be voidable for misrepresentation.

Transactions by correspondence

2.8   The parties may negotiate the contract by correspondence without meeting face to face. If the buyer fraudulently adopts the identity of another person, known to the seller, with whom the seller intends to make the contract, the sale to the actual buyer is void.

> *Cundy v Lindsay 1878*
> Blenkarn, a dishonest person, wrote to C from '37 Wood St, Cheapside' to order goods and signed the letter so that his name appeared to be 'Blenkiron & Co', a respectable firm known to C, with their offices at 123 Wood St. The goods were consigned to Blenkiron & Co at 37 Wood St. and Blenkarn re-sold the goods to L. C sued L for conversion to recover the value of the goods (for which L had already paid Blenkarn in good faith).
>
> *Held:* C intended to sell only to B & Co: the contract was void and no title passed to Blenkarn. The mistake over the Wood St address was reasonable. L was liable to C for the value of the goods.

Face to face transactions

2.9   When the parties meet face to face it is generally inferred that the seller intends to sell to the person whom he meets. The latter may mislead the seller as to the buyer's creditworthiness by assuming a false identity, but even if he takes the identity of a real person about whom the seller makes enquiries, there is no mistake of identity which renders the contract void. It is merely voidable for misrepresentation and the loss falls on the seller.

> *Phillips v Brooks 1919*
> A rogue entered a jeweller's shop, selected various items which he wished to buy and proposed to pay by cheque. The jeweller replied that delivery must be delayed

until the cheque had been cleared. The rogue then said that he was Sir George Bullough, a well known person, and the jeweller checked that the real Sir G.B. lived at the address given by the rogue. The rogue then asked to take a ring away with him and the jeweller accepted his cheque and allowed him to have it. The rogue pledged the ring to a pawnbroker, who was sued by the jeweller.

Held: the action must fail. The jeweller had intended to contract with the person in the shop. There was no mistake of identity which made the contract void but only a mistake as to the creditworthiness of the buyer. Good title had passed to the rogue until the contract was avoided.

Documents mistakenly signed

2.10 The law recognises the problems of a blind or illiterate person who signs a document which he cannot read. If it is not what he supposes he may be able to repudiate it as not his deed (*non est factum*). The relief is not now restricted to the blind or illiterate but will not ordinarily be given to a person who merely failed to read what it was within his capacity to read and understand.

2.11 The following conditions must be satisfied in order to repudiate a signed contract as *non est factum*.

(a) There must be a fundamental difference between the legal effect of the document signed and that which the person who signed it believed it to have.

(b) The mistake must have been made without carelessness on the part of the person who signs.

> *Foster v Mackinnon 1869*
> An elderly man of feeble sight was asked to sign a guarantee. He had done so before. The document put before him to sign was in fact a bill of exchange which he signed as acceptor. The bill was later negotiated to the plaintiff. M repudiated it as non est factum.
>
> *Held:* the document signed was so different from what it was believed to be that a defence of *non est factum* could be available.

2.12 In a *non est factum* case the person who signs will usually rescind the contract (for misrepresentation) between himself and the person who puts forward and misdescribes the document. The defence of *non est factum* need only be raised when an honest third party has acquired rights. Again, this is because a contract is void for *non est factum* (so no rights were acquired) whilst it is voidable for misrepresentation.

3   EQUITABLE RELIEFS FOR MISTAKE

3.1 The equitable remedy of rectification may be claimed when a document does not correctly express the common intention of the parties. A party who applies for rectification must show that:

(a) the parties had a 'common intention', though it need not have become a binding agreement, and they retained that common intention at the time of signing the document; and

(b) the document does not correctly express their common intention.

> *Joscelyne v Nissen 1970*
> J lived in the same house with his married daughter N. J agreed to transfer his car hire business to N and N undertook as part of the bargain to pay all the household expenses including the electricity, gas and coal bills due in respect of the part of the house occupied by J. The bargain, not amounting at that stage to a contract, was then expressed in a written agreement which made no reference to N's liability to pay the household bills.

Held: J was entitled to have the written agreement rectified so that it referred to N's liability to pay the household bills.

3.2 It is also possible occasionally to obtain other equitable relief for mistake if it does not render the contract void. No general principle can be deduced from such cases except that such relief is only likely to be given to relieve unfairness. Unless it is unfair, a party who has made a non-operative mistake must abide by his contract. Equity will sometimes impose a *compromise* on the parties.

> *Solle v Butcher 1950*
> Extensive improvements were made to what had been a rent-controlled flat. Both landlord and tenant believed (common mistake) that the flat had therefore ceased to be subject to rent control. It was let at a rent of £250 per annum. The original controlled rent was £140 p.a. but if the landlord had served a notice on the tenant in time he could have had the controlled rent increased to almost £250 p.a. on account of the improvements. After the period for claiming increased rent had expired it was discovered that the flat was still subject to rent control. The tenant sought to recover the excess rent and the landlord to rescind the lease.
>
> *Held:* the tenant should have the choice between a surrender of the lease and accepting a new lease at a controlled rent increased to make allowance for the landlord's improvements.

4 THE NATURE OF MISREPRESENTATION

4.1 A statement made in the course of pre-contract negotiations may become a term of the contract. If it is a term of the contract and proves to be untrue, the party who has been misinformed may claim damages for breach of contract. If, however, the statement does not become a term of the contract and it is untrue, the party misled may be able to treat it as a *misrepresentation* and rescind (avoid) the contract, or in some cases, recover damages. The contract is voidable for misrepresentation.

4.2 A misrepresentation is:

   (a) a representation of *fact* which is *untrue;*
   (b) made by one party to the other *before the contract* is made;
   (c) which is an *inducement* to the party misled actually to enter into the contract.

Representation of fact

4.3 In order to analyse whether a statement may be a misrepresentation, it is first of all necessary to decide whether it could have been a representation at all.

   (a) A statement of fact is a representation.
   (b) A statement of law, intention, opinion or mere 'sales talk' is not a representation.
   (c) Silence does not usually constitute a representation.

Statement of opinion

4.4 *A statement of opinion or intention is a statement that the opinion or intention exists, but not that it is a correct opinion or an intention which will be realised.* In deciding whether a statement is a statement of fact or of opinion, the extent of the speaker's knowledge as much as the words he uses determines the category to which the statement belongs.

> *Bisset v Wilkinson 1927*
> A vendor of land which both parties knew had not previously been grazed by sheep stated that it would support about 2,000 sheep. This proved to be untrue.
>
> *Held:* in the circumstances this was an honest statement of opinion as to the capacity of the farm, not a statement of fact.

Statement of intention

4.5   *A statement of intention, or a statement as to future conduct, is not actionable.* An affirmation of the truth of a fact (a representation) is different from a promise to do something in the future. If a person enters into a contract or takes steps relying on a representation, the fact that the representation is false entitles him to remedies at law. However, if he sues on a statement of intention - a promise - he must show that that promise forms part of a valid contract if he is to gain any remedy.

> *Maddison v Alderson 1883*
> The plaintiff had been the defendant's housekeeper for ten years. She had received no wages in this period. She announced that she wished to leave and get married. She alleged that the defendant had promised that, if she stayed with him, he would leave her in his will a life interest in his farm. She agreed to remain with him until he died. He left a will which included this promise, but because it had not been witnessed it was void. She claimed that the promise to make a will in her favour was a representation.
>
> *Held:* 'the doctrine of estoppel by representation is applicable only to representations as to some state of facts alleged to be at the time actually in existence, and not to promises *de futuro*, which, if binding at all, must be binding as contracts'. There was no contract in existence. A sincerely stated intention is not misrepresentation when it is not carried out.

Silence

4.6   As a general rule neither party is under any duty to disclose what he knows. If he keeps silent that is not a representation. But there is a duty to disclose information in the following cases.

(a)   What is said must be complete enough to avoid giving a misleading impression. A half-truth can be false: *R v Kylsant 1931*

(b)   There is a duty to correct an earlier statement which was true when made but which becomes untrue before the contract is completed: *With v O'Flanagan 1936*.

(c)   In contracts of 'extreme good faith' (*uberrimae fidei*) there is a duty to disclose the material facts which one knows. Non-disclosure can lead to the contract being voidable for misrepresentation. Three types of contract carry a duty *uberrimae fidei*, which means that failure to disclose material facts makes the contract voidable.

  (i)   Contracts of insurance (hence failure to disclose, say, a speeding conviction may invalidate motor insurance cover).

  (ii)   Contracts preliminary to family arrangements, such as land settlements.

  (iii)   Contracts where there is a fiduciary relationship, such as exists between solicitor and client, or partner and partner.

Statement made by one party to another

4.7   Although in general a misrepresentation must have been made by the misrepresentor to the misrepresentee there are two exceptions to the rule.

(a)   A misrepresentation can be made to the *public in general*, as where an advertisement contains a misleading representation.

(b)   The misrepresentation need not be made directly on a one-to-one basis - it is sufficient that the misrepresentor knows that the *misrepresentation would be passed on* to the relevant person.

> *Pilmore v Hood 1873*
> The defendant fraudulently misrepresented the turnover of his pub so as to sell it to X. X had insufficient funds and so repeated the representations, with the defendant's knowledge, to the plaintiff. On the basis of this the plaintiff purchased the pub.

Held: the defendant was liable for fraudulent misrepresentation even though he had not himself misrepresented the facts to the plaintiff.

Inducement to enter into the contract

4.8   Since to be actionable a representation must have induced the person to enter into the contract, it follows that he must have:

(a)   known of its existence;
(b)   allowed it to affect his judgment; and
(c)   been unaware of its untruth.

4.9   *If the plaintiff was not aware of the misrepresentation, his action will fail.*

Horsfall v Thomas 1862
The plaintiff made a gun to be sold to the defendant and, in making it, concealed a defect in the breech by inserting a metal plug. The defendant bought the gun without inspecting it. The gun exploded and he claimed that he had been misled into purchasing it by a misrepresentation (the metal plug) that it was sound.

Held: the defendant had not inspected the gun at the time of purchase and the metal plug could not have been a misleading inducement because he was unaware of it, and therefore did not rely on it when he entered into the contract.

5   TYPES OF MISREPRESENTATION

5.1   Misrepresentation is classified (for the purpose of determining what remedies are available) as:

(a)   *fraudulent* - a statement made with knowledge that it is untrue, or without believing it to be true, or recklessly, careless whether it be true or false;

(b)   *negligent* - a statement made in the belief that it is true but without reasonable grounds for that belief; or

(c)   *innocent* - a statement made in the belief that it is true and with reasonable grounds for that belief.

Fraudulent misrepresentation

5.2   An *absence of honest belief* is essential to constitute fraud.

Derry v Peek 1889
The plaintiff and other directors of a company published a prospectus inviting the public to apply for shares. The prospectus stated that the company (formed under a special Act of Parliament) had statutory powers to operate trams in Plymouth, drawn by horses or driven by steam power. The Act required that the company should obtain a licence from the Board of Trade for the operation of steam trams. The directors assumed that the licence would be granted whenever they might apply for it. But it was later refused.

Held: the directors honestly believed that the statement made was true and so this was not a fraudulent misrepresentation. The false representation was not made knowingly, without belief in its truth or recklessly, and so the directors escaped liability.

Negligent misrepresentation

5.3   Negligent misrepresentation may be at common law (involving breach of a duty of care owed) or under the statutory protection of the Misrepresentation Act 1967 (when the defendant must disprove his negligence). Under the Act no duty of care need be shown.

5.4   In 1963 the House of Lords reached an important decision, by which it held that in certain instances an action in tort for negligent misstatement might be possible.

> *Hedley Byrne & Co Ltd v Heller & Partners Ltd 1964*
> The plaintiffs were advertising agents acting for a new client E. If E defaulted on payment, the plaintiffs would themselves be liable. They checked E's financial position by asking their bank to make enquiries of E's bank (the defendants). Relying on the replies they placed orders and suffered substantial losses when E went into liquidation.
>
> *Held:* the action failed because the defendants were able to rely on a disclaimer. However, had it not been for this, an action for negligence would have succeeded. Liability for negligent statements depends upon the existence of a 'special relationship'; the defendants knew what the information was to be used for.

5.5   Actions for fraudulent and negligent misrepresentation lie in the law of tort.

Misrepresentation Act 1967

5.6   At the same time as case law on negligent misrepresentation was developing as outlined above, the Law Reform Committee recommended that damages should be given for negligent misrepresentation. Their recommendations resulted in the Misrepresentation Act 1967.

5.7   Under s 2(1) of the Act, where a person has entered into a contract after a misrepresentation has been made to him by another party to the contract and has as a result suffered loss, then, if the person making the misrepresentation would be liable to damages if the misrepresentation had been made fraudulently, he will be liable to damages notwithstanding that the misrepresentation was not made fraudulently. He will escape liability if he can prove that he had reasonable grounds to believe, and did believe, up to the time the contract was made, that the facts represented were true.

5.8   This puts the burden of proof on the person making the representation, the representor. He will be deemed negligent and liable to pay damages unless he can disprove negligence.

5.9   This suggests that it may be more advantageous for a plaintiff to bring a claim under the Act than at common law.

> *Howard Marine and Dredging Co Ltd v A Ogden & Sons (Excavations) Ltd 1978*
> The defendants required two barges for use in an excavation contract. During negotiations with the plaintiffs, the plaintiff's marine manager stated that the payload of two suitable barges was 1,600 tonnes. This was based on figures given by Lloyds Register, which turned out to be in error. The payload was only 1,055 tonnes. The defendants stopped paying the hire charges and were sued. They counterclaimed for damages at common law and under the Misrepresentation Act 1967.
>
> *Held:* the court was unable to decide on whether there was a duty of care (in the common law action), but the plaintiffs had not discharged the burden of proof under the Act, as shipping documents in their possession disclosed the real capacity.

Innocent misrepresentation

5.10   An innocent misrepresentation is any misrepresentation made without fault.

6   REMEDIES FOR MISREPRESENTATION

6.1   There is a fundamental principle that the effect of a misrepresentation is to make a contract *voidable* and not void. The contract remains valid unless set aside by the representee. This means that the representee may choose either to *affirm* the contract or to *rescind* it. In some instances, there may be a right to *damages*, either instead of, or in addition to, the remedy of rescission. The available remedies vary depending on the *type* of misrepresentation.

Rescission

6.2   Rescission entails setting the contract aside as if it had never been made. A contract is rescinded if the representee makes it clear that he refuses to be bound by its provisions; it is then terminated *ab initio*. The representee does not have to rescind - he may alternatively affirm the contract by:

(a)   declaring his intention to proceed with it; or
(b)   doing some act from which such an intention may reasonably be inferred.

6.3   To rescind a contract, the representee simply makes it clear that he refuses to be bound by the contract. The general rule is that he must communicate his decision to the misrepresentor, but there are two exceptions to this.

(a)   If property has been delivered to the misrepresentor as a result of the misrepresentation, it is enough simply to take the property back again.

(b)   If the misrepresentor disappears so that communication is not possible, the representee may announce his intention to rescind by some overt act that is reasonable in the circumstances.

> *Car & Universal Finance Co Ltd v Caldwell 1965*
> A car was purchased from the defendant by a rogue with a fraudulent cheque. The seller was unable to communicate with the rogue, but informed the police and the AA of the fraud. The rogue had resold the car. (The rogue had fraudulently misrepresented that the cheque would be honoured.)
>
> *Held:* the seller had rescinded the contract by taking all reasonable steps and the rogue did not transfer good title to the plaintiffs in a subsequent sale.

Loss of the right to rescind

6.4   The equitable principle of rescission seeks to ensure that the *parties should be restored to their position as it was before the contract was made*. The right to rescind is lost in any of the following circumstances.

(a)   If the party misled *affirms the contract* after discovering the true facts he may not afterwards rescind. For this purpose it is not necessary that he should expressly affirm the contract. Intention to affirm may be implied from conduct indicating that the party is treating the contract as still in operation.

> *Long v Lloyd 1958*
> The plaintiff bought a lorry for £750 after the defendant had described it as being in first class condition. On the plaintiff's first business journey, the dynamo failed, an oil seal leaked, a wheel cracked and the vehicle returned only 5 miles to the gallon. The plaintiff told the defendant of the problems; the latter agreed to pay half the cost of the dynamo but denied knowledge of any other problems. On the next business journey the lorry broke down and was declared by an expert to be unroadworthy. The plaintiff sought to rescind the contract.
>
> *Held:* acceptance of a financial contribution, together with the embarking upon the second journey, constituted affirmation of the contract.

(b) If the parties can no longer be restored to substantially the *pre-contract position*, the right to rescind is lost.

> *Clark v Dickson 1858*
> The contract related to a business which at the time of the misrepresentation was carried on by a partnership. It was later reorganised as a company and the plaintiff's interest in the business was with his consent converted into shares. He later sought to rescind.
>
> *Held:* the conversion of the plaintiff's interest in the partnership into shares in the company was an irreversible change which precluded restoration to the original position. The right to rescind had been lost.

(c) If the *rights of third parties,* such as creditors of an insolvent company, would be prejudiced by rescission, it is too late to rescind. In the *Car and Universal Finance* case, rescission occurred before the intervention of a *bona fide* purchaser.

> *White v Garden 1851*
> A rogue bought 50 tons of iron from the defendant by persuading him to take a fraudulent bill of exchange. He resold the iron to the plaintiff, who acted in good faith, and the defendant delivered the iron to the plaintiff. When the bill was dishonoured the defendant seized and removed some of the iron.
>
> *Held:* the defendant was liable in the tort of conversion; he had purported to rescind the contract too late.

(d) *Lapse of time* may act as a bar to rescission.

> *Leaf v International Galleries 1950*
> The plaintiff, in 1944, bought from the defendant an oil painting of Salisbury Cathedral for £85. The defendants had told him that the painting was by Constable, but when he tried to sell it five years later, Christie's told him that this was not the case. He immediately sued for rescission of the contract.
>
> *Held:* rescission was in theory possible, as a simple exchange of painting and purchase money could restore the previous position. The court treated the statement as an innocent (non-fraudulent) representation and refused to rescind because of the passage of time.

Exercise

In many cases, rescission is simply effected when the misrepresentee makes it clear that he refuses to be bound by the contract. When may it be advantageous to bring legal proceedings for an order for rescission?

Solution

Legal action may be desirable if the fraudulent party ignores the cancellation of the contract and fails to return what he has obtained under it. It may be necessary for a formal document, such as a lease, to be set aside by court order. There might also be a possibility that innocent third parties may act on the assumption that the contract still exists.

Damages

6.5 Rescission is a general remedy for misrepresentation. The right to damages is not generally available, but depends on showing that the statement made by the representor is either fraudulent or negligent. It should be noted that damages for misrepresentation are not the same as damages for breach of contract.

(a) In contract, the purpose of damages is to put the injured party in the position he would have enjoyed if the contract *had been* performed.

(b) In tort, the purpose is to restore the injured party to the position he was in *prior to* the tort being committed.

Fraudulent misrepresentation

6.6   In a case of *fraudulent* misrepresentation the party misled may *in addition to,* or *instead of,* rescinding the contract recover damages for any loss by a common law action for the tort of deceit. Damages will be measured by the 'out-of-pocket' rule, which involves measuring the loss directly flowing from the deceit. This may include damages for loss of profits: *Doyle v Olby (Ironmongers) 1969.*

Negligent misrepresentation

6.7   The injured party may (under the 1967 Act) claim damages for any actual loss caused by *negligent* misrepresentation. It is then up to the party who made the statement to prove, if he can, that he had reasonable grounds for making it and that it was not in fact negligent: *F and B Entertainments v Leisure Enterprises 1976*

6.8   An action at common law is also possible, damages recoverable being measured by reference to common law rules. As noted above, under the rules of tort damages are intended to put the injured party in the position he would have been in if he had never entered the contract. Whatever the type of misrepresentation, unforeseeable as well as foreseeable losses are recoverable, provided the losses are not too remote: *Royscot Trust Ltd v Rogerson & Others 1991*

Innocent misrepresentation

6.9   In a case of misrepresentation the party misled may under the 1967 Act, be awarded damages in lieu of rescission if the court considers it equitable to do so. The remedy of damages is discretionary, and as a rule is not awarded for innocent misrepresentation. An indemnity - different from damages - may be awarded, indemnifying the misrepresentee against any obligations necessarily created by the contract.

7   ILLEGALITY

7.1   Some types of contract cannot be enforced in a court of law because they are unlawful in themselves or disapproved as contrary to public policy. Some types of illegal contracts are also void. The following categories may be distinguished.

(a)   *Contracts void by statute,* including restrictive trading agreements and resale price maintenance agreements.

(b)   *Contracts which are illegal and void by statute,* for example cartel agreements.

(c)   *Contracts void at common law on the grounds of public policy,* of which the most important are contracts in restraint of trade.

(d)   *Contracts which are illegal and void at common law as contrary to public morals or the interests of the state,* including agreements to commit a crime or tort (such as assault or defrauding the Revenue), contracts to promote sexual immorality and contracts to promote corruption in public life.

7.2   Since all such contracts are *void,* neither party can enforce them by legal action. In general, money paid or property transferred under a contract which is merely void may be recovered. If the void part can be separated from the other terms without rendering the agreement meaningless, then the remainder may be valid. But if the contract is also *illegal* the courts will not (subject to some exceptions) assist a party to recover his money or property.

The effects of an illegal contract

7.3   If the contract is obviously illegal at its inception or if the contract appears to be legal but both parties intend to accomplish an illegal purpose by it, neither has an enforceable right at law against the other.

Pearce v Brooks 1866
The plaintiffs, who were coachbuilders, let a carriage described as 'of a somewhat intriguing nature' to a prostitute. They knew that she was a prostitute and the jury found (although the plaintiffs denied it) that they also knew that she intended to parade along the streets in the carriage as a means of soliciting clients and would pay for the carriage out of her immoral earnings. She failed to pay the agreed amount and they sued to recover it.

Held: although the letting of a carriage is not obviously unlawful, to do so to facilitate known immoral purposes is an illegal and void contract which will not be enforced.

7.4   If the contract is legal at its inception and one party later performs his side of it for illegal purposes, the other innocent party may recover money paid and property transferred or payment for services rendered (while in ignorance of the illegality).

Clay v Yates 1856
A printer agreed with an author to print copies of the author's book. The printer was unaware that the book contained libellous material. He discovered the libel after he had printed part of the book and refused to do any more. He claimed the value of work done but the author refused to pay for incomplete performance.

Held: the printer was justified in ceasing work on the book and could recover payment for work done.

Restraint of trade contracts

7.5   Contracts in restraint of trade are the most important examples of contracts which are void at common law. Any restriction on a person's normal freedom to carry on a trade, business or profession in such a way and with such persons as he chooses is a restraint of trade.

7.6   A restraint of trade is treated as contrary to public policy and therefore void unless it can be justified under the principles explained below. If a restraint is void the remainder of the contract by which the restraint is imposed is usually valid and binding - it is merely the restraint which is struck out as invalid. The general policy of the law is against upholding any restrictions on a person's freedom to work or carry on a trade, but there are some exceptions.

7.7   The objection to a restraint of trade is that it denies to the community useful services which would otherwise be available. On the other hand, it is recognised that a restraint may be needed to protect legitimate interests. A restraint of trade may therefore be justified and be enforceable if:

(a)   the person who imposes it has a legitimate interest to protect;
(b)   the restraint is reasonable between the parties as a protection of that interest; and
(c)   the restraint is also reasonable from the standpoint of the community.

Nordenfelt v Maxim Nordenfelt Guns and Ammunition Co Ltd 1984
The plaintiff had developed a new firing mechanism for guns and carried on, among other things, a business manufacturing these guns and their ammunition. When he sold the assets and goodwill of the business he entered into an agreement, later duplicated when the business merged with another, that he would not engage directly or indirectly in a wide number of gun-related activities or any other competing business for 25 years except on its behalf.

Held: the covenant as it related to guns and the business sold was valid because the business connection was worldwide and it was possible to sever this undertaking from the rest of the agreement. The term as to competition was void since it went much further than could reasonably be required to protect the business.

Restraints on employees

7.8   An employer may (in consideration of the payment of wages) insist that the employee's services shall be given only to him while the employment continues. But any restraint imposed on the employee's freedom to take up other employment (or to carry on business on his own account) *after* leaving the employer's service is void unless it can be justified.

7.9   Such a restraint, if reasonable in its extent, may be valid if it is imposed to prevent the employee from making use of the trade secrets or trade connections (business goodwill) of the employer, since these are interests which the employer is entitled to protect.

7.10   The courts may have to consider what constitutes *legitimate interests*. An employee who has access to *trade secrets* such as manufacturing processes, or even financial and commercial information which is confidential, may be restricted to prevent his using it after leaving his present job. In contrast to trade secrets the employer has no right to restrain an employee from exercising a *personal skill* acquired in the employer's service.

> *Forster & Sons v Suggett 1918*
> As works manager the defendant had access to technical know-how of his employer's business of making glass bottles. His contract of employment provided that for five years after leaving his employer's service he would not carry on or be interested in the manufacture of glass bottles in the UK or other glass-making similar to that of his employer's business.
>
> *Held:* it must be shown (and in this case it had been) that the employee had access to secret manufacturing processes. The restraint was valid.

> *Morris v Saxelby* 1916
> On leaving school the defendant entered the drawing office of the plaintiff (a manufacturer of cranes and lifting gear) as an apprentice and rose to become head of a department. He had some limited knowledge of the employer's technical secrets but essentially he became a skilled draftsman in engineering design work. He undertook that for seven years after leaving his employment he would not engage in any similar business in the UK.
>
> *Held:* this was a restraint on the use by the defendant of technical skill and knowledge acquired in the service of the plaintiff. He should not be prevented from earning his living by the use of it and the plaintiff had no right to be protected from the competition of a former employee using his own skills. The restriction was also unreasonably wide and was void.

Restraints on vendors of businesses

7.11   A purchaser of the goodwill of a business obviously has a right to protect what he has bought by imposing restrictions to prevent the vendor doing business with his old customers or clients. But the restraint must protect the business sold and it must not be excessive.

> *British Reinforced Concrete Engineering Co v Schelff 1921*
> The defendant carried on a small local business of making one type of road reinforcement. He sold his business to the plaintiffs, who carried on business throughout the UK in making a range of road reinforcements. He undertook not to compete with them in the sale or manufacture of road reinforcements.
>
> *Held:* the restraint was void since it was widely drawn to protect the plaintiff from any competition by the defendant. In buying the defendant's business they were only entitled to protect what they bought - a local business making one type of product and not the entire range produced by them in the UK.

7.12   For goodwill to be protected it must actually exist. The courts will not allow 'protection of goodwill' to be a smokescreen for barefaced restraint of competition.

Vancouver Malt & Sake Brewing Co Ltd v Vancouver Breweries Ltd 1934
The defendant was licensed to brew beer but in fact only produced sake. It sold its business and agreed to a term restraining it from brewing beer for 15 years. It later began to produce beer and the purchaser sought to enforce the restraint.

Held: since the seller did not, at the time of sale, produce beer the purchaser only paid for tangible assets because there was no beer-brewing goodwill to sell. The purchaser had not provided consideration for the promise not to produce beer and so he could not enforce it.

Chapter roundup

- The general rule is that a party to a contract is not discharged from his obligations because he is mistaken as to the terms of the contract or the relevant circumstances. There are a number of exceptional circumstances in which 'operative mistake' may render the contract void.

- Common mistake occurs where the parties are both mistaken as to some fundamental point, for example the existence of the subject matter of the contract. Mutual mistake occurs where the parties, without realising it, are at cross-purposes. Unilateral mistake arises where one party is mistaken and the other is aware of it.

- A *representation* is a statement made in pre-contract negotiations, intended to induce the other party to enter into the agreement; it may or may not subsequently become a contract term

- A contract entered into following a misrepresentation is voidable by the person to whom the misrepresentation was made. A misrepresentation is a statement of fact which is untrue, made by one party to the other in order to induce the latter to enter into the agreement, and a matter of some importance actually relied upon by the person misled.

- Fraudulent misrepresentation is a statement made knowing it to be untrue, not believing it to be true or recklessly, careless whether it be true or false. Negligent misrepresentation is a statement made in the belief that it is true but without reasonable grounds for that belief. Innocent misrepresentation, the residual category, is any statement made in the belief that it is true and with reasonable grounds for that belief.

- Certain contracts cannot be enforced in a court of law because they are unlawful or contrary to public policy. Contracts in restraint of trade are the most important examples of contracts which are void at common law.

Test your knowledge

1   What is *res sua*? (see para 2.2)

2   Outline the facts of *Phillips v Brooks 1919* (2.9)

3   What is *non est factum*? (2.10)

4   What are the conditions for rectification to be ordered? (3.1)

5   What is a misrepresentation? (4.2)

6   What is a contract *uberrimae fidei?* (4.6)

7   What are the two categories of negligent misrepresentation? (5.3)

8   How may the representee affirm a contract following a misrepresentation? (6.2)

9   List four situations in which the right to rescind is lost. (6.4)

10 What is a restraint of trade? (7.5)

Chapter 19

DISCHARGE OF CONTRACT

This chapter covers the following topics.

1   Performance

2   Breach of contract

3   Agreement

4   Frustration

Introduction

The coverage of the law of contract in Chapters 11 to 16 (Part E) of this Study Text addresses the requirements of the syllabus for the *Introduction to English and European Community Law* examination paper. The syllabus is designed to provide an introduction to the law of contract and provides coverage of binding agreements with reference to the doctrines of privity and formalities.

A greater understanding of the law of contract developed through further study of the subject area will inevitably be to the student's advantage. In this part of the Study Text we provide additional material on the law of contract to extend your knowledge of this subject area. You will study these areas in greater depth in the pre-professional examination in *Business Law*.

In this chapter we describe the ways in which a contract may be terminated. In Chapter 23 we look at remedies for breach of contract.

---

1   PERFORMANCE

1.1   This is the normal method of discharge. Each party fulfils or performs his contractual obligations and the agreement is then ended. As a general rule contractual obligations are discharged only *by complete and exact performance*. A party who does not perform perfectly is not entitled to claim payment or performance from the other party.

> *Cutter v Powell 1795*
> The defendant employed C as second mate of a ship sailing from Jamaica to Liverpool at a wage for the complete voyage of 30 guineas [£31.50]. The voyage began on 2 August, and C died at sea on 20 September, when the ship was still 19 days from Liverpool. C's widow sued for a proportionate part of the agreed sum.
>
> *Held:* C was entitled to nothing unless he completed the voyage.

1.2   In this case the defendant might appear to have profited to an undue degree, since he obtained part of what the plaintiff contracted to deliver without himself having to pay anything. Although such cases can be justified on their facts, the courts have developed a number of exceptions to the rule to ensure that the interests of both parties are protected. The *exceptions* are as follows.

(a)   The doctrine of substantial performance
(b)   Where the promisee accepts partial performance
(c)   Where the promisee prevents performance
(d)   Where time is not of the essence
(e)   Severable contracts

Substantial performance

1.3   The doctrine of *substantial performance* may be applied, especially in contracts for building work and the like. If the building contractor has completed the essential work and in doing so has completed a very large part of it, he may claim the contract price less a deduction for the minor work outstanding. This may also be regarded as a deduction of damages for breach of warranty when the contract price is paid.

> *Hoenig v Isaacs 1952*
> The defendant employed the plaintiff to decorate and furnish his flat at a total price of £750. There were defects in the furniture which could be put right at a cost of £56. The defendant argued that the plaintiff was only entitled to reasonable remuneration.
>
> *Held:* the defendant must pay the balance owing of the total price of £750 less an allowance of £56, as the plaintiff had substantially completed the contract.

Partial performance

1.4   The promisee may accept partial performance and must then pay for it. For example, A orders a dozen bottles of beer from B; B delivers ten which is all he has in stock. A may reject the ten bottles but if he accepts them he must pay for ten bottles at the appropriate rate.

1.5   The principle here is that although the promisor has only partially fulfilled his contractual obligations, it may sometimes be possible to infer the existence of a fresh agreement by which it is agreed that payment will be made for work already done or goods already supplied. Mere performance by the promisor is not enough; it must be open to the promisee either to accept or reject the benefit of the contract.

Prevention of performance

1.6   The promisee may prevent performance. In that case the offer (*tender*) of performance is sufficient discharge. For example, if the buyer will not accept delivery of the contract goods and the seller sues for breach of contract, the seller need only show that he tendered performance by offering to deliver.

1.7   If one party is prevented by the other from performing the contract completely he may sue for damages for breach of contract, or alternatively bring a *quantum meruit* action to claim for the amount of work done.

> *Planché v Colburn 1831*
> The plaintiff had agreed to write a book on costumes and armour for the defendants' 'Juvenile Library' series. He was to receive £100 on completion. He did some research and wrote part of the book. The defendants then abandoned the series.
>
> *Held:* the plaintiff was entitled to 50 guineas as reasonable remuneration on a *quantum meruit* basis.

Time of performance

1.8   If one party fails to perform at the *agreed time* he may perform the contract later - the contract continues in force, unless prompt performance is an essential condition (' time is of the essence'). In that case the injured party may refuse late performance and treat the contract as discharged by breach. Where time is not of the essence the injured party may claim damages for any loss or expense caused by the delay but must accept late performance.

1.9　If the parties expressly agree that '*time is of the essence*' and so prompt performance is to be a condition, that is conclusive and *late performance does not discharge obligations*. If they make no such express stipulation the following rules apply.

(a)　In a commercial contract, time of performance (other than the time of payment) is usually treated as an essential condition: *Elmdore v Keech 1969*

(b)　If time was not originally of the essence, either party may make it so by serving on the other (after the time for performance has arrived) a notice to complete within a reasonable time.

Charles Rickards Ltd v Oppenheim 1950
The contract was to build a Rolls-Royce chassis by 20 March. When this period expired without delivery the purchaser agreed to wait another three months. As the chassis had still not been built by 29 June, he served a notice requiring completion by 25 July at the latest; if this were not done he would cancel the order. He did cancel it but the makers tendered delivery three months after he had done so.

Held: although the purchaser had at first waived his rights (by the three month extension) he could, by serving reasonable notice to complete, make time of the essence and treat the contract as discharged if there was no performance within the period of the notice. He had done so and was justified in refusing delivery.

Severable contracts

1.10　The contract may provide for performance by instalments with separate payment for each of them (a *divisible* or *severable* contract).

Taylor v Laird 1856
The plaintiff agreed to captain a ship up the River Niger at a rate of £50 per month. He abandoned the job before it was completed. He claimed his pay for the months completed.

Held: he was entitled to £50 for each complete month. Effectively this was a contract that provided for performance and payment in monthly instalments.

2　BREACH OF CONTRACT

2.1　A party is said to be in breach of contract where, *without lawful excuse,* he does not perform his contractual obligations precisely. A person has a lawful excuse not to perform primary contractual obligations (that is, what he promised to do under his side of the bargain) where:

(a)　performance is impossible, perhaps because of some unforeseeable event;
(b)　he has tendered performance but this has been rejected;
(c)　the other party has made it impossible for him to perform;
(d)　the contract has been discharged through frustration (discussed later); or
(e)　the parties have by agreement permitted non-performance.

Repudiatory breach

2.2　A *repudiatory breach* occurs where a party indicates, either by words or by conduct, that he does not intend to honour his contractual obligations. A repudiatory breach is a serious actual breach of contract. It does not automatically discharge the contract - indeed the injured party has a choice.

(a)　He can elect to treat the contract as repudiated by the other, recover damages and treat himself as being discharged from his primary obligations under the contract. This is termination of the contract for repudiatory breach.

(b)　He can elect to affirm the contract.

2.3　'Where there is a contract to be performed in the future, if one of the parties has said to the other in effect "if you go on and perform your side of the contract I will not perform mine", that in effect, amounts to saying "I will not perform the contract". In that case the other party may say "you have given me distinct notice that you will not perform the contract. I will not wait until you have broken it, but I will treat you as having put an end to the contract, and if necessary I will sue you for damages, but at all events I will not go on with the contract" ' *Mersey Steel and Iron Co v Naylor Benzon & Co 1884.*

Anticipatory breach

2.4 Repudiation may be explicit or implicit. A party may break a condition of the contract merely by declaring in advance that he will not perform it when the time for performance arrives, or by some other action which makes future performance impossible. The other party may treat this as anticipatory breach and:

(a) may treat the contract as discharged forthwith; or
(b) at his option may allow the contract to continue until there is an actual breach.

> *Hochster v De La Tour 1853*
> The defendant engaged the plaintiff as a courier to accompany him on a European tour commencing on 1 June. On 11 May he wrote to the plaintiff to say that he no longer required his services. On 22 May the plaintiff commenced legal proceedings for anticipatory breach of contract. The defendant objected that there was no actionable breach until 1 June.
>
> *Held:* the plaintiff was entitled to sue as soon as the anticipatory breach occurred on 11 May.

2.5 Where the injured party allows the contract to continue, the party guilty of anticipatory breach may subsequently change his mind and perform the contract after all. Alternatively, if the contract is allowed to continue in this way the parties may be discharged from their obligations without liability by some other cause which occurs later.

> *Avery v Bowden 1855*
> The defendant entered into a contract to charter a ship from the plaintiff to load grain at Odessa within a period of 45 days. The ship arrived at Odessa and the charterer told the plaintiff that he did not propose to load a cargo. The master remained at Odessa hoping the charterer would change his mind - that is, he did not there and then treat the contract as discharged by the charterer's anticipatory breach. Before the 45 days (for loading cargo) had expired, the outbreak of the Crimean war discharged the contract by frustration.
>
> *Held:* the shipowner, through the master, had waived his right to sue for anticipatory breach (with a claim for damages). The contract continued and had been discharged later by frustration (the outbreak of war) without liability for either party.

Termination for repudiatory breach

2.6 To terminate for repudiatory breach *the innocent party must notify the other of his* decision. This may be by way of refusal to accept defects in performance, refusal to accept further performance or refusal to perform his own obligations. The effects of such termination are as follows for the innocent party.

(a) He is not bound by his future or continuing contractual obligations, and cannot be sued on them.

(b) He need not accept nor pay for further performance.

(c) He can refuse to pay for partial or defective performance already received.

(d) He can reclaim money paid to a defaulter if he can and does reject defective performance.

(e) He is *not* discharged from the contractual obligations which were due at the time of termination.

2.7 The innocent party can also *claim damages* from the defaulter for:

(a) losses sustained by him in respect of unperformed contractual obligations due at the time of default (the defaulter is in theory still bound); and

(b) losses sustained by him regarding contractual obligations which were due in the future.

2.8 Finally an innocent party who began to perform his contractual obligations but who was prevented from completing them by the defaulter can claim reasonable remuneration on a *quantum meruit* basis.

Affirmation after repudiatory breach

2.9 If a person is aware of the other party's repudiatory breach and of his own right to terminate the contract as a result but still decides to treat the contract as being in existence he is said to have *affirmed the contract*. Such a decision should be a conscious or active one; it is not deemed to have been made purely by virtue of the fact that a person hangs on to defective goods while he or she decides what to do.

2.10 The effect of affirmation is that the *contract remains fully in force*, so each party is bound to perform existing and future obligations and may sue to enforce them. If the election is unconditional - 'I shall keep the goods despite their defects' - it may not be revoked. If it is conditional - 'I will keep the defective goods provided they are mended free of charge' - and the condition is not satisfied, it may then be terminated.

3 AGREEMENT

3.1 There is a general principle that, since a contract is created by agreement, it may be discharged by agreement, and so the parties may agree to cancel the contract before it has been completely performed on both sides. But the agreement to cancel is itself a new contract which must be made under seal or for which consideration must be given.

3.2 If there are unperformed obligations of the original contract on both sides (it is an executory contract), each party provides consideration for his own release by agreeing to release the other (*bilateral* discharge). Each party surrenders something of value.

3.3 But if one party has completely performed his obligations, his agreement to release the other from his obligations (*unilateral* discharge) requires consideration, such as payment of a cancellation fee (this is called *accord and satisfaction*). Alternatively a unilateral discharge may be given by deed.

3.4 If the parties enter into a new contract to replace the unperformed contract, the new contract provides any necessary consideration. This is called *novation* of the old contract - it is replaced by a new one.

3.5 A contract may include provision for its own discharge by imposing a *condition precedent*, which prevents the contract from coming into operation unless the condition is satisfied. Alternatively, it may impose a *condition subsequent* by which the contract is discharged on the later happening of an event; a simple example of the latter is provision for termination by notice given by one party to the other. Effectively these are contracts whereby discharge may arise through agreement.

Aberfoyle Plantations Ltd v Cheng 1960
The parties agreed in 1955 to sell and buy a plantation which included 182 acres in respect of which the leases had expired in 1950. The vendor had tried without success in the intervening years to obtain a renewal of the leases. The agreement provided that 'the purchase is conditional on the vendor obtaining a renewal' of the leases. If he was 'unable to fulfil this condition, this agreement shall become null and void'. The vendor failed to obtain the renewal.

Held: the purchaser could recover the deposit he had paid.

Head v Tattersall 1871
The plaintiff bought a horse guaranteed 'to have been hunted with the Bicester hounds', on the understanding that it could be returned within a time limit if it did not answer the description. The horse was injured and the plaintiff discovered that it had never hunted with the Bicester hounds. The plaintiff returned it and sued for the return of the price.

Held: a contract had come into existence, but the option to return the horse was a condition subsequent. The plaintiff was entitled to cancel the contract, return the horse and recover the price.

4   FRUSTRATION   12/97

4.1   If it is impossible to perform the contract when it is made, there is usually no contract at all - it is void and each party is released from performing any obligation after the frustrating event.

4.2   In addition, the parties are free to negotiate 'escape clauses' or *force majeure* clauses covering impossibility which arises after the contract has been made. If they fail to do so, they are, as a general rule, in breach of contract if they find themselves unable to do what they have agreed to do. Thus if a shipowner agrees to load his ship with guano at a certain place in West Africa, he is liable in damages even if no guano is obtainable: *Hills v Sughrue 1846.*

4.3   The rigour of this principle is modified by the doctrine that in certain circumstances a contract may be discharged by *frustration*. If it appears that the parties assumed that certain underlying conditions would continue, the contract may be frustrated if their assumption proves to be false.

4.4   An alternative theory of the doctrine of frustration is that the parties should be discharged from their contract if altered circumstances render the contract fundamentally different in its nature from the original contract made by the parties. This alternative avoids imputing to the parties assumptions which in fact never occurred to them. Contracts have been discharged by frustration in the following circumstances.

Destruction of the subject matter

4.5   In the case which gave rise to the doctrine of frustration, the subject matter of the contract was destroyed before performance fell due.

Taylor v Caldwell 1863
A hall was let to the plaintiff for a series of concerts on specified dates. Before the date of the first concert the hall was accidentally destroyed by fire. The plaintiff sued the owner of the hall for damages for failure to let him have the use of the hall as agreed.

Held: destruction of the subject matter rendered the contract impossible to perform and discharged the defendant from his obligations under the contract.

Personal incapacity to perform a contract of personal service

4.6   The principle that a physical thing must be available applies equally to a person, if that person's presence is a fundamental requirement. Not every illness will discharge a contract of personal service - personal incapacity must be established.

> *Condor v Barron Knights 1966*
> The plaintiff, aged 16, contracted to perform as drummer in a pop group. His duties, when the group had work, were to play on every night of the week. He fell ill and his doctor advised that he should restrict his performances to four nights per week. The group terminated his contract.
>
> *Held:* a contract of personal service is based on the assumption that the employee's health will permit him to perform his duties. If that is not so the contract is discharged by frustration.

Government intervention or supervening illegality

4.7   Government intervention is a common cause of frustration, particularly in time of war. If maintenance of the contract would impose upon the parties a contract fundamentally different from that which they made, the contract is discharged. In many cases of government intervention, further performance of the contract becomes *illegal*. Supervening illegality, for example owing to outbreak of war (*Avery v Bowden 1855*), or government intervention to restrain or suspend performance of the contract, is a common cause of frustration.

> *Re Shipton, Anderson & Co and Harrison Bros & Co 1915*
> A contract was made for the sale of wheat stored in a Liverpool warehouse. It was requisitioned by the government under emergency wartime legal powers.
>
> *Held:* it was no longer lawful for the seller to deliver the wheat. The contract had been discharged by frustration.

Non-occurrence of an event if it is the sole purpose of the contract

4.8   Two contrasting examples of this application of the doctrine are given by the so-called 'coronation cases'.

> *Krell v Henry 1903*
> A room belonging to the plaintiff and overlooking the route of the coronation procession of Edward VII was let for the day of the coronation for the purpose of viewing the procession. The coronation was postponed owing to the illness of the King. The owner of the rooms sued for the agreed fee, which was payable on the day of the coronation.
>
> *Held*: the contract was made for the sole purpose of viewing the procession. As that event did not occur the contract was frustrated.

> *Herne Bay Steamboat Co v Hutton 1903*
> A steamboat was hired for two days to carry passengers, for the purpose of viewing the naval review (at Spithead) and for a day's cruise round the fleet. The review had been arranged as part of the coronation celebrations. The naval review was cancelled owing to the King's illness but the steamboat could have taken passengers for a trip round the assembled fleet, which remained at Spithead.
>
> *Held:* the royal review of the fleet was not the sole occasion of the contract, and the contract was not discharged. The owner of the steamboat was entitled to the agreed hire charge less what he had earned from the normal use of the vessel over the two day period.

Interruption which prevents performance in the form intended by the parties

4.9   In some cases, the parties may make express provision for certain contingencies. However if the effect of the contingency is to frustrate the essential object of the contract, the contract will nevertheless be discharged.

> *Jackson v Union Marine Insurance Co 1874*
> The parties contracted in November 1871 for a charter of a ship to proceed immediately from Liverpool to Newport, 'damages and accidents of navigation excepted', to load cargo for San Francisco. Having sailed on 2 January, the ship went ashore off the coast of Wales on 3 January and could not be refloated for a month. Thereafter she needed repairs in Liverpool to make her fit for the voyage; these were still in progress in August. Meanwhile the charterers hired another vessel. The plaintiff claimed on his policy of insurance.
>
> *Held:* the interruption had put an end to the contract in the commercial sense - it was no longer possible to perform the contract intended. The contract was discharged by frustration. The plaintiff had no claim against the charterer and could claim from the defendants.

> *Gamerco SA v ICM/Fair Warning (Agency) Ltd 1995*
> Gamerco SA, pop concert promoters, agreed to promote a concert to be held by the defendant group at a stadium in Spain. However, the stadium was found by engineers to be unsafe and the authorities banned its use and revoked the plaintiffs' permit to hold the concert. No alternative site was available and the concert was cancelled.
>
> *Held*: the contract was frustrated because the stadium was unsafe, a circumstance beyond the control of Gamerco SA.

Exceptions

4.10   A contract is not discharged by frustration in the following circumstances.

(a)   If an *alternative mode of performance* is still possible.

> *Tsakiroglou & Co v Noblee and Thorl GmbH 1962*
> In October 1956 the sellers contracted to sell 300 tons of Sudanese groundnuts c.i.f. Hamburg. The normal and intended method of shipment from Port Sudan (on the Red Sea coast) was by a ship routed through the Suez Canal to Hamburg. Before shipment the Suez Canal was closed; the sellers refused to ship the cargo arguing that it was an implied term that shipment should be via Suez or alternatively that shipment via the Cape of Good Hope would make the contract 'commercially and fundamentally' different, so that it was discharged by frustration.
>
> *Held:* both arguments failed. There was no evidence to support the implied term argument nor was the use of a different (and more expensive) route an alteration of the fundamental nature of the contract sufficient to discharge it by frustration.

(b)   If performance becomes suddenly more *expensive*.

> *Davis Contractors v Fareham UDC 1956*
> The plaintiffs agreed to build 78 houses at a price of £94,000 in eight months. Labour shortages caused the work to take 22 months and cost £115,000. They wished to claim frustration so that they could then claim for their work on a quantum meruit basis.
>
> *Held:* hardship, material loss or inconvenience did not amount to frustration; the obligation must change such that the thing undertaken would, if performed, be a different thing from that contracted for.

(c)   If one party *has accepted the risk* that he will be unable to perform.

Budgett & Co v Binnington & Co 1891
A bill of lading provided that if the consignee could not unload his cargo within ten days, demurrage (compensation) would be payable. A strike prevented the unloading during the ten days.

Held: the consignee had accepted the risk and must pay the demurrage as agreed.

(d) If one party *has induced frustration* by his own choice between alternatives.

Maritime National Fish v Ocean Trawlers 1935
The plaintiffs entered into a contract for the hire of a trawler for use in otter trawling. They had four other trawlers of their own. They applied to the Canadian government for the necessary licences for five trawlers but were granted only three licences. They nominated three of their own trawlers for the licences and argued that the contract for the hire of the fifth trawler had been frustrated since it could not lawfully be used.

Held: the impossibility of performing the hire contract was the result of a choice made by the hirers: the trawler on hire could have been nominated for one of the three licences. This was not a case for discharge by frustration.

The Law Reform (Frustrated Contracts) Act 1943

4.11 Where a contract is frustrated, the common law rule provides that the occurrence of the frustrating event brings the contract automatically to an end forthwith. It is not void *ab initio*. It starts life as a valid contract, but suddenly comes to an end. At common law, the consequences of this can be harsh. The common law provides that the loss shall lie where it falls; money paid before frustration cannot be recovered and money payable at the time of frustration remains payable. Only in 1942 was the doctrine modified, so that, where there is a complete failure of consideration, the contract can be held void *ab initio*.

Fibrosa v Fairbairn 1942
The plaintiff placed an order for machinery to be delivered in Poland. He paid £1,000 of the contract price of £4,800 with his order. Shortly afterwards the outbreak of the Second World War frustrated the contract since the German army occupied Poland. The plaintiff sued to recover the £1,000 which had been paid.

Held: the deposit was repayable since the plaintiff had received absolutely nothing for it - there had been a total failure of consideration.

4.12 In most cases now the rights and liabilities of parties to a contract discharged by frustration are regulated by the Law Reform (Frustrated Contracts) Act 1943 as follows.

(a) Any money paid under the contract by one party to the other is (subject to rule (b) below) to be repaid. Any sums due for payment under the contract then or later cease to be payable.

(b) A party who is liable under rule (a) to repay money received (or whose entitlement to payments already accrued due for payment at the time of frustration is cancelled), may at the discretion of the court be allowed to set off (or to recover) out of those sums the whole or part of his expenses incurred in performing the contract up to the time when it is discharged by frustration. But he cannot recover from the other party his expenses insofar as they exceed sums paid or due to be paid to him at the time of discharge.

(c) If either party has obtained a valuable benefit (other than payment of money) under the contract before it is discharged, the court may in its discretion order him to pay to the other party all or part of that value. If, for example, one party has delivered to the other some of the goods to be supplied under the contract, the latter may be ordered to pay the amount of their value to him.

Chapter roundup

- The normal method of discharge is performance. Obligations of the parties in the vast majority of commercial contracts are discharged by performance. Performance must be complete and exact. There is no right to receive payment proportionate to partially completed work unless one of the recognised exceptions applies.

- Breach of a condition in a contract may lead to the entire agreement being discharged by fundamental breach, unless the injured party elects to treat the contract as continuing and merely claim damages for his loss. If there is anticipatory breach (one party declares in advance that he will not perform his side of the bargain when the time for performance arrives) the other party may treat the contract as discharged forthwith, or continue with his obligations until actual breach occurs. His claim for damages will then depend upon what he has actually lost.

- The obligations of the parties may be discharged by agreement. Because an agreement to cancel is itself a contract, the following situations arise. Bilateral discharge arises where consideration on both sides is the agreement to release the other. Unilateral discharge occurs when one party has performed his side, so he requires consideration for his agreement to release the other (accord and satisfaction) or he releases by deed (no consideration required).

- A contract may be discharged by agreement where there is a condition precedent (the contract does not come into being until the condition is satisfied) or there is a condition subsequent (the contract is agreed in advance to be discharged on the occurrence of a certain event.)

- If the parties to the contract assumed, at the time of the agreement, that certain underlying conditions would continue, the contract is discharged by frustration if these assumptions prove to be false. The contract is then fundamentally different in nature from the original agreement.

- The common law consequences of frustration are modified by the Law Reforms (Frustrated Contracts) Act 1943, which regulates the right and obligations of the parties to a contract discharged by frustration.

Test your knowledge

1   Give four situations where a party to a contract may claim payment in proportion to partially completed work. (see para 1.2)

2   What is a repudiatory breach of contract? (2.2)

3   What choice does the injured party have in the event of repudiatory breach? (2.2)

4   What is anticipatory breach of contract? (2.4)

5   What may happen if a contract is allowed to continue following anticipatory breach? (2.5)

6   What is 'accord and satisfaction'? (3.3)

7   What is the doctrine of frustration? (4.3, 4.4)

8   Outline the facts of *Krell v Henry 1903* and *Herne Bay Steamboat Co v Hutton 1903* (the 'coronation cases') and distinguish between them (4.8)

9   What principle does *Davis Contractors v Fareham UDC 1956* demonstrate? (4.10)

Chapter 20

REMEDIES FOR BREACH OF CONTRACT

This chapter covers the following topics

1   Damages

2   Other common law remedies

3   Equitable remedies

4   Limitation to actions for breach

Introduction

The coverage of the law of contract in Chapters 11 to 16 (Part E) of this Study Text addresses the requirements of the syllabus for the _Introduction to English and European Community Law_ examination paper. The syllabus is designed to provide an introduction to the law of contract and provides coverage of binding agreements with reference to the doctrines of privity and formalities.

A greater understanding of the law of contract developed through further study of the subject area will inevitably be to the student's advantage. In this part of the Study Text we provide additional material on the law of contract to extend your knowledge of this subject area. You will study these areas in greater depth in the pre-professional examination in _Business Law_.

In Chapter 22 we examined the ways in which a contract may be discharged. It was noted that most contracts are performed as intended by the parties. In the event of a breach of contract, the law provides a number of remedies. These are described in this chapter.

---

1   DAMAGES

_6/96, 6/98, 12/98_

1.1   Damages are a common law remedy and are primarily intended to restore the party who has suffered loss to the same position he would have been in if the contract had been performed. The remedy of damages arises as of right. Damages are compensatory and are not meant to be a punishment, which is a criminal, not a civil, measure. In addition, they should not allow the party to whom they are awarded to profit, nor to achieve a better result than he would have done under the contract - the law will not make up for a bad bargain.

1.2   Where the contract does not make any provision for damages in the event of a breach, the court will determine the damages payable. These are called _unliquidated damages_ and are calculated with reference to the following factors.

(a)   The first issue is _remoteness of damage_. Here the courts consider how far down the sequence of cause and effect the consequences of breach should be traced before they become so indirect that they should be ignored, in other words, for what kind of damage will compensation be awarded?

(b)   Secondly, the court must decide how much money to award in respect of the breach and its relevant consequences. This is the _measure of damages_, where the principle is one of _restitutio in integrum_ (restoring to the original position).

Remoteness of damage

1.3   Under the rule in *Hadley v Baxendale* (below) damages may only be awarded in respect of loss as follows.

    (a) (i) *The loss must arise naturally*, according to the usual course of things, from the breach; or

        (ii) the loss must arise *in a manner which the parties may reasonably be supposed to have contemplated*.

    (b) A loss outside the natural course of events will only be compensated if the exceptional circumstances which cause the loss are within the defendant's knowledge, actual or constructive, when he made the contract.

> *Hadley v Baxendale 1854*
> The plaintiffs owned a mill at Gloucester which came to a standstill because the main crank shaft had broken. They made a contract with the defendant, a carrier, for the transport of the broken shaft to the makers at Greenwich to serve as a pattern for making a new shaft. Delivery was to be made at Greenwich the following day. Owing to neglect by the defendant delivery was delayed and the mill was out of action for a longer period than would have resulted if there had been no delay. The defendant did not know that the mill would be idle during this interval. He was merely aware that he had to transport a broken millshaft from the plaintiffs' mill. The plaintiffs claimed for loss of profits of the mill during the period of delay.
>
> *Held:* although the failure of the carrier to perform the contract promptly was the direct cause of the stoppage of the mill for an unnecessarily long time, the claim must fail since the defendant *did not know* that the mill would be idle until the new shaft was delivered (part (b) of the rule did not apply). Moreover it was not a natural consequence of delay in transport of a broken shaft that the mill would be out of action meanwhile (part (a) of the rule did not apply). The importance of the shaft was not obvious; the miller might have a spare.

1.4   Both parts of the rule are concerned with *what the defendant must have known*.

    (a) Under the first head of the rule he is deemed to expect any normal consequence which any other person might also expect; such things are natural and ordinary consequences.

    (b) Under the second head, if the consequence of breach for which damages are claimed is abnormal, or what one would not ordinarily expect, the defendant is liable only if he knew in making the contract of the special circumstances from which the abnormal consequence of breach could arise.

> *Victoria Laundry (Windsor) v Newman Industries 1949*
> The defendants contracted to sell a large boiler to the plaintiffs 'for immediate use' in their business of launderers and dyers. Owing to an accident in dismantling the boiler at its previous site delivery, due on 5 June, was delayed until 8 November. The defendants were aware of the nature of the plaintiffs' business and had been informed that the plaintiffs were most anxious to put the boiler into use in the shortest possible space of time. The plaintiffs claimed damages for normal loss of profits of £16 per week for the period of delay and for loss of abnormal profits, assessed at £262 per week, from losing 'highly lucrative' dyeing contracts to be undertaken if the boiler had been delivered on time.
>
> *Held:* damages for loss of normal profits were recoverable since in the circumstances failure to deliver major industrial equipment ordered for immediate use would be expected to prevent operation of the plant - it was a natural consequence covered by the first head of the rule. The claim for loss of special profits fell under the second head of the rule; it failed because the defendants had no knowledge of the dyeing contracts and the abnormal profits which they would yield.

The Heron II 1969
K, a shipowner, entered into a contract for the shipment of a bulk cargo of sugar belonging to C from the Black Sea to Basra in Iraq. He was aware that C were sugar merchants but he did not know that C intended to sell the cargo as soon as it reached Basra. The ship arrived nine days late and in that time the price of sugar on the market in Basra had fallen. C claimed damages for the loss due to the fall in market value of the cargo over the period of delay.

Held: the claim succeeded. It is common knowledge that market values of commodities fluctuate so that delay might cause loss. It was sufficiently obvious that a bulk cargo of sugar owned by merchants was destined for sale to which the market value would be relevant.

Measure of damages

1.5 As a general rule the amount awarded as damages is what is needed to put the plaintiff in the position he would have achieved if the contract had been performed. If, for example, there is failure to deliver goods at a contract price of £100 per ton and at the due time for delivery similar goods are obtainable at an available market price of £110 per ton, damages are calculated at the rate of £10 per ton: Sale of Goods Act 1979 s 51 (3). This is sometimes referred to as protecting the *expectation* interest of the plaintiff.

1.6 A plaintiff may alternatively seek to have his *reliance* interest protected; this refers to the position he would have been in had he not relied on the contract.

C & P Haulage v Middleton 1983
The plaintiffs granted to the defendant a 6-month renewable licence to occupy premises as an engineering workshop. He incurred expenditure in doing up the premises, although the contract provided that he could not remove any fixtures he installed. He was ejected in breach of the licence agreement 10 weeks before the end of a 6-month term. He was allowed by the local council to use his own garage as a temporary workshop. He sued for damages.

Held: the defendant could only recover nominal damages. He could not recover the cost of equipping the premises (as reliance loss) as he would not have been able to do so if the contract had been lawfully terminated.

1.7 Expectation loss, then, is the loss of what the plaintiff would have received had the contract been properly performed. It might be agreed that the plaintiff has not lost this since he never had it but he *expected* to have it, and the courts have generally sought to put a plaintiff in the position he would have been in if the contract had been properly performed.

1.8 More complicated questions of assessing damages can arise. The general principle is to compensate for actual financial loss.

Thompson Ltd v Robinson (Gunmakers) Ltd 1955
The defendants contracted to buy a Vanguard car from the plaintiffs. They refused to take delivery and the plaintiffs sued for loss of profit on the transaction. There was at the time a considerable excess of supply of such cars over demand for them and the plaintiffs were unable to sell the car

Held: the market price rule, which the defendants argued should be applied, was inappropriate in the current market. The seller had lost a sale and was entitled to the profit which would have resulted from the purchase.

Charter v Sullivan 1957
The facts were the same as in the previous case, except that the sellers were able to sell every car obtained from the manufacturers.

Held: only nominal damages were payable.

Non-financial loss

1.9   At one time damages could not be recovered for any *non-financial* loss arising from breach of contract. In some recent cases, however, damages have been recovered for mental distress where that is the main result of the breach. It is uncertain how far the courts will develop this concept. They are unlikely to go as far as the American courts in awarding damages for distress (particularly if distress arises from the defendant's refusal to admit liability or to apologise).

> *Jarvis v Swan Tours 1973*
> The plaintiff entered into a contract for holiday accommodation at a winter sports centre. What was provided was much inferior to the description given in the defendant's brochure. Damages on the basis of financial loss only were assessed at £32.
>
> *Held:* the damages should be increased to £125 to compensate for disappointment and distress.
>
> *Ruxley Electronics and Construction Ltd v Forsyth 1995*
> A householder discovered that although he had specified maximum depth, the swimming pool he had ordered to be built was shallower than specified. He sued the builder for damages, arguing that the damages should include the cost of demolition of the existing pool and construction of a new one of the required depth. Despite its shortcomings, the pool as built was perfectly serviceable and safe to dive into.
>
> *Held*: the expenditure involved in rectifying the breach was out of all proportion to the benefit of such rectification. The client could only recover a lesser sum by way of compensation for loss of pleasurable amenity.
>
> *Alexander v Rolls Royce Motor Cars Ltd 1995*
> The plaintiff sued for breach of contract to repair his Rolls Royce motor car and claimed damages for distress and inconvenience or loss of enjoyment of the car.
>
> *Held*: breach of contract to repair a car did not give rise to any liability for damages for distress, inconvenience or loss of enjoyment.

Mitigation of loss

1.10   In assessing the amount of damages it is assumed that the plaintiff will take any *reasonable* steps to reduce or *mitigate* his loss. The burden of proof is on the defendant to show that the plaintiff failed to take a reasonable opportunity of mitigation.

> *Payzu Ltd v Saunders 1919*
> The parties had entered into a contract for the supply of goods to be delivered and paid for by instalments. The plaintiffs failed to pay for the first instalment when due, one month after delivery. The defendants declined to make further deliveries unless the plaintiffs paid cash in advance with their orders. The plaintiffs refused to accept delivery on those terms. The price of the goods rose, and they sued for breach of contract.
>
> *Held:* the seller was in breach of contract since he had no right to repudiate the original contract. But the plaintiffs should have mitigated their loss by accepting the seller's offer of delivery against cash payment. Damages were limited to the amount of their assumed loss if they had paid in advance, which was interest over the period of pre-payment. 'In commercial contracts, it is generally reasonable to accept an offer from the party in default.'

Liquidated damages and penalty clauses

1.11   To avoid calculations or disputes later over any amount payable, the parties may include in their contract a formula (*liquidated damages*) for determining the damages payable for breach. In construction contracts, for example, it is usual to provide that if the building contractor is in breach of contract by late completion a deduction is to be made from the contract price (1 per cent per week subject to a maximum of 10 per cent in all is a typical example). The formula will be enforced by the courts if it is 'a genuine pre-estimate of loss' (without enquiring whether the actual loss is greater or smaller if it appears to be a bargain to settle in advance what is to be paid).

Dunlop Pneumatic Tyre Co Ltd v New Garage & Motor Co Ltd 1915
The contract (for the sale of tyres to a garage) imposed a minimum retail price (resale price maintenance was then legal). The contract provided that £5 per tyre should be paid by the buyer if he resold at less than the prescribed retail price or in four other possible cases of breach of contract. He did sell at a lower price and argued that £5 per tyre was a 'penalty' (see below) and not a genuine pre-estimate of loss.

Held: as a general rule when a fixed amount is to be paid as damages for breaches of different kinds, some more serious in their consequences than others, that is not a genuine pre-estimate of loss and so it is void as a 'penalty'. But the general rule is merely a presumption which does not always determine the result. In this case the formula was an honest attempt to agree on liquidated damages and would be upheld, even though the consequences of the breach were such as to make precise pre-estimation almost impossible.

Ford Motor Co (England) Ltd v Armstrong 1915
The defendant had undertaken not to sell the plaintiff's cars below list price, not to sell Ford cars to other dealers and not to exhibit any Ford cars without permission. A £250 penalty was payable for each breach as being the agreed damage which the plaintiff would sustain.

Held: since the same sum was payable for different kinds of loss it was not a genuine pre-estimate of loss and was in the nature of a penalty. (Unlike the *Dunlop* case the figure set was held to be excessive.)

2   OTHER COMMON LAW REMEDIES

Action for the price

2.1   If the breach of contract arises out of one party's failure to pay the contractually agreed price due under the contract, the creditor should bring a personal action against the debtor to recover that sum.

2.2   This is a fairly straightforward procedure but is subject to two specific limitations. The first is that an action for the price under a contract for the sale of goods may only be brought if property has passed to the buyer, unless the price has been agreed to be payable on a specific date: s 49 Sale of Goods Act 1979.

2.3   Secondly, whilst the injured party may recover an agreed sum due at the time of an anticipatory breach, whether or not he continues the contract then, sums which become due after the anticipatory breach may not be recovered unless he affirms the contract - that is, he carries on with his side of the bargain. Even where he does affirm the contract, he will be unable to recover the price if:

(a)   the other party withholds its co-operation so that he cannot continue with his side in order to make the price due; or

(b)   the injured party had no reason or 'legitimate interest' in continuing his obligations other than to claim damages. Such a legitimate interest may be obligations which have arisen to third parties.

Quantum meruit

2.4   In particular situations, an equitable claim may be made on a *quantum meruit* basis as an alternative to an action for damages for breach of contract.

2.5   The phrase *quantum meruit* literally means 'how much it is worth'. It is a measure of the value of contractual work which has been performed. The aim of such an award is to restore the plaintiff to the position he would have been in *if the contract had never been made*. It is a restitutory award.

2.6   By contrast, an award of damages aims to put the plaintiff in the position he would have been in *if the contract had been performed*. It is a compensatory award.

2.7   *Quantum meruit* is likely to be sought where one party has already performed part of his obligations and the other party then repudiates the contract (repudiatory breach). Provided the injured party elects to treat the contract as terminated, he may claim a reasonable amount for the work done.

> *De Bernardy v Harding 1853*
> The plaintiff agreed to advertise and sell tickets for the defendant, who was erecting stands for spectators to view the funeral of the Duke of Wellington. The defendant cancelled the arrangement without justification.
>
> *Held:* the plaintiff might recover the value of services rendered.

3   EQUITABLE REMEDIES

Specific performance

3.1   The court may at its discretion give an equitable remedy by ordering the defendant to perform his part of the contract instead of letting him 'buy himself out of it' by paying damages for breach. This is specific performance.

3.2   *Specific performance will only be ordered in a case where the common law remedy of damages is inadequate.* An order will be made for specific performance of a contract for the sale of land since the plaintiff may need the land for a particular purpose and would not be adequately compensated by damages for the loss of his bargain. He could not obtain another piece of land which is identical. For this reason specific performance of a contract for sale of goods is unlikely to be ordered unless the contract is one for the sale of land.

Injunction

3.3   An injunction is (in this context) also a discretionary court order and an equitable remedy, requiring the defendant to observe a negative restriction of a contract. An injunction may be made even to enforce a contract of personal service for which an order of specific performance would be refused.

> *Warner Bros Pictures Inc v Nelson 1937*
> The defendant (the film star Bette Davis) agreed to work for a year for the plaintiffs and not during the year to work for any other film or stage producer nor 'to engage in any other occupation' without the consent of the plaintiffs. She came to England during the year to work for a British film producer. The plaintiffs sued for an injunction to restrain her from this work and she resisted arguing that if the restriction were enforced she must either work for them (indirectly it would be an order for specific performance of a contract for personal service which should not be made) or abandon her livelihood.
>
> *Held:* the court would not make an injunction if it would have the result suggested by the defendant. But the plaintiffs merely asked for an injunction to restrain her from working for a British film producer. This was one part of the restriction accepted by her under her contract and it was fair to hold her to it to that extent. But the court would not have enforced the 'any other occupation' restraint. Moreover, an English court would only have made an injunction restraining the defendant from breaking her contract by taking other work in England.

3.4   An injunction is limited to enforcement of contract terms which are in substance negative restraints. It is immaterial that the restraint, if negative in substance, is not so expressed.

> *Metropolitan Electric Supply Co v Ginder 1901*
> The defendant contracted to take all the electricity which he required from the plaintiffs. They sued for an injunction to restrain him from obtaining electricity from another supplier.
>
> *Held:* the contract term (electricity only from the one supplier) implied a negative restriction (no supplies from any other source) and to that extent it could be enforced by injunction.

Rescission

3.5   Strictly speaking the equitable right to rescind an agreement is not a remedy for breach of contract - it is a right which exists in certain circumstances, such as where a contract is voidable for misrepresentation, duress or undue influence.

4   LIMITATION TO ACTIONS FOR BREACH

4.1   The right to sue for breach of contract becomes statute-barred after six years from the date on which the cause of action accrued, which is usually the date of the breach, not the date on which damage is suffered: s 5 Limitation Act 1980. The period is twelve years if the contract is by deed: s 8. The plaintiff's rights merely cease to be enforceable at law.

4.2   An action consisting of or including damages for personal injuries is limited after three years: s 11. The Latent Damage Act 1986 provides that in non-personal injury claims where damage is latent (undiscoverable), the limitation period will be either the usual six-year period or (if longer) three years from the date that the plaintiff discovered or should have discovered the damage. The Act also provides for a 'long stop' - a bar on all claims (except personal injury claims) brought more than fifteen years from the act or omission alleged to constitute the negligence.

4.3   Where the claim can only be for the equitable reliefs of specific performance or injunction, the Limitation Act 1980 does not apply. Instead, the claim may be limited by the equitable doctrine of delay or 'laches'.

> *Allcard v Skinner 1887*
> Under the influence of a clergyman, the plaintiff entered a Protestant convent in 1868 and, in compliance with a vow of poverty, transferred property worth about £7,000 to the Order by 1878. In 1879 she left the order and became a Roman Catholic. Six years later she demanded the return of £1,671, the unexpended balance of her gift, claiming *undue influence* by the defendant, the Lady Superior of the Protestant sisterhood.
>
> *Held:* this was a case of undue influence for which a right of rescission may be available, since, among other things, the rule of the Order forbade its members from seeking the advice of outsiders. But the plaintiff's delay of six years (after leaving the Order) in making her claim debarred her from setting aside the gift and recovering her property.

Extension of the limitation period

4.4   The limitation period may be extended if the debt, or any other certain monetary amount, is either acknowledged or paid in part before the original six (or twelve) years has expired: s 29. Hence if a debt accrued on 1.1.90, the original limitation period expired on 31.12.95. But if part-payment was received on 1.1.94, the debt was reinstated and does not then become 'statute-barred' until 31.12.99.

(a) *Acknowledgement.* The claim must be acknowledged as existing, not just as possible, but it need not be quantified. It must be in writing, signed by the debtor and addressed to the creditor: s 30.

(b) *Part payment.* To be effective, the part payment must be identifiable with the particular debt, not just a payment on a running account.

Chapter roundup

- Damages are a common law remedy intended to restore the party who has suffered loss to the position he would have been in had the contract been performed. The two tests applied to a claim for damages relate to remoteness of damage and measure of damages.

- Remoteness of damage is tested by the two limbs of the rule in *Hadley v Baxendale 1854.* The first part of the rule states that the loss must arise either naturally, according to the usual course of things, from the breach or in a manner which the parties may reasonably be supposed to have contemplated, in making the contract, as a probate result of its breach. The second part of the rule provides that a loss outside the usual course of events will only be compensated if the exceptional circumstances which caused it were within the defendant's actual or constructive knowledge when he made the contract.

- The measure of damages is that which will compensate for the loss incurred. It is not intended that the injured party should profit from a claim. Damages may be awarded for financial or non-financial loss.

- A simple action for the price to recover the agreed sum should be brought if breach of contract is failure to pay the price. But property must have passed from seller to buyer, and complications arise where there is anticipatory breach.

- A *quantum meruit* is a claim (in quasi-contract) which is available as an alternative to damages; the injured party in a breach of a contract may claim the value of his work or, literally, 'what he has earned'. The aim of such an award is to restore the plaintiff to the position he would have been in had the contract never been made. It is a restitutory award.

- An order for specific performance is an equitable remedy; the party in breach is ordered to perform his side of the contract. Such an order is only made where damages are inadequate compensation, such as in a sale of land, and where actual consideration has passed.

- An injunction is an equitable remedy which requires that a negative condition in the agreement be fulfilled.

Test your knowledge

1   What is the rule on remoteness of damage in *Hadley v Baxendale 1854* (see para 1.3)

2   Outline the facts of *Thompson Ltd v Robinson (Gunmakers) Ltd 1953* and *Charter v Sullivan 1957,* showing why the results were different (1.8)

3   What is the general principle of mitigation of loss? (1.10)

4   What are liquidated damages? (1.11)

5   What are the two limitations on the creditor's right to bring an action for the price? (2.2, 2.3)

6   Distinguish between a restitutory award and a compensatory award (2.5, 2.6)

7   How long after the cause of action occurred does the right to sue for breach of contract become statute-barred? (4.1)

Part G
Torts

Chapter 21

NEGLIGENCE

This chapter covers the following topics.

1 Tort and other wrongs

2 The tort of negligence

3 Duty of care

4 Breach of duty of care

5 Consequential harm

6 Occupiers' liability

7 Negligent misstatement

8 Breach of statutory duty

9 Torts of strict liability

Introduction

Tort is an important branch of the law regulating business conduct. In this chapter, we introduce the concept of tort, distinguishing it from criminal liability and liability in contract.

The chapter describes the tort of negligence, the most significant tort in modern times. The application of negligence to the occupancy of premises is also examined.

Finally, torts of strict liability and actions for breach of statutory duty are discussed.

In Chapter 23 we will examine the defences to an action in tort and the remedies available.

1 TORT AND OTHER WRONGS

1.1 There is no entirely satisfactory definition of tort. The main principle is that the law gives various rights to persons, such as the right of a person in possession of land to occupy it without interference or invasion by trespassers. When such a right is infringed the wrongdoer is liable in tort.

1.2 Tort is distinguished from other legal wrongs.

(a) A tort is a civil wrong and the person wronged sues in a civil court for compensation (or injunction against repetition). The plaintiff's claim generally is that he has suffered a loss such as personal injury at the hands of the defendant and the defendant should pay damages.

(b) In tort no previous transaction or relationship need exist: the parties may be complete strangers as when a motorist knocks down a pedestrian in the street. The claim in tort is based on the general law of duties and rights.

1.3 The same event can easily give rise to more than one legal liability. A road accident may lead to proceedings for both crime and tort and even in contract if, say, the driver is a hired chauffeur. Bad professional advice may give rise to liability both in tort and in contract.

Wrong and damage

1.4   When a plaintiff sues in tort claiming damages as compensation for loss he must normally prove his loss. But the necessary basis of his claim is that he has suffered a wrong. If there is no wrong (*injuria*) for which the law gives a remedy, no amount of loss (*damnum*) caused by the defendant can make him liable. *Damnum sine injuria* (loss not caused by wrong) is not actionable.

> *Electrochrome v Welsh Plastics 1968*
> The defendant's lorry, driven carelessly, crashed into a fire hydrant. As a result the water supply to the plaintiff's factory nearby was cut off. The factory had to close until the supply was restored. The plaintiff claimed damages for his loss.
>
> *Held:* the fire hydrant was not the plaintiff's property and so, in spite of his loss, no legal wrong had been done to him for which he could hold the defendant liable.

1.5   In some torts it is necessary to establish both wrong and loss resulting from it; this is the rule in the important tort of negligence. But in other cases it suffices to prove that a legal wrong has been done and damages (possibly nominal in amount) may be recovered without proof of any loss (*injuria sine damno*). Substantial damages maybe awarded where the loss is serious, but difficult to quantify in money terms, eg in case of damage to reputation by defamation.

Cause and effect

1.6   When the plaintiff claims damages for the loss caused by the defendant's wrongful act or omission, two main issues of cause and effect may have to be considered.

   (a)   Was the loss caused by a wrongful act or omission of the defendant himself? It may be a case of inevitable accident or there may be contributory negligence on the part of the plaintiff.

   (b)   If the sequence of cause and effect was unquestionably begun by the defendant, how far down the ensuing chain of consequences should the court go in identifying the loss for which the plaintiff is entitled to recover damages? In tort (as in contract) it is necessary to have rules on remoteness of damage.

2   THE TORT OF NEGLIGENCE   *6/95, 12/97*

2.1   In the law of tort the concept of negligence appears in two different senses.

   (a)   There is a distinct tort of negligence which is (briefly) causing loss by a failure to take reasonable care when there is a duty to do so.

   (b)   The defendant may not wish to inflict injury but by his carelessness he allows it to happen. The wrong is unintentional but negligent and so the defendant is held to be at fault for the negligent doing of a wrong.

2.2   There are some torts of 'strict liability' where it need not be shown that the defendant acted intentionally or negligently. If he creates a particular situation (of inherent risk) he is liable if harm results from it. This principle is illustrated by the rule in *Rylands v Fletcher* later in this chapter.

2.3   Most torts are wrongful *acts*. There can however be liability for an *omission*, or a failure to act in circumstances where there is a duty to do so. For example, the occupier of premises who knows that they are in a dangerous condition may be liable in tort if he fails to make the premises safe and a visitor is injured in consequence.

2.4   As explained above, many torts may be committed by mere carelessness rather than intentionally. But in modern times the law has developed a *tort of negligence in itself* which is liability for a failure to take proper care to avoid inflicting foreseeable injury. It has become the most important and far-reaching of modern torts.

2.5   To succeed in an action for negligence the plaintiff must prove three things.

(a)   The defendant owed him (the plaintiff) *a duty of care* to avoid causing injury to persons or property.

(b)   There was a *breach of that duty* by the defendant.

(c)   *In consequence* the plaintiff suffered *injury or damage* or (in some cases) financial loss.

3   DUTY OF CARE   *12/94, 6/95, 6/96, 12/96, 6/97, 6/98, 12/98, 6/99*

3.1   In the famed case of *Donoghue v Stevenson* the House of Lords ruled that a person might owe a duty of care to another with whom he had no contractual relationship at all.

Donoghue v Stevenson 1932
A purchased from a retailer a bottle of ginger beer for consumption by A's companion B. The bottle was opaque so that its contents were not visible. B drank part of the contents from the bottle and topped up her glass with the rest. As she poured it out the remains of a decomposed snail emerged from the bottle. She became seriously ill, and sued C, the manufacturer, who argued that as there was no contract between himself and B he owed her no duty of care and so was not liable to her.

Held: C was liable to B. Every person owes a duty of care to his 'neighbour', to 'persons so closely and directly affected by my act that I ought reasonably to have them in contemplation as being so affected'. In supplying polluted ginger beer in an opaque bottle the manufacturer must be held to contemplate that the person who drank the contents of the bottle would be affected by the consequences of the manufacturer's failure to take care to supply his product in a clean bottle.

Development of the doctrine

3.2   This narrow doctrine has been much refined in the sixty-odd years since the snail made its celebrated appearance. For any duty of care to exist, it was stated in *Anns v Merton London Borough Council 1977* that three points must be proved.

(a)   There must be a sufficient relationship of proximity or neighbourhood between the parties (defendant and plaintiff).

(b)   The former should be able reasonably to foresee that carelessness on his part may damage the latter.

(c)   If harm is reasonably foreseeable, is it right that the law should allow that duty to result in liability? In particular, liability for the acts of independent third parties has been restricted.

3.3   The comments made in *Anns* suggest that objective forseeability leads automatically to a duty of care and that a defendant who satisfies the foresight test is therefore liable unless there are reasons (eg public policy) why he should not be liable. In *Murphy v Brentwood DC 1990*, a case with facts similar to *Anns*, the House of Lords seems to have overruled its own decision in the earlier case, and the test of liability has been tightened, both by this case and by the *Caparo* case (see below). The *Murphy* case suggests that a duty of care will be based upon the need for proximity, a principle similar to that in *Donoghue v Stevenson* itself.

3.4   The decision in *Caparo Industries plc v Dickman and Others 1990* (see paragraph 7.7) has also cast doubt on whether a single general principle of negligence can provide a practical test which may apply to every situation. In particular, the concepts of foreseeability or neighbourhood are little more than convenient labels to attach to different specific situations before the court which, on detailed examination, it recognises as giving rise to a duty of care. It is likely therefore that, whilst the principles in paragraph 3.2 will continue to underlie the tort of negligence, categories of negligence will be increased slowly: there will be no massive extension of the concept of duty of care.

Current state of the doctrine

3.5   The cases below indicate the current uncertainty as to how far the principles of negligence extend.

Third parties

3.6   There is generally no duty to take care to prevent third parties from doing damage - mere foreseeability of damage is not enough.

> *Perl v Camden LBC 1983*
> Thieves entered an empty house owned by the defendant and broke through from there into the adjacent property, stealing a number of high-value items.
>
> *Held:* although it was foreseeable that such an event may occur, because there was no special relationship by which the house-owner could control the acts of the thieves, no duty of care to the plaintiffs arose.
>
> *Lamb v London Borough of Camden 1981*
> By their negligence, the defendants had caused damages to the foundations of the plaintiff's house so that his tenant had to vacate it. Two sets of squatters then moved in, causing much damage, until strong barricades prevented further intrusion.
>
> *Held:* the damage was reasonably foreseeable but was only 'possible' rather than 'likely to occur' and the workmen who damaged the water main which damaged the foundations could not, at the time, have foreseen the damage which would be wreaked by squatters. The defendants were therefore not liable.

3.7   But if the defendant is in control of third parties he has a duty of care in the exercise of that control.

> *Home Office v Dorset Yacht Club 1970*
> DY's property was damaged by a number of boys who escaped at night from a Borstal institution. The escape was due to lack of care by the guards for whom the Home Office was responsible.
>
> *Held:* the Home Office was vicariously liable for the negligence of its staff as it owed a duty of care to persons whose property it could be foreseen might be damaged if the boys escaped.

Economic loss

3.8   One of the most uncertain areas in the law on negligence is how far and in what circumstances there is liability for financial (usually called 'economic') loss, if it is not the direct consequence of physical damage caused by negligence. The most common example of economic loss is where a person who has suffered physical damage makes a claim for loss of business profits while the damage is put right.

3.9   But in the last twenty years successful claims have been made for loss of profits both in cases where the root cause was physical damage and in cases where no actual physical damage occurred at all.

> *Ross v Caunters 1980*
> A solicitor gave negligent advice to a testator and drew up a will carelessly. A gift to the plaintiff (an intended beneficiary) failed as a result.
>
> *Held:* the solicitor owed a duty of care to beneficiaries since it was reasonably foreseeable that they would be damaged by negligent advice. The beneficiary could therefore sue for loss since he was actually in mind when the solicitor drew up the will.

3.10 Liability to pay damages for economic loss is limited to situations where the parties are linked by some special relationship, such as solicitor and beneficiary or takeover bidder and accountant. In the *Caparo* case the situation was analysed as being one where the defendant knew:

(a) of the nature of the transactions which the plaintiff had in mind;

(b) that the advice or information would be communicated to the plaintiff; and

(c) it was likely that the plaintiff would rely on that advice or information when deciding whether to go ahead with the transaction in mind.

3.11 If the courts can identify a special relationship 'akin to contract' between plaintiff and defendant, a claim for loss of profits may succeed. This case is generally regarded as exceptional.

> *Junior Books v Veitchi Co Ltd 1983*
> The defendants were sub-contractors engaged to lay a floor in the plaintiff's factory. Their contract was with the main contractor, not with the plaintiff. The floor was defective and had to be replaced (pure economic loss, as the only damage was to the product itself).
>
> *Held:* the defendants owed the plaintiffs a duty of care. They were not producing goods for an unknown consumer; they were working for a particular person whose identity was known and who was relying on their skill and judgement as flooring contractors.

3.12 The special nature of the *Junior Books* case has been stressed in subsequent decisions, which have reverted to the award of damages for economic loss only where that loss is attached to physical loss.

> *Muirhead v Industrial Tank Specialities Ltd 1986*
> The plaintiffs, wholesale fish merchants, purchased lobsters in the summer with the intention of selling them at Christmas when prices were higher. The pumps which they purchased to oxygenate the water were inadequate. The lobsters died.
>
> *Held:* the death of the lobsters was reasonably foreseeable and this loss was recoverable. The additional losses were purely economic and were not recoverable.

Omission and commission

3.13 Generally there is no liability for a mere *omission to act*. There is a basic distinction between causing something and failing to prevent it happening. However, an 'assumption of responsibility by a professional person' may give rise to liability in respect of negligent omissions as much as negligent acts of commission, as where a solicitor who has been instructed to draw up a will simply omits to do so: *White v Jones 1995*.

Nervous shock

3.14 There is a duty to take care not to cause nervous shock to a person who one can foresee might suffer in that way from one's negligence. But the liability is not to everyone who may in fact be affected.

(a) There is a duty of care not to cause nervous shock by putting a person in fear for his own safety or by making him an actual witness to an act of negligence by which he suffers nervous shock, such as seeing his house on fire: *Attia v British Gas Plc 1987*.

(b) When a person is injured by negligence, his relatives who learn of the accident immediately afterwards and suffer shock can recover (there is a duty not to alarm or distress them). Otherwise a person who does not witness the event cannot usually claim that a duty of care was owed to him even if he suffers shock as a result.

McLoughlin v O'Brien 1982
A woman called to a hospital where her husband and three children were receiving emergency treatment shortly after an accident of which she was informed by a witness to it. She suffered nervous shock.

Held: there was a duty to her as likely to be affected and so she could recover. This follows *Hambrook v Stokes 1925* (mother heard the sound of an accident in the road where her children were playing). Distinguished from *Bourhill v Young 1943* (passenger in a tram heard but did not see an accident in the road alongside the tram: she saw the messy consequences afterwards; not within the range of persons contemplated as likely to be affected).

(c) If the plaintiff has been put in peril of physical impact, it is immaterial that the impact did not happen if physical injury is in fact caused by the shock arising from the peril.

Page v Smith 1996
The plaintiff was involved in a minor collision with another vehicle while driving his car. Although he was not injured physically, the accident led to a recurrence of myalgic encephalomyelitis (ME) from which he had previously suffered. As a result he was left permanently and chronically fatigued and unlikely to ever work again.

Held: 'since the defendant was admittedly under a duty of care not to cause the plaintiff foreseeable physical injury, it was unnecessary to ask whether he was under a separate duty of care not to cause foreseeable psychiatric injury' (Lord Lloyd). The plaintiff was in the same position as any other road accident victim with a cause of action in negligence, and the defendant had to take his victim as he found him - including his latent predisposition to ME.

(d) A distinction can be drawn between those who witness an event by dint of attending it and those who witness it via a simultaneous television broadcast.

Alcock and Others v Chief Constable of South Yorkshire Police 1991
Numerous spectators at a football match were injured or killed due to being crushed in crowded stands. Various relatives, who had proved the infliction of various psychiatric illnesses and had established that it was the defendant's actions which caused such infliction, brought an action for damages for nervous shock.

Held: the shock must be caused by the actual sight or sound of the accident or its immediate aftermath and not by the result of a communication from a third party. Even the watching of live television broadcasts would not normally satisfy the sight or sound requirement, especially as current broadcasting guidelines prohibit the transmission of pictures of the death and suffering of recognisable individuals. There would be a rebuttable presumption that the sight or sound requirement would be satisfied in the case of spouses or parents, but every case would be examined on its merits.

Emergency services

3.15 Fire authorities generally owe no duty of care in tort to individual property owners when fighting a fire: *Nelson Holdings Ltd v British Gas plc and others 1997*.

3.16 The decision in the *Nelson* case was arrived at by considering a number of earlier cases.

(a) In *Capital Counties plc v Hampshire County Council and Others 1996* it was held that the fire authority owed the plaintiffs a duty of care not to commit positive acts of negligence.

(b) In *Church of Jesus Christ of Latter Day Saints (Great Britain) v Yorkshire Fire and Civil Defence Authority 1996* it was held that it would not be fair, just and reasonable, and would be contrary to public policy to impose a duty.

(c)   In *John Munroe (Acrylics) Ltd v London Fire and Civil Defence Authority and Others 1996* it was held that ordinarily there was not sufficient proximity between the fire authority and an individual property owner for the duty to arise.

The judge concluded that it was not fair or reasonable to impose a duty of care. There was a risk that such a duty would lead to defensive fire fighting. It was inevitable that fire officers would deal with some fires more successfully than with others and it would be intolerable if, in the difficult and dangerous emergency situation in which they were often required to operate, the fire services were subject to the risk of having their every action crawled over in litigation in an attempt to recreate from the ashes of the disaster precisely what happened and how.

3.17   The existence of a duty of care is not excluded by the existence of a contractual relationship.

> *Henderson v Merrett Syndicates Limited 1994*
> The plaintiffs were 'Names' (underwriting members) at Lloyds. They alleged that the defendants had been negligent in their conduct of the Names' business and were also in breach of contract.
>
> *Held:* although subject to some criticism, the concept of 'assumption of responsibility' has been used to assess whether a plaintiff falls within the category of persons to whom the maker of a statement owes a duty of care. This concept was present in *Hedley Byrne* (see later in this chapter). The court attributed to this assumption of responsibility a tortious liability and found that this liability was not excluded by the contract. A tortious duty of care may therefore arise not only in cases where the relevant services are rendered gratuitously, but also where they are rendered under a contract.

3.18   Similarly, a term in a JCT building contract requiring an employer to insure against the risk of a fire could not be relied on by a contractor to escape liability for a fire caused by his own negligence: *Barking and Dagenham LBC v Stamford Asphalt Co Ltd and Another 1997.*

4   BREACH OF DUTY OF CARE

4.1   The standard of reasonable care requires that the person concerned should do what a reasonable man 'guided upon those considerations which ordinarily regulate the conduct of human affairs' would do and abstain from doing what a reasonable man would not do. The standard of 'a reasonable man' is not that of an average man - for instance, the standard of a 'reasonable' car driver is a very high standard indeed.

4.2   The rule has been developed as follows.

(a)   In considering what precautions should be taken or foresight applied, the test is one of knowledge and general practice existing at the time, not hindsight or subsequent change of practice.

> *Roe v Minister of Health 1954*
> A doctor gave a patient an injection taking normal precautions at that time. The drug was contaminated and the patient became paralysed. At the time of the trial seven years later medical practice had been improved to avoid the risk of undetected contamination (through an invisible crack in a glass tube).
>
> *Held:* the proper test was normal practice based on the state of medical knowledge at the time. The doctor was not at fault in failing to anticipate later developments.

(b)   A person who professes to have a particular skill, eg in a profession, is required to use the skill which he purports to have. But an error of judgement is not automatically a case of negligence: *Whitehouse v Jordan 1981.*

(c)   In broad terms, a claim against a professional person will fail if he or she can point to a body of opinion that supports the approach taken. In *Bolitho v City and*

Hackney Health Authority 1997, The House of Lords introduced an important qualification to this principle The courts will henceforth be entitled to consider whether that body of opinion was reasonable.

(d) In deciding what is reasonable care the balance must be struck between advantage and risk. The driver of a fire engine may perhaps exceed the normal prudent speed on his way to the fire but not on the way back.

(e) If A owes a duty of care to B and A knows that B is unusually vulnerable, a higher standard of care is expected. For example, B might be a child, an inexperienced employee given risky work to do, or a person with a 'thin skull'.

Paris v Stepney Borough Council 1951
P was employed by K on vehicle maintenance. P had already lost the sight of one eye. He was hammering metal. It was not the normal practice to issue protective goggles to men employed on this work since the risk of eye injury was small. A chip of metal flew into P's eye and blinded him.

Held: although industrial practice did not require the use of goggles by workers with normal sight, there was a higher standard of care owed to P because an injury to his remaining good eye would blind him. S had failed to maintain a proper standard of care in relation to P.

Res ipsa loquitur

4.3 It rests on the plaintiff to show both that the defendant owed him a duty of reasonable care and that the defendant failed in that duty. In some circumstances the plaintiff may argue that the facts speak for themselves (*res ipsa loquitur*) - that want of care is the only possible explanation for what happened and negligence on the part of the defendant must be presumed.

4.4 To rely on this principle the plaintiff must first show that:

(a) the thing which caused the injury was under the management and control of the defendant; and

(b) the accident was such as would not occur if those in control used proper care.

Scott v London & St Katharine Docks Co 1865
S was passing in front of the defendant's warehouse. Six bags of sugar fell on him.

Held: in the absence of explanation it must be presumed that the fall of the bags of sugar was due to want of care on the part of the defendants. Principles (a) and (b) above were formulated in this case.

Easson v LNE Railway Co 1944
A four year old boy fell through the open door of a train seven miles from its last stopping place.

Held: the principle of res ipsa loquitur did not apply since the railway company was not sufficiently in control of the doors of the train. After it left the last station a passenger might have opened the door.

5   CONSEQUENTIAL HARM   *6/95, 12/95, 6/96, 6/97, 12/98*

5.1 A claim for compensation for negligence will not succeed if the third element (damage or loss) is not proved. In deciding whether a claim should be allowed, the court considers whether:

(a) the breach of duty gave rise to the harm (fact); and whether
(b) the harm was too remote from the breach (law).

5.2   A person will only be compensated if he has suffered actual loss, injury, damage or harm as a consequence of another's actions. The claim will not be proved if:

(a)   the plaintiff followed a course of action regardless of the acts of the defendant;

(b)   a third party is the actual cause of harm;

(c)   a complicated series of events takes place such that no one act was the cause of all the harm; or

(d)   an intervening act by the plaintiff or a third party breaks the 'chain of causation' (*novus actus interveniens*).

5.3   Having decided whether harm arose from a breach of duty, the court will finally look at whether the harm which occurred was reasonably foreseeable; this is the question of remoteness of damage.

Remoteness of damage

5.4   When a person commits a tort with the intention of causing loss or harm which in fact results from the wrongful act, that loss etc can never be too remote a consequence. Damages will be awarded for it.

5.5   If the sequence of cause and effect includes a new act (called *novus actus interveniens*) of a third party or of the plaintiff, it may terminate the defendant's liability at that point - further consequences are too remote and he is not required to pay compensation for them. But where the intervening act is that of a third party who could be expected to behave as he did in the situation arising from the defendant's original wrongful act, the intervening act does not break the chain.

> *Scott v Shepherd 1773*
> A threw a lighted firework cracker into a crowded market. It landed on the stall of B who threw it away and it landed on the stall of C who threw it away and it hit D in the face and blinded him in one eye. D sued A.
>
> *Held:* there was no break in the chain of causation from A's intentional wrongful act and he was liable to D.

Reasonable foresight

5.6   If the intervening act is that of the plaintiff himself and he acts unreasonably, for example, by taking an avoidable and foreseeable risk of injury to himself, that breaks the chain (or if it does not it may reduce his claim for loss by his contributory negligence).

5.7   When there is a sequence of physical cause and effect without human intervention, the ultimate loss is too remote (so that damages cannot be recovered for it) unless it could have been reasonably foreseen that some loss of that kind might occur as a consequence of the wrong.

> *The Wagon Mound 1961*
> A ship (the Wagon Mound) was taking on furnace oil in Sydney harbour. By negligence oil was spilled onto the water and it drifted to a wharf 200 yards away where welding equipment was in use in the repair of another ship. The owner of the wharf at first stopped work because of the fire risk but later resumed working because he was advised that sparks from a welding torch were unlikely to set fire to furnace oil. Safety precautions were taken. A spark fell onto a piece of cotton waste floating in the oil and this served as a wick, thereby starting a fire which caused damage to the wharf. The owners of the wharf sued the charterers of the Wagon Mound, basing their claim on an earlier decision that damage caused by a direct and uninterrupted sequence of physical events is never too remote even though it could not reasonably be foreseen.

Held: the claim must fail. The earlier decision was overruled and the reasonable foresight test laid down. Pollution was the foreseeable risk: fire was not. This was a decision of the Privy Council on appeal from Australia and as such only a persuasive precedent for English courts. But as it was a decision of the most senior English judges it is always applied in cases where the claim is for negligence.

Hughes v Lord Advocate 1963
Workmen left lighted paraffin lamps as a warning sign of an open manhole in the street. Two small boys took one of the lamps as a light and went down the manhole. As they clambered out the lamp fell into the hole and caused an explosion in which the boys were injured. Evidence was given that a fire might have been foreseen but an explosion was improbable.

Held: the defendants were liable for negligence in leaving the lamps where they did. A risk of fire was foreseeable and the explosion must be regarded as 'an unexpected manifestation of the apprehended physical dangers'. It was not (as it was in the *Wagon Mound* Case) damage of an entirely different kind.

Doughty v Turner Manufacturing Co 1964
An asbestos cement lid accidentally fell into a cauldron of sodium cyanide at a temperature of 800 degrees Centigrade. The intense heat caused a chemical change in the asbestos lid as a result of which there was an explosion. The plaintiff was injured by the eruption of molten liquid. The chemical reaction leading to the explosion was previously unknown to science.

Held: a splash of sodium cyanide was foreseeable but a violent explosion was not. The result was unforeseeable and therefore too remote.

5.8   Similarly, in *Gillon v Chief Constable of Strathclyde Police and Another 1996* it was held that it would be unreasonable to require the proprietors of a football ground to erect a barrier between the players and the pitchside track. There was a foreseeable risk that a police constable watching the spectators at a football match would be injured by a player who was impelled off the pitch in the course of the game, but the risk was so small that a reasonable man would not guard against it.

5.9   In cases of physical injury which is more serious than would normally be expected because the plaintiff proves to be abnormally vulnerable, the defendant is liable for the full amount of injury done. This is the 'thin skull' principle: if A taps B on the head and cracks B's skull because it is abnormally thin, A is liable for the fracture.

5.10   If the plaintiff suffers avoidable loss because his lack of resources prevents him from taking costly measures to reduce his loss, he may still recover damages for it.

Smith v Leech Braine & Co 1962
A workman was near a tank of molten zinc in which metal articles were dipped to galvanise them. One article was allowed to slip and the workman was burnt on the lip by a drop of molten zinc. The burn activated latent cancer from which he died three years later. His widow sued for damages.

Held: damages for a fatal accident would be awarded. Some physical injury (the burn on the lip) was a foreseeable consequence. The defendants must accept liability for the much more serious physical injury (cancer) caused by their negligence.

Exercise 1

Walter is employed by X Ltd. Because of his employer's negligence he sustains a broken leg. What is the company's liability if he is left with a severe limp because of an error made by the surgeon who sets his leg in plaster?

Solution

X Ltd would probably plead that the surgeon's actions are a *novus actus interveniens*. Although such mistakes are made from time to time, they are comparatively rare, and the actions of the surgeon are entirely outside the company's control. This defence is likely to succeed (following *Hogan v Bentinck Collieries*) and the company's liability will be limited to compensation for the broken leg.

5.11   It should be emphasised that *all* torts are subject to the remoteness rules, not just negligence. In practical terms the issue is more likely to arise in the case of negligence.

6   OCCUPIERS' LIABILITY

12/96, 12/98

6.1   An occupier of premises is any person (not necessarily the owner) who has control or possession of them. Occupation may be shared by two or more persons.

6.2   By statute (Occupiers' Liability Acts 1957 and 1984) an *occupier* owes a duty ('a common *duty of care*') to all *visitors* to the *premises* and must take such precautions as are necessary to make the premises reasonably safe for the purpose for which the visitor is permitted to enter them.

6.3   An occupier of premises is the person who has control of the premises. Ownership alone is not sufficient to constitute occupancy. In *Wheat v Lacon & Co Ltd 1966* it was held that the owners of a public house, which was managed by a manager, were nevertheless occupiers of it because of the degree of control they exercised over it.

6.4   A visitor is a person who:

(a)   enters the premises with the actual or implied permission (or invitation) of the occupier; or

(b)   is a person such as a health inspector who has a legal right of entry.

6.5   A person who enters to do business with the occupier is deemed to have implied permission although he may in fact not wish to see the visitor - as an example, a casual call by a sales representative hoping to sell his products to the occupier would make him a visitor. But there is no duty of care to a visitor who, after entering the premises, exceeds the limits of the permitted purpose, say by straying into parts of the building unconnected with his visit; he then becomes a trespasser.

6.6   Premises include not only land and buildings, but also fixed and moveable structures. Case law suggests that this definition is wide enough to include a mechanical digger, scaffolding and a lift.

6.7   The duty of care may vary with the visitor. An occupier is entitled to assume that lawful visitors will display ordinary prudence while on his premises, s 2.

(a)   If the visitor is a specialist, for example a technician called in to do repairs, he is deemed to be aware of special risks incidental to his calling (eg no liability for the death by carbon monoxide poisoning of two sweeps called in to close a hole in a boiler chimney: *Roles v Nathan 1963*).

(b)   If he is a child, a higher standard of care is imposed on the occupier.

6.8   The occupier may discharge his duty to visitors:

(a)   *by taking reasonable measures*, such as repair work, to eliminate a hazard. He is not responsible for faulty work of an independent contractor, brought in to do specialist work. But he should inspect it. Thus an occupier will not be liable for the unsafe state of a lift due to negligence of the specialist firm employed to repair it but he remains liable when a school cleaner leaves slippery ice on a step (not a specialist task);

(b) *by giving warnings* where a warning is enough to enable the visitor to be reasonably safe. A visitor who ignores a warning may be consenting to the risk or may be guilty of contributory negligence. But a warning is not a sufficient precaution in some cases. It depends on the facts.

6.9 The occupier may in theory limit his liability to visitors on his premises by contract. But any such exclusion or limitation is restricted by the Unfair Contract Terms Act 1977 which among other provisions renders void a 'notice given to persons general' purporting to exclude or restrict liability for death or personal injury resulting from negligence. The position of employees is protected by the Health and Safety at Work Act 1974 and related statutes and regulations.

Occupier's liability to trespassers

6.10 The Occupiers' Liability Act 1984 has replaced the common law rules governing the duty of occupiers of premises to persons other than visitors. Prior to 1984, the occupier's duty to trespassers was to act with common sense and humanity. This required all the surrounding circumstances to be considered, for example the seriousness of the danger, the type of trespasser likely to enter, and in some cases the resources of the occupier.

6.11 There is no satisfactory definition of 'trespasser'. It may include the innocent as well as the malicious. Broadly speaking it is a person who knows he does not intend communication with the occupier or anyone else on the premises.

> *British Railways v Herrington 1972*
> The local management of British Rail were aware that children gained entry to an electrified railway line through a broken-down fence which divided the line from land open to the public. British Rail merely reported the matter to the police but did not repair the fence. A child of six was injured on the line.
>
> *Held:* the occupier's duty must be set by reference to the particular circumstances of the trespassers. A warning may be sufficient for an adult but it falls short of the duty of common humanity owed to a child to safeguard it from accessible and tempting perils on the occupier's land.

6.12 The main provisions of the 1984 Act are set out below.

Duty owed

6.13 The occupier owes a duty if:

(a) he is aware of the danger or has reasonable grounds to believe that it exists; and

(b) he knows or should know that someone is in (or may come into) the vicinity of the danger; and

(c) the risk is one against which he may reasonably be expected to offer that person some protection.

Duty broken

6.14 The duty is to take such care as is reasonable in all the circumstances to see that the person to whom a duty is owed does not suffer injury on the premises by reason of the danger.

Damage

6.15 The occupier can only be liable for injury to the person. The Act expressly provides that there can be no liability for loss or damage to property.

Warnings

6.16   The duty may be discharged (in appropriate cases) by taking reasonable steps to give warning of the danger.

6.17   The 1984 Act does not significantly change the common law, although it does weight the balance more heavily against the occupier: all the circumstances remain relevant. It is therefore unlikely that Herrington's case would be decided differently under the Act and the outcome of other cases will still be difficult to predict.

6.18   A person using a right of way across land is neither a licensee nor an invitee and is therefore not a visitor. The occupier of the land is under no liability to users of the right of way for failure to keep it in good repair: *McGeown v Northern Ireland Housing Executive 1994*. Thus the 1984 Act applies to entrants other than trespassers.

Defective Premises Act 1972

6.19   This Act imposes on landlords a general liability, say to tenants' visitors, arising from a landlord's failure to repair the premises. It also imposes a statutory obligation on those who provide dwellings (landlords, builders, developers, local authorities etc) to ensure that each dwelling is fit for habitation. Furthermore, any work done (where a dwelling house is not built under an NHBC guarantee) must be carried out in a workmanlike or professional manner using proper materials A vendor of a house has similar duties towards a buyer and other persons reasonably expected to be affected.

6.20   Actions arising under the 1972 act lie in tort. S 1 of the Act imposes 'strict liability' (see Section 9) regarding fitness for habitation while the duty imposed on landlords under s 3 requires proof of negligence on the part of the defendant.

7   NEGLIGENT MISSTATEMENT   *6/94, 6/98*

7.1   There is a duty of care not to cause economic loss by negligent misstatement, but the duty exists only where the person who makes the statement foresees that it may be relied on. There must therefore be a *special relationship*. To establish such a special relationship the person who makes the statement:

(a)   *must do so in some professional or expert capacity which makes it likely that others will rely on what he says.* This is the position of an accountant providing information or advice in a professional capacity (or indeed any other person 'professing' special knowledge, skill and care), but the principle was recently extended to a friendly relationship with business overtones.

Chaudry v Prabhakar 1989
A friend of the plaintiff undertook (as a favour) to find a suitable car for her to buy; the plaintiff stipulated that any such car should not have been involved in an accident. The friend (who knew more about cars than the plaintiff did) failed to enquire of the owner of a car (which had, to the friend's knowledge, a straightened or replaced bonnet) whether it had been in an accident. In fact the car had been in a serious accident and it was unroadworthy and worthless. The plaintiff sued the friend for £5,500.

Held: the friend owed a duty to take such care as was reasonable in the circumstances and had broken that duty; there had been a voluntary assumption of responsibility against the background of a business transaction; hence the friend was liable for the plaintiff's loss.

Coulthard v Neville Russell 1997
The Court of Appeal held that, as a matter of principle, auditors could owe a duty of care to client company directors to advise them that intended payments might breach the financial assistance provisions of the Companies Acts even if advice on

the matter was not specifically sought. Whether a duty was owed in a particular case would depend on the facts.

(b)   *must foresee that it is likely to be relied on by another person.*

Hedley Byrne v Heller and Partners 1964
HB were advertising agents acting for a new client E. If E failed to pay bills for advertising arranged by HB then HB would have to pay the advertising charges. HB through its bank requested information from E's bank (HP) on the financial position of E. HP returned non-committal replies which were held to be negligent misstatement of E's financial resources. In replying HP expressly disclaimed legal responsibility.

Held: there is a duty of care to avoid causing financial loss by negligent misstatement where there is a 'special relationship'. HP were guilty of negligence having breached the duty of care but escaped liability by reason of their disclaimer.

This case is the principal, original authority on this point.

7.2   The House of Lords in this case adopted Lord Denning's tests of a special relationship laid down in *Candler v Crane Christmas 1951*.

> 'A special relationship is one where the defendant gives advice or information and the plaintiff relies on that advice. The defendant should realise that his words will be relied on either by the person he is addressing or by a third party'.

7.3   It is almost certain that advice given on a social occasion cannot give rise to a duty of care, unless the person giving it realised (or should have realised) that it was going to be relied upon.

7.4   The principle of liability for negligent misstatement has been refined in the area of professional negligence to take account of the test of *reasonable foresight* being present to create a duty of care.

JEB Fasteners Ltd v Marks, Bloom & Co 1982
The defendants, a firm of accountants, prepared an audited set of accounts showing stock valued at £23,080. It had been purchased for £11,000, but was nevertheless described as being valued 'at the lower of cost and net realisable value'. Hence profit was inflated. The auditors knew there were liquidity problems and that the company was seeking outside finance. The plaintiffs were shown the accounts; they doubted the stock figure but took over the company for a nominal amount nevertheless, since by that means they could obtain the services of the company's two directors. At no time did MB tell JEB that stock was inflated. With the investment's failure, JEB sued MB claiming:

(a)   the accounts had been prepared negligently; and

(b)   they had relied on those accounts; and

(c)   they would not have invested had they been aware of the company's true position; and

(d)   MB owed a duty of care to all persons whom they could reasonably foresee would rely on the accounts.

Held: MB owed a duty of care (d) and had been negligent in preparing the accounts (a). But even though JEB had relied on the accounts (b), they would not have acted differently if the true position had been known (c), since they had really wanted the directors, not the company. Hence the accountants were not the cause of the consequential harm and were not liable.

7.5   This case implied that an auditor should 'reasonably foresee' that he has a legal duty of care to a stranger. The decision was confirmed in *Twomax Ltd and Goode v Dickson, McFarlane & Robinson 1983*, where the auditors had to pay damages to three investors who purchased shares on the strength of accounts which had been negligently audited.

7.6   But the *JEB Fasteners* case also reinforces the important point that the person suing for negligent misstatement must actually have relied on the advice. There is no case if he would have proceeded come what may.

The Caparo decision

7.7   The case below has made considerable changes to the tort of negligence as a whole, and the negligence of professionals in particular.

> *Caparo Industries plc v Dickman and Others 1990*
> In March 1984 Caparo Industries purchased 100,000 Fidelity shares in the open market. On 12 June 1984, the date on which the accounts were published, they purchased a further 50,000 shares. Relying on information in the accounts, which showed a profit of £1.3 million, further shares were acquired. On 25 October the plaintiffs announced that they owned or had received acceptances amounting to 91.8% of the issued shares and subsequently acquired the balance. Caparo claimed against the directors (the brothers Dickman) and the auditors for the fact that the accounts should have shown a loss of £460,000. The plaintiffs argued that the auditors owed a duty of care to investors and potential investors in respect of the audit. They should have been aware that in March 1984 a press release stating that profits would fall significantly had made Fidelity vulnerable to a takeover bid and that bidders might well rely upon the accounts.
>
> *Held:* the auditor's duty did not extend to potential investors nor to existing shareholders increasing their stakes. It was a duty owed to the body of shareholders as whole.

7.8   In the *Caparo* case the House of Lords decided that there were two very different situations facing a person giving professional advice:

(a)   preparing advice or information in the knowledge that a particular person was contemplating a transaction and was expecting to receive the advice or information in order to rely on it to decide whether or not to proceed with the transaction (a special relationship); and

(b)   preparing a statement (such as an audit report) for more or less general circulation which could forseeably be relied upon by persons unknown to the professional for a variety of different purposes.

7.9   It was held therefore that a public company's auditors owed no duty of care to the public at large who relied on the audit report in deciding to invest - and, in purchasing additional shares, an existing shareholder was in no different position to the public at large. There was insufficient proximity. This line has been maintained in a recent case.

> *Abbot and Others v Strong and Others 1998*
> The High Court decided that a circular issued by a company to its shareholders in connection with a rights issue, allegedly containing misleading profits forecast and an allegedly negligent letter from the company's accountants confirming the forecast was properly compiled, did not lead to the accountants having a duty of care to the shareholders who acquired shares in the rights issue.

7.10   In *MacNaughton (James) Papers Group Ltd v Hicks Anderson & Co 1991*, it was stated that, in the absence of some general principle establishing a duty of care, it was necessary to examine each case in the light of the concepts of:

(a)   foreseeability;
(b)   proximity; and
(c)   fairness.

The absence of a general principle establishing a duty of care was now acknowledged by the courts, so the court had to consider whether it was fair, just and reasonable for a legal duty of care to arise in the particular circumstances of each case. Lord Justice Neill set out the matters to be taken into account in considering this.

(a) The purpose for which the statement was made.

(b) The purpose for which the statement was communicated.

(c) The relationship between the maker of the statement, the recipient and any relevant third party.

(d) The size of any class to which the recipient belonged.

(e) The state of knowledge of the maker.

(f) Any reliance by the recipient.

7.11 The *Caparo* decision was re-affirmed in *Anthony v Wright 1995*, where it was held that auditors did not, save in exceptional circumstances, owe a duty of care to anyone other than the company in respect of their audits. In this case they did not owe such a duty to certain investors. Exceptional circumstances might be found if the auditors had a special relationship with a third party and if they had intended that the third party should rely on the audit. In this case, however, although the investors were beneficiaries under trusts of which the company was trustee, and of whose existence the auditors were fully aware, the auditors apparently had not assumed any responsibility towards the investors and there was no intention that the investors should rely on their audits.

7.12 In spite of these decisions, it is still possible for professional advisers to owe a duty of care to an individual. The directors and financial advisors of the target company in a contested takeover bid were held to owe a duty of care to a known take-over bidder in respect of financial statements and other documents prepared for the purpose of contesting the bid: *Morgan Crucible Co plc v Hill Samuel Bank Ltd and others 1990*. It was found that the directors and financial advisers of the target company had made express representations to a known bidder, intending that the bidder should rely on those representations. In this case they owed the bidder a duty of care not to be negligent in making representations which might mislead him.

7.13 A more recent case highlights the need for a cautious approach and careful evaluation of the circumstances when giving financial advice.

ADT Ltd v BDO Binder Hamlyn 1995
Binder Hamlyn was the joint auditor (along with McCabe & Ford) of BSG. In October 1989, BSG's audited accounts for the year to 30 June 1989 were published. Binder Hamlyn signed off the audit as showing a true and fair view of BSG's position. ADT was thinking of buying BSG and, as a potential buyer, sought Binder Hamlyn's confirmation of the audited results. On 5 January 1990, the Binder Hamlyn audit partner, Martyn Bishop, attended a meeting with John Jermine, a director of ADT. This meeting was described by the judge as the 'final hurdle' before ADT finalised its bid for BSG. At the meeting, Mr Bishop specifically confirmed that he 'stood by' the audit of October 1989, thereby reconfirming the true and fair view given in that audit. ADT proceeded to purchase BSG for £105m on the strength of Binder Hamlyn's advice. It was subsequently alleged that BSG's true value was only £40m. ADT therefore sued Binder Hamlyn for the difference, £65m plus interest.

Held: Binder Hamlyn assumed a responsibility for the statement that the audited accounts showed a true and fair view of BSG. Furthermore, ADT relied to its subsequent detriment on the information provided by Mr Bishop. Since the underlying audit work had been carried out negligently, Binder Hamlyn was held liable for the difference in the amount paid by ADT and true value of BSG, amounting to £65m.

7.14 This situation was different from *Caparo* since the court was concerned with the purpose of the *statement* made at the meeting and not with the purpose for which the audit had been performed. Binder Hamlyn appealed against the decision but in 1997 reached an out of court settlement with ADT.

7.15 Another case on duty of care had parallels with the ADT decision, but the Court of Appeal found for the accountants:

> *Peach Publishing Lt v Slater & Co 1997*
> The defendant represented at a meeting that a set of management accounts of a company that the plaintiff was seeking to acquire were 'right'. It later turned out that the accounts were inaccurate.
>
> *Held:* the Court of Appeal decided that on the facts of the case that the defendant had not assumed responsibility to the plaintiff for the accuracy of the information. There was evidence that at the meeting the plaintiff was not seeking assurance on the accounts as an end in itself, but in order to obtain a warranty from the vendor. Thus there is no automatic link between the giving of an assurance and the finding of liability.

7.16 During 1997, there were some other important clarifications of the law affecting accountants' liability in the area of responsibility towards non-clients. The following two cases both concerned authors' liability to part of a group for losses incurred elsewhere in the group.

> *Barings plc v Coopers & Lybrand 1997*
> Barings collapsed in 1995 after heavily loss-making trading by the general manager of its Singapore subsidiary, BFS. BFS was audited by the defendant's Singapore firm, which provided Barings directors with consolidation schedules and copy of the BFS audit report. The defendant tried to argue that there was no duty of care owed to Barings, only to BFS.
>
> *Held:* A duty of care was owed to Barings, as the defendants must have known that their audit report and consolidation schedules would be relied upon at group level by the parent company.
>
> *BCCI (Overseas) Ltd v Ernst & Whinney 1997*
> In this case, the defendants audited the group holding company's accounts, but not those of the plaintiff subsidiary. The plaintiff tried to claim that the defendants had a duty of care to them.
>
> *Held:* no duty of care was owed to the subsidiary because no specific information is normally channelled down by a holding company's auditor to its subsidiaries.

7.17 The High Court decided in *Yorkshire Enterprise Ltd and Another v Robson Rhodes 1998* that two companies that invested venture capital in a shopfitting company were entitled to damages from the shopfitter's auditors on the basis of negligent misstatements made by them. The court has tended to find liability in accountants where they knew the users and the specific use to which the information would be put, and had consented to involvement in the transaction. The courts will punish auditors who fail to check the accuracy of the specific information that they are providing.

7.18 The High Court has decided in *Sasea Finance Ltd v KPMG 1998* that an auditor who through negligence fails to see that a company is insolvent, with the result that the company, with the auditor's approval, pays a dividend, could be liable to the company for the amount paid out.

7.19 UK accountancy firms have been investigating ways of limiting liability in the face of increasing litigation. KPMG, for example, incorporated its audit practice in 1995. Ernst & Young and Price Waterhouse are considering offshore registration as limited partnerships.

7.20 Large firms also campaigned for a reform of the law of joint and several liability, on the grounds that auditors are often sued for the whole of a company's losses even though they may only be peripherally responsible. In February 1996 the Law Commission said that such a reform would be 'wrong in principle'. The debate continues.

8   BREACH OF STATUTORY DUTY

8.1   When a statute imposes a duty - such as the employer's duty to fence dangerous machinery - it is usually a criminal offence not to comply. A private person may sue on his own behalf for breach of statutory duty if he is a member of a class which the statutory duty was intended to protect. Statutes sometimes expressly state that no person is to have a right to sue for breach of the duty.

8.2   The plaintiff must show that:

(a)   the statute was intended to give a civil remedy for its breach;

(b)   the defendant had a duty imposed by that statute; and

(c)   the defendant was in breach and as a consequence the plaintiff suffered harm which arose out of the breach and was not too remote.

8.3   In particular, the wrong complained of must be one which was contemplated by statute.

> *Gorris v Scott 1874*
> A statute provided that animals on board ship must be kept in pens (to prevent the spread of contagious diseases). Sheep were washed overboard in a storm. The owner sued for damages on the ground that if the sheep had been securely penned as the law required the loss would not have occurred.
>
> *Held:* the claim must be dismissed. The duty to pen was not imposed to prevent the loss complained of.

8.4   Breach of statutory duty is important in the present day since a large volume of claims are brought by employees claiming breach of safety rules by their employers. The Factories Act 1961 is an important piece of legislation in this area.

Factories Act 1961

8.5   The Act applies only to a *factory*, which is a place where manufacturing or processing work is carried out. A 'factory' includes buildings ancillary to a place of manufacture and also a slaughterhouse, a laundry, a shipyard, a film set and premises where packing takes place (among other specified categories): s 175.

8.6   Premises are not a factory unless the following conditions are satisfied.

(a)   The substantial purpose for which the premises are used include manual labour. For example, a chemist's shop was not a factory although one member of its staff was a porter doing manual work.

(b)   The work is done in the course of trade or for purposes of gain, An industrial laboratory for testing materials is part of the factory but a laboratory at a technical college which tests materials is not a factory.

8.7   The occupier of a factory has an absolute duty to fence securely all *prime movers* (that is, machines which provide power, say by driving belts to the manufacturing machinery), all transmission machinery and every dangerous part of any machinery. There is strict liability for failing to do so. Machinery is dangerous if it can be reasonably foreseen that injury to any person can occur in the ordinary course of use.

> *Close v Steel Company of Wales 1961*
> C was using an electric drilling machine. The drill shattered and a fragment flew into his eye.
>
> *Held:*
>
> (a)   It was not dangerous machinery since the harm caused was not reasonably foreseeable.

(b) When there is a duty to fence machinery the fencing is sufficient if it prevents the body of the operator from coming into contact with the machine. It is not generally necessary to fence so as to prevent fragments of machinery or material from flying out.

8.8 Among particular points the following should be noted.

(a) It is no defence to show that there is no practicable means of fencing the machines. If they cannot be used when adequately fenced, then they should not be used at all.

(b) The fencing should be substantial and kept in position at all times when the machine is in motion but not when it is being examined, lubricated etc.

(c) Machines brought into a factory for repair etc are not part of the factory machinery and there is no duty to fence them in. But the duty to fence does arise as soon as a machine is installed ready for use as part of the factory plant even though it is not yet in commercial use.

(d) The duty to fence may apply to a moveable machine such as a mobile crane.

(e) It is only the dangerous parts which need to be fenced. If that is done there is no duty to fence the rest of the machine.

(f) There is generally no duty to fence merely because a moving part of a machine is near some stationary object which is not part of the machine and so there is a risk of crushing between the two.

(g) A fence is sufficiently secure even though it does not prevent reckless employees from circumventing it:

> *Carr v Mercantile Produce Co 1949*
> A woman employee forced her hand through a hole three inches in diameter to remove dough from a moving part of a machine used to make macaroni and her fingers were injured.

> *Held:* the machine was securely fenced and the employer was not liable.

9   TORTS OF STRICT LIABILITY

9.1 In many torts the defendant is liable because he acted intentionally or at least negligently. He may escape liability if he shows that he acted with reasonable care. That is essentially the position in the tort of negligence itself. But there are also torts which result from breach of an absolute duty - the defendant is liable even though he took reasonable care.

9.2 The outstanding example of a tort of strict liability is the rule in *Rylands v Fletcher*.

'Where a person who, for his own purposes, brings and keeps on land in his occupation anything likely to do mischief if it escapes, he must keep it in at his peril, and if he fails to do so he is liable for all damage naturally accruing from the escape.'

> *Rylands v Fletcher 1868*
> F employed competent contractors to construct a reservoir to store water for his mill. In their work the contractors uncovered old mine workings which appeared to be blocked with earth. They did no more to seal them off and it was accepted at the trial that there was no want of reasonable care on their part. When the reservoir was filled, the water burst through the workings and flooded the mine of R on adjoining land.

> *Held:* F was liable, and the principle quoted above was laid down.

9.3 Many industrial processes entail the artificial ('non-natural') accumulation of water, gas or other materials which may cause damage if they escape. In such cases the occupier of the land is liable even if the escape occurs without negligence or want of care on his part. It has, however, been held in a more modern case (*British Celanese v Hunt 1969*) that not every escape of industrial materials gives rise to this strict liability. Industrial activities, as distinct from the accumulation of materials, can be a natural use of the land and so be outside the rule.

9.4 Polluters may be strictly liable for the tort of nuisance. However forseeability of damage is required for there to be liability for nuisance.

> *Cambridge Water Co v Eastern Counties Leather plc 1994*
> The defendant, a firm involved in the tanning industry, stored organochlorines on its premises. The only foreseeable damage at the time was that someone working there might become overcome by fumes. The chemical seeped into the ground and a nearby public water supply borehole, over a mile away, became polluted. The plaintiff, who had to spend nearly £1 million developing a new source of supply to meet an EC directive on the quality of water, made claims in nuisance and based on the rule in *Rylands v Fletcher*.
>
> *Held:* the defendants were not liable. The plaintiffs had a right to extract water from beneath their land and liability for interference with this right was strict. However, the House of Lords decided unanimously that there could be no liability for unforeseeable damage.

9.5 It was argued in this case that the liability in *Rylands v Fletcher* is not intended to be any more strict than liability in nuisance. In *The Wagon Mound*, it was held that foreseeability of damage was essential for liability in nuisance. In addition, the language used in *Rylands v Fletcher* itself implies that damage must be foreseeable: 'anything likely to do mischief'. In giving judgement in the *Cambridge Water Co* case, the House of Lords made it clear that *Rylands v Fletcher* was broadly an extension of the principles of nuisance to cases of isolated escape from land. Thus the decision in *The Wagon Mound* should extend to determining whether there is liability in cases such as the *Cambridge Water Co* case.

9.6 The decision in the *Cambridge Water Co* case reduces the significance of *Rylands v Fletcher* and suggests that liability will in future be very close to 'ordinary' negligence liability, with foreseeability being a requirement.

Exercise 2

For the purposes of the Occupiers' Liability Act 1957, who is a lawful visitor?

Solution

Visitors are persons lawfully on the premises, such as customers in shops and factory inspectors. A trespasser will be deemed to be a lawful visitor for the purposes of the Act if he has been granted implied permission by the occupier's habitual acquiescence to a known trespass.

9.7 Torts of strict liability at common law are rare, but statutes often impose duties of this nature. An example would be the Consumer Protection Act 1987.

Chapter roundup

- The law give various rights to persons, such as the right of a person in possession of land to occupy it without interference or invasion by trespassers. When such a right is infringed the wrongdoer is liable in tort.

- Negligence is the most important modern tort. To succeed in an action for negligence the plaintiff must prove three things. He must show that the defendant owed him (the plaintiff) *a duty of care* to avoid causing injury to persons or property. He must show that there was a *breach of that duty* by the defendant. He must show that *in consequence* the plaintiff suffered *injury or damage* or (in some cases) financial loss.

- In the landmark case of *Donoghue v Stevenson 1932* the House of Lords ruled that a person might owe a duty of care to another with whom he had no contractual relationship at all. The doctrine has been refined in subsequent rulings, but the principle is unchanged.

- A specific application of the principles of negligence is demonstrated by the law relating to occupiers' liability, enshrined in the Occupiers' Liability Acts 1957 and 1984.

- A person who has suffered damage as the result of a breach of a statutory duty may have an action in tort. Industrial safety legislation tends to dominate this area of the law.

- Some torts are classified as torts of strict liability. This type of liability does not depend upon proof of fault.

Test your knowledge

1   What is a tort of strict liability? (see para 2.2)

2   Outline the facts of *Donoghue v Stevenson 1932*. (3.1)

3   What is *res ipsa loquitur* ? (4.3)

4   How may remoteness of damage affect a claim in tort? (5.4 - 5.5)

5   Who is an occupier of premises? (6.3)

6   Outline the facts of *Caparo v Dickman and Others 1990*. (7.7)

7   What must the plaintiff show in an action for breach of statutory duty? (8.2)

8   What is the rule in *Rylands v Fletcher 1868*? (9.2)

Now try illustrative question 17 at the end of the Study Text

Chapter 22

NUISANCE AND DEFAMATION

This chapter covers the following topics.

1 Private nuisance

2 Defences to an action for private nuisance

3 Public nuisance

4 Defamation

5 An action for defamation

6 Defences to an action for defamation

Introduction

In this chapter we consider two particular torts, nuisance and defamation.

---

1 PRIVATE NUISANCE

6/95

1.1 Nuisance may be of two types - public and private. In private nuisance the central idea is that of interference with the plaintiff's enjoyment of his property. Public nuisance does not require any 'invasion' of private land, rather the annoyance of the general public.

1.2 *Private nuisance* is unlawful interference with the plaintiff's use of his property or with his health and comfort or convenience. It often takes the form of emitting noise, smell or vibration - it is essentially an indirect form of interference. If A throws garden rubbish over the fence into B's garden that is trespass; if A burns his rubbish by a series of smoky bonfires which causes real discomfort to B that may be private nuisance.

What constitutes private nuisance ?

1.3 It is important to note that private nuisance is unlawful interference. Many of the actions which constitute private nuisance are themselves lawful; it is only when they cause interference to such a degree as to be unreasonable that they become unlawful. Examples of interference which has been held to be unlawful are set out below.

(a) Physical damage to the plaintiff's land by flooding: *Sedleigh-Denfield v O'Callaghan 1940*.

(b) Encroachment onto the plaintiff's land by tree roots: *Davey v Harrow Corporation 1958*.

(c) Interference with the comfort of the plaintiff through smell: *Bone v Seal 1975*.

1.4 In private nuisance cases it is often necessary to strike a balance between the convenience and interests of two parties which conflict. The following factors may enter into the decision.

(a)   If the activity causes significant physical damage to property it will generally be restrained as private nuisance. If it merely causes personal discomfort the advantages and disadvantages may be balanced to determine whether the activity complained of is so unreasonable as to amount to nuisance.

(b)   Causing intentional discomfort to a neighbour is very likely to be restrained as unreasonable.

> *Christie v Davey 1893*
> C and D occupied adjoining semi-detached houses with a common party wall. D objected to the sounds of C's activities as a music teacher. He made very loud noises, shouting and banging metal trays to annoy C.
>
> *Held:* C's music lessons were a reasonable use of her house; D's deliberate racket done purely to annoy was unreasonable. D was restrained from this conduct by means of an injunction.

Physical damage

1.5   Where the plaintiff can establish actual damage to land or property, he is not normally required to show an additional element of interference.

> *St Helens Smelting Co v Tipping 1865*
> Fumes from a copper smelting works damaged shrubs belonging to the plaintiff, who lived on an estate in a manufacturing area.
>
> *Held:* although locality was an important consideration where nuisance takes the form of interference with the occupier's comfort and enjoyment (one should not expect to breathe the clean air of the Lake District in an industrial town such as St Helens), the nature of the locality is irrelevant where the nuisance causes physical damage to property. An occupier is entitled to protection from physical damage wherever he lives.

Interference with comfort

1.6   Where there is no element of physical damage, and the alleged nuisance consists of interference with the occupier's comfort and convenience, it is for the courts to balance the conflicting interests of plaintiff and defendant. The test has been stated to be whether the interference is an 'inconvenience materially interfering with the ordinary comfort physically of human existence, not merely according to elegant or dainty modes and habits of living, but according to plain and sober and simple notions among the English people' : *Walter v Selfe 1851*.

> *Halsey v Esso Petroleum Co Ltd 1961*
> The defendant operated an oil depot. The plaintiff lived nearby. Acid damaged clothing hanging out to dry in his garden and the paintwork of his car parked on the highway. Noise from the depot's boilers and from oil tankers arriving and departing during the night interfered with his sleep.
>
> *Held:* the defendants were liable for private nuisance for the damage to clothes and the noise from the depot. (They were also liable for *public* nuisance for the damage to the motor vehicle and the noise of the oil tankers.)

1.7   By contrast in *Hunter and Others v Canary Wharf Ltd 1997* it was held that a landlord was generally entitled to build on his land as he wished and, accordingly, would not be liable in nuisance because a large building he had erected had interfered with television reception.

Abnormal sensitivity

1.8   If the plaintiff or the plaintiff's property has some abnormal sensitivity, he will be unable to restrain an interference from which a person of normal sensitivity would not require protection.

Robinson v Kilvert 1889
The plaintiff manufactured brown paper on his premises, which were situated directly above the defendant's premises. Heat from the defendant's manufacturing process damaged the brown paper, which was sensitive to heat. Ordinary paper would not have been affected.

Held: the defendant was not liable, because his action was lawful and the plaintiff was carrying on an exceptionally delicate operation.

Malice

1.9   As noted above (*Christie v Davey 1893*) actions motivated by malice may constitute nuisance. Even in the case of the plaintiff's abnormal sensitivity, malice may tip the balance towards the defendant's conduct being unreasonable.

Hollywood Silver Fox Farm Ltd v Emmett 1936
The plaintiffs bred silver foxes, which become very nervous during their breeding season and may, if disturbed, devour their own young. The defendant discharged guns on his own land in order to interfere with the foxes' breeding.

Held: the defendant was liable - he had been motivated by the malicious intention of causing damage. His argument that the noise was no more than a reasonable landowner might create during the course of shooting failed.

2   DEFENCES TO AN ACTION FOR PRIVATE NUISANCE

Prescription

2.1   The right to commit private nuisance may be acquired by prescription. The defendant must show that the actions causing the nuisance have been carried on for 20 years. The actions must have been carried on as of right: *nec vi, nec clam, nec precario* (neither forcibly, nor secretly, nor with permission).

2.2   The actions must have amounted to an actionable nuisance for the full 20 year period.

Sturges v Bridgman 1879
The plaintiff built a consulting room in his garden for use in his medical practice. The defendant operated machinery in his business as a confectioner; this created noise which caused interference to the plaintiff. The defendant pleaded prescription as a defence.

Held: although the defendant's business had continued for over 20 years, it only constituted a nuisance from the time that the consulting room was built. The defence was not available.

Statutory authority

2.3   The defendant may plead that an activity which causes interference is authorised by statute. He must demonstrate that the interference is inevitable and that he has not been negligent. Negligence here means behaviour without reasonable regard and care for the interests of other persons.

Allen v Gulf Oil Refining Ltd 1981
The plaintiffs alleged that noise, smell and vibrations from an oil refinery caused a nuisance. The Gulf Oil Refining Act 1965 (a private Act of Parliament) authorised the defendants to make compulsory purchases of land for the construction of a refinery, but did not authorise the construction or use of the refinery.

Held: construction and operation of the refinery were impliedly authorised by statute.

Consent

2.4   Consent may be a defence to an action.

> *Kiddle v City Business Properties Ltd 1942*
> The plaintiff was a tenant of part of premises of which the defendant landlord also retained part. The landlord's guttering overflowed and water damaged the plaintiff's stock.
>
> *Held:* the tenant had, by becoming tenant of part of the premises, consented to run the risk of nuisance arising from the condition of that part of the premises retained by the landlord, in the absence of negligence on the part of the landlord.

Act of God and act of a third party

2.5   Act of God or act of a third party may constitute a defence.

Coming to the nuisance

2.6   'Coming to the nuisance', a claim that the plaintiff acquired land with knowledge of an existing nuisance, is no defence: *Sturges v Bridgman 1879*. It would be unreasonable to expect someone not to purchase a property because a neighbour is committing an actionable nuisance.

Remedies

2.7   There are three remedies available to a victim of private nuisance.

(a)   An award of *damages* may be made. This will be calculated on the same basis as an award of damages for other torts.

(b)   The award of an *injunction* is, as an equitable remedy, discretionary: *Miller v Jackson 1977*. In spite of this the courts will usually grant an injunction where the nuisance is continuing. Principles have been laid down to determine when damages should be awarded instead of an injunction: *Shelfer v City of London Electric Lighting Co 1895*. 'If the injury to the plaintiff's legal rights is small, and is one which is capable of being estimated in money, and is one which can be adequately compensated by a small money payment, and the case is one in which it would be oppressive to the defendant to grant an injunction,' then damages will be substituted.

(c)   The third remedy is *abatement*. Abatement can be defined as removal of the nuisance by the victim. This is, as might be expected, not a remedy encouraged by the law. Notice must usually be given to the wrongdoer, except where there is an emergency or where the nuisance can be removed without entering the wrongdoer's land, for example to remove tree roots and branches: *Lemmon v Webb 1895*. The abater cannot use force and should use the remedy only if this can be done peaceably.

> *Perry v Fitzhowe 1846*
> The defendant demolished the plaintiff's inhabited house because the building interfered with the defendant's easement of pasture over the plaintiff's land.
>
> *Held:* abatement was no defence.

3   PUBLIC NUISANCE

3.1   Public nuisance may be defined as follows. 'Any nuisance which materially affects the reasonable comfort and convenience of life of a class of Her Majesty's subjects. The sphere of the nuisance may be described generally as the neighbourhood; but the question whether the local community within that sphere comprises a sufficient number of persons to constitute a class of the public is a question of fact in each case': *Attorney-General v PYA Quarries 1957*. An action for public nuisance is conceptually different from an action for private nuisance, even though the two may arise from the same conduct: *Halsey v Esso Petroleum Co Ltd 1961*.

3.2 Public nuisance is essentially a criminal act for which the person at fault may be prosecuted. A criminal action ensues, involving either prosecution or an action by the Attorney-General on behalf of the public. A plaintiff who wishes to commence an action in *tort* for public nuisance must show that he has suffered 'particular damage' beyond the damage sustained by the general public.

3.3 Various types of public nuisance are now governed by statute and have lost their significance in the law of tort. Legislation includes the Public Health Acts 1936 and 1961, the Clean Air Acts 1956 and 1968 and the Environmental Protection Act 1990. Most cases of public nuisance in modern times concern obstruction of the highway or danger to the highway.

Obstruction of the highway

3.4 The public has a right of passage along the highway. Interference with this right by means of obstruction constitutes public nuisance. The test is one of whether the defendant's action is unreasonable.

> *Dymond v Pearce 1972*
> The defendant parked his lorry overnight on a dual-carriageway. The vehicle was parked under a street lamp and its lights were left on. The plaintiff, a pillion passenger on a motor cycle, was involved in a collision with the lorry.
>
> *Held:* this was an unreasonable action as it had been done solely for the defendant's convenience. (The plaintiff's action failed because the *cause* of the accident was the motor cyclist's failure to look where he was going, not the parking of the lorry.)

3.5 The courts will consider whether the obstruction could have been avoided.

> *Silservice v Supreme Bread 1949*
> The defendant sold fresh bread. Queues formed each day to buy the bread; the crowd spilled onto the road.
>
> *Held:* there was no other way in which the defendant could conduct his business. There was no public nuisance.

> *Lyons v Gulliver 1914*
> The defendant owned a theatre. Queues formed which obstructed access to the plaintiff's premises.
>
> *Held:* the accumulation of people could have been avoided if the defendant had opened his doors earlier. He was liable; even though he had not intended the crowd to gather, this was the probable consequence of his actions.

Danger to the highway

3.6 This may take the form of an obstruction which is dangerous, for example an unlit spiked barrier: *Clark v Chambers 1878*. It may also take the form of danger from buildings or premises adjoining the highway. 'If owing to want of repair, premises on a highway become dangerous and therefore a nuisance, and a passer by or neighbouring owner suffers damage by their collapse, the occupier, or the owner if he has undertaken the duty of repair, is answerable whether he knew or ought to have known of the danger or not': *Wringe v Cohen 1940*.

> *Tarry v Ashton 1876*
> A lamp projecting over the highway fell on a passer-by.
>
> *Held:* this was public nuisance.

4 DEFAMATION

6/94, 12/97, 6/99

4.1 As with other rights of individuals, limits are placed on freedom of speech, both to avoid disorder and to protect the reputations of others. The most important of these restrictions is the *law of defamation*. The essence of a defamatory statement is that it *damages the reputation* of the person defamed, and:

(a) lowers his standing in society;

(b) causes him to be shunned or avoided; or

(c) makes imputations which are damaging to him in his profession, business or occupation.

4.2 Mere insults or 'abuse', spoken in the heat of a quarrel, are not necessarily defamatory, though the distinction is not always easy to make. To say to a man 'You devil!' might not be defamatory, but to say of him that 'He is a born criminal' probably would be. The law against defamation serves to protect 'interests in reputation', reputation being the estimation other people have of you. Injury to one's own self-respect, pride or dignity without further publication is not defamation.

4.3 Defamation then involves the publishing of a statement which has the effect of causing 'right- minded persons' to think less of the person or to avoid him. If a person makes a statement - written or spoken - which is 'defamatory', he may be liable to the person he has defamed, unless one of a number of recognised defences is available. If a High Court judge allows, it is possible to bring a criminal prosecution for a particularly offensive statement; in general, however, the remedy for defamation is a *civil action* to recover damages. Less often an injunction, which is a prohibition against the repetition of a defamatory statement, may be obtained.

Libel and slander

4.4 There are two distinct forms of defamatory statement.

(a) A *libel* is typically made in writing, but it includes other statements made in a form which is likely to be disseminated widely or continuously, such as a film made for public exhibition (both sound and visual effects may be libellous), a programme broadcast by radio or television, a play (s 4 Theatres Act 1968) and effigies.

> *Yousoupoff v MGM Pictures Ltd 1934*
> A film was produced in England depicting the rape of a lady by Rasputin, and his subsequent murder. The lady had been romantically linked with one of his murderers. The plaintiff, who was married to one of Rasputin's murderers, alleged that people thought she was the lady who had been raped.
>
> *Held:* a talking film, even where the defamation is only in pictures, is libellous. Hence the plaintiff did not have to show special damage to obtain her damages.

(b) A *slander* is typically spoken, or in some other transitory form, such as a gesture.

4.5 The distinction between these forms is important, since slander cannot be a criminal offence, whereas libel may be. In addition, many actions for slander will only produce a remedy if 'special loss' is proved by the plaintiff, whereas libel is actionable *per se*.

4.6 A person may sue without proof of damage if a slander:

(a) casts aspersions on his integrity or competence in his profession;

(b) alleges that he has committed a criminal offence punishable by imprisonment (*Gray v Jones 1939*);

(c) imputes unchastity to a woman (Slander of Women Act 1891); or

(d) imputes that he suffers from venereal disease or some other contagious disease.

4.7   'Special loss' must be proved in any other case of alleged slander to gain a remedy. This may be easier for a business client to prove; telling a supplier that his customer is a crook may lead to the latter losing a contract and so incur special expense in loss of profit or in finding another supplier. But mental suffering and social ostracism leading to loss of habitual hospitality have been seen as special losses for individuals.

4.8   You should note that *each occasion on which a statement is made can be a separate case of defamation* - there may be liability for a defamatory statement each time it is made, by whomever it is made. The defence of 'privilege' (as described later) is sometimes available to a person who repeats what was said by someone else (eg a newspaper reporter); but in principle it is no defence to assert that the statement is only a repetition and not an original statement - 'he said it, I didn't!'

4.9   A defamatory statement is assumed to be untrue, unless the person who made it can show that it is true - the defamed person is given the benefit of the doubt. With one minor exception a *true statement is not defamatory* since a person is not entitled to protect his reputation against the truth, even if the statement is made with malice. (The exception arises where a statement is made about a criminal conviction where the person has been 'rehabilitated' under the Rehabilitation of Offenders Act 1974. The defence of justification will not succeed if such a statement is prompted by malice.)

4.10   Normally an action for defamation is brought by an *individual* to protect his reputation. Previously it was held that a local authority, being a corporate body, had a *corporate reputation* - for conduct or performance - and might sue if it is defamed in that respect: *Bognor Regis UDC v Campion 1972*. However, in *Derbyshire County Council v Times Newspapers plc 1993* the House of Lords held that the public interest in free speech gives priority to the critic of the elected local authority. It is not clear whether a *company* can sue for defamation of its corporate reputation.

4.11   You should note, however, that an unincorporated body, such as a trade union, is merely an association of its individual members and officers - it has no corporate reputation to protect. A trade union may only sue for defamation if it is a 'special register' body within the meaning of s 10 Trade Union and Labour Relations (Consolidation) Act 1992 : *Electrical Electronic Telecommunications and Plumbing Union (EETPU) v Times Newspapers Ltd 1980*.

5   AN ACTION FOR DEFAMATION

5.1   To succeed in an action for defamation, the plaintiff must show that:

(a)   the statement complained of was *defamatory*;
(b)   that it was *understood* to refer to him (the plaintiff); and
(c)   was *published* so that third parties became aware of its contents.

What is defamatory?

5.2   It is the *sense of the statement, as reasonably understood by those to whom it was communicated,* which determines whether it is defamatory. In other words, it does *not* have to be shown:

(a)   that the defendant intended to damage the plaintiff's reputation; or even
(b)   that he was aware of its defamatory nature.

5.3   This means that a statement may be defamatory by reason of facts which are unknown to the person who makes the statement. This is a risk to which newspapers are often exposed in reporting statements by others. The Press are given certain other defences, but mere innocence of intent to defame (or ignorance that a statement is defamatory) is not of itself a defence.

5.4   The statement must be both *false* and *capable of being construed in a defamatory way*. It is up to the judge to decide whether a statement *can* be defamatory (question of law). The jury decides whether it was (question of fact). This presents a number of problems.

Natural and ordinary meaning of words

5.5   This is deemed to be what an ordinary person would infer presuming he or she had no special information. But while some words - such as 'dishonest' or 'promiscuous' - can imply only one thing, many others - such as a popular euphemism, 'fun-loving' - may have different inferences for different persons depending on their dispositions. The judge therefore attempts to draw the most 'ordinary' inference, which is the one that most right-minded people would draw. It is not necessarily the literal meaning, nor will the judge set out to read something into a statement which is not reasonably there: *Sim v Stretch 1936*.

Fact and opinion

5.6   A statement of fact which proves to be false and which may be construed in a defamatory way - such as 'X is a thief' - can clearly lead to a claim for defamation. However, a statement of opinion - 'I believe that X will be struck off as a dentist for adultery with a patient' - is also defamatory.

Innuendo

5.7   A statement which on the face of it cannot have a defamatory meaning inferred may still qualify if the plaintiff can prove:

(a)   that the statement contains a wider meaning; *and*

(b)   that reasonable people with special knowledge could and would infer such a meaning from the words or from facts which are represented in the words; *and*

(c)   that certain particular people with special knowledge did so infer; *and*

(d)   that those persons knew of the special facts before or at the time of publication.

> *Tolley v Fry 1931*
> Fry, a chocolate manufacturer, published an advertisement which was a drawing of Tolley, a famous amateur golfer, making a shot with a verse which said in effect that both Fry's chocolate and Tolley's golf were excellent. Tolley objected to the advertisement, which had been published without reference to him, on the grounds that those who saw it would conclude that Tolley had accepted a fee from Fry for his permission, thus compromising his amateur status.
>
> *Held:* the advertisement did indeed convey the innuendo of which Tolley complained: it was therefore defamatory, since it tended to lower his reputation.

Did the statement refer to the plaintiff?

5.8   On this issue also, the deciding factor is not what was *intended* by the person who makes the statement, but what was *understood* by the persons to whom the statement was made: *Bourke v Warren 1826*.

> *Hulton v Jones 1910*
> A newspaper published a humorous article describing the peccadilloes, while on holiday in France, of a churchwarden from Peckham, giving the fictitious name (it was thought) of Artemus Jones. However there was a *real* Artemus Jones (a barrister who did *not* live in Peckham and who was *not* a churchwarden). He sued the newspaper, producing evidence from some of his acquaintances that they had understood the rather distinctive name to refer to him. The newspaper's defence was that it did not even know of the plaintiff's existence.
>
> *Held:* the article must be taken to refer to the plaintiff since it had been understood in that sense. It was defamatory because it alleged sexual misconduct.

5.9   In a similar later case (*Newstead v London Express Newspaper 1931*) the paper made an unsuccessful defence that the report was a true story about another man called Newstead. However, evidence was produced that some readers who knew Newstead (the plaintiff) *took* the article to refer to him - and (unlike the other Newstead) the plaintiff had not committed bigamy, as stated in the article.

5.10 An individual may sometimes sue for a defamatory statement which was *made with reference to a class of which he is a member;* but there must be evidence that the statement was reasonably understood to *refer to the plaintiff as an individual.* Remember that an unincorporated body, such as a trade union, cannot sue for defamation on its own behalf, having no corporate reputation, nor as representative of its individual members, unless they were referred to as individuals.

> *Orme v Associated Newspaper Group Ltd 1981*
> The plaintiff was the leader in England of a religious sect ('the Moonies') and sued for damage to his own reputation arising from statements published in the newspaper about the sect in general.
>
> *Held:* on the facts, the statements could be reasonably understood to refer to the plaintiff himself (among others). However, the court went on to find that the statements were true, and therefore not defamatory.

5.11 If reference to the individual cannot be shown, the court need not decide whether or not the statement is defamatory in nature: the action has already failed.

> *Knupffer v London Express Newspaper Ltd 1944*
> The plaintiff was the head in the UK of a Russian refugee organisation, which had only 24 members in England, though it was also active in France and in the USA. The newspaper described as 'fascist' this 'minute body established in France and in the USA'. There was no mention of the English branch.
>
> *Held:* the action must be dismissed, since there was no reference to the plaintiff; it was therefore unnecessary to decide whether the term 'fascist' was defamatory.

5.12 Certain other defamatory statements may not be actionable because of their object.

  (a) A dead person cannot be defamed.

  (b) Inanimate objects, such as goods or chattels, may not be defamed - though if the statement extends from a businessman's products to his person then it may be defamatory.

Was the statement published?

5.13 For a statement to be defamatory, it must have been published. This means that some person other than the plaintiff, the defendant and the defendant's spouse must have knowledge of its contents. There is no case for defamation if the only way in which the statement is published is the action of the plaintiff himself, in showing a third party a defamatory letter which was addressed to him alone.

5.14 A person will be liable for any publication which was intended or which he could reasonably have anticipated. Case law sheds some interesting light on aspects of publication, including the following.

Letters

5.15 A letter addressed to a particular person is presumed to be published to the addressee, but the sender should anticipate in some cases that it may be read by someone else.

  (a) If a sealed letter is addressed to someone at his *home address*, it will usually be accepted that the defendant expected it to be opened by the addressee and no-one else. If someone else opens it without authorisation - such as a butler in *Huth v*

Huth 1915 - then that is not publication. However, this depends on the facts of the case.

> *Theaker v Richardson 1962*
> A defamatory letter was addressed to a married woman who was a member of the local council, along with the letter's author. It was sent in a style to suggest it was an election address. The woman's husband opened it believing this to be so.
>
> *Held:* it was a natural and probable consequence that the husband would open it and hence the statement had been published.

(b) A letter sent to someone at *work* may well be opened by a secretary: the sender/defendant will be assumed to have intended publication to a third party, unless it was marked 'private and confidential' or 'personal'.

Postcards

5.16 If a defamatory postcard has been sent through the post to the plaintiff, the law will assume that a post office employee, or some other third party, has read it.

Mechanical distributors

5.17 There is a distinction between the originators of defamatory material and those who merely disseminate it. Booksellers, libraries, newsagents etc are not generally liable for innocently spreading abroad a publication which they do not know to be defamatory. To escape liability, these 'mechanical distributors' must prove that they did not know of the libel and that there was no reason why they ought to have known of it. If the publisher asks the distributors to return all copies of a book which has been discovered to be defamatory, any distributor who ignores the request and continues to sell copies (by oversight) may be sued: *Vizetelly v Mudie's Select Library 1900*

E-mail

5.18 The increasing popularity of e-mail has created an entirely new method of communication. There have already been defamation cases where publication on the Internet of a statement that would lower someone in the minds of 'right thinking people' has been held to be libellous in Australia and the US.

This can also be applied to internal company e-mail systems. In *Eggleton v Asda 1995*, a police officer brought an action for defamation against the supermarket, alleging that a defamatory message about him was on their e-mail system.

5.19 The case law concerning e-mail is still comparatively undeveloped and untested. If a scenario relating to e-mail appears in the exam, use your knowledge as it applies to more traditional communication methods and you should produce a good answer.

6   DEFENCES TO AN ACTION FOR DEFAMATION

6.1 Available defences to an action for defamation are as follows.

(a) Consent.
(b) Justification.
(c) Fair comment.
(d) Privilege.
(e) Innocence
(f) Apology.

Consent

6.2   It is a defence that the plaintiff gave his consent, possibly only by implication, to the publication of a defamatory statement about himself *Cookson v Harewood 1932*. This sounds unlikely, but, for example, the subject of a defamatory statement made at a company meeting may fail to object to it - thereby 'consenting' to its inevitable publication in the minutes of that meeting.

Justification

6.3   *Justification* is a defence; the defendant must show that the statement was true in all material particulars. Defamation cannot be committed by telling the truth. The defendant need only prove the facts which constitute the 'sting of the charge'.

> *Alexander v North Eastern Railway Co 1865*
> A statement had been made to the effect that the plaintiff had been convicted of dishonesty and sentenced to three weeks imprisonment for failing to pay his rail fare. In fact he had been sentenced to two weeks imprisonment for non payment.
>
> *Held:* the statement could be justified.

Fair comment

6.4   For the defence of fair comment to succeed, it must be shown that the statement was:

(a)   a fair comment

(b)   on a matter of public interest, where

(c)   insofar as it gave facts they were accurate and

(d)   the defendant was not actuated by malice (improper motive) in making the statement.

6.5   This allows room for an individual - eg a writer or preacher - to speak out with an opinion on a matter of genuine concern. It is an important element of the principle of freedom of speech. The comment does not have to be true, but:

(a)   the opinion expressed on the facts must be honestly held; and
(b)   the defendant must have believed the facts to be true.

6.6   Fair comment, then, must be an opinion rather than a statement of fact - it is a particular reaction to facts, however extreme or prejudiced that reaction may be.

> *London Artists Ltd v Littler 1969*
> The defendant, an impresario, had received four letters simultaneously from the four top performers in his West End play, each of them cancelling his contract. Littler was convinced that this was a plot and sent a letter alleging this to each plaintiff, and to the press; he was sued for libel.
>
> *Held:* the matter was one of public interest and he could have made fair comment on it, but in leaping to a conclusion of a plot (which was never proved) he had made a statement of fact for which fair comment was not a defence.

Privilege

6.7   It is a defence that the statement was protected by *privilege*, which may be 'absolute' or 'qualified'. This is the most important defence in practice. The difference between absolute and qualified privilege is that absolute privilege remains available as a defence despite any evidence of malice on the part of the person who makes the statement. It enables Members of Parliament, for example, to make statements with the deliberate intention of causing prejudice to the person about whom the statement is made.

Absolute privilege

6.8   Absolute privilege is given to enable a person to make statements *in the public interest,* without fear of personal liability. It extends to:

(a)   statements made in Parliament, and papers laid before Parliament;

(b)   statements made by judge, jury, witnesses, counsel or parties in judicial proceedings and contemporary newspaper reports of those proceedings and other (fair and accurate) reports of those proceedings, such as the Law Reports;

(c)   communications between high officers of state, in the course of their official duties;

(d)   statements between solicitor and client, in some cases. (In others, only qualified privilege is given.)

Qualified privilege

6.9   The defence of qualified privilege evolved through case law. It was extended to newspapers (subject to certain conditions) by the Defamation Act 1952.

6.10   Qualified privilege is applicable to statements made *without* malice or improper intent, being statements made:

(a)   by a person who has an interest or a (social, moral or legal) duty to make it;
(b)   to a person who has a corresponding interest or duty to receive it.

This reciprocity is essential: *Adam v Ward 1917.*

6.11   Qualified privilege has been held to arise in the following cases:

(a)   common interest, eg references to prospective employers or credit agencies: *London Association for the Protection of Trade v Greenlands 1916;*

(b)   statements in protection of one's private interests: *Osborn v Thos Boulter 1930;*

(c)   statements made by way of complaint to a proper authority, eg to the Panel on Take-overs and Mergers;

(d)   professional communications between solicitor and client; and

(e)   fair and accurate reports of Parliamentary or public judicial proceedings.

6.12   If a statement to which qualified privilege might otherwise apply is made in circumstances which give it wider circulation than is necessary to protect the common interest, malice may be inferred, and the privilege will be lost.

> *Parsons v Surgey 1864*
> A shareholder of a railway company called a general meeting to which he invited non-members, including representatives of the press. At the meeting he made defamatory statements about one of the directors, who sued him. He pleaded qualified privilege.
>
> *Held:* qualified privilege would extend to communications made to other shareholders since they had a common interest in the affairs of the company. But the privilege was lost owing to the invitation to the press and other publicity about the meeting.

6.13   Comments made in protection of one's own interests and fair and accurate reports of parliamentary and judicial proceedings are protected by qualified privilege. But a statement published by, or on behalf of, a candidate for election to Parliament or to a local authority is *not* privileged, because of the candidate's vested interest in prejudicing the public's opinion. A statement might, however, be defended as a 'fair comment' on a matter of public interest.

Qualified privilege and the Press

6.14   The difficulty which confronts a newspaper in pleading common law 'qualified privilege' is that usually it has no duty (in the legal sense) to its readers to disclose the information which it prints. It is not a sufficient defence to show that the material is 'of interest' to readers. But s 7 Defamation Act 1952 offers newspapers and broadcasters statutory qualified privilege in respect of various types of report.

6.15   For the purpose of this defence, a 'newspaper' is defined as a publication which:

(a)   contains public news and comment thereon; and

(b)   is published in the UK at intervals of not more than 36 days.

6.16   The list of newspaper reports to which qualified privilege is given under the Act is divided into two parts.

6.17   Part 1 comprises reports of:

(a)   public proceedings of foreign legislatures and courts;

(b)   the contents of UK public registers and notices published by order of the courts; and

(c)   British courts martial.

6.18   It is unnecessary to give this protection to newspaper reports of the proceedings of the UK Parliament and courts since these already have absolute privilege. Where a report is covered by Part 1, the plaintiff need not be given the opportunity of rebuttal in the newspaper itself.

6.19   Part 2 lists mainly the reports of various kinds of meetings, whose appearance in the newspapers may be protected, including reports of:

(a)   public meetings - meetings *bona fide* and lawfully held in the UK to discuss a matter of common concern, whether or not admission to the meeting is restricted;

(b)   meetings of almost very kind of common interest association - artistic, scientific, religious, learned, commercial, professional, athletic or recreational - insofar as the report related to the conduct of members, officers or employees of the association. If a meeting of an association defames someone not directly associated with it, a newspaper does not have qualified privilege to report that statement;

(c)   meetings of local authorities and of their committees;

(d)   meetings of public (but not of private) companies, including corporate bodies formed under royal charter or special statute (though most companies are formed under the Companies Act).

6.20   Additional conditions apply to the reports covered by Part 2. Unlike those of Part 1, they enjoy qualified privilege only if the newspaper has responded to a request by the plaintiff's that it publish a reasonable letter of statement explaining or contradicting the original report. Note that:

(a)   this point only arises if the plaintiff makes a request for an opportunity to publish a rebuttal; and

(b)   the newspaper must make an adequate and reasonable response. If it distorts or suppresses the plaintiffs rebuttal, with selective quotation, long delay or illegible print, it might lose the protection of privilege.

Innocence

6.21   As noted above, mechanical distributors of a libel may plead *innocent defamation*. Similarly, printers or publishers could formerly establish a defence based on Section 4 of the Defamation Act 1952; this required the publication of a suitable apology and was a little-used defence. This defence was repealed by the Defamation Act 1996 and replaced by an offer to make amends. Under the new procedure the offer is one to pay *compensation*, as distinct from merely costs and expenses and to publish a correction and apology. The disseminator of defamatory material must show the following.

(a)   He was not the author, editor or publisher of the statement.

(b)   He took reasonable care in relation to its publication.

(c)   He did not know, and had no reason to believe, that what he did caused or contributed to the publication of a defamatory statement.

6.22   These principles may soon be tested in cases involving 'e-mail libel'; the question has arisen as to whether service providers are liable in defamation.'

Apology

6.23   If the statement was published in a newspaper or other periodical, the paper may plead *apology*, by showing that it:

(a)   published the statement without malice or gross negligence;
(b)   has since published a full apology; and
(c)   has paid a sum of money into court as an offer of compensation.

In other words, it has 'made amends' for its error.

Chapter roundup

- Nuisance may be of two types - public and private. In private nuisance the central idea is that of interference with the plaintiff's enjoyment of his property. Public nuisance does not require any 'invasion' of private land, rather the annoyance of the general public.

- As with other rights of individuals, limits are placed on freedom of speech, both to avoid disorder and to protect the reputations of others. The most important of these restrictions is the law of defamation. The essence of a defamatory statement is that it damages the reputation of the person defamed.

Test you knowledge

1   What is meant by private nuisance? (see para 1.2)

2   Outline the facts of *Halsey v Esso Petroleum Co Ltd 1961*, showing that you understand the distinction between private nuisance and public nuisance. (1.6, 3.1)

3   What will be the position if the actions of a defendant in an action for private nuisance are motivated by malice? (1.9)

4   List three defences to an action for private nuisance? (2.1 - 2.6)

5   What is the remedy of abatement? (2.7)

6   What is public nuisance? (3.1)

7   Distinguish between libel and slander (4.4)

8   What three things must a plaintiff in an action for defamation show? (5.1)

9   What are the facts of *Hulton v Jones 1910*? (5.8)

10   List four defences to an action for defamation (6.1)

Now try illustrative question 18 at the end of the Study Text

Chapter 23

DEFENCES AND REMEDIES

This chapter covers the following topics.

1 Vicarious liability

2 General defences to an action in tort

3 Contributory negligence

4 Limitation of actions

5 Damages in tort

6 Non-monetary remedies

7 Other matters

Introduction

In Chapter 21 the law of tort was introduced. In this chapter we describe the defences to an action in tort and the remedies available. Before looking at these, we introduce the concept of vicarious liability.

---

1 VICARIOUS LIABILITY   *12/94, 6/96, 12/97*

1.1 The person who actually commits a tort (called a *tortfeasor*) is always liable for his wrong. Others may be jointly and severally liable with him under the principle of vicarious liability. If, for example, a partner commits a tort either with the authority of the other partners or in the ordinary course of the firm's business, the other partners are liable with him.

1.2 The most important application of the principle of vicarious liability is to the relationship of employer and employee. It is often not worthwhile to sue the employee for damages since he is unable to pay them. The employer however has greater resources and may also have insurance cover.

1.3 To make the employer liable for a tort of the employee it is necessary that:

(a) there is the relationship between them of employer and employee; and
(b) the employee's tort is committed in the course of his employment.

The employee remains liable as a joint tortfeasor and has an obligation to indemnify his employer where the latter has to pay damages. The employers liability is 'strict', ie does not depend on proof of fault on his part.

Relationship of employer and employee

1.4 The existence of the employer/employee relationship is usually fairly obvious. It is characterised by such features as a contract of service and the deduction by the employer of PAYE and national insurance from the employee's gross pay. However in certain cases it is not clear whether a person is an employee or an independent contractor, and the courts have devised certain tests to establish whether the employer/employee relationship exists in such situations. The distinction is important because, if it does not, there is no vicarious liability except in certain special cases.

Intention of the parties

1.5   The parties therefore are obliged to reach an express understanding as to whether or not there is a contract of employment. But their expressed intentions do not necessarily prevail.

> *Ferguson v John Dawson & Partners 1976*
> A builder's labourer worked 'on the lump' - he was paid his wages without deduction of income tax or National Insurance contributions and worked as a self-employed contractor providing services. But his 'employer' could dismiss him, decide on which site he would work, direct him as to the work he should do and also provided the tools which he used. He was injured in an accident and sued his employers on the basis that they owed him legal duties as their employee.
>
> *Held:* on the facts taken as a whole, he was an employee working under a contract of employment.

> *Massey v Crown Life Assurance 1978*
> M was originally employed by an insurance company as a departmental manager; he also earned commission on business which he introduced. At his own request he changed to a self-employed basis. Tax etc was no longer deducted by the employers but he continued to perform the same duties. The employers terminated these arrangements and M claimed compensation for unfair dismissal on the basis that he had continued to be an employee.
>
> *Held:* as he had opted to become self-employed and his status in the organisation was consistent with that situation, he must abide by his decision. His claim to be a dismissed employee failed.

Tests applied by the courts

1.6   In borderline cases such as these it can be unclear whether a person is an employee or an independent contractor. The tests of *control, integration* into the employer's organisation, and *economic reality* (or the multiple test) are applied in such cases.

The control test

1.7   Has the employer *control* over the way in which the employee performs his duties?

> *Mersey Docks & Harbour Board v Coggins & Griffiths (Liverpool) 1947*
> Stevedores hired a crane with its driver from the harbour board under a contract which provided that the driver (appointed and paid by the harbour board) should be the employee of the stevedores. Owing to the driver's negligence a checker was injured. The case was concerned with whether the stevedores or the harbour board were vicariously liable as employers.
>
> *Held:* in the House of Lords, that the issue must be settled on the facts and not on the terms of the contract. The stevedores could only be treated as employers of the driver if they could control in detail how he did his work. But although they could instruct him what to do, they could not control him in how he operated the crane. The harbour board (as 'general employer') was therefore still the driver's employer.

The integration test

1.8   If the employee is so skilled that he cannot be controlled in the performance of his duties, was he appointed and assigned to his duties by the employer - was he *integrated* into the employer's organisation?

> *Cassidy v Ministry of Health 1951*

The full-time assistant medical officer at a hospital carried out a surgical operation in a negligent fashion. The patient sued the Ministry of Health as employer. The Ministry resisted the claim arguing that it had no control over the doctor in his medical work.

Held: in such circumstances the proper test was whether the employer appointed the employee, selected him for his task and so integrated him into the organisation. If the patient had chosen the doctor the Ministry would not have been liable as employer. But here the Ministry (the hospital management) made the choice and so it was liable.

The multiple test

1.9   Is the employee *working on his own account?*

Ready Mixed Concrete (South East) v Ministry of Pensions & National Insurance 1968
The driver of a special vehicle worked for one company only in the delivery of liquid concrete to building sites. He provided his own vehicle (obtained on hire purchase from the company) and was responsible for its maintenance and repair. He was free to provide a substitute driver. The vehicle was painted in the company's colours and the driver wore its uniform. He was paid gross amounts (no tax etc deducted) on the basis of mileage and quantity delivered as a self-employed contractor. The Ministry of Pensions claimed that he was in fact an employee for whom the company should make the employer's insurance contributions.

Held: in such cases the most important test is whether the worker is working on his own account (the *entrepreneurial* test or *multiple* test). On these facts the driver was a self-employed transport contractor and not an employee.

Other factors

1.10   Other significant factors are as follows.

(a)   Does the employee use his own tools and equipment or does the employer provide them?

(b)   Does the alleged employer have the power to select or appoint its employees, and may it dismiss them?

(c)   Payment of salary is, as mentioned above, a fair indication of there being a contract of employment. But there are exceptions. A person may still be an employee if he is paid no salary but derives his income solely from commission or tips. A person may receive a salary but not be an employee - for instance, Members of Parliament.

(d)   Working for a number of different people is not necessarily a sign of self-employment. A number of assignments may be construed as a series of employments: *Hull v Lorimer 1994.*

1.11   In difficult cases, the court will also consider whether the 'employee' can delegate all his obligations (in which case, there is no contract of employment), whether there is restriction as to place of work, whether there is an obligation to work and whether holidays and hours of work are agreed.

O'Kelly v Trusthouse Forte Plc 1983
The employee was a 'regular casual' working when required as a waiter in the banqueting department of the Grosvenor Hotel. There was an understanding that he would accept work when offered and that the employer would give him preference over other more 'casual' employees, though they were all paid at the same rate. The industrial tribunal held that there was no contract of employment because the employer had no obligation to provide work and the employee had no obligation to accept work when offered. The Employment Appeal Tribunal however held that there had been a sequence of contracts of employment on each occasion.

Held: the Court of Appeal reinstated the finding of the industrial tribunal since it was a reasonable conclusion drawn from the particular facts. Whether there is a contract of employment is a question of law but it depends entirely on the facts of each case; here there was no 'mutuality of obligations' and hence no contract.

Torts committed in the course of employment

1.12 The employer is only liable for the employee's torts committed in the course of employment. Broadly the test here is whether the employee was doing the work for which he was employed. If so the employer is liable even in the following circumstances.

(a) If the employee disobeys orders as to how he shall do his work.

> *Limpus v London General Omnibus Co 1862*
> The driver of an omnibus intentionally drove across in front of another omnibus and caused it to overturn. The bus company resisted liability on the ground that it had forbidden its drivers to obstruct other buses.
>
> *Held:* the driver was nonetheless acting in the course of his employment.:
>
> *Beard v London General Omnibus Co 1900*
> The same employer forbade bus conductors to drive buses. A bus conductor caused an accident while reversing a bus.
>
> *Held:* the employer's instructions served to demarcate the limits of the conductor's duties. He was not, when driving, doing the job for which he was employed and so the employers were not liable.

(b) If, while engaged on his duties, the employee does something for his own convenience.

> *Century Insurance v Northern Ireland Road Transport Board 1942*
> A driver of a petrol tanker lorry was discharging petrol at a garage. While waiting he lit a cigarette and threw away the lighted match. There was an explosion.
>
> *Held:* the employer was liable since the driver was, at the time of his negligent act, in the course of his employment.
>
> *Warren v Henleys 1948*
> A petrol pump attendant became involved in a quarrel with a customer over payment for petrol and hit him.
>
> *Held:* the employer was not liable since the assault was not within the scope of the employment. It is not easy to distinguish this from the Century case above, but main difference in the *Warren* case is that it was a violent personal act completely unconnected with the employees' duty to sell petrol.

1.13 If the employer allows the employee to use the employer's vehicle for the employee's own affairs, the employer is not liable for any accident which may occur. There is the same result when a driver disobeys orders by giving a lift to a passenger who is injured.

> *Twine v Bean's Express 1946*
> In this case there was a notice in the driver's part of the van that the firm's drivers were forbidden to give lifts. The passenger was killed in an accident.
>
> *Held:* the passenger was a trespasser and in offering a lift the driver was not acting in the course of his employment.
>
> *Rose v Plenty 1976*
> The driver of a milk float disobeyed orders by taking a thirteen year old boy round with him to help the driver in his deliveries. The boy was injured by the driver's negligence.

Held: the driver was acting in the course of his employment (presumably because the boy was not a mere passenger but was assisting in delivering milk).

1.14 In the numerous cases about the use of vehicles the courts have tended to widen the scope of the employer's liability by holding that if he provides a vehicle for the employee's use, the latter may be the employer's agent if he gives a fellow employee a lift (though it is not within the scope of his employment to do this: *Vandyke v Fender 1970*). So also if a vehicle is lent for the joint purposes of employer and employee, such as where the employer wishes to have his car delivered to a destination to which the employee (who drives it) wishes to go: *Ormrod v Crossville Motor Services 1953*. The law on this subject is full of narrow distinctions.

1.15 If the employee, acting in the course of his employment, defrauds a third party for his own advantage the employer is still vicariously liable.

Lloyd v Grace Smith & Co 1912
L was interviewed by a managing clerk employed by a firm of solicitors and agreed on his advice to sell property with a view to reinvesting the money. She signed two documents by which (unknown to L) the property was transferred to the clerk who misappropriated the proceeds.

Held: the employers were liable. It was no defence that acting in the course of his employment the employee benefitted himself and not them.

1.16 Where the employer is held to be vicariously liable, he may seek indemnity for the costs from his employee: *Lister v Romford Ice and Cold Storage Co 1957*.

Independent contractors

1.17 A person who has work done not by his employee but by an independent contractor, such as a freelance plumber used by a builder, is vicariously liable for torts of the contractor in the following special circumstances. In such cases the employer is personally liable in tort.

(a) If the operation creates a hazard for users of the highway, eg repair of a structure adjoining or overhanging a pavement or road.

(b) If the operation is exceptionally risky.

Honeywill & Stein v Larkin Bros 1934
Decorators who had redecorated the interior of a cinema brought in a photographer to take pictures of their work. The photographer's magnesium flare set fire to the cinema.

Held: in commissioning an inherently risky operation through a contractor the decorators were liable for his negligence in causing the fire.

(c) If the duty is personal. For example, an employer has a common law duty to his employees to take reasonable care in providing safe plant and a safe working system. If he employs a contractor he remains liable for any negligence of the latter in his work.

(d) If there is negligence in selecting a contractor who is not competent to do the work entrusted to him.

(e) If the operation is one for which there is strict liability.

2   GENERAL DEFENCES TO AN ACTION IN TORT

2.1 In an action for a particular tort the defendant may be able to rely on a defence applicable to that tort, such as justification in an action for defamation or that he took reasonable care if he is sued for negligence. But those particular defences are not available in every tort action. For example, reasonable care is no defence in a tort of strict liability. There are, however, general defences which may be pleaded in any action in tort. Of these general defences the most important is consent.

Consent

2.2   *Volenti non fit injuria* (no wrong is done to a person who consents to it) is the maxim which describes consent as a defence in tort (sometimes abbreviated merely to *volenti*). It must however be *true* consent, which is more than mere knowledge of a risk, and also a consent which is *freely given.*

2.3   In some cases the plaintiff expressly consents to what would otherwise be a wrong. For example a hospital patient awaiting a surgical operation is asked to give his written consent to the operation, that is to being cut by the surgeon's knife etc. But more often the consent is merely the voluntary acceptance of a risk of injury.

ICI v Shatwell 1965
Two experienced shotfirers were working in a quarry. Statutory rules imposed on them (not their employer) a duty to ensure that all persons nearby had taken cover before making a dangerous test. As their electric cable was too short they decided to make the test without taking cover before doing so. There was a premature explosion and both were injured. They sued the employer.

Held: (in the House of Lords) they had consented to the risk. The employer was not liable since it had not been negligent nor had it committed or permitted a breach of statutory duty over safety procedures. The injured men were trained for their work and properly left to carry out safety procedures of which they were well aware. (Lower courts, however, had taken the view that there had been negligence of the employer modified as to 50 per cent by contributory negligence of the employees - very much a borderline case).

2.4   Consent in taking a normal risk may be implied. A competitor in a boxing contest or a rugby match gives an implied consent to the risks incidental to the sports played fairly in accordance with its rules - even if the actual injury is exceptional.

Simms v Leigh Rugby Football Club 1969
Northern rugby league rules required that any wall or other obstacle should be at least seven feet from the touchline. S was tackled fairly but broke his leg against a concrete wall 7ft 3ins from the touchline. He sued the home club.

Held: the defendants were not at fault since their pitch complied with the rules. S by playing on such a pitch consented to the risk of injury in these circumstances.

2.5   However, in *Smaldon v Whitworth and Another 1996* it was held that a *referee* in a rugby match owed a duty of care in negligence to ensure that scrummages did not collapse dangerously.

2.6   In the same way a spectator at a motor race, or an employee engaged on inherently dangerous work, such as a test pilot of experimental aircraft or a steeplejack, is deemed to accept the inherent risks. But an employee, by accepting a job or continuing in it, does not consent to abnormal or unnecessary risks created by his employer merely because the employee is aware of them.

Smith v Baker & Sons 1891
S was put to work by B (his employer) in a position where heavy stones were swung over his head on a crane. Both S and B were aware of the risk. S was injured by a falling stone.

Held: S could recover damages. In working in circumstances of known risk he was not deemed to consent to the risk of the employer's negligence. This principle has been developed in later cases to impose on the employer a common law duty to provide a safe working system.

2.7   In other circumstances it has to be decided on the facts how far knowledge implies consent.

> *Dann v Hamilton 1939*
> D and H drove with others to a party at which H became very drunk. On their return to their original starting point in H's car, the party dispersed but H offered to drive D to her home nearby and she accepted. In this last part of the journey there was a serious accident due to the negligent driving of H.
>
> *Held:* D was aware of the potential danger of an accident but she had not, by virtue merely of her knowledge, assented to it. However, damages were reduced because of her contributory negligence.
>
> *Morris v Murray 1990*
> The plaintiff and defendant spent all afternoon drinking together with another man. Despite the fact that the weather was poor, the two decided to go flying in a plane owned by the defendant, who piloted it. He took off downwind and uphill; in such conditions a different runway into the wind should have been used. The plane crashed, killing the defendant and severely injuring the plaintiff, who sued the former's estate. On his behalf his administrators claimed volenti non fit injuria and/or contributory negligence on the part of the plaintiff.
>
> *Held:* right from the beginning the drunken escapade was fraught with danger and, although drunk, the plaintiff knew what he was doing. It was very foreseeable that such an escapade would end tragically and so, by embarking on the flight, the plaintiff had implicitly waived his rights in the event of injury consequent on the deceased's failure to fly with reasonable care. In contrast to *Dann v Hamilton* the plaintiff had no reason to be involved in the escapade and every opportunity for avoiding it.

Rescue cases

2.8   A person who accepts a risk in order to effect a 'rescue' does not lose his rights against the defendant if he is injured since his consent to the risk was constrained and not freely given. But the principle only applies when the risk is taken in order to safeguard others from the probability of injury for which the defendant is responsible.

> *Haynes v Harwood & Son 1935*
> The defendant's driver left his horse-drawn van unattended in a street. The horses bolted and a policeman (the plaintiff) ran out of the nearby police station to stop the horses since there was risk of injury to persons, including children, in the crowded street. He suffered injury in taking this action. The defendant pleaded *volenti.*
>
> *Held:* the policeman had not forfeited his claim by exposing himself to the risk, since consent to the risk was not freely given, and the risk was taken to safeguard others from injury that would have been the defendant's fault.
>
> *Cutler v United Dairies 1933*
> An unattended horse-drawn van bolted into an empty field. The driver called for help and a spectator who responded was injured.
>
> *Held:* the spectator had consented to the risk. He was not impelled by the need to save others from danger. His claim was barred by his consent.

2.9   If a person creates a hazard through his own negligence and a rescuer is injured, there need not be an exceptional risk over and above the inherent risks of rescue for that person to be liable for damages.

> *Ogwo v Taylor 1987*
> The defendant negligently set fire to his roof. Despite being well-protected, a fireman was badly scalded by steam produced by the water from his hose hitting the flames.

Held: the defendant's action created a real risk of injury to others, of which scalding was only one. He was therefore liable for damages.

2.10   A person who creates a risk of personal injury to others cannot contract out of his liability for personal injury or death, for instance by giving notice (in circumstances of 'business liability'): Unfair Contract Terms Act 1977.

Accident

2.11   Accident is a defence only if it could not have been foreseen nor avoided by any reasonable care of the defendant.

> *Stanley v Powell 1891*
> P a member of a shooting party fired at a pheasant. A pellet glanced off a tree and injured a beater (the plaintiff).
>
> *Held:* P was not liable for the reasons given above.

Act of God

2.12   Act of God, which is an unforeseeable catastrophe, is a special type of unavoidable accident. This defence is rarely available.

Statutory authority

2.13   If a statute requires that something be done, there is no liability in doing it unless it is done negligently. If a statute merely permits an action it must be done in the manner least likely to cause harm and there is liability in tort, for nuisance, if it is done in some other way.

Act of State

2.14   If a person causes damage or loss in the course of his duties for the State, he may claim Act of State. But it is not a defence in any case where the plaintiff is a British subject or the subject of a friendly foreign power (eg the US).

> *Buron v Denman 1848*
> D was captain of a British warship who had a general duty to suppress the slave trade. He set fire to a Spanish ship carrying slaves and released them. The Crown later ratified his act.
>
> *Held:* neither D nor the Crown were liable.

Necessity

2.15   An act which causes damage may be intentional. If this is so, the defence of necessity may be raised, provided:

(a)   the act is reasonable - such as shooting a dog to prevent it worrying sheep; and either

(b)   the act was done to prevent a greater evil; or

(c)   it was done to defend the realm.

Mistake

2.16   An intentional act done out of mistake may occasionally be defendable if it was reasonable. Such a case may be where a person makes a citizen's arrest in the reasonable and sincere belief that the plaintiff committed a crime.

Self defence

2.17 Similarly, self-defence is a valid defence if the defendant acted to preserve himself, his family or his property, so long as the act was reasonable and in keeping with the nature of the threat. But if a blow is struck in response only to verbal attack, there is no defence.

2.18 Lastly, no claim for damages will succeed if both plaintiff and defendant were engaged in illegal activity at the time of the damage, and it arose naturally out of that activity. Hence a burglar could not sue his getaway driver for damages when the latter crashed the car: *Ashton v Turner 1980.*

3   CONTRIBUTORY NEGLIGENCE

3.1 If the damage suffered as a result of negligence was partly caused by contributory negligence of the plaintiff his claim is proportionately reduced: Law Reform (Contributory Negligence) Act 1945.

3.2 The defendant need not prove that the plaintiff owed him a duty of care. It is sufficient if part of the damage was due to the plaintiff's failure to take reasonable precautions to avoid a risk which he could foresee. If a motor cyclist, injured in a crash caused by the negligence of another driver, suffers avoidable hurt by failure to wear a crash helmet (which is compulsory by law) that is contributory negligence (*O'Connell v Jackson 1971*), which will reduce damages by 15% if injury would have been less and 25% if it would not have happened at all had the helmet been worn: *Froom v Butcher 1976.* So too is failure of a front seat passenger in a car to use a seat belt (even before it became compulsory).

The test of contributory negligence is what caused the damage, not what caused the accident.

3.3 There is however a standard of reasonableness. Mere failure to take a possible precaution or even thoughtlessness or inattention are not contributory negligence, unless there is a failure to do what a prudent person should do to avoid or reduce a foreseeable risk, If the plaintiff is a workman working at a monotonous task or in factory noise which may dull his concentration, due allowance is made in determining whether he is guilty of contributory negligence. A child of any age may be guilty of contributory negligence but in deciding whether he has been negligent the standard of reasonable behaviour is adjusted to take account of his inexperience.

> *Yachuk v Oliver Blais 1949*
> A boy of nine bought petrol from a garage stating falsely that his mother's car had run out of petrol down the road. It was supplied in an open margarine tub. The boy (and his friend of seven who accompanied him) wished in fact to play Red Indians. They set fire to the petrol and the elder boy was badly burned. The garage pleaded contributory negligence.
>
> *Held:* the garage was negligent in selling the petrol in this way. There was no evidence that the boys realised the danger of what they did and so it was not a case of contributory negligence.

3.4 The contributory negligence of an adult who accompanies a child is not a defence to an action by the child.

Employer/employee relationship

3.5 In the special circumstances of the employer/employee relationship, certain principles relating to contributory negligence have been developed by the courts. Due allowance is made for ordinary human failings. In particular:

(a)   an employee is not deemed to consent to the risk of injury because he is aware of the risk. It is the employer's duty to provide a safe working system;

(b)   employees can become inattentive or careless in doing work which is monotonous or imposes stress. This factor too must be allowed for in the employer's safety precautions;

(c)   it is not always a sufficient defence that the employer provided safety equipment etc. The employer has some duty to encourage if not to insist on its proper use. Much depends on the nature of the risk and the experience and responsibility (or want of it) of the employee.

(d)   many dangers can be caused by carelessness or other fault of an otherwise competent employee, possibly by his mere thoughtlessness. It is the employer's duty to be watchful and to keep such tendencies in check;

(e)   employees do not work continuously. The employer's duty is to take reasonable care for their safety in all acts which are normally and reasonably incidental to the day's work.

> *Davidson v Handley Page 1945*
> A woman employee went to wash her tea-cup after use. She slipped on a slippery surface and was injured.
>
> *Held:* the employer had failed in his duty to take reasonable care to provide safe premises. The employee's injury had occurred in the course of her employment and the employer was liable.

4   LIMITATION OF ACTIONS

4.1   The right of action in tort is generally barred by lapse of time six years after the right of action accrues: Limitation Act 1980. But where the claim is for personal injury resulting from negligence, a limitation period of three years runs from the time when the right of action accrued or (if later), from the date when the plaintiff first knew of it. The purpose of this rule is to allow a plaintiff to sue when the consequences of a tort only become apparent long after the tort is committed.

4.2   The Latent Damage Act 1986 provides that in non-personal injury claims where damage is latent (undiscoverable), the limitation period will be either the usual six year period or (if longer) three years from the date that the plaintiff discovered or should have discovered the damage. The Act also provides for a 'long-stop' - a bar on all claims (except personal injury claims) brought more than fifteen years from the act or omission alleged to constitute the negligence.

5   DAMAGES IN TORT

5.1   The rules on remoteness of damage in tort have already been considered. The amount of damages is based on the principle of compensating the plaintiff for his financial loss and not of punishing the defendant for his wrong. But there are several categories of damages related to the circumstances.

Ordinary damages

5.2   Ordinary damages are assessed by the court as compensation for losses which cannot be positively proved or ascertained, and depend on the court's view of the nature of the plaintiff's injury.

Special damages

5.3   Special damages are those which can be positively proved, such as damage to clothing, cars etc.

Exemplary damages

5.4   Exemplary or aggravated damages are intended to punish the defendant for his act, and to deter him and others from a similar course of action in the future. These damages are only rarely awarded, eg where in a defamation case the defendant raises the defence of justification but loses. In *Rookes v Barnard 1964* the House of Lords set down that exemplary damages could only be awarded for torts where the defendant calculated to make more money from the tort than he would have to pay in damages (as is sometimes the situation in newspaper libel cases), where a government official acts oppressively, arbitrarily or unconstitutionally, or where statute permits.

Nominal damages

5.5   Nominal damages are given where the plaintiff has suffered injury, but has suffered no real damage (eg trespass to land without damage to that land).

6   NON-MONETARY REMEDIES

Injunction

6.1   This is an order by the court which requires an individual to refrain from doing a certain act, or orders him to do a certain act. There are two types of injunction.

(a)   *Interlocutory injunctions*: these are awarded before the hearing of an action so as to preserve the status quo. Here, the plaintiff enters into an undertaking to pay the defendant for any loss arising out of the granting of the injunction.

(b)   *Perpetual injunctions*: these are granted after the full hearing and continue until revoked by the court.

6.2   Failure to comply with an injunction is a contempt of court, which then empowers the court to fine the person in default or imprison him until his contempt is purged, when he apologises and promises not to breach the court order again in the future.

7   OTHER MATTERS

Death of the plaintiff or injured party

7.1   Death used to put an end to tortious claims, as common law rules provided that, firstly, death of either party extinguished the defendant's tortious liability, and secondly, a third party could not bring an action in respect of the death of another as the result of a tort. However, this was often a source of injustice and has now been remedied by statute.

7.2   The Law Reform (Miscellaneous Provisions) Act 1934 provides that on the death of any person all causes of action vested in him survive for the benefit of his estate. This applies to all torts except defamation. Under the Act, it is the action of the deceased which is brought. It is brought by the deceased's personal representative.

7.3   The Fatal Accidents Act 1976 makes it possible for a dependant to bring an action where the death of the person upon whom the dependency exists has been caused by the tort of another, provided that the person killed would have been able to bring an action and recover damages for such tort. An action may be brought on behalf of the defendants by the administrator or executor of the deceased's estate, or a dependant may sue in his or her own name.

Joint tortfeasors

7.4   If two or more persons are jointly liable in tort, such as employer and employee in a situation of vicarious liability of the former for acts of the latter, either or both may be sued.

7.5   If one joint tortfeasor is required to pay damages he may usually recover a contribution from the other(s) - they should share the liability equally: Civil Liability (Contributions) Act 1978. But in some cases one joint tortfeasor, because he is primarily responsible, is liable to indemnify the other. In such a case the right of indemnity overrides any claim for contribution against the person entitled to be indemnified.

Chapter roundup

- Other parties may be jointly and severally liable with the tortfeasor under the principle of vicarious liability. The principle is most usually encountered in the realm of the employer/employee relationship. Two factors must be considered: the nature of the relationship and actions performed in the course of employment. An independent contractor may also be liable in certain specific circumstances.

- There are a number of general defences which may be pleaded in any action for tort. The most important of these is consent.

- If the damage suffered as a result of negligence was partly caused by contributory negligence of the plaintiff the claim is proportionately reduced: Law Reform (Contributory Negligence) Act 1945.

- The right of action in tort is generally barred by lapse of time six years after the right of action accrues: Limitation Act 1980. But where the claim is for personal injury resulting from negligence, a limitation period of three years runs from the time when the right of action accrued or (if later), from the date when the plaintiff first knew of it.

- The amount of damages is based on the principle of compensating the plaintiff for his financial loss and not of punishing the defendant for his wrong. There are several categories of damages related to the circumstances.

Test your knowledge

1   What two conditions are necessary for an employer to be vicariously liable for the tort of an employee? (see para 1.3)

2   What three tests do the courts apply to decide whether a person is an employee or an independent contractor? (1.7-1.9)

3   Describe and distinguish *Limpus v London General Omnibus Co 1862* and *Beard v London General Omnibus Co 1900*. (1.12)

4   What is a 'general defence'? (2.1)

5   List five general defences besides consent. (2.11 - 2.17)

6   What is an injunction ? (6.1)

7   What are the rules on tortious claims on the death of the plaintiff? (7.2, 7.3)

Now try illustrative question 19 at the end of the Study Text

Illustrative questions and suggested answers

1   LEGAL PROCEEDINGS

(a)   Explain the difference between civil law and criminal law.

(b)   Whilst driving in the course of employment you cause damage to another vehicle and it is alleged that you are to blame. What legal proceedings may arise from the incident? In which courts would these proceedings take place? What is the possible outcome of these proceedings?

2   COURTS AND TRIBUNALS

Explain which court or tribunal would settle the following matters. Indicate in each instance any provisions existing for an appeal.

(a)   A claim for damages of £10,000 for negligence.
(b)   A prosecution for failure to fence dangerous machinery.
(c)   A claim for compensation for unfair dismissal.
(d)   An action to recover a debt of £100.

3   DELEGATED LEGISLATION

What is meant by delegated legislation? Outline the forms that delegated legislation may take, its advantages and any controls that exist over its use.

4   EC LAW

(a)   Outline the sources from which a judge may draw the legal rules to apply in deciding a case.

(b)   What is meant by European Community Law? Explain the extent to which this is a source of English law.

5   CHOSES

Define choses in action and choses in possession. How may each type be transferred?

6   LAND

What legal estates and interests in land are capable of being created in accordance with the provisions of the Law of Property Act 1925?

7   TRUSTS

(a)   Outline the conditions which must be satisfied if a trust is to qualify as a charitable trust. To what extent might a trust for the benefit of the employees of a particular organisation and their families qualify for charitable status?

(b)   In what ways do charitable trusts differ from private trusts?

8   THE THREE CERTAINTIES

In connection with the creation of a trust, the 'three certainties' are usually necessary. Describe what is meant by the three certainties, giving an example of each type and indicating the effect of failure of each certainty.

9   TRUSTWORTHY

(a)   How are the first trustees of an express trust appointed?
(b)   Discuss whether the first trustees are obliged to accept office.
(c)   What standard of care is required of a trustee?

10   AVAILABLE CAPITAL

Henry and George propose to establish a small retail business in which they will invest all their available capital. They will run the business between them. They are practical men who wish to avoid 'fuss' and who like to keep their financial affairs to themselves. Advise them on the most suitable form of business organisation to meet their requirements.

11   **CONTRACTING**

Explain with examples:

(a)   the distinction between void, voidable and unenforceable contracts; and

(b)   the effect of this distinction when goods are subsequently transferred to third parties.

12   **ACCEPTED OFFER**

A contract comes into being when an offer is accepted. Discuss:

(a)   the forms that an acceptance may take;

(b)   when an acceptance may be effective without actual communication to the person making the offer.

13   **AGREEMENT**

(a)   'Where an agreement between two parties is of a business nature the courts will presume an intention of enter into legal relations.' How far would you agree that this is a true statement of the law?

(b)   Philip made an offer to Susan, his cousin, to provide maintenance for her at the rate of £300 a month if she would give up her job as a typist in the civil service and study to be a chartered secretary. Susan agreed to accept Philip's offer and in September 19X4 she gave up her job and enrolled as a student on a course. In August 19X9 Susan had still not passed her final examinations and so Philip advised here that he was no longer prepared to support her while she continued her studies.

In the context of the above information explain the legal significance of:

(i)   Philip's offer; and
(ii)   Susan's acceptance.

14   **PROMISES**

Explain whether Paul is required by the law of contract to fulfil his promises in the following situations:

(a)   He promises to sell an expensive car to Arthur for £10.

(b)   He returns home to find that his house windows have been cleaned by Bernard and he promises to pay Bernard £1 for his work.

(c)   He agrees to pay Charles £100 for painting his house within three weeks and he later promises a further £20 if Charles finishes the job on time.

(d)   He promises to deliver goods to David in return for a payment to him of £50 by Eric.

(e)   He promises to release Frank from a debt of £500 if Frank pays him £400.

15   **TEENAGER**

Consider the enforceability of the following agreements entered into by E, aged 17:

(a)   he books a holiday with a travel agent, paying £20 down and promising to pay £5 per month for six months. After paying £30 in all, E has his holiday and thereafter refuses to pay any more;

(b)   he buys 50 shares from a limited company promoted by his friend;

(c)   he borrows £100 from F, pretending that he is 19 years of age, and spend £50 on a record player, £20 on shirts and the remaining £30 on paying his fees at a college where he is studying to be a chartered secretary.

16   **IMPLIED TERMS**

Describe how terms may be implied into a contract.

17   HOLE IN THE ROAD

A firm of contractors is engaged in road repairs. During the course of the work, the following incidents take place. Discuss the possible liability of the contractors for the injuries.

(a)   A labourer employed by the contractors omits to fence a hole in the road. A cyclist falls into the hole and is injured.

(b)   A lorry with a driver is hired to carry away waste material. Whilst doing this, the driver knocks down and injures a pedestrian.

(c)   A sub-contractor is engaged for work with electric cables. His carelessness leads to a small boy being electrocuted.

18   EXTREMISTS

At a meeting of the Association of Alternative Trade Unions, a debate became very heated on the issue of extremist infiltration. One speaker stated that 'these unions within unions are a corrupt cancer on the vital organs of trade union democracy and all those self seeking infiltrators, who are well known to us, ought to be publicly denounced for what they are.'

Another speaker named several trade unions which he alleged suffered from such infiltration. The following day several newspapers and the radio news broadcasts reported these statements verbatim. One newspaper, 'The Daily Buglecall', also named several union officials and activists whom it identified with extremist infiltration.

Consider whether any person has been defamed and outline any defences to an action for defamation in the circumstances.

19   JASPER

Jasper is the proprietor of a large garage. What is his liability, if any, in each of the following situations?

(a)   One of his employees is taking a car for a test drive when it skids out of control on to the wrong side of the road and damages another car coming in the opposite direction.

(b)   A car that has just been repaired is being driven away by a customer when the car door falls off and injures a pedestrian.

(c)   Jasper suggests that a customer change his vehicle insurance company in order to get better terms. The customer does so and suffers loss when the recommended company later fails and is unable to meet his claim.

1   LEGAL PROCEEDINGS

(a)   *Civil law* exists to enable a person, ie individuals or corporate bodies such as companies, to obtain redress or protection if their legal rights are infringed or threatened. Such proceedings are brought against the person alleged to be at fault. The usual result of successful civil action is the award of damages as compensation or a court order instructing the defendant to do or to abstain from doing something, eg a newspaper might be ordered not to publish a libellous statement or to pay damages if it has already done so. The action is brought before a judge in a civil court under civil procedure as a case between private persons to do justice between them. The rules of evidence are less stringent than in criminal cases: the case has to be proved only on the *balance of probabilities.*

A *crime* is an act prohibited by law in the interests of society, even though its immediate effect (eg in a case of manslaughter) is injury to a particular person. The State, through the director of public prosecutions or the Crown Prosecution Service, institutes a criminal prosecution with the object of obtaining a conviction and a suitable punishment by imprisonment or a fine. Criminal proceedings are brought in courts which have criminal jurisdiction, usually a magistrates' court or (for serious offences) a crown court (where a judge sits with a jury). The accused person is presumed to be innocent until the prosecution proves by evidence *beyond reasonable doubt* that he is guilty. If the prosecution cannot prove his guilt he is entitled to be acquitted.

(b)   On the facts given, the driver at fault may have been guilty of a driving offence, ie a crime, such as careless driving. The police to whom the incident should be reported will investigate and if the facts indicate a driving offence, will charge him. A prosecution will then be brought, probably in the local magistrates' court. If the driver is found guilty he is likely to be fined and his driving licence will be endorsed with a record of the conviction. The magistrates have power to award compensation (up to £5,000) to avoid duplication of legal proceedings. But if the accused person has already been found liable in a civil court to pay damages that decision is in no way conclusive as to his guilt on a criminal charge for which a different standard of proof is required.

The owner of the damaged vehicle (or if it is insured his insurers after compensating him) may sue the driver at fault in civil proceedings to recover damages. Unless the claim exceeds £25,000 the action will almost certainly be brought in a county court. Any compensation awarded in criminal proceedings would of course go to reduce the civil damages which might be awarded. The claim would be based on tort, ie negligence (want of due care) by the driver at fault.

Since the accident occurred while the driver was acting as an employee the action could be brought against his employer under the principle of vicarious liability. The employer or his insurers would be able to pay the damages even though the driver perhaps could not do so.

2   COURTS AND TRIBUNALS

(a)   An action for negligence is a civil proceeding based on the law of tort. The limit of county court jurisdiction in tort is £25,000 (up to £50,000 if the court so decides). Hence the action would be heard in the county court. If the county court, having considered:

(i)   the financial substance of the action;

(ii)   whether questions of public interest are raised;

(iii)   the complexity of the facts; and

(iv)   whether transfer is likely to result in a speedier trial (though not this criterion alone), decides it is more appropriate for the case to be transferred to the High Court, this can be done.

From the county court either party may appeal to the High Court (Chancery Division) or the Court of Appeal (Civil Division). From the Court of Appeal there is a further right of appeal (but only with leave of the Court of Appeal or the House of Lords) to the Judicial Committee of the House of Lords.

(b)   This is a criminal prosecution which would usually take place in a magistrates' court (provided it is an offence triable summarily or either way). From that court the accused, if convicted, may appeal to the Crown Court. If, however, objection is made to the magistrates' decision (to convict or to acquit) on a point of law, either party can ask the magistrates to state their findings in a written case stated and appeal to a Divisional Court of the High Court to decide whether the point of law was correctly decided.

If the offence were very serious (an indictable offence) the magistrates would conduct committal proceedings with a view to a trial of the case before the Crown Court.

(c) A claim for compensation for unfair dismissal is made before an employment tribunal which consists of a legally qualified chairman and two other members chosen from a panel nominated by employers associations and by trade unions respectively. From an industrial tribunal either party may appeal to the Employment Appeal Tribunal which has a High Court judge as chairman and two other members representing employers and employees respectively. From the EAT, there is a further right of appeal to the Court of Appeal (Civil Division) and thence finally to the Judicial Committee of the House of Lords.

(d) This is a civil action for debt. The county court of the district in which the debtor resides or carries on business has jurisdiction to hear the case. From a county court there is a right of appeal either to the High Court (Chancery Division) or to the Court of Appeal (Civil Division) and thence to the House of Lords.

As the debt is less than £5,000 the county court district judge could hear the case as an arbitrator sitting in a 'small claims' court. As a general rule, no costs are recoverable except the cost of issuing the summons (as an inducement against using legal advocates in such cases).

3 DELEGATED LEGISLATION

The only source of statute law is Parliament which enacts Acts of Parliament and may, in doing so, give delegated authority to make additional rules of law.

An Act of Parliament begins as a Bill which must pass through a sequence of discussions (including consideration of the Bill clause by clause in Committee) in both the House of Commons and the House of Lords before the Bill receives royal assent and becomes an Act. This procedure usually takes about six months (since the successive stages are taken at intervals) and absorbs several days of debate in each House. This factor limits the output of Acts of Parliament to about 70 a year.

In most Acts there is a section which authorises an appropriate person or body to make subordinate rules for specified purposes. In this way a Minister (in practice civil servants acting under his instructions) may prepare *statutory instruments* to fill in the details or to modify an Act. A local authority may similarly be authorised to make bye-laws in its area. A nationalised industry such as British Rail may also be given power to make bye-laws. A professional body such as the Law Society may have power to make rules binding on its members. The Sovereign acting on the advice of the Privy Council has authority to make *Orders in Council* in an emergency or to deal with some international problem (such as the economic sanctions against Rhodesia (now Zimbabwe) from 1965 to 1980).

The advantages of delegated legislation are that by this means the output of detailed law can be greatly increased, with speed, flexibility and effective definition of detail. Some 3,000 statutory instruments, some very short but others rather longer, are issued every year. Parliament does not have time to deal with all this lawmaking.

Delegated legislation is not put through the slow-moving parliamentary procedure of scrutiny and debate. It can be produced in a hurry when needed. Insofar as delegated legislation fills in detail, which is its main purpose, it can be altered from time to time by making a new regulation. Each year, for example, the financial limits on compensation for unfair dismissal are increased to allow for the effect of inflation on earnings. Many details are very technical, for example, some accounting practices applicable to company accounts. These are best discussed and agreed between the ministries and business and professional groups.

The standard method of control is to require (in giving authority to make delegated legislation) that the new rules shall either require positive approval (by a single vote) in Parliament or more often shall be open to Parliamentary challenge for say 40 days before coming into effect.

Delegated legislation must be kept within the limits of the powers given by the relevant Act. If it appears to exceed those limits anyone may challenge the rules in a court of law asking for a declaration that the rules are *ultra vires* (in excess of the delegated lawmaking power) and void.

4 EC LAW

(a) In presenting his case to the courts a barrister specifies the rules of statute or case law on which he relies. He usually reads the section of an Act of Parliament or a passage from a judgment in an earlier case if he relies on it as part of his argument. He also develops his points by legal argument. The judge listens to both sides and then explains (in a judgment) the reasons for his conclusions.

If the dispute before the court depends on a statute (or delegated legislation made under powers given by an Act of Parliament) the judge has to consider in the light of the arguments and any previous decisions (precedents) put to him by counsel what those statutory words mean. A statute usually contains an interpretation section which sets out what certain defined expressions used in the statute are intended to mean. For example, s 741 Companies Act 1985 states that 'director' includes any person occupying the position of director, by whatever name called. There is also a general Interpretation Act 1978 which provides, for example, that a singular word (such as 'person') also includes its plural (persons).

There are a number of general principles of interpretation of statutes which the court may have to apply. The most basic and important of these rules is that usually any word should be given its ordinary meaning as found in a dictionary in preference to a less obvious meaning (but an interpretation section of the statute can override that). There are subsidiary rules of interpretation such as the golden rule (make sense of it if possible), the contextual rule, the mischief rule etc.

If the point at issue is related to delegated legislation the court may be asked to decide whether the 'statutory instrument' is invalid because it has been made in excess of (*ultra vires*) the delegated power to make it. Secondly, the counsel, in presenting their case to the court, are likely to cite 'precedents', which are earlier decisions on the same issue given in a previous case. The judge will decide whether these are genuine precedents to which he should turn for guidance.

When an earlier case is cited as a precedent it is necessary to extract from it the reasons given for the decision in that case (called the ratio decidendi). Only that reason can be a precedent. The court will also consider whether the facts of the earlier case are so like those of the present case as to make the earlier decision a relevant precedent.

The court will also consider whether a relevant precedent is binding or only persuasive. A decision of a superior court such as the House of Lords or the Court of Appeal is binding on a High Court judge. The Court of Appeal is also bound by earlier decisions of that court. If it is not a binding precedent the court will give it due attention as a persuasive precedent but need not follow it. It sometimes happens that decisions of foreign, eg Commonwealth or US, courts are persuasive only. Finally, if there is a ruling of the European Court on the point at issue, an English court would usually follow it.

(b)   The United Kingdom has been since 1 January 1973 a member of the European Community and a party to the Treaty of Rome by which the European Community was established in 1957 and to related treaties under which the European Coal and Steel Community and the European Atomic Energy Community were established. These three treaties were merged in 1965 and operate as binding obligations on member states.

The treaties give powers to the Council of Ministers to issue regulations and directives to member states. Regulations are 'self-executing' - they are immediately effective as law binding persons within (or even trading within) the territory of the Communities. The prohibition of restrictive practices in trade in manufactured goods is effected by regulations (issued mainly under Article 85 of the Treaty of Rome). An infringement of these regulations which apply to trade between member states, is punishable by fine imposed by EC authorities in Brussels even though no national, ie UK, law has been enacted to give them direct effect as law. The UK did of course pass its own European Communities Act 1972 to bring treaties and regulations, then existing or yet to be made, into operation in UK territory.

The general programme of harmonisation of law throughout the Community is carried forward by the issue of directives which state in general terms the principles to which the national law of each member state should conform. The governments of member states then propose legislation, framed with due regard to their system of law, to bring their law into conformity with the EC directive.

The council and the Commission of the Community may make decisions on particular issues which are binding on those to whom they are addressed. They may also issue advisory recommendations and opinions. The principles expressed in directives may also be relied on in proceedings before national courts: *Van Duyn v Home Office 1974*.

In legal proceedings before national courts a party may raise the question whether the local law conforms to a relevant provision of the EC law. The court may then seek an opinion from the European Court on the issue raised and will then apply the ruling in the proceedings before. A number of such cases have related to local law requiring equal pay for men and women engaged on similar work. One such case was *Macarthy v Smith 1980* where a woman employee successfully challenged the UK Equal Pay Act 1970 since the Act did not permit a comparison with the wage paid to her male predecessor in the same job.

More recently, the *Factortame* litigation has demonstrated the supremacy of EC law over UK law. A claim was brought against the UK Parliament on the grounds that certain provisions of the Merchant Shipping Act 1988 were in direct contravention of Article 52 of the Treaty of Rome. Pending a decision from the European Court of Justice the House of Lords suspended the relevant provisions. The ECJ ruled that the 1988 Act was in breach of Article 52 and the Act will, as a result, be amended.

5   CHOSES

Choses in action

The terms choses in action and in possession belong to the law of property. 'Choses' is an old French word for 'things' (property). English law, for historical reasons, divides property into numerous categories, of which there are two major sub-divisions. The first of these is the distinction between real and personal property. Land is the only form of real property, all others, including things in action and in possession, are personal property.

A further division is between tangible and intangible property. Things in action are essentially intangible property; they are abstract things, such as shares or a bank balance. The owner of a thing in action cannot enforce his rights to it by seeking or keeping possession. Rights are protected through the courts. A bank customer will seek to enforce his rights to the money in his account in the courts if the bank refuses, wrongfully, to honour his cheques.

Things in possession is a residual category, also known as 'chattels' or moveable property. They are distinguished from real property, land, in that the owner's claim is against the person who wrongfully interferes with these rights personally, and his rights may be satisfied by payment of value, as opposed to return of the property itself. Things in possession must be distinguished from leasehold land or 'chattels real'. Thus 'things' cars, jewellery, clothes - are all things in possession.

Choses in possession

The assignment of choses in possession is often preceded by a contract, particularly if the object is valuable. However, for the actual transfer, all that is necessary is delivery of the thing to the transferee, with the intention that ownership as well as possession is being transferred. A contract is not necessary, but there is often a written document recording that ownership has been transferred. Some types of personal property, such as ships, require a particular procedure to be followed to transfer ownership.

Things in action cannot, as intangible things, be transferred by delivery. Instead they are assigned by a written document. S 136 Law of Property Act 1925 prescribes the conditions necessary for 'statutory transfer' of a thing in action. The assignment must be in writing, the document signed by the assignor. There must also be an absolute transfer of the thing, the assignor retaining no interest in it and there being no conditions attached to the transfer which might interfere with this. The assignor must also notify the person whose obligation to him created the thing of the assignment. He will then make payment to the transferee; if he is not notified of the change he will be able to discharge his obligations by payment to the assignor.

Where an equitable thing in action is not transferred in accordance with this procedure, but the intention to transfer is clear, equity will give effect to the transfer. Certain kinds of thing in action, such as debentures and shares, require special procedures to effect their transfer.

6   LAND

Before 1926 there were several different classes of interest over land, each carrying its own rights and duties. The Law of Property Act 1925 simplified this situation considerably by recognising only two types of legal estate and five types of legal interest. An estate in land gives the owner a right to possess the land - the right of occupation. An interest gives a right over land to the non-owner. It does not give a right of possession but it is a valid right against other persons.

Legal estates

There are two legal estates in land: freehold ownership and leasehold ownership. A freeholder has the fee simple absolute in possession, and so may transfer ownership at death at his own will; there are no overriding conditions to his ownership and he has an immediate right of occupation. A leasehold is a term of years; it can however be of any duration (eg 999 years), provided it is defined or terminable. The essential difference is that a lease comes to an end, whereas a freehold goes on forever. The immediate holder of that freehold may transfer it, or die, but the right of ownership continues. Leaseholds are carved out of the freehold and will be absorbed by it when the lease ends (a landlord's or freeholder's rights are *in reversion* because possession reverts to the freeholder when the lease expires). The lease may be transferred, in which case the new holder will have privity of lease with the freeholder; he will be a party to the lease agreement although he did not take part in its creation.

Legal interests

The 1925 Act also created five legal interests in land. An *easement* is a right or privilege enjoyed by one person over the land of another. It is a restriction of the landowner's rights to use his land. The right may be, for example, to light (perhaps preventing the development of the land) or it may be to remove the produce of the land (grazing or shooting rights); this latter type of right is called *profit a prendre*.

The second type of legal interest is the *legal charge*, and may be given by a mortgagor to a mortgagee as security for a loan of money. If the landowner mortgagor defaults on the loan then the mortgagee has the right to take various steps to reclaim his money, the most direct being the sale of the land and satisfaction of the debt from the proceeds. The landowner is entitled to receive any excess payment received.

The other legal interests are a *rentcharge, a charge imposed on land by law and a right of entry*. A rentcharge is a right, not arising from a lease, to receive rents from the landowner. This type of interest is gradually being abolished by the Rentcharges Act 1977. A right of entry is a right to reclaim possession given to a lessor or to a person entitled to a rentcharge in the event of default.

7 TRUSTS

(a) The essential feature of a charitable trust is that it must be established for a purpose which is recognised by law as charitable.

The definition of charitable purposes is derived, through much case law, from the preamble to the Charitable Uses Act 1601. It comprises trusts for: the relief of poverty; the advancement of education; the advancement of religion; and other purposes beneficial to the community not falling under those heads. The Recreational Charities Act 1958 was passed to remove uncertainty by declaring that charities of that type were indeed charitable.

Secondly, with the exception of charities for the relief of poverty, it must be shown that the charity will benefit the public or some section of the public and not a restricted group only. Thus a trust for the education of the descendants of employees of one company was too restricted to be accorded charitable status: *Oppenheim v Tobacco Securities Trust 1931*. The exception from this rule for trusts to relieve poverty was reviewed and confirmed by the House of Lords in *Dingle v Turner 1972*, where it was held that a trust to pay pensions to employees of a company who were in need was a valid charitable trust. A trust for the education of children of employees would not be.

Thirdly, a charitable trust is one which is exclusively for charitable purposes. Thus a trust for 'charitable or benevolent purposes' is not a charitable trust in the legal sense since it may apply to benevolent purposes which are not charitable: *Chichester Diocesan Fund v Simpson 1944*.

(b) Apart from the positive requirements described above, charitable trusts differ from private trusts in two essential respects.

First, the general rule which requires *certainty of objects* (beneficiaries) does not apply to charitable trusts. The essence of a charity is that it is for the public benefit (in particular ways). The persons who are to benefit cannot be, and are not required to be, defined individually or as a class. If it is not possible, or becomes impossible, to apply the trust funds to the particular charitable purpose declared the court has power, under the *cy-pres* doctrine, to authorise the use of the trust funds for some similar purpose.

The second main remission of normal trust law in relation to charitable trusts is that the *rule against perpetuities* does not apply to the duration of a charitable trust. It is essential that trust property should vest in the charitable trust within the perpetuity period. But once it is subject to such a trust, it may continue so indefinitely. A private trust on the other hand must be so framed that within the permitted perpetuity period, (often 80 years though there are alternatives), vested interests will exist in the trust property which will bring it to an end when those interests fall into possession.

There are a number of external special features of charitable trusts. As there are no identifiable individual 'objects' (beneficiaries) the right to apply to the court to enforce the duties of the trustees is given to the Attorney General as representative of the community. Trustees of charities are required to register with the Charity Commissioners and to submit their accounts to them: Charities Act 1960. Charities, and gifts to charities, enjoy a number of remissions from taxes on income and capital transactions.

The maximum number of trustees of a private trust is four if the trust comprises land or if the power to appoint additional trustees is exercised (the power is limited to raising the number to four). This limit does not however apply to trustees of a charitable trust.

The trustees of a private trust must exercise their powers by unanimous decision - a majority decision is not permitted and is not binding on the minority. This rule too does not apply to trustees of a charity.

8   THE THREE CERTAINTIES

A trust will only be valid if the three certainties, as laid down by Lord Langdale in *Knight v Knight 1840*, are present. They are:

(a)   certainty of words;
(b)   certainty of subject matter; and
(c)   certainty of objects.

Certainty of words

The words used need not be formal, indeed there is no obligation for a settlor to use the word trust. The words must be imperative and show that a trust was intended. The problems that arise normally do so when trusts or wills have been drafted without professional advice and use precatory words such as 'in the hope', 'requesting', 'beseeching'. In *Re Adams and Kensington Vestry 1884* a testator gave all his property to his wife absolutely, 'in full confidence that she will do whatever is right as to the disposal thereof between my children'. It was held that the wife might take the property free from any trust as the precatory words 'in full confidence' were insufficient indication of the intention to create a trust.

However, a bequest such as '£10,000 to Albert in trust for my cousin Jane' clearly creates a trust in favour of Jane.

Certainty of subject matter

This implies that the property which is the subject of the trust must be certain and that the interests of the beneficiaries are ascertainable.

For example, a bequest of 'such sum as is necessary to enable Albert to live in comfort' is uncertain and there is no trust. If, on the other hand, the bequest is of 'such one of my six horses as Albert shall select', it is valid and the trust will be confirmed as soon as Albert chooses a particular horse.

If the beneficial interest is clearly vested in a beneficiary, but he is directed to apply unascertained parts of it for the benefit of others, the principal beneficiary takes all, the others being disregarded: *Curtis v Rippon 1820*. However, if all the beneficial interests are uncertain (eg 'all my shares in trust, some for Alberta and the rest for Carol') then the property may be held on resulting trust for the settlor but more probably the maxim 'equality is equity' will apply and there will be an equal division between the beneficiaries.

Certainty of objects

The trust must have beneficiaries able to enforce it. If there are no beneficiaries it is a trust of imperfect obligation and is void - the property being normally held on resulting trust for the settlor. Where there are beneficiaries, their identity must be reasonably certain and a trust in favour of 'Albert and his relatives' is certain as far as Albert is concerned, but is void as regards his relatives. However, if the trust is a discretionary trust, then provided it is possible to say with certainty that a given person is or is not a member of a class that benefits under the trust, the trust will not fail for uncertainty.

9   TRUSTWORTHY

(a)   The first trustees are, most commonly, appointed by the settlor either in the trust instrument or the will.

If the trust was set up during the lifetime of the settlor and he has not named trustees, or if they are named but are dead or refuse to act, then if the trust instrument nominates some person to appoint trustees that power can be used and, that failing, the appointment will be made by the court on the basis of the equitable maxim 'the court will not allow a trust to fail for want of a trustee'. The settlor, as such, has no further power to make appointments unless he is also a trustee or a person named in the trust instrument.

In a will trust the testator will either name his trustees or, if not, the executors of the estate become the trustees of any will trust. When the estate has been distributed except for the gifts on trust, the executors should transfer the property to themselves as trustees. Where real property is involved this requires a vesting assent: *Re King's Will Trusts 1964*. As far as personal property is concerned vesting would probably be assumed, but a vesting assent is desirable. The executors could appoint other trustees if they did not wish to act.

On an intestacy those who apply successfully for letters of administration hold the deceased's property on trust for sale and distribution among the statutory next of kin after payment of funeral and testamentary expenses and debts (s 33 Administration of Estates Act 1925).

(b)   The first trustees are not obliged to take office. So long as a trustee has done no act indicating an intention on his part to accept the trusteeship, he is at liberty to disclaim. Disclaimer may be made: (i) by deed, (ii) by writing, (iii) orally, or (iv) by inactivity for a period of time since appointment, provided the trustee has never acted as such. Disclaimer must be of the whole trust and not just part. Disclaimer should be by deed which provides good and unambiguous evidence. The effect of disclaimer is to vest the whole of the trust property in the co-trustee(s), and he (or they) may then administer the trust without the agreement of the person disclaiming.

(c)   As regards the standard of care required of a trustee Lord Watson said in *Learoyd v Whiteley 1887* 'As a general rule the law requires of a trustee no higher degree of diligence in the execution of his office than a man of ordinary prudence would exercise in the management of his own affairs. Yet he is not allowed the same discretion in investing the moneys of the trust as if he were a person *sui juris* dealing with his own estate.

Businessmen of ordinary prudence may, and frequently do, select investments which are more or less of a speculative nature; but it is the duty of a trustee to confine himself to the class of investments which are permitted by the trust and likewise to avoid all investments of that class which are attended with hazard.'

In complying with this general standard of care a trustee is bound to make his investments in such a way that those entitled to income obtain a reasonable sum and yet the capital is preserved for those entitled in remainder. Thus, even an authorised investment may, in particular circumstances, be unjustified and amount to a breach of the trustees' duty of impartiality.

A paid trustee, who is usually a professional trustee, is expected to apply that professional skill. He will be expected to do more of the work and delegate less and will not normally be able to shelter behind s 61 of the Trustee Act 1925 (power of court to excuse a trustee from a breach of trust where he has acted honestly and reasonably).

This apart, there is no significant difference between the standard of diligence expected of the paid and the amateur trustee.

10   AVAILABLE CAPITAL

The choice lies between trading as a partnership and forming a registered company to carry on the business.

Partnership

Partnership is merely a relation between the partners. The two men will be the joint proprietors. They can make whatever arrangements between themselves that suit them best and few formalities or publicity are required.

The drawback of trading as partners is that each partner has unlimited liability for the debts of the firm. They therefore risk personal bankruptcy if the firm becomes insolvent. They should also realise that each partner is an agent of the other and the latter is bound by all contracts made by the former in carrying on in the usual way business of the kind carried on by the firm.

Company

If Henry and George prefer to carry on business through a company with limited liability (of members) they restrict their financial risks to losing their investment if the company fails. If they seek to raise a loan, eg from a bank, to finance the business they could (unlike a partnership) offer security in the form of a floating charge over the assets (including current assets such as stock in trade and trade debts) of the company. But if they cannot or do not offer security in that way the lender may well insist that Henry and George should assume personal liability by giving guarantees of the loan to the company.

In forming a company they must conform to the numerous rules of company law. They will incur greater expenses on formation, throughout the life of the company (there is a requirement to file an annual return and audited accounts), and on its dissolution, although the fees are not excessive.

More publicity will have to be given to its affairs, in particular with regard to its directors and charges on its assets.

As managers of the company's business Henry and George should arrange to be appointed its directors. They then share collective responsibility (as the board of directors) for making contracts on behalf of the company (but not each other) as their principal. The directors' powers to make contracts are determined by the articles of association. But the directors cannot have wider powers than the company itself: if they exceed those limits the contract will be *ultra vires* and void, though the other party will probably be able to enforce it against the company under s 35(1) and s 35A and B Companies Act 1985.

11   CONTRACTING

(a)   To constitute a legally binding agreement there must be offer and acceptance, consideration and intention to create legal relations. Even if those elements are present the contract may be affected by factors including mistake, lack of personal capacity or illegality.

The absence of a necessary element or the presence of an invalidating factor may make the agreement void. It is then no contract at all. This is the result if the parties agree to buy and sell goods which unknown to them both have ceased to exist: *Couturier v Hastie 1852*. There is then no obligation on either side and no transfer of property.

A contract which is voidable exists at the outset but one party has the option to declare it void. If he does so the contract is rescinded at this point but usually without retrospective effect. If for example a party is induced to enter into a contract by misrepresentation he has the right (unless it has meanwhile been lost) to avoid the contract. However, in this case it is a valid contract until avoided and property transferred under it cannot usually be recovered from third parties.

There are few necessary formalities for making contracts. However, a contract for the sale or other disposition of land or an interest in land is unenforceable unless it is in writing: s 2 Law of Property (Miscellaneous Provisions) Act 1989.

An unenforceable contract is a contract. If therefore a party to it does something in performance of it, such as paying a deposit as part payment of the purchase price he cannot recover it if he later refuses to continue with the contract: *Monnickendam v Leanse 1923*.

A contract may also become unenforceable if either party fails to enforce his rights for six (or in some contracts twelve) years. His rights are then barred by limitation.

(b)   If the contract is void but legal a party who has transferred property under it may recover his property from a third party even if the latter has bought and paid for it: *Cundy v Lindsay 1978*.

If however the contract is void for illegality he cannot usually recover it (though there are exceptions).

When property is transferred under a voidable contract and the transferee in turn transfers it to a third party, eg by re-sale, before the contract is avoided the original transferor cannot recover it from the third party since the original transferee has good title under a contract still in force at the time of resale: *Phillips v Brooks Ltd 1919*.

This is also the position when property transferred under an unenforceable contract passes to a third party.

12   ACCEPTED OFFER

(a)   The minimum requirement of acceptance is that the offeree shall by some act indicate that he accepts the offer. There is no acceptance by mere passive inaction: *Felthouse v Bindley 1863*.

The act of acceptance may be but need not be expressed in words, spoken or written. Mere conduct which indicates agreement to the offer suffices: *Brogden v Metropolitan Railway Co 1877*.

If however the offeror stipulates that he requires acceptance of a particular kind eg by letter and the offeree does not accept in that way but in some other way it is necessary to decide whether the prescribed method of acceptance was the only effective type. The offeror may say that no alternative of acceptance suffices; if he does so that is the result. If he merely indicates how he prefers the acceptance to be made, eg by registered letter, an acceptance by some other means such as an unregistered letter which is actually received is sufficient. In these circumstances the offeror has suffered no detriment by the use of a different method. If however he had requested acceptance in writing so as to have a record, verbal acceptance would probably not suffice.

(b) It is usually necessary that the offeree should communicate his acceptance to the offeror and the acceptance takes effect when the offeror receives it. The offeror may however by his offer indicate that an act of acceptance shall be effective without communication to him: *Carlill v Carbolic Smoke Ball Co 1893.*

By requesting a reply by letter or even by sending his offer by letter the offeror may by implication constitute the post office his agent to receive the acceptance by letter on his behalf. If the offeree posts a letter, properly stamped and addressed to the offeror, his acceptance is complete as soon as it is posted even if it is delayed or lost in the post: *Household Fire Insurance Co Ltd v Grant 1879.*

If however the terms of the offer or the nature of the transaction suggest that the offeror did not intend acceptance by letter to be complete before he receives the letter the courts will readily conclude that there was no acceptance until the letter reached the offeror: *Holwell Securities Ltd v Hughes 1974.*

The postal acceptance rule applies only to contracts by letter. It does not affect an offer and acceptance by telex. In that case acceptance is effective when it reaches the telex terminal of the offeror: *Entores Ltd v Miles Far East Corporation 1955.*

13 AGREEMENT

(a) A contract is an agreement which is legally binding and so can be enforced (or damages obtained for its breach) in a court of law. One of the essential elements of a legally binding agreement is that the parties should have intended, when they made their agreement, to be bound by it as a legal obligation.

It is always open to the parties to state expressly that they intend or do not intend, as the case may be, to create 'legal relations' - a legally binding contract. The court will accept that their intention, so expressed, is genuine and will be guided by their declaration. For example in *Rose & Frank v J R Crompton & Bros 1923* an agreement stated that it was not 'subject to legal jurisdiction' in the UK. It was held not to be binding.

In many cases however the parties do not express their intention. The courts have then to deduce what their intention really was. If the agreement relates to a business transaction the courts will usually deduce that the parties intended to create legal relations, unless (as in the cases above) there is an express statement to the contrary: *Edwards v Skyways 1964*. A business agreement may also be held to lack intention to create legal relations if it is so imprecise that it could not be effectively enforced. This is often the position with agreements made between employers and trade unions on procedure for negotiating settlement of disputes.

(b) (i) This is an offer which may be converted into a binding contract if Susan (the offeree) accepts it.

(ii) Acceptance of an offer is an essential part of a contract. However there is no legal rule which requires acceptance to be in a particular form. It may be in writing, or by word of mouth or even by conduct. The offeror may indicate how his offer is to be accepted. If he insists on acceptance in one particular way acceptance in any other way will not create a contract.

On the facts given the offer requires acceptance by conduct - Susan is invited to give up her job and enrol as a student. She has done this and so her conduct is a sufficient acceptance: *Carlill v Carbolic Smoke Ball Co 1893.*

14 PROMISES

When a party to a contract undertakes to perform obligations under the contract the obligations are binding on him only if he has received consideration (or if the contract is made by deed). Each of the five parts of the question raises detailed applications of the principle that consideration is an essential element of a binding contract.

(a) Consideration must have some economic value but it need not be of a value equal to that of the promise given. It is common practice in formal agreements to state that consideration of a nominal amount (50p or £1) has been received so that there is a clear admission that sufficient consideration has been received. In the present case £10 is sufficient consideration to make the promise binding although it is 'inadequate' ie less than the value of the car.

(b) Consideration may be a promise given in exchange for a promise (executory consideration) or an act (or forbearance) in exchange for a promise (executed consideration). Executed consideration must however be given after the promise to which it relates. A promise to pay for what has already been done is given for past consideration which is generally insufficient to make the promise binding: *Re McArdle 1951.*

Past consideration is sufficient however to support an acknowledgement of a statute-barred debt or to constitute value for a bill of exchange. A promise to pay for work already done is only binding if the work was done at the promisor's request, or otherwise in circumstances such that a promise to pay is implied at the time when the work is done: *Re Casey's Patents 1892.*

If Paul had asked Bernard to clean his windows and Bernard was a professional window-cleaner the promise to pay could be binding for the reason given above. Otherwise it is not binding since the work is past consideration when the promise is given.

(c)   A promisee's performance of obligations which already bind him under a contract with the promisor, is no consideration for the latter's promise of additional payment merely for doing what the promisee already has to do. Charles gave no consideration for the promise of the extra £20. He merely does what is already promised to Paul: *Stilk v Myrick 1809.* Recently the courts' view appears to have changed: *Williams v Roffey Bros and Nicholls (Contractors) Ltd 1990.* In this case, a promise to pay a sum of money additional to that already agreed upon in the contract, in return for the fulfilment of existing obligations, was held to be binding. It was held that both parties derived benefit from this promise, as the defendant (the main contractor), in achieving his sub-contractor's timely completion, himself avoided penalty payments which he would otherwise have had to make.

(d)   The contract is between Paul and Eric since it is they who gave consideration to each other. A third party (David) who benefits from the performance of the contract but gives no consideration cannot enforce it. He is not party to the contract and consideration does not move from him: *Tweddle v Atkinson 1861.* Eric, if he pays £50, can enforce delivery of the goods to David but David himself cannot do so.

(e)   Acceptance of part payment of an existing debt is no consideration for a promise to forego the balance: *Foakes v Beer 1884.*

If however the promise is given with the intention that the promisee should act on it (otherwise than by making part payment) and he does act on it and cannot, if the promise is withdrawn, be restored to his original position the principle of promissory estoppel prevents the promisor from retracting his promise: *Central London Property Trust v High Trees House 1947.* This principle is normally restricted to waiver of periodic payments of rent or hire purchase instalments where the promisee assumes that the arrangement continues on the basis of his reduced (or nil) payment. The party who agrees to accept reduced payments or none at all cannot after the relevant period has expired then retrospectively demand the unpaid balance.

15   TEENAGER

In all the problems given E is a minor, being under the age of 18 years.

(a)   If the travel agent can show that the holiday was 'necessary' to E, having regard to his condition in life and actual requirements at the time of booking and taking the holiday E must pay a reasonable sum for it. 'Necessaries' are not confined to goods but may include services; a holiday could qualify as a necessary but the travel agent may have difficulty in showing that it was. If he cannot do so his claim will fail

Even if the travel agent fails to show that the holiday was a necessary it would not be open to E to claim back the £30 which he has paid since he has had the benefit of the holiday.

(b)   A contract to buy shares in a company is voidable by a minor during his minority or within a reasonable time after attaining his majority. Thus if E has only paid part of the nominal value of the shares he could avoid the contract so that he will not be liable for any future calls on the shares. It will not be possible for E, however, to recover the money he has paid because he has received some consideration, being the allotment of the shares: *Steinberg v Scala (Leeds) Limited.*

(c)   A contract for the repayment of money lent is unenforceable under the Minors' Contracts Act 1987, and this is so even though the infant has falsely represented himself to be of full age: *Leslie v Sheill 1914.* If, however, the lender can show that the money borrowed by infant has been spent on necessaries, he has the same right of recovering the money he has lost as the tradesman would have had if he had not been paid.

In the problem it is likely that F could show that the £20 spent on shirts and £30 on instruction in accountancy are necessaries and so he would be able to recover this part of the sum borrowed by E, provided that these were reasonable prices.

16 IMPLIED TERMS

As a general principle, the parties to a contract may by their offer and acceptance include in their contract whatever terms they prefer. However the law may in appropriate circumstances modify these express terms in a number of ways. Terms may be implied by custom, by the courts or by statute. The Chartered Institute of Management Accountants have published a legal glossary in which they define an implied term as follows. 'A term deemed to form part of a contract even though not expressly mentioned by the parties. Some such terms may be implied by the courts as necessary to give effect to the presumed intentions of the parties or as following trade practice in that type of business. Other terms may be implied by statute, for example, the Sale of Goods Act.'

Custom

The parties may be considered to enter into a contract subject to a custom or practice of their trade. But any express term overrides a term which might be implied by custom.

In *Hutton v Warren 1836,* the defendant landlord gave the plaintiff, a tenant farmer, notice to quit the farm. He insisted that the tenant should continue to farm the land during the period of notice. The tenant asked for 'a fair allowance' for seeds and labour from which he received no benefit (as he left before harvest time). It was held that, by custom, he was bound to farm the land until the end of the tenancy; he was also entitled to a fair allowance for seeds and labour. In contrast, in the case of *Les Affreteurs v Walford 1919,* a charter of a ship provided expressly for a 3% commission payment to be made 'on signing the charter'. There was a trade custom that it should only be paid at a later stage. The ship was requisitioned by the French government before the charterparty began, and so no hire was earned. It was held that an express term prevails over a term otherwise implied by custom. The commission was payable on hire.

A more recent example is provided by the case of *British Crane Hire v Ipswich Plant Hire 1974,* demonstrating that this is still relevant. Both firms were in the business of hiring out cranes and heavy plant. IPH hired a crane from BCH for use on marshy ground. BCH sent IPH a copy of their standard conditions, which were similar to those used throughout the trade and which provided that the hirer would be liable for all expenses arising out of the crane's use. Before these were signed, the crane sank into the marshy ground and BCH claimed from IPH the expenses which it (BCH) incurred in recovering the crane. The claim succeeded because:

(a) both parties were in the same trade;
(b) they had equal bargaining power; and
(c) there was evidence that they both understood that BCH's standard conditions would apply.

Statute

Terms may be implied by statute. In some cases the statute permits the parties to contract out of the statutory terms (for instance the terms of partnership implied by the Partnership Act 1890 may be excluded). In other cases the statutory terms are obligatory: the protection given by the Sale of Goods Act 1979 to a consumer who buys goods from a trader cannot be taken away from him.

The terms implied by Sale of Goods Act 1979 represent one of the most important examples of terms being implied into a contract by statute. A sale of goods may be subject to statutory rules on the following.

(a) The effect of delay in performance (s 10).
(b) Title, or the sellers' right to sell the goods (s 12).
(c) Description of the goods (s 13).
(d) Quality of the goods (s 14(2)).
(e) Fitness of the goods for the purpose for which they are supplied (s 14(3)).
(f) Sale by sample (s 15).

The Unfair Contract Terms Act 1977 prohibits or restricts the possibility of modifying these statutory rules (other than those on time) by the use of exclusion clauses as follows. It is not possible to exclude or restrict:

(a) the statutory terms on the seller's title - his right to sell - in any circumstances; nor

(b) the statutory terms relating to contract description or sample, quality or fitness for a purpose (ss 13-15) when the buyer is dealing as consumer. In a contract under which the buyer is *not* dealing as a consumer, that is when seller and buyer are both engaging in the transaction in the course of business, ss 13-15 may be excluded or restricted, but only if the exclusion or restriction satisfies a requirement of *reasonableness.*

The courts

Terms may be implied if the court concludes that the parties intended those terms to apply and did not mention them because they were taken for granted, or because they were inadvertently omitted. The court may then supply a further term to prevent the failure of the agreement and to implement the manifested intention of the parties. The contract is given 'business efficacy'. In *The Moorcock 1889*, the owners of a wharf agreed that a ship should be moored alongside to unload its cargo. It was well known to both wharfingers and shipowners that at low water the ship would ground on the mud at the bottom. At ebb tide the ship settled on a ridge concealed beneath the mud and suffered damage. It was held that it was an implied term, though not expressed, that the ground alongside the wharf (which did not belong to the wharfingers) was safe at low tide since both parties knew that the ship must rest on it. '*Prima facie* that which in any contract is left to be implied and need not be expressed is something so obvious that it goes without saying; so that, if while the parties were making their bargain an officious bystander were to suggest some express provision for it in their agreement they would testily suppress him with a common "Oh, of course" ': *Shirlaw v Southern Foundries 1939*. This type of implied term is sometimes referred to as a term *implied in fact*.

The court may also imply terms to maintain a standard of behaviour, even though the parties may not have intended them to be included. This is sometimes referred to as a term *implied in law*. In *Liverpool City Council v Irwin 1977*, the defendants were tenants of a maisonette in a tower block owned by the plaintiffs. There was no formal tenancy agreement. The defendants withheld rent, alleging that the plaintiffs had breached implied terms because *inter alia* the lifts did not work and the stairs were unlit. The council argued that there were no implied terms. It was held that it was necessary to consider the obligations which 'the nature of the contract itself implicitly requires'. Tenants could only occupy the building with access to stairs and/or lifts, so terms needed to be implied on these matters. A term was implied that the landlord would keep these parts reasonably safe.

17   HOLE IN THE ROAD

(a)   Where someone is injured in an accident he may have a remedy in compensation if he can show that what happened to him was due to another person's 'negligence' - negligence being a civil wrong or 'tort'.

In this context the cyclist will first have to prove that, as someone closely and directly affected by the labourer's conduct, he was owed a duty of care by him (under the 'neighbour' principle in *Donoghue v Stevenson*); there seems little doubt about that being so here.

The next question is whether that duty was discharged. And again, the answer is clear; someone who leaves unfenced a hole that he has dug in the road has obviously failed to meet the standard of care practised by the reasonable man.

Lastly, the cyclist satisfies the condition that he has suffered a reasonably foreseeable loss due to the breach of the duty of care. In these circumstances, it should be possible to bring a successful action in negligence against the labourer.

However, there will not be much point to such an action if - as is highly probable - the labourer lacks the resources to meet the award that is made against him. The cyclist might be better advised therefore to sue the labourer's employer - the contractors.

An employer is vicariously liable for the wrongful acts of his employee under a contract of service, if they were carried out in the course of employment. In the present case, though not all the facts are known, the labourer probably was employed under a contract of service and the tort probably occurred in the course of his employment - he had not radically departed from doing the work that he was employed to do but was, in all likelihood, merely performing an authorised act in a wrongful manner.

If this is correct, then the cyclist may sue the contractors, provided he can establish the negligence of the labourer. The contractors, theoretically, may in turn be indemnified by the labourer, though in practice this is unlikely to happen.

(b)   Assuming that the driver is held to have been negligent - based on the criteria outlined above - there is a further possibility here that the contractors will be vicariously liable.

It may be the case that the lorry-driver's permanent employer (not the contractors) will be liable. The leading case on this issue, *Mersey Docks and Harbour Board v Coggins and Griffiths Ltd (1947)*, indicates that liability is presumed to remain with the permanent or general employer, unless control over the method of work is plainly evidenced as having been transferred to the temporary employer. The burden of proof is on the permanent employer to rebut the usual presumption.

In the present case, the one thing supporting the view that liability passed to the contractors is the fact that a lorry driver's work is not very specialised and hence could potentially be controlled by the contractors. On the other hand, where machinery is hired together with the worker, it is more likely that the original employer will continue to be liable.

It is difficult to say what the outcome would be here, but the authorities appear to suggest that the odds are on the contractors being protected.

Another possibility is that neither the contractors nor the permanent employers will be vicariously liable. This will be so if the wrongful act occurred while the labourer was engaged on a detour or 'frolic of his own', such that he could not be said to have been acting in the course of his employment: *Beard v London General Omnibus 1929*.

(c)   Although an employer is often liable for the acts of an employee who is engaged under a contract of service, there is normally no vicarious liability with respect to independent contractors employed under a contract for services. Where the courts have had difficulty in making this distinction, they have invoked the control, organisation and multiple tests.

Here there is little doubt that the electrician is an independent contractor: his specialised work evidently cannot be controlled by the contractors, he is not an integral part of their organisation and the economic reality of the contractual relationship implies a contract for services.

Despite this, the contractors may not be immune if the facts suggest one of those exceptional situations where an employer can be liable for the wrongful acts of an independent contractor. This may well be so since a person who performs work on or adjoining the highway which poses a danger to the public is responsible for the torts of his (independent) contractor. A similar liability also arises where the contractor is assigned work which is particularly hazardous: *Honeywill and Stein v Larkin Bros 1934*.

For these reasons, the contractors probably are liable for the evident negligence of the electrician - and it is unlikely to make any difference that the boy may have been a trespasser: Occupiers' Liability Act 1984. Technically, however, the liability is not vicarious, since it arises from a breach of a duty owed to the injured party by the employer.

18   EXTREMISTS

The statements made at the meeting by the two speakers are defamatory in that they are damaging to the reputation of the individuals concerned, and they have been published to the other persons present at the meeting. However, the remaining objection to an action for defamation is that the statements do not refer to a person in the legal sense, since a trade union is not a corporate body but a mere association of individuals. One cannot defame a trade union itself: *Electrical Electronic Telecommunications and Plumbing Union v Times Newspapers 1980*.

Individual officials of the union named by the second speaker might perhaps sue, alleging that his remarks were aimed at and understood to refer to them. But unless the evidence that they were identified was reasonably clear, such an action would probably fail since, as a principle, a defamatory remark about a class of persons does not give to any one of them a right to sue for defamation of himself: *Knupffer v London Daily Express Newspaper Co Ltd 1944*.

If the speakers *were* sued, they would also rely on the defence of 'qualified privilege'. The meeting was a private meeting. Speakers at it had a duty to state their views on matters of common concern, and other members had an interest in hearing what they had to say. The plaintiffs might assert that the speakers had lost the defence of qualified privilege by reason of their *malice*, indicated by the strong language which they used. But there are a number of cases in which it has been accepted that a speaker who expresses strong feelings is not on that account to be treated as actuated by malice.

The reports

The newspapers are protected by 'qualified privilege' insofar as they publish fair and accurate reports of a meeting of an association of this type. Since this protection is given by Part II of the Schedule to the Defamation Act 1952, however, they must publish any reasonable letter or statement in rebuttal which the plaintiffs may require them to publish. The defence of qualified privilege is also lost if the statement is made maliciously, but there is nothing to suggest it in this case. The protection given by the Defamation Act 1952 to newspapers also extends, on a similar basis, to broadcasts made in the United Kingdom.

One of the newspapers *The Daily Buglecall* has, however, gone further than publishing verbatim reports of the meeting. It has named various individual trade union officials, in connection with the allegations made at the meeting - where apparently no names were given. If these officials sue the newspaper on that account, the only defence available would be 'justification' ie that the allegations were true. It is always risky to rely on this defence since it will fail unless all material particulars of the allegation can be proved. The damages awarded will then be much larger because of the repeated assertion of the defamatory statement.

19   JASPER

(a)   The question does not state what was the cause of the accident. It is likely however that it was due either to the unsafe condition of the car, which was out on a test run, or to bad driving. In what follows it is assumed that it was an accident which could have been avoided by taking reasonable care.

A person owes a duty of reasonable care to those who are likely to be affected by the consequences of his negligence: *Donoghue v Stevenson 1932*. The test is one of proximity and a person who fails to take care is liable to the person injured by his carelessness if he should have foreseen this result, unless there is reason for limiting or excluding liability.

On the assumption that there was a lack of reasonable care there is liability for damage or injury to other persons on the road since that is the foreseeable consequence and the damage is of a foreseeable type: *The Wagon Mound 1961*.

If the accident was due to the defective condition of the car resulting from bad work in the garage or from the driver's negligence, the employer is liable in either case under the principle of vicarious liability. This principle imposes liability on an employer for negligence of an employee carried out of the course of his employment. Either the mechanic or the driver was negligent in the work he did; the employer is vicariously liable in each case.

(b)   It is not stated that the door fell off because the repair work, for which the employer is again vicariously liable, was done without proper skill and care.

However, in cases of unexplained accidents the doctrine of res ipsa loquitur is applied. If the object which causes the accident is in the charge of the defendant and the accident would not have happened if proper care had been taken then 'the thing speaks for itself' - it is treated as a case of negligence even though the exact cause is unknown: *Scott v London and St Katharine Docks Co 1865*. If of course there is an alternative and equally probable explanation which negatives the defendant's negligence he may rely on that possibility, which he need not prove was the actual case, to negative the res ipsa loquitur presumption: *Easson v LNE Railway Co 1944*.

(c)   There is a duty to take care in making statements particularly on financial matters. However, under the general proximity test, the duty is owed only to persons who will be prejudiced by misleading information and who are known to the person making the statement to rely on his special knowledge in the relevant field.

In the leading case (*Hedley Byrne & Co Ltd v Heller & Partners Ltd 1964*) there was no doubt that the person to whom the statement (a banker's reference or status report) was made would treat it as reliable information from a well-trained source. If there had not been an effective disclaimer the bank would have been liable for issuing a misleading opinion.

It is unlikely that Jasper would be liable if his advice was given carelessly, without taking care to ensure that the other insurers were financially sound. If of course he well knew that the other insurers were already in difficulty and intentionally deceived his customer it would be a case of deceit. In that case the statement is made not negligently but fraudulently and Jasper would be liable for his deceit.

Glossary,
List of cases
and Index

This glossary contains short definitions of some key legal words and phrases.

Acceptance A positive act by a person accepting an offer so as to bring a contact into effect.

Accord and satisfaction Agreement and consideration.

Actus reus Guilty act. One of the two requirements normally present in a crime, the other being *mens rea*.

Ad idem Of the same (mind or intention). A requirement for a valid contract.

Administrative tribunals Special 'courts' set up to settle disputes.

Agent A person authorised to act for another (the principal) and bring that other into legal relations with a third party.

Anticipatory breach Renunciation by party to a contract of his contractual obligations before the date for performance.

Appeal A request to a higher court by a person dissatisfied with a decision of a lower court that the previous decision be reviewed.

Arbitration A means of settling a dispute outside the courts.

Assignment Transfer of rights and liabilities.

Auction A type of contract for the sale of property.

Bill The draft of a proposed statute.

Bill of exchange A type of order to pay money.

Bona fide In good faith

Bye-law Type of delegated legislation.

Capacity The ability or power of a person to enter into legal relationships or carry out legal acts.

Care, duty of The care owed by one person to another which, if broken, may give rise to an action for negligence.

Case stated A particular form of appeal.

Caveat emptor Let the buyer beware.

Certorari A prerogative order.

Chancery division A division of the High Court.

Charterparty A contract between the shipowner and the charterer whereby a ship is hired for a period of time or for a particular voyage.

Codification The replacement of common law rules by statute which embodies those rules.

Commercial court A specialised court.

Common law The body of legal rules developed by the common law courts and now embodied in legal decisions.

Condition Term vital to a contract. Breach of a condition destroys the basis of the contract.

Condition precedent Specific type of contract term.

Condition subsequent Specific type of contract term.

Consideration That which is given, promised or done by a party to a contract.

Consolidation The passing of an Act to 'tidy up the law'.

Contract An agreement which the law will recognise and enforce.

Council on Tribunals Statutory body which overseas the workings of administrative tribunals.

Counsel's opinion The advice of a barrister on a specialised or difficult point of law which may be obtained by a solicitor before advising his or her client on whether or not to proceed with his or her action.

Counterclaim When court proceedings are begun by the plaintiff serving details of his claim upon the defendant, the defendant may reply with a counterclaim alleging that he or she is the injured party. For example, he or she may allege that he or she did not pay for the goods because they were defective.

County court Inferior civil court.

Court of Appeal Appeal court divided into two divisions.

Covenant A clause in a deed whereby a person promises to do, or refrain from doing, a specific act.

Custom Unwritten law which formed the basis of common law.

Damages The sum claimed or awarded in a civil action in compensation for the loss or injury suffered by the plaintiff.

De facto As a matter of fact, disregarding questions of right or title.

De jure As a matter of law.

Decision Secondary source of EC law.

Defendant The person against whom a civil action is brought or who is prosecuted for a criminal offence.

Delegated legislation Rules of law made by subordinate bodies to whom the power to do so has been given by statute.

Directive Secondary source of EC law.

Divisional court A court in the High Court.

Enabling act A statute which establishes a framework within which some subordinate body, often a minister, is 'enabled' or empowered to fill in the details by delegated legislation.

Equity A source of English law consisting of those rules which emerged from the Court of Chancery.

Estoppel If a person, by his words or conduct, leads another to believe that a certain state of affairs exists and that other alters his or her position to his or her detriment in reliance on that belief, the first person is estopped (prevented) from claiming later that a different state of affairs existed. Thus if a principal, by honouring contracts made by his or her agent, induces a third party to believe that the agent possesses certain authority, the principal will be bound by later contracts of a similar nature made by the agent even if they are unauthorised.

Exclusion clause Contract clause purporting to exclude or restrict liability.

Ex gratia By way of favour or gift.

Ex parte Of the one part or one side.

Executed That which takes place at the present time.

Executory That which is to take place at some future time.

Expressio unius est exclusio alterius To state one thing is to exclude others.

Fraud Using misrepresentation to obtain an unjust advantage in the knowledge that it is untrue, without belief in its truth or recklessly, not caring whether it be true or false.

Freedom of contract Principle that parties may contract on the terms which they choose.

Frustration Discharge of contract by some outside event which makes further performance impossible in the form anticipated.

Fundamental breach Doctrine developed by the courts as a protection against unreasonable exemption clauses in contracts.

Good faith Fair and open action without any attempt to deceive or take advantage of knowledge of which the other party is unaware.

Guarantee A promise to answer for the debt or default of another.

Habeas corpus You have the body.

High Court Civil court with extensive jurisdiction.

Implied term Term deemed to form part of a contract even though not expressly mentioned by the parties.

In personam An action *in personam* is one seeking relief against a particular person.

In rem An action *in rem* is one brought in respect of property.

Indemnity Security against or compensation for loss.

Industrial tribunals Local tribunal dealing with disputes between employer and employee.

Injunction An order of the court directing a person not to carry out a certain act.

Inns of Court There are four such Inns - Grays, Lincoln's, Middle Temple and Inner Temple - which intending barristers must join and which have the exclusive privilege of conferring the status of barrister.

Intention to create legal relations Element necessary for an agreement to become a legally binding contract.

Interpretation clause Most statutes and statutory instruments include a clause, either at the beginning or the end, which defines the meaning to be given to words or phrases used in the enactment.

Invitation to treat Indication that a person is prepared to receive offers with a view to entering into a binding contract.

Judgment The sentence or order of the court.

Judicial review Application to the High Court for relief from a wrongful act.

Justice of the Peace A magistrate, normally without legal qualifications, appointed by the

Lord Chancellor to adjudicate in a Magistrates' Court.

Law Commission Two Commissions were set up in 1965, for England and Wales and for Scotland, as permanent bodies charged with the task of keeping the law under review and proposing reforms where necessary. There are five full-time Commissioners, a High Court judge as chairman and four other legal practitioners or academic lawyers. Normal practice is to publish a working paper first to invite comment and then a final report, often with a draft bill included which embodies the proposed reforms.

Law Lords The name given to the ten life peers or Lords of Appeal in Ordinary who, together with the Lord Chancellor and any other peers who have held high judicial office, sit in the House of Lords as the final court of appeal. In practice, five will normally sit.

Law Merchant Early mercantile customs.

Law Reports The principal reports of decided cases

Law Society The statutory body governing the solicitors' branch of the legal profession.

Leapfrog procedure Procedure by which appeal from the High Court may go directly to the House of Lords.

Legal aid A statutory scheme administered by the Law Society for assisting applicants with the cost of legal proceedings, either in whole or in part. It may cover preliminary legal advice or it may extend to the actual court proceedings. The applicant must show that he or she cannot afford to proceed because his or her disposable capital and disposable income are below prescribed amounts. In civil actions he or she must also show that he or she has an arguable case whilst in criminal prosecutions the charge must be serious or complex.

Legal person A human being (natural person) or a corporate body (artificial person) having rights and duties recognised by law.

Lien A right to retain possession of property until a debt has been paid.

Lifting the veil (of incorporation) A company is normally to be treated as a separate legal person from its members. 'Lifting the veil' means that the company is identified with its members or directors or that a group of companies is to be treated as a single commercial entity. An example of this is to prevent fraud.

Limitation of actions By statute, proceedings must be commenced within a certain period of time from the date when the action could first have been brought.

Limited liability Limitation of the liability of members to contribute to the assets of a business in the event of a winding up.

Liquidated damages Fixed sum agreed by parties to a contract and payable in the event of a breach.

Listed Quoted on a recognised stock exchange.

Mandamus We command.

Member Shareholder of a company.

Mens rea Guilty mind.

Minor A person under the age of eighteen.

Misrepresentation False statement made with the object of inducing the other party to enter into a contract.

Natural person A human being with rights and duties recognised by the law as opposed to an artificial person such as a corporate body.

Negligence This may refer to the way in which an act is carried out, that is carelessly, or to the tort which arises when a person breaches a legal duty of care that is owed to another, thereby causing loss to that other.

Negotiability Quality possessed by certain documents representing claims to money which may be transferred by delivery (and in some cases endorsement).

Negotiable instrument A document which is negotiable, for example a bill of exchange or a cheque.

Novation Transaction whereby a creditor agrees to release an existing debtor and substitute a new one in his or her place.

Obiter dictum Something said by the way.

Objects clause A clause in a company's memorandum of association which sets out the 'aims' and 'purposes' of the company.

Offer Express or implied statement of the terms on which the maker is willing to be contractually bound.

Order in Council A form of delegated legislation.

Partnership The relation which subsists between persons carrying on a business in common with a view of profit. Every partner is liable without limit for the debts of the partnership. In the absence of any written agreement, matters such as profit sharing are determined by the Partnership Act 1890.

Past consideration Something already done at the time that a contractual promise is made.

Penalty clause Clause in a contract providing for a specific sum to be payable in the event of a subsequent breach.

Per se By itself.

Plaintiff The person who complains or brings an action asking the court for relief.

Possession Actual physical control over property with the intention of maintaining that control.

Precedent A previous court decision.

Prerogative order An order made by the High Court.

Presumption A rule of evidence.

Prima facie At first sight or on first impressions.

Private company A company which may not offer shares to the public, and which has not been registered as a public company.

Privity of contract The relation between two contracting parties which allows either to sue the other for breach.

Prohibition A type of court order.

Promise Voluntary understanding by one person to another to perform or abstain from performing a certain act.

Public company A company registered as such under the Companies Act. The principal distinction between public and private companies is that only the former may offer shares to the public.

Quantum meruit As much as he has deserved.

Quasi contract Resembling a contract but not really a contract.

Queen's Bench Division Division of the High Court.

Ratio decidendi The reason for the decision.

Re In the matter of.

Rectification An equitable remedy.

Regulation A secondary source of EC law.

Remoteness of damage Relationship between a wrongful act and the resulting damage which determines whether or not compensation may be recovered. Different principles apply in contract and in tort.

Repudiation Rejection or renunciation.

Rescission The act of repudiation of a contract. An equitable remedy.

Restitutio in integrum Restoring to the original position.

Restraint of trade Restriction upon a trade or business which is *prima facie* void at common law.

Restrictive Practices Court A special court with High Court status.

Royal Assent Final stage in the process by which a Bill becomes an Act.

Sale of goods A contract whereby the seller transfers or agrees to transfer the property in goods for a money consideration called the price.

Share A member's stake in a company's share capital.

Small claim A claim not exceeding £1,000 may be brought within the quicker, cheaper and more informal arbitration procedure within the county court.

Specific performance A type of court order.

Standard form contract Contract where the terms are drawn up by the stronger party

Standard of proof The extent to which the court must be satisfied by the evidence presented.

Statute-barred Inability to pursue an action because proceedings were not started within the period prescribed by statute.

Statutory instrument Form of delegated legislation.

Subject to contract Qualified acceptance pending making of a more formal agreement.

Subpoena Under penalty (for refusal).

Summons Generally an order to appear before a court but used particularly of the document which begins County Court proceedings and of the order to appear before a Magistrates' Court when the accused is not arrested.

Supreme Court of Judicature Established by the Judicature Acts 1873-75, it consists of the Court of Appeal and the High Court.

Tender Offer, particularly of goods or money.

Title Legal right to possession or ownership of property.

Tort A wrongful act.

Trade union An organisation of employees formed to regulate relations between employer and employees.

Trust An arrangement by which the legal owner of a property has an obligation to administer it for the benefit of the beneficiary who has an equitable interest in it.

Uberrimae fidei Of utmost good faith.

Ultra vires Beyond their powers. In company law this term is used in connection with transactions which are outside the scope of the objects clause and therefore, in principle at least, unenforceable.

Unenforceable Not actionable in a court

Unfair dismissal Termination of a contract of employment in breach of certain statutory rights given to the employee.

Vicarious liability Liability for the wrongful acts of another.

Void Having no legal effect.

Voidable Capable of being rendered void at the option of one of the parties, but valid until the option is exercised.

Waive Give up a claim or right, such as the right to receive notice.

Warranty Minor term in a contract.

Writ A written command.

Wrongful dismissal Breach of contract of employment by the employer without justification and without appropriate notice.

BPP Publishing

Scott v London & St Katharine Docks Co 1865, 252

Scott v Shepherd 1773, 253

Scriven Bros v Hindley & Co 1913, 212

Sedleigh-Denfield v O'Callaghan 1940, 266

Sellack v Harris 1708, 89

Sen v Headley 1989, 97

Sergeant v National Westminster Bank 1990, 110

Shadwell v Shadwell 1860, 175

Shanklin Pier Ltd v Detel Products 1951, 162, 179

Shelfer v City of London Electric Lighting Co 1895, 269

Shirlaw v Southern Foundries 1939, 189, 201

Silservice v Supreme Bread 1949, 270

Sim v Stretch 1936, 273

Simms v Leigh Rugby Football Club 1969, 285

Simpkins v Pays 1955, 165

Smaldon v Whitworth and Another 1996, 285

Smith v Baker & Sons 1891, 285

Smith v Eric S Bush 1989, 207

Smith v Hughes 1871, 196

Smith v Leech Braine & Co 1962, 254

Solle v Butcher 1950, 214

SS Ardennes (Cargo Owners) v SS Ardennes (Owners) 1951, 197

St Albans City and District Council v International Computers Ltd 1994, 207

St Helens Smelting Co v Tipping 1865, 267

Stanley v Powell 1891, 287

Steinberg v Scala (Leeds) Ltd 1923, 183

Stevenson v McLean 1880, 155

Stilk v Myrick 1809, 174

Stoke-on-Trent CC v B & Q plc 1991, 49

Street v Mountford 1985, 62

Strong v Bird 1874, 97

Sturges v Bridgman 1879, 268, 269

Tamplin v James 1880, 211

Tarry v Ashton 1876, 270

Taylor v Caldwell 1863, 229

Taylor v Laird 1856, 226

Tebbs v Carpenter 1816, 107

The Heron II 1969, 236

The Moorcock 1889, 189, 201

The Wagon Mound, 264

The Wagon Mound 1961, 253

Theaker v Richardson 1962, 275

Thomas v Thomas 1842, 172

Thompson Ltd v Robinson (Gunmakers) Ltd 1955, 236

Thompson v LMS Railway 1930, 202

Thrupp v Collett 1854, 101

Tinn v Hoffmann 1873, 157, 159

Tolley v Fry 1931, 273

Tsakiroglou & Co v Noblee and Thorl GmbH 1962, 231

Tulk v Moxhay 1848, 66, 178

Tweddle v Atkinson 1861, 171

Twine v Bean's Express 1946, 283

Twomax Ltd and Goode v Dickson, McFarlane & Robinson 1983, 258

Unit Construction Co Ltd v Bullock 1960, 131

Van Duyn v Home Office 1974, 48

Vancouver Malt & Sake Brewing Co Ltd v Vancouver Breweries Ltd 1934, 223

Vandyke v Fender 1970, 284

Vauxhall Estates v Liverpool Corporation 1932, 27

Vestey v Inland Revenue Commissioners (Nos 1 and 2) 1980, 39

Victoria Laundry (Windsor) v Newman Industries 1949, 235

Vizetelly v Mudie's Select Library 1900, 275

Walford v Miles 1991, 167

Walter v Selfe 1851, 267

Warner Bros Pictures Inc v Nelson 1937, 239

Warren v Henleys 1948, 283

Webb v Earl of Shaftesbury 1802, 108

Welby v Drake 1825, 175

Wheat v Lacon & Co Ltd 1966, 255

White v Garden 1851, 219

White v Jones 1995, 249

Whitehouse v Jordan 1981, 251

Williams v Carwardine 1833, 159

Williams v Roffey Bros & Nicholls (Contractors) Ltd 1990, 174

With v O'Flanagan 1936, 215

Wood v Robarts 1818, 175

Woodar Investment Development Ltd v Wimpey Construction (UK) Ltd 1980, 178

Woolfson v Strathclyde Regional Council 1978, 133

Wringe v Cohen 1940, 270

Yachuk v Oliver Blais 1949, 288

Yates Building Co v R J Pulleyn & Sons (York) 1975, 157

Yorkshire Enterprise Ltd and Another v Robson Rhodes 1998, 261

Young v Bristol Aeroplane Co 1944, 38

Yousoupoff v MGM Pictures Ltd 1934, 271

ORDER FORM

To order your ICSA books, you can phone us on 020 8740 2211, email us at *publishing@bpp.co.uk*, fax us on 020 8740 1184, or cut out this form and post it to us at the address below.

To: BPP Publishing Ltd, Aldine House, Aldine Place
London W12 8AW

Tel: 020 8740 2211
Fax: 020 8740 1184

Forenames (Mr / Ms): _____ Surname: _____

Daytime delivery address: _____

_____

Post code: _____ Date of exam (month/year):_____

	Price (£) 9/99 Text	Price (£) 3/99 Kit	Quantity Text	Quantity Kit	Total £
Foundation					
Business Economics	18.95	10.95			
Quantitative Techniques	18.95	10.95			
Introduction to English and EU Law	18.95	10.95			
Organisation and the Human Resource	18.95	10.95			
Information Systems	18.95	10.95			
Pre-Professional					
Introduction to Accounting	19.95	10.95			
Business Law	19.95	10.95			
Management Principles	19.95	10.95			
Managing Information Systems	19.95	10.95			
Professional Stage One					
Professional Administration	20.95	10.95			
Management Practice	20.95	10.95			
Corporate Law	20.95	10.95			
Financial Accounting	20.95	10.95			
Professional Stage Two					
Administration of Corporate Affairs	20.95	10.95			
Company Secretarial Practice	20.95	10.95			
Corporate Finance and Taxation (FA 99) (10/99)	20.95	10.95			
Management Accounting	20.95	10.95			

Postage and packaging:

UK: Texts £3.00 for first plus £2.00 for each extra

   Kits £2.00 for first plus £1.00 for each extra

Europe (inc ROI): Texts £5.00 for first plus £4.00 for each extra

   Kits £2.50 for first plus £1.00 for each extra

Rest of the World: Texts £20.00 for first plus £10.00 for each extra

   Kits £15.00 for first plus £8.00 for each extra

Total [   ]

We aim to deliver to all UK addresses inside 5 working days. Orders to all EU addresses should be delivered within 6 working days. All other orders to overseas addresses should be delivered within 8 working days.

I enclose a cheque for £ _____ **or charge to Access/Visa/Switch**

Card number [ ][ ][ ][ ][ ][ ][ ][ ][ ][ ][ ][ ][ ][ ][ ][ ][ ][ ]

Start date (Switch only) _____ **Expiry date** _____ **Issue no. (Switch only)**___

Signature _____

REVIEW FORM & FREE PRIZE DRAW

All original review forms from the entire BPP range, completed with genuine comments, will be entered into one of two draws on 31 January 2000 and 31 July 2000. The names on the first four forms picked out on each occasion will be sent a cheque for £50.

Name: _____   Address: _____

_____

_____

How have you used this Text?
(Tick one box only)

☐ Home study (book only)

☐ On a course: college _____

☐ With 'correspondence' package

☐ Other _____

Why did you decide to purchase this Text?
(Tick one box only)

☐ Have used complementary Kit

☐ Have used BPP Texts in the past

☐ Recommendation by friend/colleague

☐ Recommendation by a lecturer at college

☐ Saw advertising

☐ Other _____

During the past six months do you recall seeing/receiving any of the following?
(Tick as many boxes as are relevant)

☐ Our advertisement in *Chartered Secretary*

☐ Our brochure with a letter through the post

Which (if any) aspects of our advertising do you find useful?
(Tick as many boxes as are relevant)

☐ Prices and publication dates of new editions

☐ Information on Text content

☐ Facility to order books off-the-page

☐ None of the above

Have you used the companion Practice & Revision Kit for this subject?   ☐ Yes   ☐ No

Your ratings, comments and suggestions would be appreciated on the following areas

	Very useful	Useful	Not useful
Introductory section (How to use this Study Text, etc)	☐	☐	☐
Introduction to chapters	☐	☐	☐
Syllabus coverage	☐	☐	☐
Exercises and examples	☐	☐	☐
Chapter roundups	☐	☐	☐
Test your knowledge quizzes	☐	☐	☐
Illustrative questions	☐	☐	☐
Content of suggested answers	☐	☐	☐
Glossary and index	☐	☐	☐
Structure and presentation	☐	☐	☐

	Excellent	Good	Adequate	Poor
Overall opinion of this Text	☐	☐	☐	☐

Do you intend to continue using BPP Study Texts/Kits?   ☐ Yes   ☐ No

Please note any further comments and suggestions/errors on the reverse of this page.

Please return to: ICSA Range Manager, BPP Publishing Ltd, FREEPOST, London, W12 8BR

REVIEW FORM & FREE PRIZE DRAW (continued)

Please note any further comments and suggestions/errors below

FREE PRIZE DRAW RULES

1   Closing date for 31 January 2000 draw is 31 December 1999. Closing date for 31 July 2000 draw is 30 June 2000.

2   Restricted to entries with UK and Eire addresses only. BPP employees, their families and business associates are excluded.

3   No purchase necessary. Entry forms are available upon request from BPP Publishing. No more than one entry per title, per person. Draw restricted to persons aged 16 and over.

4   Winners will be notified by post and receive their cheques not later than 6 weeks after the relevant draw date. Lists of winners will be published in BPP's *focus* newsletter following the relevant draw.

5   The decision of the promoter in all matters is final and binding. No correspondence will be entered into.